Human Behavior and Environment

ADVANCES IN THEORY AND RESEARCH

Volume 4
Environment and Culture

Human Behavior and Environment

ADVANCES IN THEORY AND RESEARCH

Human Behavior and Environment

ADVANCES IN THEORY AND RESEARCH

Volume 4
Environment and Culture

EDITED BY

IRWIN ALTMAN
University of Utah
Salt Lake City, Utah

AMOS RAPOPORT
University of Wisconsin
Milwaukee, Wisconsin

AND

JOACHIM F. WOHLWILL
Pennsylvania State University
University Park, Pennsylvania

PLENUM PRESS · NEW YORK AND LONDON

Library of Congress Cataloging in Publication Data

Main entry under title:

Human behavior and environment.

Includes bibliographies and indexes.
1. Environmental psychology — Collected works. I. Altman, Irwin. II. Wohlwill,
Joachim F.
BF353.H85   301.31   76-382942
ISBN 0-306-40367-6 (v. 4)

© 1980 Plenum Press, New York
A Division of Plenum Publishing Corporation
227 West 17th Street, New York, N.Y. 10011

Printed in the United States of America

Articles Planned for Volume 5
TRANSPORTATION AND ENVIRONMENT
Editors: Joachim Wohlwill, Peter Everett, and Irwin Altman

Contributors

JOHN R. AIELLO • Department of Psychology, Rutgers—The State University, New Brunswick, New Jersey

JOHN W. BERRY • Department of Psychology, Queens University, Kingston, Ontario, Canada

JOHN W. BENNETT • Department of Anthropology, Washington University, St. Louis, Missouri

RICHARD W. BRISLIN • East–West Center, Culture Learning Institute, Honolulu, Hawaii

SIDNEY N. BROWER • Planning Commission, Department of Planning, City of Baltimore, 222 East Saratoga Street, Baltimore, Maryland

AMOS RAPOPORT • Department of Architecture, University of Wisconsin-Milwaukee, Milwaukee, Wisconsin

MILES RICHARDSON • Department of Geography and Anthropology, Louisiana State University, Baton Rouge, Louisiana

IGNACY SACHS • Le Centre International de Recherche sur l 'Environnement et le Développement, Ecole Pratique des Hautes Etudes, 54 Boulevard Raspail, Paris, France

JOHN H. SORENSEN • Department of Geography, University of Hawaii, Honolulu, Hawaii

DONNA E. THOMPSON • Department of Psychology, George Peabody College, Vanderbilt University, Nashville, Tennessee

GILBERT F. WHITE • Institute of Behavioral Science, University of Colorado, Boulder, Colorado

Preface

Following upon the first two volumes in this series, which dealt with a broad spectrum of topics in the environment and behavior field, ranging from theoretical to applied, and including disciplinary, interdisciplinary, and professionally oriented approaches, we have chosen to devote subsequent volumes to more specifically defined topics. Thus, Volume Three dealt with *Children and the Environment*, seen from the combined perspective of researchers in environmental and developmental psychology. The present volume has a similarly topical coverage, dealing with the complex set of relationships between culture and the physical environment. It is broad and necessarily eclectic with respect to content, theory, methodology, and epistemological stance, and the contributors to it represent a wide variety of fields and disciplines, including psychology, geography, anthropology, economics, and environmental design. We were fortunate to enlist the collaboration of Amos Rapoport in the organization and editing of this volume, as he brings to this task a particularly pertinent perspective that combines anthropology and architecture.

Volume Five of the series, presently in preparation, will cover the subject of behavioral science aspects of transportation.

Irwin Altman
Joachim F. Wohlwill

Contents

CHAPTER 3

CULTURAL ECOLOGY AND
INDIVIDUAL BEHAVIOR

JOHN W. BERRY

CHAPTER 4

PERSONAL SPACE, CROWDING, AND
SPATIAL BEHAVIOR IN A CULTURAL CONTEXT

JOHN R. AIELLO

DONNA E. THOMPSON

CHAPTER 5

TERRITORY IN URBAN SETTINGS

SIDNEY N. BROWER

CHAPTER 6

CULTURE AND THE URBAN STAGE: THE NEXUS OF SETTING, BEHAVIOR AND IMAGE IN URBAN PLACES

MILES RICHARDSON

CHAPTER 7

HUMAN ECOLOGY AS HUMAN BEHAVIOR: A NORMATIVE ANTHROPOLOGY OF RESOURCE USE AND ABUSE

JOHN W. BENNETT

CHAPTER 8

NATURAL HAZARDS:
A CROSS-CULTURAL PERSPECTIVE

JOHN H. SORENSEN
GILBERT F. WHITE

CHAPTER 9

CULTURE, ECOLOGY, AND DEVELOPMENT: REDEFINING PLANNING APPROACHES

IGNACY SACHS

Introduction

The growth of a field of research and scholarship is signaled by many events, including an outpouring of research, theory, and methodological contributions. But the establishment of a field is also reflected in institutional events, such as the founding of new organizations, the convening of conferences, the appearance of books and journals, and the formation of professional societies. So it is that we have witnessed in recent years the birth and growth of research on comparative or cross-cultural aspects of human behavior.

This is not to say that the comparative study of culture, contemporaneously or historically, is a totally new endeavor. Historians, anthropologists, and others have been engaged in such work for many years. But the volume and intensity of research have accelerated in the past decade, and scholars have emerged in many disciplines whose *primary* interest is in the comparative analysis of culture. If present trends continue, the cross-cultural analysis of behavior will surely become more than a sideline or fragmentary specialty within one or the other of the social sciences. Needless to say, this burgeoning interest has been accompanied by issues of theory development and research methodology that are unique to the comparative study of cultures.

In addition to research productivity, several institutional events have occurred in the past decade. Alongside mainstream disciplinary organizations to which cross-cultural scientists belong, there presently are a number of interdisciplinary societies. The goals of these organizations are diverse; some publish journals, some hold conferences, others produce informal newsletters, some sponsor monographs and other volumes. The number of these organizations is increasing, their memberships are rising, and they appear to be thriving. Such groups include the International Association of Cross-Cultural Psychology, The Society for Cross-Cultural Research, and The Society for Psychological Anthropology. Journals that are geared primarily to comparative analysis of

1

cultures include *Ethos,* and *The Journal of Cross-Cultural Psychology.* At the same time anthropology journals, books, and monographs continue to deal with various cross-cultural topics.

Another signal of the "arrival" of a field on the intellectual scene is the appearance of a major compendium of knowledge. The past decade has seen a steady increase in the number of books on cross-cultural topics, culminating in 1979 and 1980 with the publication of what is likely to be a major reference work, a five-volume *Handbook of Cross-Cultural Psychology,* under the general editorship of Harry Triandis. Although its emphasis will be on psychological aspects of cross-cultural issues, the scope of this compendium will be broad and interdisciplinary, and it will contain knowledge gleaned from studies done by psychologists, anthropologists, psychiatrists, sociologists, and others.

The present volume deals with one aspect of this mushrooming field, namely, the relationship between culture and the physical environment. Here again, the analysis of culture–environment relationships is not a new topic of study. Indeed, the understanding of culture from the perspective of physical anthropology, cultural anthropology, behavioral geography, and history has *always* necessitated an appreciation of culture–environment linkages. Within anthropology, furthermore, these linkages have become the focus of analyses by cultural ecologists who stress the influence of natural environments, and by cognitive- and symbolic-oriented anthropologists, who emphasize the influence of culture on the selection and shaping of environments. Yet there often has been neglect of the crucial role of cultural variables as important determinants and mediators of the interaction between people and environments. For example, what is perceived as desirable or undesirable environmental quality is culturally variable, as are standards of crowding, privacy, environmental aesthetics, satisfactory living conditions, and the like. Similarly, physical environments are often endowed with unique cultural meanings and symbolisms that are reflected in the design of dwellings, neighborhoods, settlements, and even whole landscapes.

The fact that a culture affects and is affected by its physical environment is not a new idea. What is new, however, is the growing interest in cross-cultural or comparative analysis of culture–environment linkages, and the quest to understand how these linkages are similar and different among cultures. Indeed, there is a virtual absence of knowledge about cross-cultural aspects of environment–behavior relationships. While there are innumerable examples of culture–environment bonds in the ethnographic literature, such as in descriptions of housing and community design, agricultural techniques, and beliefs about the nature of the world and universe, there is little by way of *comparative* analysis of such topics. Moreover, even the rare analyses that are available tend to neglect important dimensions and variables. One is hard pressed, for example, to find thorough comparative analyses of territorial practices in different cultures, community and home designs, perceptions and world views regarding nature, etc. Perhaps the point is best illustrated by positive examples. Rapoport's (1969) analysis of home designs in relation to environmental, technological, and cultural variables stands out as a unique piece of cross-cultural comparative work. He has since begun to extend such analyses to urban settings (Rapoport, 1977). There are also a number of comparative studies of the relationship between ecology, food gathering and growing techniques, and social structure, based on analyses of cultures in the Human Relations Area Files (see Chapter 3). Additionally, we find more limited efforts, such as Altman's (1977) treatment of privacy from a cross-cultural perspective, or Gould's (1973) research on environmental preferences of people from different European and African countries.

The present volume is intended to address some of these issues, and to begin to fill some of the gaps in our knowledge, by illustrations of the types of research that have been done on culture–environment relationships and by suggestions for additional directions of research. To provide readers with some insight into the range of topics in the field and possibilities for culture–environment research, we selected topics in terms of several criteria. First, we considered it important to portray the interdisciplinary nature of the field and the diversity of approaches that have been used to study culture–environment relationships. Thus, the authors in the volume include psychologists (Berry, Brislin, Aiello, Thompson), geographers (Sorensen, White), environmental designers (Brower, Rapoport), anthropologists (Bennett, Richardson, Rapoport), and an economist (Sachs).

Second, we wished to illustrate how culture–environment relationships occur at many levels of scale. The microlevel of scale is exemplified by Berry's analysis of the perceptual and cognitive facets of individual behavior in relation to qualities of the physical environment and culture (Chapter 3). Another level of scale is illustrated in the chapter by Aiello and Thompson, who examine personal spacing and crowding in interpersonal relationships from a cross-cultural perspective (Chapter 4). At still another level of scale, Brower (Chapter 5) analyzes urban neighborhoods as territories, and Richardson (Chapter 6) examines the town square or plaza in relation to cultural similarities and differences. At a still larger scale, Bennett (Chapter 7), Sorensen and White (Chapter 8), and Sachs (Chapter 9) deal with the relationship between culture and broad aspects of the physical environment, such as environmental hazards, resources, utilities, and economic development. In a very broad treatment, Rapoport (Chapter 1) discusses a number of issues, comparing the application of cultural-event knowledge at several levels of scale, all of which are interrelated as parts of a single environmental system.

Another criterion for inclusion of contributions in the volume relates to the methodology of cross-cultural research. It became evident quickly to a number of early researchers in the field that the standard laboratory experiments of psychologists, the participant observation techniques of sociologists and anthropologists, or the methods of interview, survey, and archival analysis could not always be easily applied in cross-cultural research. The comparison of information across cultures, problems of translation of language and meaning from one culture to another, the differing accessibility to information in various cultures, and numerous other technical problems heightened the sensitivity of researchers to the limitations of simple application of existing methodologies in cross-cultural settings. And, as a general methodological issue, the "emic–etic" dilemma became salient. How was one to understand a culture from a strictly etic orientation, where one's own cultural or theoretical framework was used to categorize and interpret the behavior of others? Yet, if one adopted a strictly emic orientation, examining a culture solely from its perspective, how could one evolve cross-cultural generalizations? The emic–etic and other methodological issues of cross-cultural research are discussed in detail by Brislin (Chapter 2), and they also appear in several other chapters as recurring themes.

A major goal of the book was to integrate research knowledge and theories in the culture–environment field, to stimulate new thinking and research, and to make available summaries of findings in representative areas of study. While all chapters do this to some extent, a number of them were specifically directed at substantive and theoretical topics.

In Chapter 3, Berry adopts a model of cultural ecology to examine aspects of cognitive and perceptual styles in different cultures. His model links individual psychological functioning with various facets of culture and environment.

Aiello and Thompson (Chapter 4) analyze the range of existing research and theory on the popular topics of personal spacing and crowding. In their summary and integration of this work they also point to major lines of theorizing that are relevant to a cross-cultural perspective.

In Chapter 5, Brower summarizes his own research and intervention studies on territoriality, and also outlines related research by others.

Richardson (Chapter 6) adopts an anthropological and sociological perspective to analyze the design, functions, and symbolisms of community centers, such as town squares and plazas, in relation to cultural values and historical influences.

Bennett (Chapter 7) examines resource utilization in relation to cultural, environmental, and psychological factors. He offers a conceptual model that includes such variables, and applies his analysis to cultures differing in technological development and social structure.

Chapter 8, by Sorensen and White, examines cultural responses to destructive environmental events, such as floods, earthquakes, and volcanoes. In addition to a review of a considerable portion of the literature on this topic, they propose a social-systems model to account for human responses and coping and adaptations to such striking environmental events.

Another general issue that is implicit, and occasionally explicit throughout the volume, is that a comparative analysis of culture–environment also requires a historical perspective. Since the variety of cultures over the course of history is far greater than that existing today, and since the spectrum of culture–environment relations, solutions, and adaptations is quite broad, we must also be aware of the need for a comparative historical dimension to the problems of people and environments.

We also considered it important to examine the application of cross-cultural research to the design of environments in different cultures. How does one achieve an effective design process, given the emic–etic issue and the problems of understanding another culture at the level of the individual, the group, the community, and the society? Without offering pat solutions, Rapoport (Chapter 1) addresses several facets of this topic in terms of the theory that design is dependent on context, and hence is culture-specific. Brower (Chapter 5) and Sachs (Chapter 8) also address design and planning issues at the urban neighborhood scale and at regional and national scales respectively. Although these chapters adopt rather different conceptual orientations—Rapoport adopts a broad cultural perspective, Brower works from the base of the concept of territoriality, and Sachs uses an economic orientation—these application-oriented chapters all opt for a translation process that is clearly attentive to the structure and functioning of cultures in relation to their unique physical environments.

In summary, the chapters in this volume attempt, collectively, to provide a multidisciplinary approach that examines culture–environment relationships at several levels of scale, that addresses cer-

tain crucial issues of theory and research methodology, and that highlights some problems and possibilities for application of cross-cultural
knowledge to the design of environments.

A cross-cultural analysis of environment–behavior relationships is
an exciting venture in its own right. It may also eventually change the
nature of environment–behavior research by increasing the participant
disciplines that deal with cultural and cross-cultural analysis, by making
the field more international, and by expanding the variety of people and
cultures that are studied. Furthermore, cross-cultural analysis may also
facilitate better understanding of our own culture, by placing it in the
perspective of other social systems. And, eventually, comparative
analysis of cultures may increase our understanding of other social entities, especially if we can achieve a delicate etic–emic balance of developing general principles of environment—behavior relationships
concurrently with an understanding of cultures on their own terms and
as specific social systems.

If these efforts succeed, we may not only better appreciate how
cultures are different from one another, but, equally important, we may
discover how diverse human social systems are similar and how they
share certain generic qualities and concerns. In so doing, we may take a
small step toward understanding one of these perennial issues, namely,
the balance between cultural variability and uniqueness among social
groups and the more universal and common characteristics of cultures.

REFERENCES

Altman, I. Privacy regulation: Culturally universal or culturally specific. *Journal of Social Issues*, 1977, 33, 66–84.
Gould, P. R. On mental maps. In R. N. Downs & D. Stea (Eds.), *Image and environment: Cognitive mapping and spatial behavior*. Chicago: Aldine, 1973, pp. 182–220.
Rapoport, A. *House form and culture*. Englewood Cliffs, N.J.: Prentice-Hall, 1969.
Rapoport, A. *Human aspects of urban form: Towards a man–environment approach to the urban form and design*. New York: Pergamon, 1977.

Cross-Cultural Aspects of Environmental Design

AMOS RAPOPORT

INTRODUCTION

In considering the relationship between culture and environmental design this chapter will suggest that these two are intimately related and that cultural differences must be considered in tracing environmental effects and in stating design requirements. Since culture is variable, designed environments respond to variable definitions of needs and priorities as expressed in varying schemata: environments are culture specific. In being so they are congruent with specific life-styles. For one thing, both designs and life-styles can be seen as resulting from sets of choices among many alternatives which even the most severe constraints make possible. These choices reflect certain ideal images and schemata, i.e., both environments and life-styles are shaped by cultural "templates." At smaller scales this process results in sets of cues which are encoded in the environment and help guide behavior. In order to be useful cues need to be decoded—if they cannot be decoded, then environments are effectively meaningless—another reason for the culture specific nature of environments.

The variability of environments and cultures in response to the much smaller number of climatic, ecological, and material forces is due to the relatively low criticality of built environments which allows the

AMOS RAPOPORT • Department of Architecture, University of Wisconsin-Milwaukee, Milwaukee, Wisconsin 53201.

use of built environments, in the broadest sense (as of other aspects of material culture), to assert and establish group identity, i.e., the variety of environments reflects the complexity of culture. Built environments are thus intimately related to the images and schemata of groups, which is made evident by the rather remarkable fact that recognizable cultural landscapes emerge from the individual decisions of innumerable individuals. This could only happen if members of such groups do, in fact, share conceptual models of ideal environments as settings for ideal people leading ideal lives; these must also covary in nonrandom ways.

The variety of environments and the importance of meanings, and their use to establish group identity so that they come to stand for groups, suggests that designed environments are much more than physical objects or prosthetic or economic devices. Two things follow. One is that environmental design research must be cross-cultural and historical—it must use the largest possible range of examples in order validly to generalize. The second is that in order to understand man–environment interaction one must get beyond material aspects of the environment—the nature of culture, of environments and their relationships must play a central role.

The first step in such a process is to conceptualize terms such as culture, environment, and environmental design. Not only are these terms too broad but they are frequently used rather loosely. In order to be useful they must be clearly conceptualized. I thus begin with a discussion of the nature of the two principal terms—culture and environmental design. The purpose is not to define them but rather to suggest one useful way of dealing with such global terms. Having done this, the next step is to bring these two terms together—to discuss their relationship and then to deal with some of the characteristics of this relationship. This is done by considering the variability of these relationships and hence the cultural specificity of the resulting environments. Within this framework it then becomes possible to discuss how one might design for culture and what aspects of the cultural core might need to be supported by culture-specific design and how. Finally it becomes possible to suggest lines of important future research needed to make such a design approach feasible.

Two points should be made about this argument. First, the topic is so broad and varied that this treatment of it represents merely one possible approach—not *the* approach. Second, in order not to lose too much of the complexity of the topic, too simplistic and linear an argument must be avoided. The approach is thus almost cyclic: a large although still limited number of themes is discussed from different perspectives, in different contexts, and, by moving back and forth among them, the linkages and relationships among its parts are exposed in their multidimensional fullness. The intent is to provide a conceptual approach, a way of thinking about the problem which will allow further exploration of these central, although hitherto relatively neglected aspects of man–environment interaction.

CULTURE

Anthropologists agree about the centrality of "culture" in defining humanity. Beyond that, however, they disagree much more. Thus definitions of culture abound. In 1952, Kroeber and Kluckhohn produced a sizable book reviewing definitions and concepts of culture and since then the stream of definitions and conceptualizations has continued unabated; a new book, including these more recent efforts, would be significantly larger.

For our purposes, however, it is enough to suggest that all definitions fall into one of three general views of culture. One defines it as a way of life typical of a group, the second as a system of symbols, meanings, and cognitive schemata transmitted through symbolic codes, the third as a set of adaptive strategies for survival related to ecology and resources. Increasingly, these three views are seen not as being in conflict but rather as complementary. Thus, designed environments of particular cultures are settings for the kind of people which a particular group sees as normative, and the particular life-style which is significant and typical, distinguishing the group from others. In creating such settings and life-styles, an order is expressed, a set of cognitive schemata, symbols, and some vision of an ideal are given form—however imperfectly; finally, both the life-style and symbolic system may be part of the group's adaptive strategies within their ecological setting.

For our purposes, then, culture may be said to be about a group of people who have a set of values and beliefs which embody ideals, and are transmitted to members of the group through enculturation. These lead to a world view—the characteristic way of looking at the world and, in the case of design, of *shaping* the world. The world is shaped by applying rules which lead to systematic and consistent choices (to be discussed below) whether in creating a life-style, a building style, a landscape, or a settlement. These latter two are, after all, the result of individual decisions and acts of many people which yet add up to a recognizable whole: if one knows the ordering system, or code, it is possible to say that this is an Indian or Italian city, a Mexican or Australian landscape. Habits, manners, food, roles, and behavior also result from such choices. All the elements mentioned show—or should show—regularities due to the common, underlying schemata and should be mutually illuminating.

At the same time, "culture" as a concept is too broad to relate to environmental design and it is, therefore, useful to consider how it might be subdivided. One proposal (Rapoport, 1973; 1976a, p. 25) is that culture typically leads to a particular world view. World views reflect ideals and lead to choices but are still difficult to use (e.g., Jones, 1972; Szalay & Maday, 1973; Szalay & Bryson, 1973)—particularly in relation to environments. Values are one aspect of world views and, while easier to identify and to analyze, are still rather too complex, at this stage, to link directly to built environments. Values are frequently embodied in images and these can be studied (Rapoport, 1977) but it is useful to carry the analysis further. Values result in particular life-styles—the ways in which people characteristically make choices about how to behave, what roles to play, how to allocate resources. This has been used successfully in relation to artifacts and built environments, as in the concept of *genre de vie* in French cultural geography, in environmental design research (e.g., Michelson & Reed, 1970), and in marketing and advertising.

At one level of analysis, activities and activity systems are an even more specific aspect of life-style which may offer a most useful entry point into relating culture and environments via human behavior. Starting with activities, it should be possible to work through the sequence and to identify more easily differences in life-style, values, images, world views and, eventually, culture as they relate to the built environment, particularly if we go beyond the surface manifest aspects of these activities to their underlying meanings, which then introduce their guiding images and schemata. This will be discussed in more detail below when we consider some of the mechanisms linking culture and environment. First, however, let us consider briefly the concept of environment and environmental design.

ENVIRONMENTAL DESIGN

All man-made environments are designed in the sense that they embody human decisions and choices and modify the world in some purposeful way. In that sense, since there are few places left on earth which humanity has not altered in some way, much of the earth is really designed. Designed environments obviously include places where forests have been planted or cleared, fields laid out in certain patterns, rivers diverted; the placement of roads, dams, pubs, and cities are all design; roadside stands and secondhand car lots are design, as is the work of a tribesman burning off, laying out a camp or village, or building a dwelling.

When we say that these are all designed environments what do we mean by "environment?" This is another term which is too broad to be used successfully. Different conceptualizations have been proposed (e.g., Ittelson, 1960; Lawton, 1970; Moos, 1974; Rapoport, 1977), all of which discuss the components of this term. Before discussing the latter, one can suggest that the environment can be seen as a series of relationships between things and things, things and people, and people and people. These relationships are orderly, i.e., they have a pattern and a structure—the environment is *not* a random assemblage of things and people any more than culture is a random assemblage of behaviors and beliefs. Both are guided by schemata or templates, as it were, which organize both people's lives and the settings for these. Hence the patterns and organizations have commonalities which are the subject matter of our topic. In the case of the environment the relationships are primarily, although not exclusively, spatial—objects and people are related through various degrees of separation in and by space. But, when environments are being designed, *four* elements are being organized: (1) space, (2) meaning, (3) communication, and (4) time.

Although all environments constitute complex interrelationships among these, it is useful conceptually to separate them and to discuss them as though separate, since this results in a better understanding of the nature of environments and the differences in their design.

Planning and design at all scales—from regions to furniture groupings—can be seen as the *organization of space* for different purposes and according to different rules which reflect the activities, values, and purposes of the individuals or groups doing the organizing. At the same time space organization also reflects ideal images, representing the congruence (or, in cases where the system ceases to work, the lack of it) between physical space and social, conceptual, or other kinds of spaces (Rapoport, 1970a, 1977). This great variety of possible "types" of space, and the fact that different groups, whether cultures or subcultures such as designers and the lay public, "see" space differently, makes any definition of space difficult. Intuitively, however, space is the three-dimensional extension of the world around us, the intervals, distances and relationships between people and people, people and things, and things and things. Space organization is, then, the way in which these separations occur and is central in understanding, analyzing, and comparing built environments. It is a more fundamental property of such environments than is shape, the materials which give it physical expression and other characteristics, which can more usefully be seen as an aspect of the *organization of meaning*. The organization of meaning can then be separated from the organization of space, both conceptually and in fact.

Although space organization itself expresses meaning and has communicative properties, meaning is often expressed through signs, materials, colors, forms, size, furnishings, landscaping, maintenance, and the like. If we conceptualize spatial organization primarily as the organization of fixed feature elements, then meaning is often expressed through the organization of semifixed feature elements such as the above. People themselves, their dress, hairstyles, proxemics, kinesics, and other nonverbal behaviors are aspects of the nonfixed elements of the environment. In contemporary situations, where people generally do not directly shape their environments, semifixed elements become particularly important and play a major role in personalization and other ways of expressing individual and group identity. This is reinforced by the fact that behavior and the organization of nonfixed elements is frequently quickly reflected in changes in semifixed elements whereas fixed-feature elements remain unchanged or change very slowly. Although in traditional settings meaning systems coincided with spatial organization (which is why archaeology "works"), the former may represent a separate, noncoinciding symbolic system, as it frequently seems to do in modern cities where eikonic and symbolic meaning systems become semi-independent of the spatial system (Carr, 1973; Choay, 1970–71; Venturi, Scott-Brown, & Izenour, 1972).

Thus both spatial and other systems of cues may identify settings, which then become indicators of social position, ways of establishing group or social identity, and ways of indicating expected behavior—but only if the cues communicate, i.e., are comprehensible and can be decoded (Rapoport 1977, 1978d)—an important aspect of culture–environment relations. It also helps if the various systems are congruent since they then reinforce one another, redundancy is high and meanings are clearest and strongest: low congruence and low redundancy, or conflicting systems, lead to environments which communicate less clearly. For example, there are situations where location in urban space, for example, centrality, indicates location in social space and others where it does not (e.g., Rapoport, 1977; Stanislawski, 1950). There are also reversals, so that in the United States central location today often indicates low status, and is seen as undesirable, whereas in Italy it still indicates very high status and is most desirable (e.g., Schnapper, 1971). In all these cases a misreading of the code will lead to the wrong conclusions and inappropriate behavior. Even when spatial location communicates, this is reinforced by other cues—the kinds of people seen, shops, levels of maintenance, front/back behavior, and many other noticeable differences (Rapoport, 1977). It may also further be stressed by the street layout, e.g., regular in the center vs. irregular on the periphery, and the materials used, e.g., man-made at the center and natural at the periphery with the former in each case indicating higher status (e.g., Richardson, 1974). In such cases the message is much clearer but, once again, depends on culture-specific codes, in the last example one stressing the distinction between the conceptual domains of culture (high status) and nature (low status).

Such differences in the meaning of center also influence behavior and the organization of *subjective* space—helping to explain the apparently contradictory findings about the relationship between subjective distance and direction of downtown in the United States and Britain (Rapoport, 1977).

An important reason why congruence between these systems is desirable is that the meaning of settings helps communication, i.e., social communication among people (whereas meaning is communication from the *environment* to people). Thus, specific organization of space and meaning reflect and influence the *organization of communication*. Who communicates with whom, under what conditions, how, when, where, and in what context is an important way in which built environment and social organization are related. Both are culturally variable: the nature, intensity, rate, and direction of interaction vary as do the settings appropriate to it. Thus, if people notice and understand cues in the environment identifying particular settings, they know how to behave appropriately, i.e., the context and the situation are established (Rapoport, 1978d). Of course, people also need to be prepared to act appropriately (a problem not encountered in traditional cultures), but if the cues are not noticed or, if noticed, not understood, appropriate behavior becomes impossible. This phenomenon occurs in situations of culture unfamiliarity.

Finally, people live in time as well as space—the environment is also temporal—and can, therefore, also be seen as the *organization of time*, reflecting and influencing behavior in time. They may be understood in at least two major ways. The first refers to large-scale, cognitive structuring of time such as linear flow vs. cyclic time; future orientations vs. past orientation (e.g., Doob, 1971; Yaker, Osmond, & Cheek, 1971); the future as an improvement over the past vs. the future as likely to be worse (e.g., Kearney, 1972). This influences behavior and decisions and, through those, environments so that in India the cyclic view of time (as opposed to our linear conception) has helped preserve elements which otherwise would have disappeared and also shaped the character of cities (Sopher, 1964). In the case of the United States and Britain, their respective future and past orientations have also led to very different cultural landscapes (Lowenthal, 1968; Lowenthal & Prince, 1964, 1965). Such time structuring also influences how time is valued and, hence, how finely it is subdivided into units. Thus, we advertise watches as being accurate to within one second a year, whereas in traditional Pueblo culture a week was the smallest relevant time unit (e.g., Ortiz, 1972). Such cultural differences clearly influence the second major way in which cultural differences in the organization of time can be considered—the tempos and rhythms of human activities, i.e., the number of events per unit time and the distribution of activities in time (day and night, weekday and restday, seasonal, profane vs. sacred times, and so on) respectively. Tempos and rhythms distinguish among groups and individuals who may have different temporal "signatures" and they may also be congruent or incongruent with each other. Thus, people may be separated in time as well as, or instead of, space and groups with different rhythms occupying the same space may never meet, groups and different tempos may never communicate. Groups with different rhythms may also conflict, as when one group regards a particular time as quiet and for sleep, another for noise and boisterous activity (e.g., Rapoport, 1977). Cultural conflicts and problems may often be more severe at the temporal level than at the spatial, although clearly spatial and temporal aspects interact and influence one another: people live in space-time.

The purpose of structuring space and time is to organize and structure communication (interaction, avoidance, dominance, etc.), and this is done partly through organizing meaning. The organization of communication also influences the organization of the other three variables. In organizing these four variables, choices are made and alternatives eliminated, and these choices tend to lead to an approximation of an image or schema. This I have called the choice model of design and these organizations can also be seen as physical expressions of cognitive domains (Rapoport, 1976a,b, 1977); designed environments encode, give expression to and, in turn, influence social, cognitive, and other environments.

In traditional situations, the organization of these four variables was more uniform and coincided more. For example, temporal organizations were more uniform because based on natural diurnal or seasonal cycles. At the same time, in any given culture, most people accepted the ritual/ religious calendar.

Temporal and spatial organization also worked together. For example, among Australian aborigines, darkness and the location of fires in front of each family's dwelling area in the camp meant that people could not see each other at night. This was used to develop a particular system of conflict resolution through verbal means which tends to break down when lighting is introduced, or when the camp spatial organization is altered, with consequent increases in stress and aggression (Hamilton, 1972).

In terms of meaning, there was much greater sharing of symbols and the cues which communicated them—most people agreed about them and, at the same time, the space/meaning congruence was strong and clear. Communication was much more predictable being fixed and prescribed, enforced by sanctions, and related to membership in various groups—and the other organizations expressed and reinforced this clarity.

The environments of various cultures can thus be conceptualized in terms of the organization of these four variables, their specific expressions and devices used, the degree of congruence, and so forth. This conceptualization, combined with that proposed for culture, suggests a way of starting to relate these two major elements.

THE RELATIONSHIP OF CULTURE AND ENVIRONMENTAL DESIGN

The system of rules of any given culture leads to systematic choices about which elements are important. Such elements will then tend to vary and also be given different emphasis. This may apply to the environment where various physical devices may be used for similar ends, similar physical devices may indicate different things, environmental quality components may vary and, if similar, may be ranked differently (Rapoport, 1977). This may also apply to life-styles, so that people make choices among available alternatives and may allocate their limited resources—material, temporal, or symbolic—differently (e.g., Michelson & Reed, 1970). Potentially, one could develop an approach whereby the elements and characteristics of both environments and life-styles could be described by profiles expressing differential choices, and the congruence or lack of congruence between them studied (for a small, beginning attempt see Rapoport, 1977, p. 18).

Note that choices are among possible alternatives; what is possible is partly a function of the ecological milieu, partly of cultural interpretations thereof. The specific nature of the choices made tends to be lawful, reflecting the culture of the people concerned. In fact, one way of looking at culture is in terms of the most common choices made. It is this

lawfulness of the choices which makes places recognizably different
from one another; makes dress, behavior, what one eats and table manners, structuring of space, time, meaning, and communication all
noticeably different. These consistent choices result in *style*—whether of
built environment or of life.

In making choices, certain values, norms, criteria, and assumptions
are used. These are often embodied in ideal schemata: built environments and the life they enclose all, in some way, reflect and encode
these schemata—however imperfectly (Rapoport, 1977, p. 15ff). Groups
stress different things, rank them differently, and relate them differently, so that, for any group, there is a *core* of elements which are
important and define the group to itself and to others and which are not
easily given up. There are also peripheral elements which are more
easily given up and sometimes willingly changed. Their disappearance
does not threaten the integrity of the culture, whereas a sudden and
forcible change in the core is disruptive and potentially destructive,
because it upsets homeostasis (Rapoport, 1978b,c). This suggestion will
be considered later when the implications of this approach to design are
considered in more detail. At this point it will be useful briefly to consider a few of the many possible mechanisms linking culture and environmental design.

Some of these have already been implictly discussed: life-style—
with all this implies; social organization and family structure; cognitive
schemata or domains; meanings, symbols, and rituals; temporal organizations. Many of these can be grouped into *occasions*—who does what,
with whom, when and in what context, and where—i.e., which settings
are appropriate. Clearly, occasions exist without specific physical settings or markers, but these latter are useful. When settings provide
physical cues, and encode the ideas implicit in the situation, they become a useful mnemonic, they reinforce behavior by reminding people
how to act, how to behave, what is expected of them; they also provide
props and supportive elements appropriate to the situations. Built environments go beyond that, however. They also make ideas visible, signify power or status, express and support cosmological schemata, encode value systems, they separate domains, differentiating between
here/there, men/women, private/public, inhabitable/uninhabitable,
sacred/profane, front/back, and so on. The physical distinctions among
places and settings not only express the various purposes they serve:
they also communicate appropriate behavior. Built environments thus
provide a spatiotemporal framework for occasions and activities, and
remind people what these activities are (Rapoport, 1978d,e). But they

only do all these things if they are legible, i.e., if the meaning is appropriate to the culture and its activities.

At this point we may return to the notion of activities as a useful starting point—particularly since activity systems in space and time have been much used by planners and environmental designers and because they can easily be related to behavior setting systems (Rapoport, 1977). When used, however, activities have been overly generalized, i.e., cultural differences have been neglected and also only their manifest aspects have been considered. Yet activities, even at the level of so-called basic needs, seem extremely variable (Rapoport, 1969a) and this variability increases as one moves away from the manifest aspects to what have been called their latent aspects (Zeisel, 1969). This variability means that one must deal with specifics, so that, for example, while sitting is a universal activity, whether one sits on the floor or on chairs has major implications for behavior, manners, dress, furniture design, room furnishings, and many aspects of house and garden design—as a comparison of Chinese and Japanese houses will quickly reveal (Fitzgerald, 1965). Furthermore, who sits with whom or avoiding whom, when, during which occasions, and so on will influence many aspects of larger setting systems. Thus, through considering differences among apparently simple molecular activities such as cooking, eating, playing, sleeping, shopping—even sheltering—we can eventually get to more molar concepts such as life-style, images, values, and, eventually, world views, subcultures, and cultures as they relate to built environments.

The following schema may be suggested. Any activity can be analyzed into four components (Rapoport, 1977):

1. The activity proper
2. The specific way of doing it and where it is done
3. Additional, adjacent or associated activities which become part of the activity system
4. Symbolic aspects and meaning of the activity

Consider cooking. The activity is one of converting raw food into cooked food—a human activity so basic that it is often used to distinguish between the basic domains of culture and nature (e.g., Lévi-Strauss, 1970). The specific way of cooking may involve frying, roasting, baking, or whatever; the use of special kinds of utensils or ovens; the use of special settings; standing, squatting, and so on. Associated activities may include socializing, exchanging information, listening to music, or whatever. The symbolic meaning of cooking may be ritual; a way of acquiring status—as among Puerto Rican women (e.g., Zeisel, 1969); a way of asserting some special social identity or membership of a group—as among the Apache (e.g., Esber, 1972a,b); a way of enculturating or socializing children (e.g., Rapoport, 1978a; Ricci, 1972).

Similar arguments can be made for drinking alcoholic beverages, eating, shopping, and many other activities. Consider shopping. This is basically the exchange of money (or goods) for goods. The specific way of shopping may vary, with major implications for the design of the setting—supermarket or bazaar—its relationship to the city, the sensory interaction with both goods and people in the various sense modalities. Activities associated in the activity system may include talking, eating, socializing, getting messages to people, finding out what goes one. Finally, the symbolic meaning may be display, conspicious consumption, shopping as recreation, or a way for women to get out of the house.

It is the difference among these four aspects of apparently simple activities which leads to specific forms of settings, differences in their relative importance, the amount of time spent in them, who is involved and so on—in fact all the kinds of things which influence built form. An important, unresolved question is the degree of constancy due to people as members of a single species and the variability due to culture; this will be discussed later.

This schema goes beyond the distinction made between manifest and latent function in the built environment (Zeisel, 1969) although, in effect, (1) and (2) above are mainly manifest while (3) and (4) fit into the latent category. By being specific, however, it can be suggested that the variability of (2), (3), and (4) leads to differences in form and the differential success of various designs. In fact, acceptability and choice (including habitat selection [cf. Rapoport, 1977]) would appear to be most related to (3) and (4) which are closest to the cultural core and most likely to be embodied in images.

This typology also relates in an interesting way to the hierarchy of levels of meaning ranging from the concrete object, through the use and value objects to the symbolic object (Gibson, 1950, p. 198–199; 1968, p. 91ff.) and which I have found useful elsewhere (Rapoport & Hawkes, 1970; Rapoport, 1970a,b,c; 1976a,b). In that case also, the variability increases as one moves to the symbolic end of the scale, which seems most closely related to environmental choices and the effects of the environment on people—desirable or undesirable.

These variable activities occur in systems of settings which are also variable (Rapoport, 1977). What often relates systems of activities to systems of settings are the social institutions which cultures develop (e.g., King, 1976). These link occasions, activity systems, and their appropriate systems of settings. Not only are specific settings different, but also the rules associated with them: acceptable or unacceptable activities, who is admitted or excluded, when they are used and so on, and how they are related—linked or divided—how their meanings are indicated, the means whereby they are differentiated from other settings. The most significant type of setting system is the house–settlement system and one can show that there is great cultural and subcultural variability in the elements, and relationships among them, of such systems, some of which are not intuitively obvious and may even be counterintuitive (Rapoport, 1977, p. 298–315). Again, one finds that such differences can generate conflicts, as when streets are defined by one group as places for interaction and by others as merely for passage (Becker, 1973; Rapoport, 1969a), or as in the case of reversal of behaviors and cues appropriate to front and back domains. Thus, when fronts are not well maintained, lawns or their equivalents absent, or behavior defined by one group as inappropriate to front regions takes place in them, this may not only lead to conflict but to the definition of areas as slums—with serious planning and design implications (Rapoport, 1977; see also Brower this volume). Similar problems may occur when the transitions among domains are unclear or inappropriate; when time organization is substituted for space organization in situations where there is no knowledge of how to use such devices; where defenses against stress generally or for achieving privacy are similarly inappropriate—in fact, at any time when there is major incongruence between activities and settings, for whatever reason (sudden changes in cultural core elements, large conceptual distance among elements [Rapoport, 1978c] or when major and uncontrollable changes upset homeostasis). This gets us to the question of the effects of design on people and the notion of culture-specific design. But before turning to these, it is useful to examine the variability of culture–environment relations in more detail.

THE VARIABILITY OF CULTURE–ENVIRONMENT RELATIONS

Even a quick look at a few examples suggests that culture–environment relations vary to the extent that some may be almost reversals of others. For example, such reversals can occur over time, so that mountains, which were seen as evil and to be avoided, suddenly become, in the eighteenth century, beautiful and sublime—and to be sought out (Nicolson, 1959). Similarly, ancient ruins in Rome lost their negative associations as pagan and the devil's work and, with the Renaissance, came to symbolize a golden age. The meanings of settlement and wilderness generally have also changed over time, to the extent that a reversal occurred so that settlements, initially the humanized, sacred space *par excellence* (contrasting with profane wilderness) become "profane" space with wilderness becoming "sacred" (Tuan, 1974, pp. 104–105). Thus, we find a general process of definition into domains such as nature/culture, us/them, men/women, private/public, front/back, good/bad, sacred/profane, and so on (often with a middle term present which resolves this binary opposition), but the *meanings* attached to these domains shift and may reverse. Once imposed, such meanings influence land use and legislation, even in United States urban areas such as Boston (e.g., Firey, 1961) or Western wilderness areas (Erickson, 1977).

Such shifts and reversals help explain the differential location of settlements and dwellings as particular groups select or avoid plains or mountains, seacoasts or interiors, suburbs or cities, different neighborhoods within cities, large cities or rural areas (Rapoport, 1977). Activity systems also show these influences as groups avoid certain areas defined as hazardous. For example, Eskimos avoid areas defined as dangerous because profane and full of evil spirits (Burch, 1971), whereas modern urbanites avoid those areas thought to be dangerous because of crime (*New York Times*, 1971) (see Rapoport, 1977, for this comparison; see also Downs & Stea, 1977, p. 16). Once again the process is general: the human mind tends to categorize the environment into domains and to label some as undesirable or unusable, avoiding those, while frequenting those defined as usable or desirable (Rapoport, 1976b); the specifics are variable, however.

Given a common process but differing specifics, it follows that, in selecting or designing environments, people make choices so as to match their images of desirable places, appropriate for the kinds of people which the particular culture sees as normative and for the kind of life-style which it regards as significant and typical of the group, distinguishing it from other groups. Although the process is constant, the resulting environments differ greatly. This raises a topic of great generality—if cultures and their environments differ, is there any uniformity? This is, of course, an extremely old and fundamental problem among students of culture—the variability of cultures vs. the psychic unity of humanity, and we shall return to it since it should also be a central problem in environmental design research. It is, in fact, a major reason for adopting a cross-cultural approach.

Clearly, in this chapter, I have generally stressed one particular model of the relation of culture to environment—what might be called a cognitive congruence model, suggesting that environments are approximations to cognitive schemata held by people in a culture. In this I have stressed two of the three major definitions of culture: that dealing with cognitive schemata and symbolic meanings, and that concerned with ways of life, because these are related: settings house particular life-styles, and both environments and life-styles are the result of choices among alternatives based on common schemata. I have generally ignored the third major category of definitions of culture—that stressing adaptive strategies within particular ecological settings.

There are two reasons for this. The first is that cultures often persist even when ecological milieus change; they, and particularly their cores, are resistant to change. In terms of design one is less interested in how, or why, particular cultural patterns began than in what they are at a particular moment in time. Although ecology, resources, and sociopolitical variables may, indeed, influence culture, this is less important for our purpose than the fact that a culture exists with all the elements which make it up. It is, of course, also important to discover which of these are likely to change quickly or slowly, much or little, and the likely courses of change and development (and to design in an open-ended manner for these changes)—but all these begin with the existing situation.

The second reason is that in examining many examples of environments it appears that sociocultural variables are primary, with ecological ones, such as climate, materials, and ways of making a livelihood secondary, constraining, or modifying (Rapoport, 1969a),[1] although for a balanced approach they cannot be neglected.

It also seems that these various factors play different roles in large-scale and small-scale environments. For example, if we consider Australian aborigines and Northwestern Coast Indians of North America, we find that among the latter the settlement pattern seems to be determined by ecological and economic considerations, and houses by ritual ones; whereas among the former the dwelling responds primarily to climatic and material (i.e., ecological) forces, while the settlement pattern—in this case the movement pattern and relationships to the land—is based on ritual. In most cases, however, the example of the Northwest Coast Indians seems more typical and one could suggest a hypothesis that there is an element of scale involved. Ecology may be most important at large scales, so that agricultural patterns, land use, regional settlement patterns such as the location and distribution of settlements are greatly (although not entirely) influenced by ecological forces, possibly because

[1]In fact these relationships are rather complex, as some of the other chapters in this volume suggest. Also LeVine's (1973) consideration of the relation of culture and personality then seems relevant to attempts to relate personality and environment (e.g., the special issue of *Environment and Behavior*, Vol. 9, No. 2, June, 1977). For another potential link see Berry (1976).

of higher criticality (although there are exceptions other than the aborigines—e.g., the Dogon, Norway vs. Sweden, etc.). At smaller scales, settlement and building form and layout, possibly because of lower criticality, are mainly influenced by cognitive and other cultural factors.

Nomadism, i.e., movement itself, may also vary. Thus aboriginal movements are ritually highly significant and determined, although some would argue that even rituals have ecological significance (e.g., Rappaport 1971a,b). On the other hand the movements of Northwest Coast Indians are ecologically determined, as are those of the Basseri— although for these latter, movement itself becomes the important element replacing ritual (Barth, 1961; see also Rapoport, 1978c).

Australian aborigines also value ritual sites much more than resource sites and protect them more, whereas in Western culture the opposite is true. This was, in fact, a major problem since incoming settlers could not grasp aboriginal relationship to the land. This led to the denial of land rights to aborigines, since they did not appear to own, or even value, land in terms of the Western stress on material rather than symbolic resources; this is an example of culturally "illegible" codes.

Resources themselves are also culturally defined. As Zimmermann once said: "Resources are not; they become" (cited in Hewitt & Hare, 1973, p. 29). Thus, cultures will differentially "see" resources and pick different ecological niches. They will use those selectively to give material expression to organizations of space and meaning which reflect the organization of time and communication and are related to cognitive domain definition. Different materials will be used and they will be contrasted in different ways to create meaning. Since the organization of meaning can be separated from the organization of space, new and different materials may be used to express similar domains and spatial organizations.

Since resources are culturally defined, even ecological milieus and constraints are, at least partly, subjective: we are dealing with "perceived" (or more correctly, *cognized* [e.g., Rapoport, 1977]) resources, hazards, opportunities, and costs. The ways in which resources are exploited, by whom, and for what purposes are also culturally variable.

This point is further strengthened by the fact that two cultures in an identical setting may create very different built environments (Rapoport, 1969b). It is also reinforced by considering the great variety of responses to particular climates, in traditional and "primitive" situations, so that there seems to be no systematic relation of the type of dwelling and degree of shelter to either type or severity of climate (Rapoport, 1969a).

Even if one only considers extremely cold climates, those of highest criticality, no consistent relationship is found.[2]

Even in Western cultures, although the variability is smaller, and shrinking, major variations in standards and levels of comfort can be found, including indoor temperatures, lighting levels, stair proportions, and the like (Rapoport & Watson, 1972). More generally, notions of environmental quality, which involve a comparison with standards and norms, are highly variable so that the definition of a "slum," for example, can prove fairly difficult since it seems related to culture, to notions of appropriate behavior in particular domains such as public or private and front or back; appropriate materials, landscaping standards of maintenance; mixed uses vs. separation of activities in residential areas, and so on (see Rapoport, 1977, for a review). Similar considerations have influenced the very major changes in how squatter settlements have been seen and are increasingly influencing consideration of problems of traditional cultures and environments, modernization (e.g., Bodley, 1975), and "improvements." Thus, there is increasing interest in ethnomedicine and traditional systems of medicine and psychiatry as opposed to Western ones, with clear implications for the design of appropriate settings for these activities.

Similarly, it has been shown that the replacement of a thatched, communal dwelling (the *Bohio*) used by the Motilone Indians on the border of Colombia and Venezuela, which is dark inside, with an earth floor and open cooking fires, by modern dwellings, with light, cross-ventilation, concrete floors, and separate kitchens, was not only not an improvement but had disastrous consequences—destroying the culture and leading the author to describe these "improvements" as "ethnocide" (Jaulin, 1971). Similarly, as we have already seen, the introduction of electric light into Australian aboriginal camps may totally disrupt the conflict resolution mechanism which depends on darkness (Hamilton, 1972). The provision of Australian-type dwellings for the aborigine's squatter shacks was seen as a deterioration not an improvement by the residents because sociospatial relations and inside/outside contacts were disrupted (Savarton & George, 1971). In North Africa, the provisions of running water in dwellings disrupted the function of the village well as one of the few occasions (if not the only one) for women in *purdah* to leave the house, gossip, interact, and relate to the communication network obtaining and passing information.

---

[2]This was well demonstrated in a term paper in my course in the Department of Anthropology, University of Wisconsin-Milwaukee, by Donna Wade on "House Form and Climate."

In squatter settlements outside Mexico City the attempt to improve hygiene, quality of goods, and prices by eliminating markets and travelling vendors and replacing them with shops, similarly disrupted a major latent function: the vendors acted as the primary information and communication system. The change was *not* an improvement and the final solution was a combination of market *and* shops (Rapoport, 1977).

All these examples not only stress the latent aspects of activities but also the fact that environment quality, "better" or "worse" environments, are not absolute but relative and are a matter of definition. In other words, they need to be considered emically, from inside the culture and valid for it, stressing what the people in that culture themselves emphasize, rather than in terms of an imposed etic, i.e., from the perspective of an outside observer stressing principles valid cross-culturally. Of course, both are needed for understanding: the major point is that emic aspects must be understood in order to *develop* or derive etics. For example, it seems generally valid to analyze environments as expressions of cognitive schemata and domains. However, the specific taxonomies, the particular domains, how they are grouped as being similar or different and on what basis, how various domains are related to one another and what devices are used to link, separate, modulate, or isolate them, vary and must be studied emically. This goes beyond theoretical interest and importance: for example, density and crowding will depend on the cultural definition of domains and standards, so that before comparing densities, their emic definitions must be understood (Rapoport, 1976b, 1977).

Stephen Carr once spoke of the "city of the mind", while Joachim Wohlwill reminded us that the "environment is not in the head." I would argue that it *is* the subjective environment which influences behavior, but that this subjective environment is not completely arbitrary—it does not spring full-grown from our minds like Athene from the head of Zeus: it is related to the environment "out there" in some way. Although it may be transformed it is the "objective" environment which is thus transformed. The relationship between the two is via the mechanisms which link people and environments and which constitute one of the basic three questions of man–environment research (Rapoport, 1976a).

The designer's task, in this connection, is to create environments which will help people to construct *those* environments in their heads which are appropriate, which they desire, which match their images, ideals, and cognitive styles. Only such environments are supportive of people's life-styles and activities. In other words, the designer's task is to make more predictable and effective the relationships and congruence between the "objective" and "subjective" environments.

An important question in this connection is the variability of schemata, images, and cognitive styles within groups. Clearly, members of groups are not fully homogeneous with respect to such matters (e.g., Pelto & Pelto, 1975). However, even in arguing that in any group there is variability, one can argue that this variability is less *within* a group than *among* groups. The very fact that we can speak of groups suggests this. Although not all Navaho, for example, share schemata (for one thing they show different levels of acculturation), their schemata are more alike than they are like the schemata of the Hopi—or the Temne of Sierra Leone. Similarly, the elements of the environments of a given culture are not identical—they can vary considerably—yet the environment of a particular group is identifiable as such. A related issue, therefore, is what are valid groups in any context, particularly in contemporary Western situations or situations of culture change. The conclusion seems inescapable that groups which are valid for particular purposes, for example the cross-cultural analysis of environmental differences, need to be *discovered*, not assumed *a priori*. Such groups do not necessarily have to be based on criteria such as race, nationality, ethnicity, socioeconomic status, or whatever. For various purposes, different contexts and at different times different criteria become valid as defining "homogeneous" groups—and we are dealing with *perceived* (or cognized) homogeneity, i.e., *subjectively defined homogeneity* (as I will shortly elaborate). The definition of groups, of "us" as opposed to "them," depends on different characteristics. Yet this definition has been suggested as basic to humans. One of the things that defines groups is that their members have more in common than they do with members of other groups, i.e., they share some ideals, images, cognitive schemata—and thus characteristics of their environments. Also, though this is still some time off, it should be conceptually possible to conceive of variations in schemata and environments as transforms of basic models, so that the variability is nonrandom, consistent, and related to paradigms shared by the group.

One final point needs to be made. The environment "out there" is usually man-made since few places exist in which the environment has not been designed in the sense that it has been changed in some purposeful way. Not only built environments are man-made; so are landscapes. As such, they themselves are "subjective" in the sense that they are culturally variable. As already suggested, if the code is known one can easily tell whether a city is Peruvian or French, a landscape Chinese or Italian; in a given case one can tell whether a rural or urban landscape is Indian or Mestizo (Hill, 1964; Richardson, 1974); European, African, or Indian (Larimore, 1958; Rapoport, 1977). Since cultural landscapes are the result of the individual decisions of innumerable people, the fact that they add up to such recognizable totalities strengthens the view that they embody cultural schemata—that environments are physical expressions of cognitive schemata, that they are thought before they are built.

CULTURE-SPECIFIC ENVIRONMENTS

The notion of culture-specific environments follows from that of the specificity of activities, occasions, institutions, settings, and schemata. Various specific ways of organizing these, and particular environmental organizations, are suitable and necessary for particular groups with their specific conceptual systems; cognitive styles, social relationships, and behavioral patterns. For example, culs-de-sac may foster social interaction but may be liked or disliked for that very reason by different groups (Rapoport, 1977). Shared common spaces may in some cases (e.g., traditional Indian, Latin-American, or Greek villages and towns) foster interaction; in other cases they may not only not foster such interaction but actually *discourage* it (e.g., Foddy, 1977; Michelson, 1970). The question is what the effects might be of culturally inappropriate environments, how serious these might be and, consequently, how important the consideration of cultural variables is in design.

These questions are best approached by considering briefly the effects which environments have on people, i.e., the effects of particular organizations of space, time, meaning, and communication on human behavior, well-being, or mood. If there are no effects, or if these effects are minor, then the importance of studying man–environment relations is correspondingly diminished. It is also a difficult question to answer since the evidence is often difficult to compare, is contradictory and there is no consensus or generally accepted theoretical model. However, three positions can be distinguished regarding this, one of the three basic questions of man–environment research (Rapoport, 1977). The first is environmental determinism, the view that the physical environment determines human behavior. This has been the traditional view in planning and design, the belief that changes in the forms of environments can lead to major changes in behavior, increased happiness, increased social interaction, and so on. As a reaction, a second view was put forward that the physical environment has no major effects on people but that it is the social, economic, and similar environments which are of major importance. At most, to use a geographical analogy, one could accept the possibilist view; that physical environments provide possibilities and constraints within which choices are made based on other, mainly cultural, criteria. The third position, in geography, is probabilism—the view that physical environments do, in fact, provide possibilities for choice but that they also constrain choice to the extent that some choices become much more probable than others in given physical settings.

The current view in environmental design research is similar. The built environment is seen as a setting for human activities. Such settings may be inhibiting or facilitating, they constrain choices selectively, and a particular setting may be facilitating to the extent of acting as a catalyst or releasing latent behavior, but cannot, however, determine or *generate* activities. Thus, in doing many experiments with students, I found that, if one works in a direction desired by people, then apparently minor environmental elements will have major effects in predicted directions. Working against desired behaviors, very major changes need to be introduced, and do not always work even then. Similarly, inhibiting environments will generally make certain behaviors more difficult although they will not usually block them completely; generally, though, it is easier to block behavior than to generate it. Such inhibiting effects may, under conditions of reduced competence (e.g., children, the elderly, the ill, the institutionalized [e.g., Lawton, 1970; Perin, 1970]) become much more acute and they may, in fact, become critical.

This reduced competence may be cultural as well as physical, so that groups undergoing very rapid change, groups whose culture is "marginal" and, generally, those in situations of environmental stress (Rapoport, 1978b), may be affected critically by inappropriate forms of the built environment. Such forms may, for example, prevent or destroy particular forms of family organization, prevent the formation of homogeneous groups for mutual help, disrupt social networks or certain institutions, prevent certain ritual or economic activities, eliminate highly specific privacy and conflict resolution mechanisms, require major restructuring of cognitive schemata, and so on (Rapoport, 1978c). These are compounded by lack of perceived choice and control when change is rapid and forced rather than gradual and voluntary, and when values central to the group are threatened.

All cases of reduced competence—physical, mental, or cultural— seem to have a common factor, reduced ability to cope with high levels of stress, so that the *additional* stress of overcoming inhibiting environments may become too great. There are a number of complicating factors. First, the effects of adaptation in terms of stress are frequently remote in space and time from the initial occurence and hence difficult to trace. Second, environmental effects are mediated by "filters" (Rapoport, 1977) which may be pan-human, cultural, subcultural, personal, or situational, i.e., they are part of the perceived environment and involve expectations, motivations, judgments, and meanings. Thus we are dealing with *perceived* stress, which is subjectively defined and culturally variable, so that apparently major stressors may have minor effects while apparently minor, and even benign, variables may have disastrous consequences (Rapoport, 1978b).

Notions of environmental quality, standards, and the like are also variable so that, for example, the definition of undesirable environments and the meaning of density or privacy are all fairly complex issues. It also follows that effects of particular environmental changes are not always intuitively clear or predictable. Although in conditions of heightened criticality supportive environments may be necessary, they become supportive by being *culture specific*. An important aspect of culture-specific design follows from the importance of latent aspects of activities and from the observation that people behave differently in different settings (e.g., Barker, 1968). People do so because they tend to make their behavior congruent with the norms for behavior appropriate to the setting as defined by the culture (Rapoport, 1978a,d). This implies that the built environment *provides cues for behavior*, and that it can be seen as a form of nonverbal communication, whether through fixed-feature elements (walls, floors, roofs, streets, etc.), semifixed-feature elements (furniture, furnishings, landscaping, signs, etc.), or nonfixed-feature elements (people, their dress, gestures, proxemic relationships, and so on) (cf. Hall, 1966).

People, then, act according to their reading of the environmental cues, and the code or "language" must be understood. The design of the environment can be seen partly as a process of encoding information so that users can easily decode it. If the code is not shared, not understood, or inappropriate, the environment does not communicate: its "language" may be foreign to the users. An important aspect of culture-specific environments, those culturally supportive, is thus in the organization of meaning.

The above discussion also suggests that it is possible to distinguish between direct and indirect effects of the environment. The former are those where the environment directly affects behavior, mood, satisfaction, performance, or interaction. The latter are those where the environment is used to draw conclusions about the social situation and behavior regulated accordingly—the effects are social but the cues are physical. The setting and its cues do not determine behavior, as already suggested: they just make certain behaviors more likely, they guide and constrain behavior; although any situation always presents some choice rather than eliciting an automatic response, appropriate settings restrict the range of responses. In fact, most of culture consists of habitual, routinized behavior which may often be almost automatic; the cues and rules of settings which are understood help elicit these appropriate responses (Rapoport, 1978d). This process operates particularly effectively in traditional cultures and settings: cultures could, in fact, be ranked on the basis of how well these processes operate.

In this discussion, as typically in most discussions about the effects of environments on people, there is an implicit assumption that somehow people are placed in environments which then act on them. Yet, in most cases, people select their habitat, leading to various forms of migration—international, interregional, interurban, down to the selection of a neighborhood, house, and furniture. In effect, people vote with their feet, and a major effect of environment on people is negative or positive attraction—the pushes and pulls leading to *habitat selection* which also include latent aspects; since such choice involves the matching of perceived characteristics against norms and images, it is culturally variable (Rapoport, 1977). In some cases, habitat selection is blocked and this then becomes a major environmental problem. In cases of forced habitation (urban renewal, settling nomads, institutionalization), the environment becomes more critical, and this heightened criticality, at the cultural level, means that the survival of cultures may be linked to the form of the environment so that such environments may become *negatively determining*.

We have seen that in any culture there is a core and a set of peripheral elements. It is when environments inhibit and make impossible the functioning of the core elements that the group's cultural survival may be threatened. At the same time, as already pointed out, one cannot always predict *a priori* the importance to the cultural core of particular environmental features—this needs to be discovered. Thus, it had been predicted that the Navaho hogan was a critical element to that group and their environmental well-being (Bochner, 1975), i.e., a supportive core element. Recent work, however, has suggested that this is not the case and that the *settlement* form may be much more significant (Sadalla, Snyder, & Stea, 1976). This finding is not altogether unexpected since, frequently, relationships among dwellings, between dwellings and the outside, and to other elements in the house–settlement system, are more important than the dwellings themselves, so that similar findings apply to other nomadic or seminomadic groups (Rapoport, 1978c). But this is not necessarily the case: in other instances the opposite may be true. The important thing is that *this must be discovered by analyzing the specifics of the culture and the related environments.*

Thus, in identifying where in the house–settlement system cosmological and sacred meanings are to be found, it is soon discovered that among Australian aborigines it is primarily in the landscape generally, and above all in certain sacred places within that landscape related to the various specific groups; secondarily in camps (i.e., settlements) and not at all in the dwelling itself (Rapoport, 1972). Among the Northwest Coast Indians of North America,[3] on the other hand, sacred meaning is mainly attached to the dwellings, the settlement apparently having none (Goldman, 1975; Müller, 1955—both on the Kwakiutl). Among the Ainu, finally, such meanings seem to be attached to all three—to the landscape, to the settlement, and to the dwelling (Ohnuki-Tierney, 1972). Other combinations are undoubtedly possible—in each case the significant elements and relationships among them must be discovered. Also, though for some groups spaces are most significant, for others time organization may be more critical (Rapoport, 1978c).

The specifics are the crucial consideration. Then, through an understanding of the mechanisms which primarily relate these elements and the effects likely to occur as various elements are changed, guidelines become possible for planning and design decision.

DESIGNING FOR CULTURE

Given the argument about the importance of sociocultural variables and hence the need for culture-supportive environments, designing for culture seems desirable. It also seems to be exceedingly difficult—although it should be the long range goal. Activities, however, particularly if they include latent and symbolic aspects, can provide a very useful starting point and lead fairly easily to life-style, as defined above, i.e., as the outcome of a series of choices about how to allocate temporal, material, and symbolic resources on the basis of culturally defined priorities. Design is also the result of a similar choice process, so that particular environments have qualities seen as desirable or undesirable, supportive or inhibiting. They are supportive to the extent that the systems of settings, their cues and meanings, and the rules about who is included or excluded are congruent with the activity systems, all these

[3]Ranging from the Tlingit in the north, through the Haida, Tsimshian, Kwakiutl, Bella Coola, and Nootka, to the Salish in the south.

judgments being subjective and culturally variable. Different organizations of space, time, meaning, and communication are needed to support rather than inhibit given life-styles.

Since cultures survive to the extent that children are appropriately enculturated, child-rearing is often an important aspect of life-style and, as is the case in our cities, an important criterion for both habitat selection and conflict among groups. Thus, if children are controlled by members of the larger group rather than merely the immediate family, then an inappropriate space organization, based on the control of children by the nuclear family, will not be supportive and may lead to delinquency and conflict, whether in China (Anderson, 1972; Mitchell, 1971) or among blacks in the United States (Hall, 1971; Yancey, 1971). Spaces used by children then need to be differently related to adults and *their* activities. The absence of such spaces, while inhibiting for some groups, may not have negative effects in the case of other groups and may, in fact, be a desirable aspect of their environment.

As we would expect, even more specific considerations are needed. In traditional China there were subcultural differences so that the appropriate spatial organization for one group, for whom children's play took place in house courts, was quite inappropriate for another where children played in the street (Schak, 1972). These are, of course, aspects of the more general question of the relation of environments to enculturation of children (Rapoport, 1978a), and also to children's caretakers. In different cultures different people become caretakers and need very different supportive settings with different relationships to parts of the house–settlement system. Such relationships may also have unforeseen consequences as, for example, among the inhabitants of the West End of Boston. There small children were cared for by teenage girls who hung out near shops. Teenage boys used basketball to impress girls, thus requiring courts to be located appropriately. When not so located, they were not used (Brolin & Zeisel, 1968)—i.e., there was a relationship between caretaking and basketball play.

Another example is provided by privacy (Rapoport, 1976a). If that is defined as the control of unwanted interaction, then "unwanted" and "interaction" are both culturally variable terms. How one avoids interaction, once defined, is also variable and one can suggest that there are at least five or six major mechanisms: *rules* (manners, hierarchies, avoidance, etc.); *moving away* (as in the case of nomads); *psychological means* (internal withdrawal, depersonalization, etc.); *behavioral cues* (hiding behind a paper); structuring activities in *time* (so that particular individuals and groups do not meet); *spatial separation; physical devices* (walls, doors, locks, curtains—the usual design mechanisms which can be conceptualized as privacy filters). Usually, multiple mechanisms are used, but various groups stress particular ones, as well as particular sensory modalities. The use of inappropriate mechanisms, or the emphasis on inappropriate modalities, the wrong context (who is to be avoided, when, and why) can lead to environments which are inhibiting rather than supportive (for example, nomads who use moving away as a major mechanism have great difficulty when suddenly faced with the need to use physical devices or rules [Rapoport, 1978c]). Similarly, people in a culture using spatial separation and physical devices can be subjected to major stress when they have to use temporal mechanisms (Harrington, 1965). How then does one go about achieving congruence between life-style and built environment? Certain *general* principles can be suggested. Among them:

1. The nature of the group and its characteristics, life-style, rules for behavior, environmental preferences, images, cognitive schemata, space and time taxonomies, and so on, should be established.

2. Communication and privacy needs, the mechanisms and defenses used, and the various sensory modalities stressed should be known.

3. The symbols of status as expressed in location, dwellings, and artifacts, i.e., environmental meaning, should be understood, as should the principal ways of establishing social identity.

4. The nature of the activity systems and their latent aspects need to be understood, as does their distribution in space and time, and how they are related to home range, to territorial behavior, and to the nature of territorial markers.

5. Social organization, relations, and networks, and their relation to the organization of the environment, to movement patterns, and to interaction rates and settings, should be traced.

Thus approached, environments will tend to be supportive rather than inhibiting. Supportive environments are based on some more detailed, *although still general*, principles:

(a) Those elements most important to the cultural system must receive most support and be helped to last longest, so that peripheral elements are replaced first. Thus, the cultural core must be identified.

(b) Those activities which have important latent and symbolic functions, and are critical to the culture, should be stressed and supported.

(c) The spatial organization of settlements, neighborhoods, and dwellings should be related to social organization and structure, space and time use, meanings, and the organization and control of communication and interaction. Affective and perceived density should be related to traditions, as should various groupings of dwellings, movement patterns, forms of homogeneity, and so on.

In all these cases we are dealing with systems of settings of which one of the most important is the house–settlement system (Rapoport, 1969a; 1977). As already suggested, house–settlement systems are extremely variable culturally: their components and the associated behaviors and rules need to be discovered, they cannot be foreseen *a priori*. In fact, if one starts with activity systems, even the definition of "dwelling" becomes fairly difficult and culturally variable, since the system of settings where such activities occur, their relationships, when used, according to which rules, and including or excluding whom, vary. What happens in a "house" in one culture may occur in a number of different settings within the house–settlement system in another.[4] This is partly a matter of differentiation, i.e., the number and specificity of settings, partly of how they are related (integrated or separated), how marked and contrasted, and what rules apply regarding their use.

If one begins with activities and life-styles as a way of designing culture-supportive environments, then an important question clearly is: *which* activities, their way of being carried out, associated activities, and their meanings are the most important? It is in this connection that the idea of the culture core becomes important, i.e., those elements most important to the group itself (i.e., emically). The cultural core defines a user group profile, a particular life-style and a set of important activities. Although lists of elements are not generally useful, core elements are likely to be found among the following:

1. Characteristics such as ethnicity, language, and religion
2. Family and kinship structures and child-rearing practices
3. Residence patterns, land divisions, landowning and tenure systems
4. Food habits
5. Ritual and symbolic systems
6. Ways of establishing and indicating status and social identity
7. Manners and nonverbal communication
8. Cognitive schemata
9. Privacy, density, and territoriality
10. Home range behavior and networks
11. Various institutions such as ways of working, cooperating, trading.

[4]A number of examples can be found in Rapoport (1977).

It is the elements of the culture core which are supported by supportive environments.

Two more questions could be asked: By what are they supported, and how are they supported? The answer to the first is that they are supported by various designed systems, which at one level may be visualized as related systems of settings and at a more fundamental level as particular organizations of space, time, meaning, and communication. One thus needs to go beyond the physical environment—underlying all environments, including apparently "disordered" ones, are social and conceptual ordering systems, meanings, relationships, and domains. The specific environment is the result of the ordering system and domains, the relationships among them, and the physical elements expressing them. A useful way of understanding what is supportive is thus an analysis of the existing settlements, dwellings, and house–settlement systems. In the case of developing countries, for example, one can suggest that one should analyze traditional environments, squatter settlements, modifications to urban environments, and, finally, environments of elites. This would indicate which features last longest, which are important, and how transformations occur, and hence allow both likely trajectories of environmental changes and the effects of changes to be predicted.

The answer to the second question: How do supportive environments work? is that support is given by appropriate spatial and temporal organizations, by meaningful cues, and by proper modulation of communication, i.e., the inclusion and exclusion of appropriate individuals and groups at appropriate times and in appropriate places, in appropriate situations, and using appropriate mechanisms. One of the elements which culture-specific, and hence supportive, environments make available are the appropriate defenses which the members of a particular group know how to use in order to achieve desired interaction rates (e.g., Rapoport, 1978b). An alternative interpretation is possible. It could be argued that as members of a single species, people in all cultures (with *individual* variations) have comparable interaction rates: what varies is their location and distribution in various settings in the house–settlement system, timing, and the significant others involved. If that were the case, appropriate environments would then facilitate the proper modulation of that interaction rate rather than the achievement of appropriate interaction rates.

The critical supportive elements differ in their specifics but can be analyzed in similar ways, i.e., there is the usual interplay of specificity and generality. In many cases, latent aspects and meanings are central, and it is important to consider "structurally" equivalent units so that, for example, the equivalent of a street may be the space within a compound rather than the circulation space among compounds, although the latter "looks" more like a street.

Culture-supportive environments are most clearly seen in extreme situations of rapid culture change, environmental stress, and the like— i.e., in situations of high criticality. This is an example of the general principle that, in research, it is easiest to start with extreme situations where effects are strongest and hence seen most clearly, and then move on to more "subtle" situations.

In cases of high criticality, supportive environments have several important functions. By supporting traditional and/or familiar activities they provide a safe and familiar base from which to operate; counterintuitively this may speed adaptation and modernization. Such settings also avoid the need totally to restructure cognitive schemata—a most difficult task—and thus reduce stress. This total restructuring of cognitive schemata is always difficult, but becomes particularly so when the people concerned are already under stress (Rapoport, 1978b,c). When groups are subjected to environmental stress various strategies are possible. They can change the macroenvironment (e.g., move); they can alter the physical environment at the meso- or microscale; they can change their behavior; they can change their values and perceptions and thus reduce cognitive dissonance (e.g., Adams, 1974); the group can break down, as has happened to Australian aborigines (e.g., Cawte, 1972, 1974) or the *Ik* (Turnbull, 1972).

Supportive environments are meant to prevent the latter adaptation and help with more useful adaptive strategies in given situations which partly depend on culture. In this process there is a particular adaptation which merits being discussed separately. By providing apparently minor, yet key, elements, supportive environments may help this particular adaptation known as *defensive structuring* (Siegel, 1970). The central characteristic of this response to environmental stress with which a group cannot cope is often the concentration on a few key values which give social identity to the group, reinforce solidarity, and so on—and in this process environmental elements and symbols can be most important. The provision, or retention, of such important environmental and life-style symbols may often avoid the development of other, possibly less desirable, mechanisms. In this process, the *meaning* of elements is clearly most important, as is the meaning of particular activities, and this helps explain the apparently minor character of some of them: what makes them important is their relation to the culture core.

For example, among the Mayo Indians of Sonora, Mexico, the house cross (and, to a lesser extent, some other types of crosses) are the major symbolic element in asserting and maintaining social identity, reinforcing group cohesion, communicating expectations about behavior and group boundaries to members and nonmembers alike. The orientation of houses, their relation to the settlement and to group membership is linked to this important, though apparently minor, architectural element which identifies the group. In fact, the houses seem haphazardly arranged until the system is understood (Crumrine, 1964)—i.e., until the code can be read. In this, as in other cases, ritual and processions are important and relate to the crosses (or other elements) so that periodic ceremonial movement, using such symbols, plays an essential, and hence core, role in the integration of the group and the ordering of the environment, as among the Australian aborigines, or among the Maya (e.g., Vogt, 1968, 1976). These essential environmental elements only communicate to those who understand the code.

In the case of the Apache, it is a particular form of meal organization which requires a spatial organization quite different than that used in Anglo houses. This setting is supportive for this key activity which is central to the identity and survival of the group (Esber, 1972a,b). Among Puerto Ricans in Boston a particular aesthetic complex has developed which is supportive of life-style and critical for ethnic survival (Jopling, 1974). This apparently trivial choice of particular objects, colors, and the like becomes an example of defensive structuring substituting for other responses which are blocked by the particular circumstances, social and environmental, under which this group lives. In the case of the Fang, in Africa, one finds the development of a "miniaturized" environment, a building (called the Aba Eboka) for a new syncretic religion. This building encodes the important elements of traditional cognitive schemata and supports ritual activities which likewise embody essential elements of the culture core (Fernandez, 1977). It is probably this mechanism which leads to the finding that in Argentina migrant groups succeeded when they were able to recreate traditional field layouts and settlement forms (Eidt, 1971). Homogeneity was also important—a point discussed below.[5]

We find apparently minor elements in situations closer to our own which play similar roles. Thus social identity is often communicated through environmental elements, landscaping, maintenance levels, and the like. For some groups the ability to cluster may be critical for the survival of language or culture and particular neighborhoods may be most important for particular groups (see examples in Rapoport, 1977).

---

[5]A number of other examples of this phenomenon are reviewed in Rapoport (1977).

This last point provides an example of another type of supportive setting—an area of people homogeneous along certain dimensions who, through clustering, create a supportive environment.

Homogeneous neighborhoods have been extremely prevalent throughout history as shown by both historical and archaeological data. It has been more formalized in some *places* than others (e.g., India and the Middle East) and at some *times* (e.g., periods of massive migrations or rapid culture change). It is also clear that they are more important for some groups than others (e.g., those under stress, localities, those of limited mobility), since they provide mutual support.

The variables whereby groups are defined as homogeneous have varied in different places and times, but have always resulted in areas homogeneous on the basis of these variables. Among them have been: religion, class, race, place of origin, kinship, caste, language, stage in life cycle, education, community of interests, and occupation. Increasingly today life-style is becoming a major variable. The important point is that, as already pointed out, once again, it is a *subjective definition* by the people concerned rather than any *a priori* set of variables. In other words, we are dealing with *perceived homogeneity* (Rapoport, 1977). It is this which explains an area such as LaClede Town in St. Louis, Missouri, which is often described as extremely heterogeneous on the basis of the standard measures of race, income, and the like. But the people who have chosen to live there share an ideology—of wanting to live in a "heterogeneous" area in the central city. Paradoxically, their shared "heterogeneity" on ideological grounds gives them an unusually high degree of perceived homogeneity.

It can also be suggested that when the natural processes of selection by perceived homogeneity are blocked, other forms will emerge which are less desirable because artificial rather than natural (Petonnet, 1972). These will then be based on imposed and arbitrary rather than subjectively defined criteria, and hence not work nearly as well.

If neighborhoods based on perceived homogeneity have been so prevalent there must be good reasons for them. It is quite easy to list large numbers of possible reasons, most of which are clearly related to the concept of environments supportive of specific life-styles:

- Homogeneity increases predictability or reduces unpredictability, thus reducing stress, the need to process information and hence overload.
- A homogeneous area can be a "backstage region" (to use Goffman's term) allowing people to relax and behave more naturally, once again reducing stress.

- Homogeneity reduces the perceived density of areas, again reducing information levels.
- Homogeneity allows a large number of psychological, cultural, and other "defenses" to operate much more effectively and is *in itself* a major defense.
- Homogeneity allows meanings to be taken for granted, i.e., it leads to much clearer and more effective nonverbal communication. It becomes easier to understand body language, clothing, behavior, physical cues in the environment, and to relate them to rules and hence to appropriate situations and contexts: environmental cues work more effectively.
- Homogeneity leads to agreement about temporal organization and greatly reduces conflict.
- Homogeneity leads to agreement about notions of environmental quality and hence reduced conflict about various standards such as maintenance, front lawns, children's behavior. It also makes self-governance much easier and hence enables the use of informal rather than formal rules and controls. This makes working together, cooperation, involvement, and participation much easier, and thus has implications for open-endedness. All this becomes possible due to agreement on goals based on shared values.
- Homogeneity provides mutual support at times of stress and culture change. Through the ability to share symbols, shops, language, food, festivals, rituals and religion, family and kinship, etc., environmental stress can be greatly reduced (particularly since we are dealing with *perceived* stress so that there is also agreement about what are stressors). Through the use of all these, and other, institutions such mutual support can, in fact, help cultural groups survive (e.g., Rosser & Harris, 1965; Ehrlich, 1971). These effects, of course, vary for different groups depending on the degree of stress, rapidity of change, whether the group is spacebound or not, etc.
- The existence of many homogeneous areas increases choice at the urban scale, helps habitat selection, and increases both perceived and actual control, again reducing stress.
- Homogeneity results in personalization which is not random but has a coherent character. This leads to complexity at the urban scale rather than to chaos, produces areas with distinctly different and comprehensible character, and thus helps groups, and individuals in these groups, to communicate social identity.

The notion of perceived homogeneity implies that the nature of the group which is being considered in planning and design cannot be assumed *a priori* but needs to be discovered, a conclusion already introduced. It is the life-style and culture core profile of that group which needs to be made congruent with the environmental quality variables and characteristics of the environment. Such a match is never perfect, nor can it be, since cultures change (although, as we have seen, the starting point is the existing situation). Neither should the match be perfect, since open-endedness is important. On the other hand even open-endedness is culture-specific, i.e., which elements need to be left for people to manipulate and control is, to a considerable extent, a matter of their meaning and their role in the culture core, and hence needs to be discovered rather than assumed (Rapoport, 1968).

IMPLICATIONS FOR THE FUTURE

If design for culture and cultural differences is to occur, what is needed? To conclude this chapter I will outline a few of the issues which require clarification, i.e., some needed research.

A most important first step is to consider the question of variability vs. constancy already briefly raised. More specifically, which aspects of culture and environmental design are constant and invariant, or change very slowly, and which vary and in what ways. This would help to clarify which are the baselines and constancies, if any, and which the cultural differences. If the commonalities could be defined there would be very much less left requiring specific consideration and these specifics could then be studied in more detail; design for cultural specificity would also become easier (Rapoport, 1975, p. 146). These constancies could be seen in various ways: one might consider species specific constancies, those applying to large groups and so on gradually defining the degree of variability and specificity which needs to be considered in any given case. By isolating the regularities and those elements more constant and invariant over time and across cultures, the variability which operates and is significant in any given context would be greatly reduced and could be more easily isolated, studied, and used.

The idea of establishing baselines for design based on an understanding of our species' evolutionary past is intriguing. Suggestions have recently been made that there may be such species-specific evolutionary baselines, so that particular environments may be maladaptive and that the concept of phylogenetic maladjustment may apply to humans (e.g., Boyden, 1970, 1974; cf. also Fox, 1970; Hamburg, 1975; Rossi, 1977; Tiger, 1969; Tiger & Fox, 1966, 1971; Tiger & Shepher, 1975; Washburn & Lancaster, 1968). In a very real sense human intellect, emotions, and basic social life are all evolutionary products of the hunting life, since people have been hunters for about 99% of human history. The organization of behavior and the intellectual and genetic repertoire of people are the result of hunting—we have the genetic equipment and biological and social attributes going back millions of years. Among the environmental characteristics related to this evolutionary base are: a low density level (rarely exceeding throughout human history one person per square mile) so that there may be social stress at densities much above the average at which the species evolved (Ucko, Tringham, & Dimbleby, 1972, p. 178, 443). Other characteristics are small group size and homogeneity in the group, and certain levels of environmental stimulation and challenge. In all cases, recent changes have been too rapid for behavioral adaptation, and even the 10,000 years of farming (compared with the millions of years of hunting/gathering) are too short for genetic change.

Admittedly, much of this is speculative and currently rather controversial, but it is also intuitively appealing and, in any case, it is a line of research which needs to be pursued. It is also important to understand other constancies, particularly since our own culture stresses change to an inordinate degree. Also, if apparent change and variability are an expression of invariant processes this is also extremely important because the *reasons* for doing apparently different things remain the same.

If we understand these reasons and the processes which they represent, then we may find that apparently unrelated forms, apparently different ways of doing things are equivalent, in the sense that they achieve the same objectives, are the result of similar mental processes, or are transformations of each other.

To use an example: Consider three urban forms—a dense city of courtyards, a low density urban fabric of widely separated dwellings, and a city made up of "urban villages" composed of highly homogeneous populations with strong social links. These appear very different indeed, but can all be shown to be mechanisms for controlling unwanted interaction, i.e., reduce information levels and stress and achieve desired levels of privacy (Rapoport, 1977, p. 339). Although they cannot be substituted among groups, being culture-specific, an understanding of their underlying deeper similarity is important and useful.

To establish such regularities and patterns one needs cross-cultural and historical research. In order to be valid, any theories and concepts must be based on the broadest possible sample. Much of what passes for theory in planning, design, and environmental design research is based only on the high-design tradition, ignoring those environments created by the folk or popular tradition. Yet by far the largest percentage of all built environments belong to these latter traditions. Such theories also tend to be based on evidence from the Western tradition, neglecting other cultural milieus. Finally, they tend to be based on recent research and neglect the historical dimension—particularly the remote past and the past in nonliterate and non-Western traditions. It is thus imperative to consider man–environment interaction through time and cross-culturally in order to trace regularities and patterns, and also in order that any generalizations might be valid. Generalizations based on limited samples are suspect; the broader our sample, in space and time, the more likely are we to see regularities in apparent chaos, as well as understand better those differences which are significant, i.e., the more likely are we to see patterns and relationships—and these are the most significant things for which to look.

An approach such as this, which includes a time dimension, as it must, given the astonishing antiquity of architecture and settlements (Rapoport, 1979a,b) has obvious methodological implications. If we are to use evidence of the past, then we cannot very well go and do empirical field work—we must learn to use archaeological materials and whatever exists—early travel books, ethnographic descriptions and other secondary sources, various "indirect" methods, and so on (Rapoport, 1970c).

Another task is to discover more about how particular environments can be supportive for specific activities, and also which activities are important in any given case—and why. In other words, we need to learn how to identify the cultural core and its components, and what environmental elements are most supportive of that core. This involves knowing the relationship of sociocultural variables to environment in terms of the relationship of one to many. In studying the various regularities and patterns, it may be hoped that there will be more regularities in supportive layouts and designs, i.e., variations in the many sociocultural variables discussed (and those *not* discussed) might result in a smaller number of environments. This possible relationship between the many sociocultural variables and the fewer built environments has not been investigated—but it urgently needs to be. This would help in mapping sociocultural variables against environmental variables, i.e., checking the degree of congruence or synomorphy.

Ultimately, a concern with culture-supportive design, a concern for cultural variables, and a commitment to a cross-cultural and historical approach to environmental design, goes beyond their role in helping with a deeper understanding of man–environment interaction and the development of more valid theory. There is an implicit value judgment which needs to be made explicit: that environments should be supportive of cultures because cultures should survive, that we need cultural pluralism. This seems so self-evident and axiomatic (although a different view is possible) that I do not wish to justify it too much.

But two points can be made in support of this position. One is "aesthetic"—there is value, to many people, in having diversity in lifestyles, languages, clothing, food, and environments—it makes for a richer, more complex world. There is another thought-provoking argument by Eiseley (1969). Throughout history many cultures have disappeared for various reasons. One of these is that they took a "wrong turning," made the wrong choices. What are the implications of a single, homogenized world culture, particularly if *it* should have taken the wrong turning? It is ultimately dangerous to put all our eggs into one basket—a cultural gene pool may be as important as a biological one.

REFERENCES

Adams, R. L. A. Uncertainty in nature, cognitive dissonance, and the perceptual distortion of environmental information: Weather forecasts and New England beach trip decisions. In J. H. Sims & D. D. Baumann (Eds.), *Human behavior and the environment*. Chicago: Maroufa Press, 1974, pp. 162–172.

Anderson, E. N., Jr. Some Chinese methods of dealing with crowding. *Urban Anthropology*, 1972, *1*, 141–150.

Barker, R. G. *Ecological psychology*. Palo Alto, Calif.: Stanford University Press, 1968.

Barth, F. *Nomads of South Persia: The Basseri tribe of the Khamseh confederacy*. Boston: Little, Brown, 1961.

Becker, F. D. A class-conscious evaluation (going back to Sacramento's Mall). *Landscape Architecture*, 1973, *64*, 448–457.

Berry, J. W. *Human ecology and cognitive style*. New York: Wiley, 1976.

Bochner, S. The house form as a cornerstone of culture. In R. W. Brislin (Ed.), *Topics in culture learning* (Vol. 3). Honolulu: East-West Center, 1975, 9–20.

Bodley, J. H. *Victims of progress*. Menlo Park, Calif.: Cummings, 1975.

Brolin, B. C., & Zeisel, J. Mass housing: Social research and design. *Architectural Forum*, (July/August, 1968), *129*, 66–71.

Boyden, S. V. (Ed.). *The impact of civilization on the biology of man*. Canberra: Australian National University Press, 1970.

Boyden, S. V. *Conceptual basis of proposed international ecological studies in large metropolitan areas*. Unpublished manuscript, 1974.

Burch, E. J., Jr. The non-empirical environment of the Arctic Alaskan Eskimo. *Southwest Journal of Anthropology*, 1971, *27*, 148–165.

Carr, S. *City signs and lights: A policy study*. Cambridge: M.I.T. Press, 1973.

Cawte, J. *Cruel, poor and brutal nations*. Honolulu: University of Hawaii Press, 1972.

Cawte, J. *Medicine is the law*. Honolulu: University of Hawaii Press, 1974.

Choay, F. Remarques à propos de sémiologie urbaine. *Architecture d'Aujourd'hui*, December 1970/January 1971, 42, 9–10.

Crumrine, N. R. *The house cross of the Mayo Indians of Sonora, Mexico (a symbol of ethnic identity)*. Tucson: University of Arizona Press, Anthropology Paper No. 8, 1964.

Doob, L. W. *Patterning of time*. New Haven: Yale University Press, 1971.

Downs, R. M., & Stea, D. *Maps in minds: Reflections on cognitive mapping*. New York: Harper and Row, 1977.

Ehrlich, A. S. History, ecology and demography in the British Caribbean: An analysis of East Indian ethnicity. *Southwest Journal of Anthropology*, 1971, 27, 166–180.

Eidt, R. C. *Pioneer settlement in northeast Argentina*. Madison: University of Wisconsin, 1971.

Eiseley, L. C. Alternatives to technology. In A. W. Morse & W. Cooney (Eds.), *The environment of change*. New York: Columbia University Press, 1969, pp. 165–180.

Erickson, K. A. Ceremonial landscapes of the American West. *Landscape*, (Autumn 1977), 22, 39–47.

Esber, G., Jr. Indians, architects and anthropologists: A study of proxemic behavior in a Western Apache society. *Man-Environment Systems*, March, 1972a, 2, 58.

Esber, G., Jr. Indian housing for Indians. *The Kiva*, 1972b, 3, 141–147.

Fernandez, J. W. *Fang architectonics*. Philadelphia: Institute for the Study of Human Issues, Working Paper No. 1, 1977.

Firey, W. Sentiment and symbolism as ecological variables. In G. A. Theodorson (Ed.), *Studies in Human Ecology*. Evanston, Ill.: Row, Peterson, 1961, pp. 253–261.

Fitzgerald, C. P. *Barbarian beds*. London: Cressett Press, 1965.

Foddy, W. H. The use of common residential area open space in Australia. *Ekistics*, 1977, 43, 81–83.

Fox, R. The cultural animal. *Encounter*, 1970, XXXV, 31–42.

Gibson, J. J. *The perception of the visual world*. Boston: Houghton Mifflin, 1950.

Gibson, J. J. *The senses considered as perceptual systems*. London: Allen & Unwin, 1968.

Goldman, I. *The mouth of heaven: An introduction to Kwakiutl religious thought*. New York: Wiley, 1975.

Hall, E. T. *The hidden dimension*. Garden City, N.Y.: Doubleday, 1966.

Hall, E. T. Environmental communication. In A. H. Esser (Ed.), *Behavior and environment*. New York: Plenum Press, 1971, pp. 247–256.

Hamburg, D. A. Ancient man in the twentieth century. In V. Goodall (Ed.), *The quest for man*. New York: Praeger, 1975.

Hamilton, P. *Aspects of interdependence between Aboriginal social behaviour and the spatial and physical environment*. Seminar on low-cost housing for Aborigines in remote areas. Royal Australian Institute of Architects. Canberra (February, 1972).

Harrington, M. Resettlement and self-image. *Human Relations*, 1965, 18 115–137.

Hewitt, K., & Hare, F. K. *Man and environment* (conceptual framework). Commission on College Geography, Resource Paper No. 20. Washington, D.C.: Association of American Geographers, 1973.

Hill, D. A. *The changing landscape of a Mexican municipio (Villa Las Rosas, Chiapas)*. Chicago: University of Chicago, Department of Geography Research Paper No. 91, 1964.

Ittelson, W. H. *Some factors influencing the design and function of psychiatric facilities*. Department of Psychology, Brooklyn College, 1960.

Jaulin, R. Ethnocide: The theory and practice of cultural murder. *The Ecologist*, 1971, 1, 12–15.

Jones, W. T. World views: Their nature and their function. *Current Anthropology*, 1972, 13, 79–109.

Jopling, C. F. Aesthetic behavior as an adaptive strategy. Paper given at the XLI Congreso Internacional de Americanistas, Mexico City, September, 1974.

Kearney, M. *The winds of Ixtepeji: World view and society in a Zapotec town.* New York: Holt, Rinehart & Winston, 1972.

King, A. D. *Colonial urban development: Culture, social power and environment.* London: Routledge & Kegan Paul, 1976.

Kroeber, A. L., & Kluckhohn, C. *Culture: A critical review of concepts and definitions.* Cambridge: Harvard University, Papers of the Peabody Museum, 1952, Vol. XLVII, No. 1.

Larimore, A. E. *The alien town: Patterns of settlement in Busoga, Uganda.* Chicago: University of Chicago, Department of Geography, Research Paper No. 55, 1958.

Lawton, M. P. Planning environments for older people. *AIP Journal,* 1970, *36,* 124–129.

LeVine, R. A. *Culture, behavior and personality.* Chicago: Aldine, 1973.

Lévi-Strauss, C. *The raw and the cooked* (J. & D. Weightman, Trans.) London: Jonathan Cape, 1970.

Lowenthal, D. The American scene. *Geographical Review,* 1968, *58,* 61–88.

Lowenthal, D., & Prince, H. The English landscape. *Geographical Review,* 1964, *54,* 309–346.

Lowenthal, D., & Prince, H. English landscape tastes. *Geographical Review,* 1965, *55,* 186–222.

Michelson, W. Analytic sampling for design information: A survey of housing experiences. In H. Sanoff & S. Cohn (Eds.), *EDRA,* 1970, *1,* 183–197.

Michelson, W., & Reed, P. *The theoretical status and operational usage of lifestyle in environmental research.* Toronto: University of Toronto, Center for Urban and Community Studies, Research Paper No. 36, September, 1970.

Mitchell, R. E. Some social implications of high density housing. *American Sociological Review,* 1971, *36,* 18–29.

Moos, R. H. Systems for the assessment and classification of human environments: An overview. In R. H. Moos & P. M. Insel (Eds.), *Issues in social ecology: Human milieus.* Palo Alto, Calif.: National Press Books, 1974, pp. 5–28.

Müller, W. *Weltbild und Kult der Kwakiutl Indianer.* Wiesbaden: Steiner, 1955.

The New York Times, January 24, 1971.

Nicolson, M. H. *Mountain gloom and mountain glory.* Ithaca, N.Y.: Cornell University Press, 1959.

Ohnuki-Tierney, O. Spatial concepts of the Ainu of the northwest coast of southern Sakhalin. *American Anthropologist,* 1972, *74,* 426–457.

Ortiz, A. Ritual drama and the Pueblo world view. In A. Ortiz (Ed.), *New perspectives on the Pueblos.* Albuquerque: University of New Mexico Press, 1972, pp. 135–162.

Pelto, P., & Pelto, G. H. Intracultural diversity: Some theoretical issues. *American Ethnologist,* 1975, *2,* 1–18.

Perin, C. *With man in mind.* Cambridge, Mass.: M.I.T. Press, 1970.

Petonnet, C. Réflexions au sujet de la ville vue par en desous. *L'Anné Sociologique,* 1972, *21,* 151–185.

Rapoport, A. The personal element in housing: An argument for open-ended design. *R.I.B.A. Journal,* July, 1968, pp. 300–307.

Rapoport, A. *House form and culture.* Englewood Cliffs, N.J.: Prentice-Hall, 1969a.

Rapoport, A. The pueblo and the hogan: A cross-cultural comparison of two responses to an environment. In P. Oliver (Ed.), *Shelter and society.* London: Barrie and Rockliff, 1969b, pp. 66–79.

Rapoport, A. The study of spatial quality. *Journal of Aesthetic Education* 1970a, *4,* 81–96.

Rapoport, A. Symbolism and environmental design. *International Journal of Symbology,* 1970b, *1,* 1–10.

Rapoport, A. An approach to the study of environmental quality. In H. Sanoff & S. Cohn (Eds.), *Environmental design research association first annual conference*, 1970c, 1–13.

Rapoport, A. Australian Aborigines and the definition of place. In W. Mitchell (Ed.), *Environmental design research association third annual conference*, 1972, Vol. 1, pp. 3-3-1-3-3-14. In a different form in P. Oliver (Ed.), *Shelter, sign and symbol*. London: Barrie and Jenkins, 1975, pp. 38–51.

Rapoport, A. Images, symbols and popular design. *International Journal of Symbology*, 1973, 4, 1–12.

Rapoport, A. An "anthropological" approach to environmental design research. In B. Honikman (Ed.), *Responding to social change*. Stroudsburg, Pa.: Dowden, Hutchinson & Ross, 1975, pp. 145–151.

Rapoport, A. Socio-cultural aspects of man-environment studies. In A. Rapoport (Ed.), *The mutual interaction of people and their built environment: A cross cultural perspective*. The Hague: Mouton, 1976a, pp. 7–35.

Rapoport, A. Environmental cognition in cross-cultural perspective. In G. T. Moore & R. G. Gollege (Eds.), *Environmental knowing*. Stroudsburg, Pa.: Dowden, Hutchinson & Ross, 1976b, pp. 220–234.

Rapoport, A. *Human aspects of urban form*. Oxford: Pergamon, 1977.

Rapoport, A. On the environment as an enculturating medium. In S. Weidemann & J. A. Anderson (Eds.), *Priorities for environmental design research*. Washington, D.C.: Environmental Design Research Association, 1978a, pp. 54–58.

Rapoport, A. Culture and the subjective effects of stress. *Urban Ecology*, 1978b, 3, 241–261.

Rapoport, A. Nomadism as a man-environment system. *Environment and Behavior*, 1978c, 10, 215–246.

Rapoport, A. *On the environment and the definition of the situation*. Paper given at the Ninth Annual Conference of the Environmental Design Association, Tucson, Ariz., April, 1978d.

Rapoport, A. *Sacred places, sacred occasions, sacred environments*. Paper given at the Annual Meeting of the International Society for the Comparative Study of Civilizations, Milwaukee, Wis., April, 1978e.

Rapoport, A. On the cultural origins of settlements. In A. J. Catanese & J. Snyder (Eds.), *Introduction to planning*. New York: McGraw-Hill, 1979a.

Rapoport, A. On the cultural origins of architecture. In J. Snyder & A. J. Catanese (Eds.), *Introduction to architecture*. New York: McGraw-Hill, 1979b.

Rapoport, A., & Hawkes, R. The perception of urban complexity. *AIP Journal*, 1970, 36, 106–111.

Rapoport, A., & Watson, N. Cultural variability in physical standards. In R. Gutman (Ed.), *People and buildings*. New York: Basic Books, 1972, pp. 33–53. (Originally published in the *Transactions of the Bartlett Society*, Vol. 6, 1967–1968.)

Rappaport, R. A. Ritual, sanctity and cybernetics. *American Anthropologist*, 1971a, 73, 59–76.

Rappaport, R. A. The sacred in human evolution. *Annual Review of Ecology and Systemics*, 1971b, 2, 23–44.

Ricci, K. Using the building as a therapeutic tool in youth treatment. In *New environments for the incarcerated*. Washington, D.C.: U.S. Department of Justice, Law Enforcement Aid Administration, 1972, pp. 22–32.

Richardson, M. The Spanish-American (Colombian) settlement pattern as societal expression and as behavioral cause. In H. J. Walker & W. G. Haag (Eds.), *Man and cultural heritage: Papers in honor of Fred B. Kniffen*, Geoscience and Man, Vol. V. Baton Rouge: Louisiana State University Press, 1974, pp. 35–52.

Rosser, C., & Harris, C. *The family and social change: A study of family and kinship in a South Wales town.* London: Routledge & Kegan Paul, 1965.

Rossi, A. A biosocial perspective on parenting. *Daedalus,* Spring 1977, *106,* 1–32.

Sadalla, E. K., Snyder, P. Z., & Stea, D. *House form and culture revisited.* Paper given at the Seventh Annual Conference of the Environmental Design Research Association, Vancouver, 1976.

Savarton, S., & George, K. R. *A study of historic, economic and sociocultural factors which influence Aboriginal settlements at Wilcannia and Weilmeringle, NSW.* Unpublished B. Arch. Thesis, University of Sydney, 1971.

Schak, D. C. Determinants of children's play patterns in a Chinese city: An interplay of space and values. *Urban Anthropology,* 1972, *1,* 195–204.

Schnapper, D. *L'Italie rouge et noire: Les modèles de la vie quotidienne a Bologne.* Paris: Gallimard, 1971.

Siegel, B. J. Defensive structuring and environmental stress. *American Journal of Sociology,* 1970, *76,* 11–46.

Sopher, D. Landscapes and seasons: Man and nature in India. *Landscape,* Spring, 1964, *13,* 14–19.

Stanislawski, D. *The anatomy of eleven towns in Michoacan.* Austin: University of Texas, Institute of Latin American Studies, No. X, 1950.

Szalay, L. B., & Bryson, J. A. Measurements of psychosocial distance: A comparison of American blacks and whites. *Journal of Personality and Social Psychology,* 1973, *26,* 166–177.

Szalay, L. B., & Maday, B. C. Verbal associations in the analysis of subjective culture. *Current Anthropology,* 1973, *14,* 3–28.

Tiger, L. *Men in groups.* New York: Random House, 1969.

Tiger, L., & Fox, R. The zoological perspective in social science. *Man,* 1966, *1,* 75–81.

Tiger, L., & Fox, R. *The imperial animal.* New York: Delta Books, 1971.

Tiger, L., & Shepher, J. *Women in the kibbutz.* New York: Harcourt, Brace, Jovanovitch, 1975.

Tuan, Y. *Topophilia.* Englewood Cliffs, N.J.: Prentice Hall, 1974.

Turnbull, C. M. *The mountain people.* New York: Simon and Schuster, 1972.

Ucko, P. J., Tringham, R., & Dimbleby, G. W. (Eds.). *Man, settlement and urbanism.* London: Duckworth, 1972.

Venturi, R., Scott-Brown, D., & Izenour, S. *Learning from Las Vegas.* Cambridge: M.I.T. Press, 1972.

Vogt, E. Z. Some aspects of Zanacantan settlement patterns and ceremonial organization. In K. C. Chang (Ed.), *Settlement archaeology.* Palo Alto, Calif.: National Press, 1968, pp. 154–173.

Vogt, E. Z. *Tortillas for the gods: A symbolic analysis of Zinacantecan rituals.* Cambridge: Harvard University Press, 1976.

Washburn, S. L., & Lancaster, C. S. The evolution of hunting. In R. B. Lee & I. DeVore (Eds.), *Man the hunter.* Chicago: Aldine, 1968, p. 293ff.

Yaker, H. M., Osmond, H., & Cheek, F. (Eds.). *The future of time.* Garden City, N.Y.: Doubleday, 1971.

Yancey, W. L. Architecture, interaction and social control. *Environment and Behavior,* 1971, *3,* 3–21.

Zeisel, J. *Symbolic meaning of space and the physical dimension of social relations.* Paper presented at the American Sociological Association annual meeting, September 1969.

2

Cross-Cultural Research Methods

STRATEGIES, PROBLEMS, APPLICATIONS

RICHARD W. BRISLIN

INTRODUCTION

Cross-cultural studies are necessary for the complete development of theories in environmental research since no one culture contains all environmental conditions that can affect human behavior. Likewise, no one country contains all possible types of man-made changes of the physical environment, nor all of the man-made adaptations to natural conditions such as climate, noise, air quality, and potential hazards. In addition, many places in which environmental researchers might be asked to work are in parts of the world where "development" is seen as a necessity or at least a desideratum. These places are often in countries where empirical research is not a well-established entity, hence the necessity for importing advisers from other countries. Although frequently forgotten (Fahvar & Milton, 1972), environmental assessments prepared by such advisers should include analyses of how a development project will affect a culture and even the behavior of people for whom the project was designed.

RICHARD W. BRISLIN • East-West Center, Culture Learning Institute, Honolulu, Hawaii 96848.

CROSS-CULTURAL STUDIES

All these examples point to the necessity of looking at uses of cross-cultural research for environmental studies, a link of heretofore specialized areas that has rarely been attempted (Altman & Chemers, 1980). In the broadest, and somewhat operational sense, cross-cultural studies in the behavioral/social sciences refer to "the empirical study of members of various culture (defined below) groups who have had iden- tifiable experiences that lead to predictable and significant differences (as well as similarities) in behavior. In the majority of such studies, the groups speak different languages, are governed by different political units, and reside in different geographic areas," (Brislin, Lonner, & Thorndike, 1973, p. 5: some additions made to the original wording).

Without entering into a space-consuming debate regarding what culture is, the two positions that are most frequently cited by cross- cultural specialists will be presented. Using "culture" to refer to the man-made part of the human environment, Triandis (1977a, p. 423) adds "subjective culture" to refer to people's response to the "man- made part of the environment, or to a group's characteristic way of perceiving its social environment." To form a more complete picture for environmental studies, Wohlwill's (1973) position would have to be added: that the environment exists not only "in the head" but also physically, independent of the organism. Then, "subjective culture" would be broadened to include people's responses to those natural con- ditions that *are* present in their environment.

A second definition is that suggested by the anthropologists Kroeber and Kluckhohn (1952, p. 180):

> Culture consists of patterns, explicit and implicit, of and for behavior acquired and transmitted by symbols, constituting the distinctive achieve- ments of human groups, including their embodiments in artifacts; the essen- tial core of culture consists of traditional (i.e., historically derived and selected) ideas and especially their attached values; culture systems may on the one hand, be considered as products of action, on the other as condition- ing elements of further action.

This definition seems especially helpful for the subject matter of this book because of (a) the explicit emphasis on action (i.e., in relation to the environment) and (b) the emphasis on attached value to ideas (i.e., subjective reactions to the environment). Two further ideas suggested by Kroeber and Kluckhohn are also relevant. They relate to how the above definition may change in the future as research continues: con- cern with "(c) the interrelations of cultural forms; and (d) variability and the individual" (1952, p. 180: letters added to continue order, above). Again, the Wohlwill addition would be necessary.

Readers would be misled regarding uniformity of thought in this research area if they were left with what seemed to be *the* one definition of culture. The diversity of opinion negates this possibility, although the Kroeber–Kluckhohn definition will be used throughout this chapter. But, rather than follow this lead (chosen only for organizational purposes), researchers should combine their own intuitive feelings of what "culture" is with those formal definitions they think most helpful for the purposes of a given study.

The unifying link among cross-cultural researchers is not a content area, or even a set of methods. Rather, the link consists of an "approach" to the use of empirical methods, and a willingness to work in field settings in other countries. There is no methodological problem that is completely unique to cross-cultural studies, but certain problems are so intensified that they seem unique. Cross-cultural researchers often have to work in an unfamiliar language. They have to worry whether or not the concepts they are investigating have the same meaning (the "equivalence" issue) in all cultures under investigation. Researchers also have to deal with the fact that methods which may be familiar and even definitive to them (e.g., experiments, interviews, paper and pencil testing) may be unfamiliar and even distasteful to people from other cultures. Working in field settings is often compounded by the additional time needed for visas, clearances to key institutions, health precautions, and the establishment of cooperative relationships necessary for cross-cultural studies.

OVERVIEW OF CHAPTER

A complete review of all methods that have been used by cross-cultural specialists, with possible applications for environmental researchers, is obviously impossible. Volumes have been written on cross-cultural methods (Brislin *et al.*, 1973; Triandis & Berry, 1980), and long review articles have been done on cross-cultural environmental studies (Altman & Chemers, 1980; Rapoport, 1976). Instead, certain general problems will be covered which have to be faced by virtually all cross-cultural researchers, together with potential approaches to their solution. Awareness of these problems and of the jargon surrounding them provides one of the few indentity markers of cross culturalists. However, these same markers form a barrier for environmental researchers who may want to embrace cross-cultural studies, hence their explication in this chapter. To help in the solution of more specific problems, listings of cross-cultural methods, with sources in which they are explained, will be included at the end of this chapter. The general problems are:

1. Analyzing the uses of cross-cultural research
2. The establishment of cross-cultural theoretical frameworks, combined with an avoidance of imposing extraneous frameworks upon a specific culture
3. Procedures for combining concerns with both culture-universal and culture-specific concepts
4. The plausible rival hypothesis approach, in which all potential explanations for data are analyzed
5. The analysis of archival materials (e.g., ethnographies, archaeological reports, other written documents)
6. Use of multiple methods and multiple data points
7. Dangers of explaining complex phenomena through low correlations among variables
8. Human relations in cross-cultural research

THE USES OF CROSS-CULTURAL RESEARCH

Given the difficulties in carrying out cross-cultural research, mentioned above, two easy questions to ask are, "Why do it at all? Is it worth the effort?" People involved in cross-cultural studies have suggested a number of uses for the approach (Brislin, 1976a; Strodtbeck, 1964; Whiting, 1968) which are felt to be powerful enough to compensate for the difficulties. The seven uses reviewed here center around the nature of independent variables, hypothesis generation and testing, the generation of theories, and theory validation and expansion.

EXPANSION OF INDEPENDENT VARIABLES

A frequently cited advantage of cross-cultural studies (e.g., Whiting, 1968) is that (1), the range of independent variables can be increased beyond that found in any one culture. This increase can include both quantitative and qualitative aspects of variables. With regard to quantitative aspects, some variables can be defined according to ratio *scales*, as in the number of people living in a set amount of space in studies of crowding/density; or the degree of air quality as defined by the numbers and amounts of measured pollutants. With regard to qualitative aspects, the exact *content* of independent variables also varies across cultures, and so again an increase in range can be exploited. An example is the content of the term "control of waters for fishing" in Micronesia and the United States (Johannes, 1977). In the United States and many countries of the Western world, marine resources are open to any citizen. In Micronesia, the waters are controlled by families, clans, and chiefs. The latter approach was an effective approach to conservation, but it has caused problems with the appearance of United States-based commercial fisheries in Micronesia. This central idea in cross-cultural research, different content for similar concepts, will be covered again in the next section on universal and culture-specific frameworks. The point to be made here is that the range of meaning can be used to advantage in hypothesis testing since cross-cultural similarities and differences can be predicted with knowledge of the range.

Hypothesis Generation and Testing

A use of central importance to environmental studies is that (2) cross-cultural studies force an examination of situational variables, and hence the generation of hypotheses to interrelate these variables, since such variables obviously differ from culture to culture. Just by traveling in various countries researchers can observe differences in numbers and types of man-made adaptations to the environment, presence or absence of natural features such as mountains or plains, and types of disasters for which people do and do not prepare. This sensitization is more difficult to accomplish if a person stays in only one culture, since so little variation is observed compared to that existent on a worldwide scale. Knowledge of these variables allows researchers to form hypotheses about situational effects in addition to the heretofore overemphasis on dispositional effects. Undoubtedly, key interactions between situations and dispositions can be hypothesized after such analyses.

A given culture can sometimes be looked upon as (3) an experimental treatment impossible to manipulate in a laboratory or in a field setting. This is the rationale behind Berry's (1976) approach in which aspects of the physical environment (temperature and rainfall) determine areas of the world in which cultivation is and is not possible. Where conditions are favorable, cultivation is chosen by people as a means of exploiting the environment. Where cultivation is not possible, people hunt, gather, fish, or raise animals. Children are, for course, born into the two types of societies (cultivation and noncultivation), and their experiences in them are considered to be an "experimental treatment."

Predictions are made about child-rearing practices and the perceptual/
cognitive skills that are typically developed.

At times (4), researchers will discover a trait or situation that seems
to be present in one culture but not in another, or they will be able to
document differential incidences of the same trait or situation. This discovery leads to attempts to explain the differences, formulate a
hypothesis, and test it in a more formal manner. Anderson (1972) was
struck by the fact that crowding and density in Hong Kong, involving
many more people per acre than in cities in North America or Europe,
did not seem to have the adverse effects commonly claimed. This led
him to suggest both social norms that allow people to predict the responses of the many others in the environment, and coping mechanisms
that allow people some control over access to others. The analysis of
Hong Kong–other country differences also led Anderson to suggest
positive aspects of density (lots of company, excitement, someone
around to help in times of trouble), a viewpoint that had been lacking in
analyses that did not consider cross-cultural differences.

A very practical use of cross-cultural studies is that (5) researchers
may have access to certain populations of interest which might not be
accessible in their own country. For instance, the very rich and powerful
do have some controls over environmental development, but these
people are notoriously unavailable for serious interviews in North
America. In other parts of the world, however, visiting researchers are
assigned a good deal of status and may have access to such people. Or, it
is difficult to gain access to children with nutritional problems in some
countries, but (tragically) much easier in others. Such access brings with
it special responsibilities and ethical concerns that should be examined
by researchers with as much care as their independent and dependent
variables. The power that comes with ascribed status and carte blanche
access to people can "go to one's head" and can eventually harm a
research project.

THE GENERATION OF THEORIES

After hypothesis testing, theoretical frameworks may be developed.
At some point the theory may call for certain types of variables, and (6)
researchers skilled in cross-cultural studies can often suggest such critical
variables based on knowledge of the experiences of people in various
cultures. A theory relating environmental experiences to basic perceptual processes (Deregowski, 1980; Segall, Campbell, & Herskovits,
1966), for instance, suggests that physical features which a person observes over and over again lead to the development of perceptual in-

ference habits. One part of the theory predicts that experience with viewing long, uninterrupted vistas leads to mistakes in judgments of the horizontal–vertical illusion.

Specifically, the vertical line would be judged longer than the horizontal line, when they are in fact equal. Pollnac (1977) reasoned that if experiences with open vistas is the reason, fishermen should perceive the illusion differently as the number of years of fishing experience increases:

> The ecological hypothesis... suggests that small-scale marine fishermen who make distance judgments to locate themselves with respect to available resources—in a relatively flat environment without aid of electronic or mechanical devices—will be more susceptible to the horizontal-vertical illusion. (p. 427)

Working among fishermen in Costa Rica, Pollnac found a strong relation between overestimation of the vertical line and number of years fishing.

THEORY VALIDATION AND EXPANSION

Within all disciplines there are well-established theories that can be subjected to cross-cultural tests. Such testing (7) can indicate that a theory's explanatory power can handle cross-cultural findings; it can suggest revisions and expansions of a theory; and it can also suggest that some theoretical concerns are really only indications of the importance of certain concepts within one part of the world. With regard to the latter, the overemphasis on the negative aspects of crowding has already been mentioned. With regard to expansion, Piagetian theory has been the most successful case of cross-cultural studies having a major impact on a well-established tradition (Dasen, 1972; Piaget, 1966). Much of the contribution is of interest to environmental researchers, since the proposed universality of stages has been tempered by considerations of what children actually experience in a given environment. For instance, certain environments have certain objects (e.g., nuts from trees: Price-Williams, 1961) that children can play with. Similarly, some environments demand so much time of children in certain subsistence-level societies (e.g., help with herding, farming) that these children cannot attend school and receive different forms of stimulation there. All these experiences lead to certain levels of performance on formal Piagetian tasks.

CULTURE-UNIVERSAL AND CULTURE-SPECIFIC FRAMEWORKS:
EMICS AND ETICS

If there is a piece of jargon that cross-cultural specialists use, at the
risk of shutting off communication with the uninitiated, it is "emics and
etics." Any noncommunication is unfortunate, since the terms summarize a very important and central concept and analytical tool (Berry,
1969; Irwin, Klein, Engle, Yarbrough, & Nerlove, 1977; Poortinga, 1975).
Before explaining the concept, however, a problem which can be
analyzed with the help of the analytical tool may be posed. Then emics
and etics will be introduced in their abstract form, and subsequently
applied to this specific problem. Such an approach may be the best way to
explicate this important concept.

The problem involves drought and starvation in East Africa (Talbot,
1972). A group of European consultants recommended that development projects be established to increase water availability and
grasslands for the Masai, an East African culture whose members had
long been involved in raising cattle. Instead of leading to more healthy
herds of cattle and better grazing areas, however, the development projects led to starvation for the cattle and eventually for some of the Masai.
How can this be explained? The cross-cultural concepts of emics and
etics are useful for such an analysis.

Emics and etics refer to the two goals of cross-cultural research. One
is to document valid principles in all cultures and to establish theoretical
frameworks useful in comparing human behavior in various cultures.
This is the "etic" goal, and the term comes from phonetic analysis. In
linguistics, a phonetic system is one that documents and analyzes all
meaningful sounds that are present in all languages and which integrates them into a general framework. The other goal of cross-cultural
research is to document valid principles of behavior within any one
culture, with attention given to what the people themselves value as
important as well as what is familiar to them. Such an analysis has to
reject the importation and imposition of frameworks from outside a
culture, since, by definition, a researcher cannot gain insight into emics
by using foreign tools. The tools must be indigenous. This latter type is
an emic analysis, and the term comes from phonemics. In linguistics, a
phonemic analysis documents sounds meaningful in a specific language.

An example from linguistics may be helpful. A phonetic system will
have the initial /ng/ sound, an initial /l/ sound, and an initial /r/ sound
since these are important in at least one of the world's languages. In
addition, these sounds can be integrated into a general framework based
on such concepts as activation of vocal cords, and parts of the mouth

used in making the sounds. An English phonemic system will have the /l/ and /r/ sounds, but not the initial /ng/ sound, since the latter is not a part of the English language. Japanese will not have both the /l/ and /r/ sounds since the language does not make a distinction between them (a fact that leads to ethnic jokes). English speakers thus have to put special effort into learning the initial /ng/ sound, a task that was faced by many Peace Corps volunteers assigned to Pacific island cultures. Japanese speakers have to work hard on the /1–r/ distinction, as most teachers of English as a second language will testify. The "metaphor" of emics and etics for cross-cultural research contains the elements referred to immediately above: what is present and absent, what is meaningful, what has to be given special attention because it is common in one system but not another, and what can be systematized into integrative frameworks.

Cross-cultural researchers have attempted to deal with both etics and emics in their research. A system proposed by Brislin (1976a), drawing upon earlier work by Przeworski and Teune (1966, 1970) represents such an attempt. The researcher starts by examining concepts that may have cross-cultural validity, but keeps in mind that not all *aspects* of those concepts will be the same in all cultures under study. Aspects may be different both for cultures across nations and for various cultures or subcultures within a country. In the examples, the researchers who are cited did not use the terms "emics and etics," but their analyses fit well into this conceptualization.

In discussing the effects of rangeland development on the Masai culture of East Africa, Talbot (1972) analyzed the concept "uses and care of cattle" from the perspective of the Masai and from the perspective of people from Europe and North America in charge of the development. Members of both cultures have similar conceptualizations about several core connotations, and these are the proposed etics: provision of milk, fertilizer, and demands placed on humans for caring of cattle. But in addition to this etic core, there are differences which can be called the emics within each group:

NORTH AMERICA, EUROPE EMICS	MASAI EMICS
Cattle for meat	Cattle not primarily used for meat
Cattle raised for sale	Cattle not generally raised for sale
Grazing over a large area	Grazing in small areas (to protect from predators)
	Emphasis on quantity
Emphasis on quality as much as quantity	
Other signs of wealth and prestige available besides cattle	Cattle are a major sign of wealth and prestige
Experience with conservation	Always a struggle to maintain limited herds, so no opportunity to think about conservation when large numbers of cattle are present

The emphasis on quantity was a major problem in the rangeland development projects. Prior to European contact, natural conditions such as droughts and fires effectively limited the size of herds, so the intelligent practice was to always have as many cattle as possible. But when water and grasslands became more common after development, the Masai norm of "desirability of quantity," without a self-imposed norm of "desirability of limitations for the purpose of conservation", led to herds of unreasonable size. The cattle then overgrazed and destroyed the available rangeland. In turn, cattle then died for lack of food, and the Masai themselves were faced with starvation. This case is frequently cited as an example of failure of technology (rangeland development) due to ignorance of a human variable (norm of quantity).

As a second example, the problem faced by Muttagi (1977) concerning the use of natural resources in Bombay, India, will be considered. The concept under study was "distribution and taxation of water," and there are several core connotations that could be considered etic, since they are applicable in various parts of the world: concerns for equity, practicability of delivery methods, and concerns that costs needed to collect tax revenues are not excessive. If the problem were faced in the United States, distribution and taxation would be based on variables like family income, number of dependents, and individual need for additional water (as with special job requirements). In Bombay, however, the costs of obtaining such information would be greater than the budget for the entire water delivery project. Hence, distribution and taxation were based on the type of man-made housing in which people live. The four-part typology was:

1. Pavement dwellers: no permanent home
2. Hutment and slum dwellers: homes made of indigenous materials like mud and wood
3. Dwellers in chawls, or tenement buildings of several stories
4. Better quality tenement buildings with self-contained flats (apartments) that include more amenities than buildings in category 3

Taxes increased from category 1 (no tax) to category 4 (highest tax). In actuality, there is a correlation (not perfect) between this typology and such variables as socioeconomic status. In Bombay, this emic classification, which might have direct application in very few countries of the world, led to a better solution than a costly importation of some other typology. Cross-cultural comparisons could then be made using the etic concept, "distribution and taxation of water," as long as the emic manifestations are kept in mind for each of the cultures under study.

The more general framework in which emics and etics are empirically analyzed (Brislin, 1976a) is based on the premise that most important concepts will have somewhat different meanings from culture to culture. But there may also be a common core of meaning which can form the basis for cross-cultural analysis. The development of a questionnaire or interview schedule will be used as an example. After deciding upon a concept for investigation, the researcher would write etic items meant to tap core aspects of a concept, such as "uses and care of cattle." These items should be relevant, easily understood, and readily responded to by members of all cultures under study. In addition, the researcher would write emic items meant to tap important concepts within each culture. By definition, emic items would *not* be relevant and easily understood by respondents from all cultures, but rather only by members of one or several of the cultures under study. Figure 1 summarizes the approach.

Interpretable statistical relations would be expected between core items and specific items for each culture, since a combination of core-plus-specific is the operational definition of the concept for each culture. No statistical relations are necessarily expected between specific items

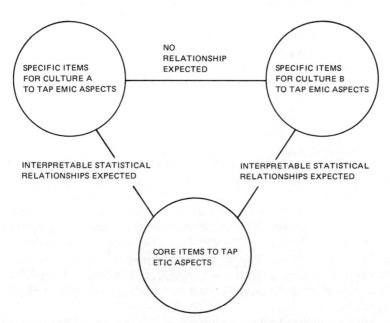

Figure 1.   Overview of method involving core items (etics) and culture-specific items (emics).

for each culture (analyzed across cultures), since they were written to suit the needs of each culture and so do not necessarily have any shared meaning.

PROCEDURES FOR USING THE EMIC-ETIC CONCEPTUALIZATION

Given acceptance of this general approach to combining concerns about culture universals and analyses of culture specifics, methods have to be developed to operationalize the approach. Put another way, the question is: "How can core/etic items and culture-specific/emic items be discovered so that the procedure can be profitably used?" Several are available. The first, a procedure that is mandatory, is for researchers to familiarize themselves with the ethnographic literature on the cultures in which they want to work. Many, many problems can be avoided, and much can be learned, if this library-oriented research step is taken. Effective organization and retrieval systems, such as the Human Relations Area Files (described by Barry, 1980), are of tremendous help in locating relevant literature on specific cultures. Data on concepts of interest can then be compared, and (together with the researchers' knowledge of their own cultures) potential emics and etics can be suggested.

If a collaboration between researchers from various countries can be established (Groenman, 1971), extensive discussions among them should yield a number of possible core items and culture-specific items. Wesley and Karr (1966) have suggested that researchers interview people who have lived in more than one of the cultures under investigation, have them reflect upon their experiences, and then analyze their responses in terms of emics and etics. Similarly, the work of Ervin-Tripp (1964) might be extended. People who have lived in more than one culture are shown pictures and are asked a series of questions about them. Although Ervin-Tripp used the Thematic Apperception Test (a series of pictures about which people tell stories) because of a desire to document different personality traits as a function of language and culture, there is no reason why pictures presenting various environmental variables cannot be shown. People would be asked to respond in one of their languages, or to answer from the perspective of one of the cultures that they know. Responses would be analyzed in terms of what is common across all responses, and what is specific to one culture and language.

Another method takes advantage of the well-established principle of learning that recognition is better than recall. Blank stares will often be the response to a direct question like, "What aspects of your environment affect human behavior?" But if people from various cultures read or listen to an analysis of environment and behavior, they can then comment on it. Much has been written about various cultures by visiting researchers, and Brislin and Holwill's (1977) study of indigenous commentary showed that educated members of those cultures can make helpful corrections and expansions on any researcher's analysis. Incidentally, that study also showed that indigenous people were sensitive to imposed frameworks and explanations, and they were also able to verbalize the need to take the perspective of members of their cultures into account.

If a group of people from various cultures can be brought together, a method expanding on the work of Triandis, Davis, and Takezawa (1965) could be used. People write items about some aspect of environment and behavior, and then rate their own items and the items of others in a Thurstone-like sorting procedure. This procedure is based on people's ratings along a scale that has 11 points. The scales have to be determined beforehand, and they have to be etic in the sense of understandable and relevant to members of all cultures. For instance, this scale could well be an etic:

IMPORTANT   UNIMPORTANT
        1   2   3   4   5   6   7   8   9   10   11

People can also indicate that a certain item cannot be rated by them since it represents a completely unfamiliar concept, or a concept that they cannot understand. Help in generating such scales may be derived from Osgood's cross-cultural work on universals of affective meaning, carried out in 30 language groups (Osgood, 1977; Osgood, May, & Miron, 1975). The people then read and rate all items, not just those written by colleagues from their own culture. Items that have wide agreement across cultures, defined by a mean with a low standard deviation, are considered etics. Items that have agreement *within* a culture, but not across cultures, are considered emics. Items that have high standard deviations both within and across cultures are set aside. The process of sharing items stimulates the development of new items, since people are reminded of certain aspects of the concept. The procedure continues until a sufficient set of etic and emic items is generated, such that the people agree that virtually all aspects of the concept have been tapped.

About those items that were set aside: further research is needed to discover what to do with them. The items cannot be used in the above procedure, as it now stands, because they are ambiguous. There are at least two reasons for ambiguity: the items are poorly written, so that they mean different things to different people, or the items are well-worded and tap ambiguous aspects of the environment. The problem is compounded because the ambiguous facets of the environment may be the most important. The fact that people *don't* know exactly how to react to some aspects may be more important than discovering those aspects that have widely shared meaning. The method described here can document the latter, but not the former.

A final approach to generating emics and etics is to use the results of the decentering procedure developed for translation between languages (Brislin, 1970; Werner & Campbell, 1970). In decentering, one bilingual translates from the source to a target version, and a second bilingual blindly translates back to the source. A third bilingual translates *that* source version, which is itself later back-translated. The procedure can be diagrammed as follows:

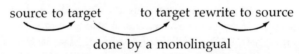

source to target to source to target to source

If a concept can "survive" the procedure, it is assumed to be etic (with respect to the two languages), since bilinguals must have words readily available in both languages to translate the concept. If a concept drops out (is not found in a back-translation), it is assumed to be emic, especially if discussions with translators indicate an absence of readily available words. If researchers are worried about generalizing from the input of bilinguals to the monolinguals who will comprise the eventual study sample, they can add steps like the following:

source to target   to target rewrite to source

done by a monolingual

Since there are no examples within environmental research of this procedure, other studies have to be examined to indicate how this approach may be used. Phillips (1960, p. 302) could not have the sentence stem "sometimes a good quarrel is necessary because" translated into the Thai language. "After much discussion the translators decided that, although it was conceivable that an American might enjoy a quarrel for its cathartic effect, the notion would be incomprehensible to a Thai." In the currently used terms, "a good quarrel" is not an etic.

What can all this effort yield? Here are some of the advantages of using one or more of the above techniques:

1. Analyzing concepts in terms of emics and etics is probably an approach that meets reality "head-on." Rather than the frequent throwing up of arms, together with complaints that concepts mean different

things in different cultures, researchers can accept this fact as reality, and then deal with it directly.

2. The procedure makes explicit what culture-specific detail is lost in cross-cultural theorizing. All experienced researchers know that they are working at a level of abstraction above the data in theory building and that they lose certain details. When researchers theorize using etics, they know what details they are not using (the emics for each culture), and they know that a complete picture for any one culture is a combination of emics and etics.

3. The procedure allows researchers to say that a phenomenon exists in one culture, but not at all, or to a much lesser degree, in another. Such information would be derived from a pattern of results showing that (a) members of one culture agree upon the frequency and meaning of a phenomenon, but also showing that (b) members of another culture give no analysis because of inability to relate to it. Such data on what is and is not present is important (e.g., cathartic quarrels in Thailand and the United States). As a practical matter, such phenomena have to be given special attention in communications across cultures, since some people involved will have no experience and so will have a difficult time understanding what is being discussed. In analyzing difficulties of such communication as it relates to friendship formation, a person from the island (atoll) of Truk said (Brislin, 1971, p. 177):

> A Trukese that has never experienced the cold winter of the U.S. could not comprehend and intelligently appreciate a Statesider telling him the terrible winter they had in Albany anymore than a person from Albuquerque that has never seen an atoll could visualize the smallness of the islets that make up an atoll.

4. If the procedures are carried out in a number of cultures, emics will appear that are similar for a subsample of the cultures; these will not be etics, since they are not valid for all cultures. Such "patterns of emics" can then motivate a search for explanatory reasons, which may take the form of similar social structures, similar climate, similar world views, and so forth.

5. The procedures make explicit another fact that all experienced researchers know: the use of any set of methods can itself be an imposed etic. One recent review (Waddell, 1977) on empirical environmental studies (White, 1974) made this point clearly:

> The community studies are... problematic because of an overriding concern with a particular geographical methodology developed out of the flood plain studies of the 1950's and an implicit, but nevertheless transparent, ideological basis. (p. 72)

> The community studies in general are characterized by strict mechanistic analyses that transmit little sense of the collectivities under investigation and lead, then, to no questionning of the basic assumptions of the research. . . . Many of the papers serve uncritically as vehicles for (a certain person's) conceptual framework and assumptions—assumptions which are of very questionable validity. (p. 74)

Potential imposition of methodologies which, by design, yield only certain sets of data will always be a threat of cross-cultural studies. With a sensitivity to emics which the present approach demands, however, researchers can constantly question themselves as to the basis of their final labels of what is emic and what is etic.

THE PLAUSIBLE RIVAL HYPOTHESIS APPROACH

Cross-cultural studies will always be threatened by many alternative explanations for any set of data which a researcher may gather. Reasons include the well-known difficulties of field research compared to laboratory research (e.g., Campbell & Stanley, 1966), *combined with* additional difficulties brought on by a willingness to work in other cultures. In cross-cultural studies there is usually an unfamiliar language with which a researcher must deal. People in the other cultures are often unfamiliar with basic data-gathering techniques such as tests and interviews, and there are rarely other studies (on a specific topic) to aid in the interpretation of a new data set. Researchers are often unaware of subtle interpersonal communication cues that *are* widely shared among members of other cultures. Hence researchers may misread a situation, or worse, offend people so that subsequent cooperation in data gathering is impossible. A willingness to deal with the alternative explanations of data that are brought about by such additional complexity is probably an entry requirement for people considering cross-cultural research.

The general approach to the problem is to engage in a plausible rival hypothesis analysis, as suggested by Campbell (1968, 1969). In doing such an analysis, researchers consider their preferred interpretation of the data along with all other potential explanations. The preferred interpretation is usually a theory-based concept, while the plausible alternatives can be both theoretical and methodological in nature. A general guide is that the researchers should be able to presuppose every criticism that a journal reviewer or editor could possibly have as a reason for rejecting the final write-up of a piece of research. Aid in presupposing methodological reasons can be derived from Lonner's (1975) content analysis of reviewer's reasons for recommendations of "accept" and "reject" with respect to publication in the *Journal of Cross-Cultural Psy-*

chology. References to common methodological problems and analyses of how to deal with them are given at the end of this chapter.

Example 1: Plausible Alternative of Age Rather than Specific Experience

Some examples from environmental research should help in explaining how this procedure is used. In his study of environment and perception which has already been reviewed, Pollnac (1977) related years of fishing experience to illusion susceptibility, and suggested a functional relation linking the two variables. An obvious plausible rival hypothesis is age, since several theories (Over, 1968) suggest relations between age and perception of illusions. Pollnac, however, gathered data on age and ruled out this explanation by showing a nonsignificant partial correlation between age and susceptibility when years of fishing are controlled. This approach of performing additional analyses to rule out alternative explanations will be common, and it means that the alternatives have to be presupposed early in the research work. The additional data have to be gathered at the same time as the primary data, since it is prohibitively expensive, and at times impossible, to return to a culture for the purpose of gathering follow-up data.

Example 2: Plausible Alternative of Familiarity with Materials

The familiarity of materials and tasks that constitute the data-gathering method will always be a plausible alternative explanation of results. Such an explanation will be especially true when researchers try to analyze underlying dispositions of people in one culture compared to people in another. A dispositional analysis, such as feelings about the inevitability and noncontrol of natural hazards, may be correct. But if the data-gathering methods involve drawing, or manipulation of objects, or participation in a simulation, then researchers must demonstrate that they can rule out differential familiarity (across cultures) with these tasks as an explanation of the results. Researchers interested in many topic areas across the range of behavioral/social sciences will have to become interested in the environment, since that is the aspect of people's lives that provides much "familiarity." For instance, in experiments on the conservation of discontinuous quantities, the normal Piagetian method is to use beads in containers. Working among the Tiv of Central Africa, Price-Williams (1961) tried this method, but found that communication difficulties were prevalent, and so he changed the material to nuts, far more common in the Tiv culture. Results showed a degree of conservation similar to acculturated European groups of children. This is one of the few studies in which European and non-Western children performed similarly on a Piagetian task (Dasen, 1972). A possible reason is that there is a variable operating, which might be called "explicit attention to communication with subjects," that is based on the researcher's familiarity with the culture and with the physical environment.

Similar concerns with familiarity as a plausible rival hypothesis will be present whenever unfamiliar methods, such as interviews or questionnaires, are used. It is easy to forget that while people in certain parts of the world may be accustomed to interviews and may be happy to fill out questionnaires, these practices are by no means universal. A subtle problem is that, due to differential familiarity with either the language of the questionnaire or with the questionnaire completion itself, the *range* of responses may be different from culture to culture. In a study involving respondents from 23 countries, Brislin and Holwill (1977) noted that people gave answers that closely followed the wording of the open-ended questions that were asked of them. Brislin was worried about charges of "fatuousness" in pointing this out, but that one detail has been discussed by other researchers more often than any other methodological point in the study. The subtle aspect of the issue is that, in studies with native speakers of English, respondents often go far beyond the wording of the questions. They do so partly because of familiarity with filling out questionnaires. Questions about natural resources are thus likely to elicit a wide range of connotations with respect to education, politics, movie stars, and so forth. But nonnative speakers, not so familiar with the language of the questionnaire or (even with a well-translated instrument) questionnaire completion, do not write about any and all thoughts that come to their minds. Rather, they are more likely to stick to the specific subject matter mentioned in the questions. In addition, they are not likely to go beyond the examples given in a questionnaire. If a question posed to Pacific Islanders asks about preparation for hazards (e.g., earthquakes, tsunamis), only a very few respondents will give examples about hazards other than the two mentioned in the question. A plausible rival hypothesis problem arises when differences across cultures are overinterpreted as a more complex, differentiated view of the environment. Responses more in line with the content of the question might be interpreted as reflecting a "cognitively simple" view. Such an interpretation would not be justified.

Example 3: Plausible Alternative of Regression Due to Sampling Problems

Sampling problems will also be troublesome, since random sampling is often prohibitively expensive, and sometimes nearly impossible, owing to the absence of population lists (or maps of households) from which to sample (Brislin & Baumgardner, 1971). "Matching" has been used as an approach to obtaining "equivalence," but it is a totally inadequate method, which only adds the plausible rival hypothesis of regression artifacts to a study (Campbell & Erlebacher, 1970; Campbell & Stanley, 1966). Space given to describing the inept procedure is justified only because it is used so often. In applying the technique, researchers try to gain equivalence by choosing people in one culture and then matching them with people in another on the basis of such variables as age, socioeconomic status, years of experience in the environment, and so forth. The procedure could also be used in the selection of research sites in an environmental study, since aspects of the environment in one culture (climate, density) could be matched with aspects in another. The procedure has probably been used, despite early analyses of its grave shortcomings (Thorndike, 1943), because of its appeal to common sense: control by searching for similar people or environmental features across cultures.

There are two problems, the first of which will hopefully appeal to common sense as much as the reason for matching in the first place. If people from one culture (B) are chosen on the basis of characteristics of people from another (A), then the B people in the study are not representative of all Bs (since they were chosen on the basis of the As). Similarly, the As that are in the final sample will not be representative of all As, since some will be discarded on the basis of no B person's being available as a match. Hence the researcher ends up with odd samples that may affect the data gathered. The argument is similar for environmental features. Assume that cultures are matched on climate for a study on the effects of rainfall. The cultures remaining in the sample will not represent all examples of level of rainfall, since some will be discarded on the basis of no match being available on climate.

The mathematical rationale for avoiding matching takes much space to present, and it has been done elsewhere (Brislin, 1976c; Campbell & Erlebacher, 1970). In general, the mathematical demonstration shows that matching causes subjects at an extreme (on a variable) to be chosen, and they regress toward the mean of the entire population on any dependent variable that is correlated with the matching variable. This regression toward the mean (a mathematical certainty) can easily be misinterpreted as having a theoretically relevant relationship to the independent variable.

Example 4: Explaining Alternative by Biased Selection of Ethnographic Studies

Although not by any means exhausting the categories of plausible rival hypotheses, one more type that is especially prevalent in cross-cultural studies will be discussed. Cross-cultural researchers *will* find differences, given the complexity of the issues with which they deal. There is a terrible temptation to explain away these differences by choosing examples from the anthropological literature that seem to support one's own suggested interpretation. The problem is that examples which do not support the interpretation are ignored. Other researchers, then, can suggest plausible alternatives based upon another set of examples, and the process can continue despite the fact that no real contribution is being made. A much better procedure is to employ a formal content analysis (Brislin, 1980; Holsti, 1968) which forces researchers to scrutinize all examples and to document their preferred interpretations in terms of widely accepted principles of sampling (of examples), coding, reliability, and validity. These concepts are explained in the next section of this chapter.

The plausible rival hypothesis approach forces researchers to think about all aspects of their data and to analyze all possible interpretations. At times, certain interpretations cannot be completely ruled out, even in well-designed studies. In such cases, these interpretations can be labeled, and indications of relative importance as targets for future research can be presented.

ARCHIVAL MATERIAL: CONTENT ANALYSIS

Although most of the examples in this chapter are based on data gathered as part of fieldwork in various cultures, good research can also be done by analyzing existing, already gathered materials. Examples of such materials are ethnographies, environmental impact statements, architectural plans, photographs, and so forth. The collection of formal techniques for dealing with such material is called "content analysis." A definition has been proposed by Janis (1949) that emphasizes what actually happens during a content analysis.

> "Content analysis" may be defined as referring to any technique (a) for the classification of the sign-vehicles, (b) which relies solely upon the *judgments* (which theoretically, may range from perceptual discriminations to sheer guesses) of an analyst or group of analysts as to which sign-vehicles fall into which categories, (c) on the basis of *explicitly formulated rules,* (d) provided that the analyst's judgments are regarded as the reports of a *scientific observer.* (Janis, 1949, p. 55, emphases in the original.)

A distinct possibility for the future is that the analysis of various materials will become more frequent. Fieldwork is very expensive, and more and more countries are placing restrictions on visiting researchers. Further, students can learn many of the basic principles of cross-cultural methodology (e.g., emics–etics, plausible rival hypotheses) through content analysis, and thus gain sophistication, so as to be better prepared for any field trip opportunity which arises.

Since long chapters have been written on content analysis (Brislin, 1980; Holsti, 1968), only basic points will be presented here. Content analysis must proceed according to explicit rules, so that a wide range of material is examined, not just that which will support a researcher's hypothesis. Content analysis is based on sorting material into categories established by a researcher, and these categories must also be formulated according to explicit rules. Findings from content analysis must also transcend the material that is analyzed, so that there is a contribution to theory development. Purely descriptive analyses are available in the literature, but readers will have no way of putting them into a framework if researchers suggest no link between their results and the work of other people.

In its actual use, content analysis can be described by four steps: (1) sampling of materials, (2) category development and subsequent sorting into them, (3) assessing reliability of the coding procedure, and (4) establishing the validity of results.

Sampling refers to decisions regarding what material is to be analyzed. This step is very important, since it determines the amount of generality a researcher can draw from the final results. For instance, if environmental impact statements prepared by governmental officials are analyzed, the researcher cannot make statements about the views of public interest groups from the private sector. Researchers should also have a good estimate of the amount of relevant material, compared to the amount of available material. Often, relevant material is not available, since it is located in an inconvenient place, has legal restrictions preventing its examination, and so forth.

In coding, the usually massive set of original material is transformed, according to a carefully prepared set of rules, into a limited number of well-defined categories. This step allows an economical reduction of the data to manageable proportions, allows the researcher to draw conclusions, and allows communication of the results to other interested individuals. In carrying out the coding, various persons (called "coders") are asked to read the original material, and to then place parts of it into the categories. Without clear categories, then, various coders cannot agree on what material should go into what category. In fact, one piece of practical advice (Holsti, 1968) is that in deciding where to put time, effort, and money, researchers usually have more success by developing clear categories than in spending long hours training coders to work with less than adequate categories.

Reliability refers to assessing the degree to which coders agree as to what material goes into what categories. Dissimilar coders are best, since a plausible rival hypothesis to agreement among similar people is that the reliability estimate cannot be generalized beyond the type of people who do the coding. If people from different cultures, with differing amounts of education, of different ages (and so forth) agree, however, then this finding provides evidence of robust categories.

Validity refers to a linkage of results from the content analysis with other, independent criteria. This step is the one most often neglected in content analysis. In assessing validity, the question to be asked is, "Do these results relate intelligibly to other indicators, and are these latter indicators also supportive of the hypothesis that stimulated the content analysis?" A good approach to assessing validity is through the use of multiple methods and multiple data points, and these procedures are covered in the next section.

Before going on, however, a massive source of cross-cultural materials (that is available for analysis) should be described. The source is the Human Relations Area Files (HRAF), available on paper or on microfilm in many large libraries (uses described by Barry, 1980; Naroll & Michik, 1980). The files contain efficiently organized material on 300 cultural units (roughly, "societies") throughout the world. Topical categories have been established, together with information regarding the location of materials related to the categories in each of the 300 cultural units. Categories of interest to readers of this book include the following: building and construction, structures, clothing, equipment and maintenance of buildings, exploitation activities (such as land use and water supply), settlements, and geography (includes climate, and topography and geology).

Much of the material in the files is not available elsewhere. Organizers have been diligent in obtaining out-of-print materials, and they have also commissioned translation of other-language source materials. There is a specialized methodological literature that has grown around use of the files (e.g., Naroll & Cohen, 1970; Naroll & Michik, 1980), and several caveats should be mentioned here. Material in the files is based on what various ethnographers reported; there is no guarantee that these ethnographers were correct regarding every statement they made. Much of the material is based on field work done many years ago, and so many of today's environmental issues will not be adequately analyzed. Further, many of the ethnographers were not specifically interested in environmental research, and so may not have given certain topics as much attention as readers of this volume may desire. Still, much material is available, and there is no better place to start one's search for background material about various cultures against which new data sets can be interpreted.

MULTIPLE METHODS AND MULTIPLE DATA POINTS

Many plausible rival explanations can be ruled out if researchers use more than one method to investigate their hypotheses. Many plausible alternatives are method bound: unfamiliarity with the materials in an experiment, a poorly translated questionnaire, unclear categories in content analysis, and so forth. But if the same hypothesis is investigated by more than one method, and if both methods yield data that are supportive, then the task of suggesting plausible alternatives is much harder (Campbell & Fiske, 1959).

For example, an area that has received a good deal of attention is the relation between environment and perception, which has been mentioned above in the review of Pollnac's (1977) research. The basic hypothesis is that experience with different types of physical environments leads to predictable differences in people's basic perceptual processes (Deregowski, 1979). Since experience is with a three-dimensional world, the perceptual tests should also be in three dimensions. However, almost all research in the area is based upon a single method: responses to two-dimensional figures. Hence, plausible alternatives of experience with depicting three dimensions on two-dimensional surfaces can easily be put forth. Realizing this difficulty, Brislin and Keating (1976) designed an experiment in which people from three cultures made perceptual judgments about objects in a three-dimensional scene. Specifically, they viewed objects set up in a nonlaboratory setting that demanded judgments from a distance of over 13 meters. Combined with similar results from parallel investigations using the more common (and easier to administer) two-dimensional stimuli (Liebowitz & Pick, 1972), the plausible alternative was ruled out by this multiple-method approach.

Multiple data points are also important. As Campbell (1961) has pointed out, differences in results based on one set of data gathered in two cultures are impossible to interpret. There are so many differences between any two cultures that claims by a researcher regarding the *one* reason for a set of results are unwarranted. The problem can be addressed by gathering multiple sets of data, as above, and/or by gathering data from more than two cultures. This latter quality is one of the main strengths of Berry's (1976; also his chapter, this volume) work. Based on data gathered from 21 culture groups in six very diverse parts of the world, Berry developed a theory relating ecology to human behavior. He developed an index of ecology based on exploitation pattern (hunting, fishing, agriculture, etc.), settlement pattern, and size of local community; and a culture index based on political stratification, social stratification, family organization, compliance–assertion ratings of child-rearing practices, and self-reports on severity of child training. Berry then made a case that all these factors can be combined into a single ecocultural index, and that this can be related to the development of individual cognitive styles. Given the consistency of the data from 21 culture groups, it is difficult to suggest *methodological* reasons why Berry obtained the results that he did. Theoretical reasons that account for the data as well as the original formulation (that cultures place demands on individuals that lead to certain cognitive styles) are likewise hard to develop. But even if an alternative theory can be formulated, understanding of human behavior is likely to increase. Put another way, data that are solid enough to persuade readers that time spent in formulating alternative explanations is worthwhile will be data that are helpful in advancing research. Data that can be dismissed on the grounds of a methodological difficulty will not motivate others to suggest theoretical explanations. A difficulty in this type of research, lack of attention to variance that is *unexplained* by the researcher's theoretical formulation, will be covered in the next section.

A third application of the multiple methods/data points approach is to predict interactions among the multiple variables (each represented by at least one data point) that are part of the study. Returning to the issue of familiarity of materials owing to their presence in certain environments, Irwin, Schafer, and Feiden (1974) found that very different conclusions could be drawn about culture and categorization if this issue was taken seriously. They discovered that Mano farmers of Liberia, West Africa, were able to sort types of rice into more categories than United States college males. The latter group, on the other hand, were able to sort cards into more categories. The interaction, then, is between culture and task.

This approach, basing interpretations on interactions, is similar to the procedure use in the classic work of Segall *et al.* (1966). They predicted different types of perceptual judgment, based on the physical environment in which people live. People in carpentered environments (many man-made buildings with large numbers of right angles) will make perceptual judgments different than those of people living in envi-

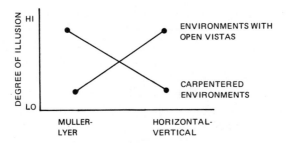

Figure 2.   Interaction between type of environment and type of visual illusion.

ronments with broad, open vistas. The operational definition of perceptual judgments consists of responses to the Müller-Lyer illusion

$$\longleftrightarrow$$

$$\succ\!\!-\!\!\prec$$

and to the horizontal–vertical illusion

The basic results (oversimplified since the sole purpose is to present the
methodological approach) can be graphed as shown in Figure 2. The interaction between type of environment and type of perceptual illusion
rules out a whole host of other explanations, such as understanding of
the instructions regarding the rather unfamiliar task of judging the
lengths of lines in visual illusions.

EXPLAINING COMPLEX PHENOMENA THROUGH LOW
CORRELATIONS AMONG VARIABLES

A number of researchers have engaged in a series of cross-cultural
environmental studies and have then suggested theories that link several variables into a causal framework. The theories undoubtedly explain
some of the variance, but not all, and the latter issue is too often ignored.
For instance, Whiting (1964) has combined the following variables (and
others; only some will be reviewed here) into a complex framework:

   a. Rainy tropical climates produce food that is low in protein.
   b. Because of the situation described in (a), mothers in such cul-

     tures are likely to nurse their children for long periods to provide the children with protein from milk.

c. The situation described in (b) leads to a long postpartum sex taboo, in which wife and husband do not have intercourse. The rationale is that the development of a new fetus would harm the mother's milk for the suckling child.

d. Cultures in which a long postpartum sex taboo is common are likely to have polygamous marriages as well as patrilocal residence.

e. In addition, as demonstrated by Whiting, Kluckhohn, and Anthony (1958), cultures with a prolonged postpartum sex taboo *and* an exclusive mother–son sleeping arrangement are also likely to have painful male initiation ceremonies as a common practice. The purpose of the ceremony, perhaps, is to break the mother–son bond so that the boy can join the adult male members of the culture in their activities.

These imaginative theoretical formulations are well worth doing. The problem comes in ignoring those cases that do not fit the model. Whiting (1964, p. 432) himself notes the problem:

> Although the above associations are for the most part statistically significant, a close look at any of the tables shows that there are many exceptional cases. Some of these are no doubt due to the operation of other factors which have not been taken into account in the study.

Even with such caveats, however, researchers simply take these theoretical formulations too seriously and do not spend needed time and effort on investigating the variance that is unexplained by these models. For instance, the contingency coefficient (Siegel, 1956, p. 196) between availability of protein and duration of postpartum sex taboo is .26 (calculated from Whiting's data, 1964, p. 428). This suggests that a great deal of variance has gone unexplained.

     Perhaps an analogy relating to a crisis in another research tradition will be helpful. Mischel (1973) had a major impact on thinking about personality measurement and theory when he pointed out that, for years, researchers have been weaving theories based on correlations of $r = .30$ between predictor and criterion. This yields a variance-accounted-for figure of .09, which is simply not high enough for the development of robust theories. Yet, few researchers paid attention to the unexplained variance until Mischel's criticism. A developing field such as cross-cultural environmental studies should benefit from the mistakes of others and should start giving attention to multiple sources of variance from the start.

There are several reasons why low correlations are the rule rather than the exception. One is the "law of the hammer": if a child receives a hammer for Christmas, suddenly everything needs hammering. Similarly, when an instrument is available, such as some of the measures of cognitive style used by Berry (1976), they are likely to be used in situations where a better (perhaps more emic) alternative is available. For the type of work done by workers in the Whiting tradition, the "instrument" is a category or code for which ratings from various cultures are already available. But when they are used, the possibility of explaining a large amount of variance is immediately diminished, since these imported instruments, by their very nature, do not tap subtleties within each culture where the variance undoubtedly hides. In the language of the early part of this chapter, there is not an emic manifestation within the culture to complement the etic. The present author has a hypothesis about these matters: cross-cultural research is so complex and frustrating that use of an already developed instrument gives a sense of confidence. To further complicate the matter, there is a need for comparative data on the same instruments to determine their usefulness as well as to obtain multiple data sets for later interpretation. If researchers develop their own emic instruments, this comparability can be lost. Like most important matters, cross-cultural research demands long and careful thought about goals and alternatives, some of them contradictory. Whatever the decision, the thinking should yield better data than the rather mindless use of already available instruments that seems to permeate cross-cultural research.

Another problem in linking variables is that theories must specify what should *not* correlate as well as what should correlate. If variables which should not be related are empirically shown to be closely associated, then the theory is called into question and modifications should follow. But researchers working in the area exemplified by the Whiting study (called "hologeistic" research) have been inattentive to the presence of significant correlations that are not called for by theories. Hence they lose a chance for possible improvement. Guthrie (1971) has suggested a method for analyzing all types of correlations, and he has designed it specifically for hologeistic studies, but his worthwhile contribution has not been widely accepted by researchers. Based on the Campbell and Fiske (1959) multitrait–multimethod matrix, Guthrie's technique involves intercorrelating a large number of variables. The format of the results generated by the technique allows a straightforward examination of correlation coefficients that are predicted and that are not predicted by a hypothesis or theory.

HUMAN RELATIONS IN CROSS-CULTURAL RESEARCH

In recent years, cross-cultural researchers have come to realize that there are special considerations in the general area of human relations that have to be dealt with carefully. The basic issue is that cross-cultural research is dependent upon the goodwill of people in various cultures, and upon the approval of administrators who can permit or deny access to certain cultures. A number of indicators suggest that there are real problems in obtaining access and in maintaining good relations with those people involved in research. Much of the analysis has been done in the field of anthropology, but the problems are common to all the behavioral/social sciences. Keesing and Keesing (1971, p. 405) pointed out that:

> Fieldwork in non-Western societies will simply not be possible for many aspiring anthropologists. The costs are rising too high, the anthropologists becoming too numerous, the places becoming too few and—perhaps— increasingly inhospitable to "being studied."

A graduate student from Fiji, in reacting to a sociological study, had an unfavorable report (in Brislin & Holwill, 1977, pp. 22–23):

> My experience in the past has been that the scholars on Indian culture, or should I call them "intellectuals," having studied the cultural patterns of Indians in India go down to the colonies and try to relate all their hypotheses upon the people of ethnic Indian background. They go there with some preconceived notions and try to search for these elements or they come across some similar notions or gestures get highly excited and jump to sweeping generalizations such as those put forth by the author in this article.

Other negative reactions have been documented by Tagumpay-Castillo (1968), who wrote from the point of view of a person who has regularly received visiting researchers. Finally, Harrington (1973) has discussed the negative reactions of a "man on the street" from Tubuai, a Pacific island. This analysis did the behavioral sciences no good, since it was published in a popular press magazine that has an estimated readership of 30,000,000 people. What can be done? Unfortunately, any suggestion can be attributed to some "holier than thou" attitude that readers may attribute to the writer. This potential attribution has probably prevented the thorough analysis that the problem demands. Here are just a few suggestions that have been put forth by people from cultures in which researchers from various countries regularly work:

1. Researchers should make efforts to assure that they are leaving something of benefit to the culture before and/or after they return to their own country. Such contributions can take the form of a trained assistant who can help with the work of local researchers; write-ups in language that people from the culture can understand; talks to local interest groups; support of local journals, if any, through publication in them; involvement of local researchers who complete the work with feelings that a true collaboration, or at least an effective and honest cooperative venture, has taken place.

2. Cross-cultural researchers will probably have to engage in studies that have an applied focus, since spokespersons in various cultures are likely to ask, "What's in it for us?" For researchers with an applied orientation, accustomed to answering this question in their own country, this will pose no problems. For more theoretically-oriented researchers, a change may be called for. Or, perhaps compromises can be made. If a large-scale survey is the method of choice, researchers can ask local officials if they would like to add some questions to the interview schedule. These could then be analyzed and written up in exchange for permission to carry out the part of the survey which reflects the researchers' interests.

3. Researchers must live up to their agreements. Representatives of some cultures are now demanding a contract-like proposal which calls for delivery of promised work by such and such a date. If researchers do not abide by the contract, *other* researchers may be denied permission in the future. In other words, there may be few penalties to the original researcher, but opportunities may be restricted for others.

Related to this point, most people who become involved in cross-cultural research in the 1980s will find a certain amount of hostility in attempting to gain permission to work in other cultures. They will be paying for the sins of their predecessors, and they will continue to do so until cross-cultural research acquires a better reputation than it has at the present time.

4. Researchers can sensitize themselves to basic customs and modes of interpersonal interaction in the cultures where they work. Customs and styles *are* different from culture to culture, and interpersonal blunders can interfere with work plans (Gudykunst, Hammer, & Wiseman, 1977; Hall, 1959).

5. Researchers must be sensitive to the nature of their own funding support. People in other cultures use the source of funding as a major determinant in deciding upon the level of cooperation which they will offer. They often assume that researchers hold views similar to those of administrators in the funding agency, even though the researchers

themselves would insist that they are doing "independent" research. And, like it or not, much cross-cultural research is viewed as being supported by the CIA (Doob, 1973; McCormack, 1976). Research projects have been ruined because this point received insufficient attention.

Human relations should be given as much attention as hypothesis formation and methodological design. The reason is survival oriented: researchers cannot test their hypotheses without the cooperation of people from other cultures. Researchers will be all dressed up, with no place to go, if administrators say "no" to a research request.

CONSIDERATIONS FOR THE FUTURE

Several suggestions may be considered here regarding future directions of the relation between cross-cultural research and environmental studies. These speculations are not quite so well developed as the methods and recommendations presented earlier, and so they should be examined with a greater-than-normal amount of care.

Exciting developments are under way in the use of multivariate statistics. These techniques are almost always used with the assistance of computers and accompanying software (programs). They permit analysis of massive amounts of data, and they reduce such data to a much smaller set of tables or figures that efficiently summarize a study's results. Brebner, Rump, and Delin (1976) used such techniques in a cross-cultural study of attitudes toward the physical environment. These researchers correctly recognized that, as with any method, care must be taken to insure proper use. In this case, they recognized that the way in which data (in a multivariate study) are combined can affect results, and they kept this point in mind when comparing their results with those of another study. Another potential problem is the suitability of data for the application of multivariate techniques. Dziuban and Shirkey (1974) observed the following about the most common technique of this sort, factor analysis:

> It has become practice for researchers to report in professional journals the results of factor and component analyses of various correlation matrices. Undoubtedly this is, at least in part, due to the accessibility of computer programs that perform these tasks.... Seldom, however, is evidence provided that the sample correlation matrices at hand are appropriate for factor-analytic methods. (Dziuban & Shirkey, 1974, p. 358)

Choice of this quote is not meant as a recommendation to avoid use of multivariate techniques. It does, however, represent a recommendation to insure that the data be studied carefully before a choice is made regarding the method of analysis. If this is not done, plausible rival hypotheses stemming from improper use of statistics can be put forward.

Fortunately, environmental research has attracted interdisciplinary attention. Psychologists, anthropologists, architects, sociologists, educators, and members of other disciplines have made contributions. Perhaps this variety of disciplines will lead to tolerance for a wide range of methodological approaches. Disciplines are sometimes differentiated on the basis of preferred method, e.g., experimentation for psychologists and participant observation for anthropologists. The borrowing of methods across disciplines, however, can yield good research. For instance, participant observation can yield insights into what concepts are important within a culture. These concepts can then be quantified and empirically tested, perhaps through experimentation or a sample survey. The time spent in participant observation helps insure that researchers are not imposing concepts from *their* culture on the one in which they are working.

Even though the bulk of the chapter has dealt with methodology, the more important part of research is the generation of hypotheses. Only after this step is completed should a method be chosen. In other words, the hypothesis should direct the choice of a method, not vice versa. Too little time is spent on hypothesis generation, so that trivial ideas are sometimes tested with very sophisticated methods. One way to generate better hypotheses is to ask for criticism from colleagues about ideas for research. Currently, colleagues are often asked to comment about methods, but rarely about the quality of the idea being examined by the method. Both cross-cultural and environmental studies will rise or fall, in terms of acceptance by the broad audience of behavioral and social scientists, on the basis of good hypotheses and eventually good theories.

BIBLIOGRAPHIC REFERENCES TO CROSS-CULTURAL RESEARCH METHODS

The following is a guide to some additional treatments of methodological issues:

1. *Overview of methodological issues common to virtually all cross-cultural studies:* Berry (1980); Brislin *et al.* (1973); Frijda and Jahoda (1966); Strodtbeck (1964).
2. *Measurement:* Guthrie (1977); Irvine (1980); Poortinga (1975).

3. *Use of the emic-etic distinction:* Berry (1969); Irwin *et al.* (1977).
4. *Validation of emics and etics:* Davidson, Jaccard, Triandis, Morales, and Diaz-Guerrero (1976); Triandis (1976).
5. *Translation between languages:* Brislin (1976b; 1980); Sechrest, Fay, and Zaidi (1972).
6. *Search for what is familiar within a culture, and subsequent use of such information in empirical studies:* Cole, Gay, Glick, and Sharp (1971); Cole and Scribner (1974).
7. *Interviewing:* Frey (1970); O'Barr, Spain, and Tessler (1973); Pareek (1980)
8. *Questionnaire design:* Brislin *et al.* (1973); Triandis (1977b).
9. *Natural observations:* Longabough (1980).
10. *Fieldwork:* Golde (1970); Goodenough (1980); several chapters in Naroll and Cohen (1970).
11. *Use of formal tests:* Brislin *et al.* (1973); Cronbach and Drenth (1972); Irvine (1980); Lonner (1976).
12. *Content analysis:* Brislin (1980); Holsti (1968).
13. *Hologeistic methods (cross-cultural surveys using anthropological data files):* Naroll and Cohen (1970); Naroll and Michik (1980).
14. *Experimentation:* Brislin *et al.* (1973); Sechrest (1977).
15. *Sampling:* Brislin *et al.* (1973); Frijda and Jahoda (1966); Sudman, 1976).

ACKNOWLEDGMENT

Key studies in the field of environment and behavior were suggested by Dr. Diane Drigot. Her assistance is gratefully acknowledged.

REFERENCES

Altman, I.. & Chemers, M. Cultural aspects of environment-behavior relationships. In H. Triandis & R. Brislin (Eds.), *Handbook of cross-cultural psychology* (Vol. 5). Boston: Allyn & Bacon, 1980.
Anderson, E. Some Chinese methods of dealing with crowding. *Urban Anthropology*, 1972, *1*(2), 141–150.
Barry, H. The Human Relations Area Files. In H. Triandis & J. Berry (Eds.), *Handbook of cross-cultural psychology*, (Vol. 2). Boston: Allyn & Bacon, 1980.
Berry, J. On cross-cultural comparability. *International Journal of Psychology*, 1969, *4*, 119–128.
Berry, J. *Human ecology and cognitive style: Comparative studies in cultural and psychological adaptation.* New York: Wiley/Halsted, 1976.
Berry, J. Introduction to cross-cultural methodology. In H. Triandis & J. Berry (Eds.), *Handbook of cross-cultural psychology* (Vol. 2). Boston: Allyn & Bacon, 1980.

Brebner, J., Rump, E., & Delin, P. A cross-cultural replication of attitudes to the physical environment. *International Journal of Psychology*, 1976, *11*, 111–118.

Brislin, R. Back-translation for cross-cultural research. *Journal of Cross-Cultural Psychology*, 1970, *1*, 185–216.

Brislin, R. Interaction among members of nine ethnic groups and the belief–similarity hypothesis. *Journal of Social Psychology*, 1971, *85*, 171–179.

Brislin, R. Comparative research methodology: Cross-cultural studies. *International Journal of Psychology*, 1976a, *11*, 215–229.

Brislin, R. (Ed.). *Translation: Applications and research.* New York: Gardner and Wiley/Halsted, 1976b.

Brislin, R. Methodology of cognitive studies. In G. Kearney & D. McElwain (Eds.), *Aboriginal cognition: Retrospect and prospect.* Canberra: Australian Institute of Aboriginal Studies, 1976c, pp. 29–53.

Brislin, R. Oral and written materials: Content analysis and translation. In H. Triandis & J. Berry (Eds.), *Handbook of cross-cultural psychology* (Vol. 2). Boston: Allyn & Bacon, 1980.

Brislin, R., & Baumgardner, S. Non-random sampling of individuals in cross-cultural research. *Journal of Cross-Cultural Psychology*, 1971, *4*, 397–400.

Brislin, R., & Holwill, F. Reactions of indigenous people to the writings of behavioral and social scientists. *International Journal of Intercultural Relations*, 1977, *1*(2), 15–34.

Brislin, R., & Keating, C. Cultural differences in the perception of a three dimensional Ponzo illusion. *Journal of Cross-Cultural Psychology*, 1976, *7*, 397–412.

Brislin, R., Lonner, W., & Thorndike, R. *Cross-cultural research methods.* New York: John Wiley, 1973.

Campbell, D. The mutual methodological relevance of anthropology and psychology. In F. Hsu (Ed.), *Psychological anthropology.* Homewood, Ill.: Dorsey Press, 1961.

Campbell, D. A cooperative multinational opinion sample exchange. *Journal of Social Issues*, 1968, *24*, 245–258.

Campbell, D. Perspective artifact and control. In R. Rosenthal & R. Rosnow (Eds.), *Artifact in behavioral research.* New York: Academic Press, 1969, pp. 351–382.

Campbell, D., & Erlebacher, A. How regression artifacts in quasi-experimental evaluations can mistakenly make compensatory education look harmful. In J. Hellmuth (Ed.), *Compensatory education: A national debate.* New York: Brunner/Mazel, 1970, pp. 185–210.

Campbell, D., & Fiske, D. Convergent and discriminant validation by the multitrait-multimethod matrix. *Psychological Bulletin*, 1959, *56*, 81–105.

Campbell, D., & Stanley, J. *Experimental and quasi-experimental design for research.* Chicago: Rand-McNally, 1966.

Cole, M., & Scribner, S. *Culture and thought: A psychological introduction.* New York: Wiley, 1974.

Cole, M., Gay, J., Glick, J., & Sharp, D. *The cultural context of learning and thinking.* New York: Basic Books, 1971.

Cronbach, L. J., & Drenth, P. J. D. (Eds.). *Mental tests and cultural adaptation.* The Hague: Mouton, 1972.

Dasen, P. R. Cross-cultural Piagetian research: A summary. *Journal of Cross-Cultural Psychology*, 1972, *3*, 23–39.

Davidson, A., Jaccard, J., Triandis, H. C., Morales, M., & Diaz-Guerrero, R. Cross-cultural model testing: Toward a solution of the emic-etic dilemma. *International Journal of Psychology*, 1976, *11*, 1–13.

Deregowski, J. Perception. In H. Triandis & W. Lonner (Eds.), *Handbook of cross-cultural psychology* (Vol. 3). Boston: Allyn & Bacon, 1980.

Doob, L. Foreword. In R. Brislin, W. Lonner, & R. Thorndike, *Cross-cultural research methods*. New York: Wiley, 1973, pp. v–vii.

Dziuban, C., & Shirkey, E. When is a correlation matrix appropriate for factor analysis? Some decision rules. *Psychological Bulletin*, 1974, *81*, 358–361.

Ervin-Tripp, S. Language and TAT content in French-English bilinguals. *Journal of Abnormal and Social Psychology*, 1964, *68*, 500–507.

Fahvar, M., & Milton, J. (Eds.). *The careless technology: Ecology and international development*. Garden City, N.Y.: Natural History Press, 1972.

Frey, F. Cross-cultural survey research in political science. In R. Holt & J. Turner (Eds.), *The methodology of comparative research*. New York: The Free Press, 1970, pp. 173–264.

Frijda, N., & Jahoda, G. On the scope and methods of cross-cultural research. *International Journal of Psychology*, 1966, *1*, 109–127.

Golde, P. (Ed.). *Women in the field: Anthropological experiences*. Chicago: Addison-Wesley, 1970.

Goodenough, W. Field methods. In H. Triandis & J. Berry (Eds.), *Handbook of cross-cultural psychology* (Vol. 2). Boston: Allyn and Bacon, 1980.

Groenman, S. Foreword. In P. Jacob, *Values and the active community*. New York: Free Press, 1971, pp. xv–xix.

Gudykunst, W., Hammer, M., & Wiseman, R. An analysis of an integrated approach to cross-cultural training. *International Journal of Intercultural Relations*, 1977, *1*(2), 99–110.

Guthrie, G. Unexpected correlations and the cross-cultural method. *Journal of Cross-Cultural Psychology*, 1971, *2*, 315–323.

Guthrie, G. Problems of measurement in cross-cultural research. In L. Loeb-Adler (Ed.), Issues in cross-cultural research. *Annals of the New York Academy of Sciences*, 1977, *285*, pp. 131–140.

Hall, E. *The silent language*. New York: Doubleday, 1959.

Harrington. R. One man's special island. *Parade*, January 7, 1973, pp. 21–22.

Holsti, O. Content analysis. In G. Lindzey & E. Aronson (Eds.), *Handbook of social psychology*, (Vol. 2, 2nd ed.). Reading, Mass.: Addison-Wesley, 1968, pp. 596–692.

Irvine, S. Tests and psychometrics. In H. Triandis & J. Berry (Eds.), *Handbook of cross-cultural psychology* (Vol. 2). Boston: Allyn and Bacon, 1980.

Irwin, M., Klein, R., Engle, P., Yarbrough, C., & Nerlove, S. The problem of establishing validity in cross-cultural measurements. In L. Loeb-Adler (Ed.), Issues in cross-cultural research. *Annals of the New York Academy of Sciences*, 1977, *285*, pp. 308–325.

Irwin, M., Schafer, G., & Feiden, C. Emic and unfamiliar category sorting of Mano farmers and U.S. undergraduates. *Journal of Cross-Cultural Psychology*, 1974, *5*, 407–423.

Janis, I. The problem of validating content analysis. In H. Laswell & N. Leites (Eds.), *The language of politics: Studies in quantitative semantics*. New York: George Stewart, 1949, pp. 55–82.

Johannes, R. Traditional law of the sea in Micronesia. *Micronesica*, 1977, *13*(2), 121–127.

Keesing, R., & Keesing, F. *New perspectives in cultural anthropology*. New York: Holt, Rinehart, & Winston, 1971.

Kroeber, A., & Kluckhohn, C. Culture. *Papers of the Peabody Museum*, 1952, *47*, No. 1.

Liebowitz, H., & Pick, H. Cross-cultural and educational aspects of the Ponzo illusion. *Perception and Psychophysics*, 1972, *12*, 403–432.

Longabough, R. Naturalistic observations. In H. Triandis & J. Berry (Eds.), *Handbook of cross-cultural psychology* (Vol. 2). Boston: Allyn and Bacon, 1980.

Lonner, W. An analysis of the prepublication evaluation of cross-cultural manuscripts: Implications for future research. In R. Brislin, S. Bochner, & W. Lonner (Eds.), *Cross-cultural perspectives on learning*. New York: Wiley/Halsted, 1975, pp. 305–320.

Lonner, W. The use of Western-based tests in intercultural counselling. In P. Pedersen, W. Lonner, & J. Draguns (Eds.), *Counseling across cultures.* Honolulu: University Press of Hawaii, 1976, pp. 170-183.

McCormack, W. Problems of American scholars in India. *Asian Survey,* 1976, *16,* 1064-1080.

Mischel, W. Toward a cognitive social learning reconceptualization of personality. *Psychological Review,* 1973, *80,* 252-283.

Muttagi, P. Tariff studies for water supply and sewerage services in greater Bombay. Bombay: Tata Institute of Social Sciences, 1977 (Sion-Trombay Road, Deonor, Bombay—400 088, India).

Naroll, R., & Cohen, R. (Eds.). *A handbook of method in cultural anthropology.* Garden City, N.Y.: Natural History Press, 1970.

Naroll, R., & Michik, G. Hologeistic studies. In H. Triandis & J. Berry (Eds.), *Handbook of cross-cultural psychology* (Vol. 2). Boston: Allyn and Bacon, 1980.

O'Barr, W., Spain, D., & Tessler, M. (Eds.). *Survey research in Africa: Its applications and limits.* Evanston, Ill.: Northwestern University Press, 1973.

Osgood, C. Objective indicators of subjective culture. In L. Loeb-Adler (Ed.), Issues in cross-cultural research. *Annals of the New York Academy of Sciences,* 1977, *285,* pp. 435-450.

Osgood, C., May, W., & Miron, M. *Cross-cultural universals of affective meaning.* Urbana: University of Illinois Press, 1975.

Over, R. Explanations of geometric illusions. *Psychological Bulletin,* 1968, *70,* 545-562.

Pareek, U. Interviewing. In H. Triandis and J. Berry (Eds.), *Handbook of cross-cultural psychology* (Vol. 2). Boston: Allyn and Bacon, 1980.

Phillips, H. Problems of meaning and translation in field work. *Human Organization,* 1960, *18,* 185-192.

Piaget, J. Nécessité et signification des recherches comparatives en psychologie génétique. *International Journal of Psychology,* 1966, *1,* 3-13. Translated into English and reprinted in J. W. Berry & P. Dasen (Eds.), *Culture and cognition.* London: Methuen, 1973.

Pollnac, R. Illusion susceptibility and adaptation to the marine environment: Is the carpentered world hypothesis seaworthy? *Journal of Cross-Cultural Psychology,* 1977, *8,* 425-434.

Poortinga, Y. Some implications of three different approaches to intercultural comparison. In J. Berry & W. Lonner (Eds.), *Applied cross-cultural psychology.* Amsterdam: Swetz and Zeitlinger, 1975, pp. 329-332.

Price-Williams, D. R. A study concerning concepts of conservation of quantities among primitive children. *Acta Psychologica,* 1961, *18,* 297-305.

Przeworski, A., & Teune, H. Equivalence in cross-national research. *Public Opinion Quarterly,* 1966, *30,* 33-43.

Przeworski, A., & Teune, H. *The logic of comparative social inquiry.* New York: Wiley, 1970.

Rapoport, A. Environmental cognition in cross-cultural perspective. In G. Moore & R. Gollendge (Eds.), *Environmental knowing.* Stroudsburg, Pa.: Dowden, Hutchinson, & Ross, 1976.

Sechrest, L. On the need for experimentation in cross-cultural research. In L. Loeb-Adler (Ed.), Issues in cross-cultural research. *Annals of the New York Academy of Sciences,* 1977 *285,* pp. 104-118.

Sechrest, L., Fay, T., & Zaidi, S. Problems of translation in cross-cultural research. *Journal of Cross-Cultural Psychology,* 1972 3(1), 41-56.

Segall, M., Campbell, D., & Herskovits, M. *The influence of culture on visual perception.* Indianapolis: Bobbs-Merrill, 1966.

Siegel, S. *Non-parametric statistics for the behavioral sciences.* New York: McGraw-Hill, 1956.
Strodtbeck, F. Considerations of meta-method in cross-cultural studies. *American Anthropologist,* 1964, *66,* 223–229.
Sudman, S. *Applied sampling.* New York: Academic Press, 1976.
Tagumpay-Castillo, G. A view from Southeast Asia. In *American Research on Southeast Asian Development: Asian and American Views.* New York: The Asia Society, 1968, pp. 20–49.
Talbot, L. Ecological consequences of rangeland development in Masailand, East Africa. In M. Farvar & J. Milton (Eds.), *The careless technology: Ecology and international development.* Garden City, N.Y.: Natural History Press, 1972, pp. 694–711.
Thorndike, R. Regression fallacies in the matched groups experiment. *Psychometrika,* 1943, *7,* 85–102.
Triandis, H. Approaches toward minimizing translation. In R. Brislin (Ed.), *Translation: Applications and research.* New York: Wiley/Halsted, 1976, pp. 229–243.
Triandis, H. Subjective culture and interpersonal relations across cultures. In L. Loeb-Adler (Ed.), Issues in cross-cultural research. *Annals of the New York Academy of Sciences,* 1977a, *285,* pp. 418–434.
Triandis, H. *Interpersonal behavior.* Monterey, Calif.: Brooks/Cole, 1977b.
Triandis, H., & Berry, J. (Eds.). *Handbook of cross-cultural psychology* (Vol. 2) *Methodology.* Boston: Allyn & Bacon, 1980.
Triandis, H. C., Davis, E., & Takezawa, S. Some determinants of social distance among American, German, and Japanese students. *Journal of Personality and Social Psychology,* 1965, *2,* 540–551.
Waddell, E. The hazards of scientism: A review article. *Human Ecology,* 1977, *5,* 69–76.
Werner, O., & Campbell, D. Translating, working through interpreters, and the problem of decentering. In R. Naroll & R. Cohen (Eds.), *A handbook of method in cultural anthropology.* New York: American Museum of Natural History, 1970, pp. 398–420.
Wesley, F., & Karr, C. Problems in establishing norms for cross-cultural comparisons. *International Journal of Psychology,* 1966, *1,* 257–262.
White, G. (Ed.). *Natural hazards: Local, national, global.* New York: Oxford University Press, 1974.
Whiting, J. Effects of climate on certain cultural practices. In A. Vayda (Ed.), *Environment and cultural behavior: Ecological studies in cultural anthropology.* Garden City, N.Y.: Natural History Press, 1969, pp. 416–455. Originally published in W. Goodenough (Ed.), *Explorations in cultural anthropology,* New York: McGraw-Hill, 1964, pp. 511–544.
Whiting, J. Methods and problems in cross-cultural research. In G. Lindzey & E. Aronson (Eds.), *Handbook of social psychology* (Vol. 2, 2nd ed.). Reading, Mass.: Addison-Wesley, 1968, pp. 693–728.
Whiting, J., Kluckhohn, E., & Anthony, A. The function of male initiation ceremonies at puberty. In E. Maccoby, T. Newcomb, & E. Hartley, *Readings in social psychology,* New York: Holt, 1958, pp. 359–370.
Wohlwill, J. The environment is not in the head! In W. Preiser (Ed.), *Environmental design research* (Vol. 2). Stroudsberg, Pa.: Dowden, Hutchinson, & Ross, 1973, pp. 166–181.

3

Cultural Ecology and Individual Behavior

JOHN W. BERRY

INTRODUCTION

Traditionally, much of the discipline of psychology has attempted to comprehend behavior as a function of stimuli impinging upon an individual. In recent years, the approach of ecological psychology has noted that the stimuli usually employed in psychology really represent only a very narrow range of all possible stimuli, and that they are excessively artificial in character; as a result, ecological psychology has emphasized the need to study behavior in more molar and naturalistic contexts. Similarly, an emerging cross-cultural psychology has argued that we should be attending to broad ranges of situations drawn from a cross section of cultures. It soon became clear, though, that sampling from new cultures also meant sampling from the new environmental contexts in which the cultures were situated. Thus, it became essential that the movement cross-culturally be accompanied by increased attention to the environmental settings of the cultures studied, a position similar to that espoused by ecological psychology.

Fortuitously, a similar movement within anthropology was developing the point of view that the forms which a culture evolves can and must be understood as adaptations to its habitat. This movement, often termed cultural ecology, has provided a valuable link and body of

JOHN W. BERRY • Department of Psychology, Queen's University, Kingston, Ontario, Canada K7L 3N6.

knowledge for psychologists wishing to trace individual behavior to its cultural and environmental bases.

This chapter will begin in the next section by briefly outlining these three developments, (ecological psychology, cross-cultural psychology, and cultural ecology), and by integrating them into a framework for understanding individual behavior in its ecological and cultural contexts. Then it will selectively review studies in the areas of cognitive style and social behavior which have been guided from this point of view. A further section will review studies of individual adaptation to environmental and cultural change, and a final section will point up some applications and future directions for work in this area.

SYSTEMATIC APPROACHES

In general psychology, an ecological approach has been promoted by Brunswik (see Hammond, 1966; Postman & Tolman, 1959, for reviews), Barker (1969), and most recently by Bronfenbrenner, (1977). Brunswik considered that behavior should be examined in its "natural-cultural habitat", and that the task of psychology is "the analysis of the interrelation between two systems, the environment and the behaving subject" (Hammond, 1966, p. 23). These interrelations are viewed as adaptations; individual behavior is a "coming to terms" with the environment (Brunswik, 1957, p. 5). Similar goals were adopted by Barker, who argued that "psychology knows how people behave under conditions of experiments and clinical procedures, but it knows little about the distribution of these and other conditions, and of their behavior resultants, outside of laboratories and clinics" (1968, p. 2). Essentially, the "psychologist-free environment of behavior" remains little known. Most recently, Bronfenbrenner (1977) has advocated an "experimental ecology," arguing that "much of contemporary developmental psychology is the science of the strange behavior of children in strange situations with strange adults for the briefest possible periods of time" (1977, p. 513).

All three writers have espoused a naturalistic approach to the study of individual behavior: the environmental context must be understood if the behavior is to be accounted for. A similar movement, that known as cross-cultural psychology, has asserted that the cultural context must also be incorporated into our psychological research: human behavior can be understood only when its cultural underpinnings are incorporated into the explanatory system. A further similarity is also evident: just as ecological psychology has urged the movement of psychologists out of the laboratory and clinic, so cross-cultural psychology has required the movement of psychologists out of their home culture into other cultural milieus. For both, this movement has effectively increased the range of independent variables—the range of habitats for behavior—requiring them to attend to phenomena and relationships hitherto ignored in general psychology.

For those primarily interested in cultural variables, many of these new phenomena and relationships were already being examined by a third emergent point of view—that of cultural ecology. One of the first expressions of this perspective (Forde, 1934) demonstrated that there were "complex relations between the human habitat and the manifold technical and social devices developed for its exploitation" (p. 460). Recent presentations of this view have argued that "culture is man's most important instrument of adaptation" (Cohen 1968, p. 1), and that cultural and environmental variables may be related in two ways (Vayda, 1969, p. xi). In one (the "weak" version), there can be a demonstration that cultural and environmental phenomena function as parts of the same system; in the other (the "strong" version), it can sometimes be shown that "environmental phenomena are responsible in some manner for the origin or development of the cultural behavior under investigation." The most recent review (Feldman, 1975) emphasizes the subtlety of these relationships, and demonstrates the ability of contemporary cultural ecologists to avoid the simplistic deterministic statements that plagued much of the earlier environmentalist thought.

Attempts have been made by the writer to integrate these three systematic approaches into one "ecocultural psychology" (Berry, 1976; in press), and these may be outlined briefly here. The ecocultural approach which has been developed over the past decade (see Berry, 1966, 1971, 1975, 1976) incorporates ecological, cultural, acculturational, and behavioral variables into a single model.

The basic elements of the model (see Figure 1) are ecological (interactions between human organisms and their habitat), cultural (group-shared patterns of behavior which are adapted to the group's habitat), and behavioral. A parallel set of elements, which is introduced through major contact with technologically dominant societies, includes the acculturative influences themselves (operating mainly through urbanization and education), the contact culture (a culture no longer simply in adaptation to its habitat, but now also under these acculturative influences), and acculturated behavior (consisting of "shifts" in behavior from previous levels, and "acculturative stress" behaviors which are novel and mildly pathological).

A basic proposition of the ecology element is that human organisms

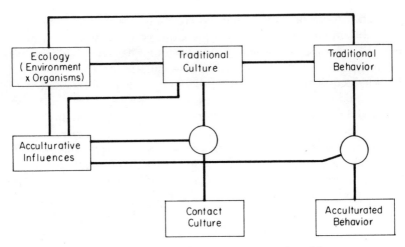

Figure 1.   An ecological-cultural-behavioral model.

(with their primary biological needs) interact with their physical environments in ways which seek to satisfy these needs. Because of variations in environmental features (e.g., temperature, rainfall, and soil quality), there will emerge variations in economic possibilities which may satisfy these needs.

A well-established dimension of varying economic pursuits is that of "exploitive pattern" (Murdock, 1969, pp. 130–131), where societies may be classified as gathering, hunting and trapping, pastoral, fishing, or varieties of agricultural. And another way of expressing this exploitive dimension is in terms of degree of "food accumulation" (Barry, Child, & Bacon, 1959); these authors have defined agricultural and pastoral pursuits as "high food accummulation," a combination of some agriculture with no pastoralism as "medium food accumulation," and hunting and gathering as "low food accumulation." The importance of this parallel classification will be explained when we discuss the socialization emphases element of the traditional culture component of the model.

Demographic patterns appear to be a function of these economic ones. For Murdock (1969), "settlement patterns" may be classified as fully nomadic, seminomadic, semisedentary, and fully sedentary; and size of population units may be arranged from small settlements (less than 50) up to towns or 50,000 or more. Both settlement pattern and population unit size are clearly related to exploitive pattern (Tables 2 and 3, pp. 144–145, Murdock, 1969), with hunting and gathering societies being predominantly nomadic or seminomadic with small population units, and agricultural and pastoral societies predominantly sedentary or semisedentary with much larger population units.

In summary, the evidence for the ecology element of the model shows that knowledge of physical environmental features allows prediction of the economic possibilities (exploitive pattern and food accumulation), which in turn allows prediction of the demographic distribution (settlement patterns and size of population units). The relationships are all probabilistic (rather than deterministic) and correlational (rather than causal). Nevertheless they are extant and are of sufficient strength to make predictions about features of the traditional culture element of the model.

In this chapter we espouse a definition of the concept of *culture* as a group's adaptation to the recurrent problems it faces in interaction with its environmental setting (cf. Edgerton, 1971). This approach in essence is a functional one, and considers that many (indeed most) features of a particular culture can be understood in terms of its particular function in the whole cultural system, and more broadly in the larger environmental context in which a people carry out their lives. Although many cultural elements are contained in the model, only two illustrative elements are examined here: stratification and socialization. Sociocultural stratification (that is, the presence of status hierarchies in a social system), may be related to a number of elements in the ecological component: two of these should suffice to illustrate the connection. In the first example, Nimkoff and Middleton (1960) have divided societies into categories of "great" or "little" social stratification, and into four exploitive patterns; of the 364 societies classed as "agriculture present," most (76%) were classed as highly stratified, while of the 73 societies classed as "hunting or gathering," most (78%) were in the low stratification category. In a second demonstration, Pelto (1968) drew a distinction between "tight" (high stratification) and "loose" (low stratification) societies, and provided both evidence and theoretical arguments for ecological correlates of this dimension. His interpretation specifies two ecological factors: the first is "high reliance on food crops," and the second is "high population density," both being associated (across many societies) with the presence of tight, highly stratified features of the society. Conversely, absence of agriculture, and the existence of low population density are associated with low levels of stratification in "loose" societies.

The second element of the traditional culture component is socialization emphases, and follows closely the work of Barry et al. (1959). These workers were able to demonstrate a clear but probabilistic relationship between an ecological variable (the degree of food accumulation in the society) and a general socialization one (societal ratings on "pressure toward compliance" vs. "assertion"). More specifically, training for "responsibility" and "obedience" correlated positively with high food accumulation, while training for "achievement," "self-reliance," and "independence" correlated negatively. Thus we have clear evidence that the degree of food accumulation is a reasonably good predictor of socialization emphases on the basis of their study: further elaborations of this relationship have provided continuing support (Barry, 1969; Barry & Paxson, 1971).

It is of interest to note that these ratings of socialization emphases are also related to another ecological variable (size of population unit), and to the other traditional cultural variable (sociocultural stratification): pressure toward compliance correlates +.43 with size of population unit, and +.56 with stratification (Barry et al., 1959, p. 61). Further evidence for this cluster of relationships is available from the same source: food accumulation correlates +.52 with size population unit, and +.74 with sociocultural stratification.

These societies rated by Barry et al. (1959) were all classified as "subsistence level," where ecological press and cultural adaptation may be more in tune with each other than in societies that participate in wider economic systems. It is important to note, then, that only in such subsistence-level societies can such ecological–cultural relationships be expected with confidence. To go beyond these societies in sampling for behavioral variation is to ignore this crucial parameter of the model.

In summary, we may label a broad ecological dimension running from agricultural interactions with the environment through to hunting and gathering interactions. Associated with the former pole is high food accumulation, high population density, and high sociocultural stratification and socialization emphases upon compliance; associated with the latter pole is low food accumulation, low population density, low stratification, and socialization practices emphasizing assertion. Societies which range along this broad ecological dimension, it is hypothesized, will vary concomitantly on these other ecological and cultural variables; this hypothesis is open to empirical check in any particular field investigation.

At the second (acculturation) level of the model, we include within the acculturative influences component such factors as experience of Western education, availability of wage employment, and the degree of urbanization which has taken place. These influences act upon the traditional culture, altering it to some extent: the culture of a people changes so that it now includes some residual elements of the traditional culture and some new forms, termed the contact culture. Continuing along the model, acculturation also influences the behavior of individuals, leaving some traditional behavior in place, but also altering it by inducing "shifts" toward new behavioral norms, and "stress" reactions; these have been termed acculturated behavior.

More recently (Berry, in press), an attempt has been made to develop a more refined model which will focus specifically on causal relationships between variables in the ecocultural setting and a variety of psychological consequences. This model (see Figure 2) represents four arcs or causal linkages between environment and behavior. The structure of the model places the four environmental contexts at the left and the effects at the right. Toward the top of the model are natural and holistic contexts and effects, while at the bottom they are more experimental (controlled and reductionistic).

Looking in detail at the environmental contexts, the *ecological context* is the "natural-cultural habitat" of Brunswik, or the "preperceptual world" of Barker. It consists of all the relatively permanent characteristics which provide the context for human action, and includes the "ecological," "traditional culture," and "acculturational influences" components of the research model employed earlier (Berry, 1975, 1976).

Nested in this ecological context are two levels of the "life space" or "psychological world" of Lewin (1936). The first, the *experiential context*, is that pattern of recurrent experiences which provide a basis for learning; it is essentially the set of independent variables which cross-cultural psychology tries to spot as being operative in a particular habitat in the development of behavioral characteristics. These variables include such day-to-day experiences as child-rearing practices, occupational training, and general education. The other, the *performance context*, is the limited

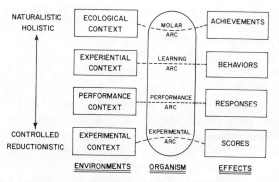

Figure 2.   A model of relationships among environmental contexts, the organism, and behavioral effects at four levels.

set of environmental circumstances which may be observed to account for particular behaviors. These are immediate in space and time, and include those features of a setting, such as a specific role or social interaction, which can influence how a person will respond in that setting.

The fourth context, the *experimental context,* represents those environmental characteristics, such as a test item or stimulus condition, which are designed by the psychologist to elicit a particular response or test score. The experimental context may or may not be nested in the first three contexts; the degree to which it is nested represents the ecological validity of the task.

Paralleling these four contexts are four effects. The first, *achievements,* refers to the complex, long-standing, and developed behavior patterns which are in place as an adaptive response to the ecological context. It includes established and shared patterns of behavior which can be discovered in an individual or distributed in a cultural group.

The second, *behaviors,* are the molar behaviors which have been learned over time in the recurrent experiential context. Included are the skills and traits and attitudes which have been nurtured in particular roles, or acquired by specific training or education, whether formal or informal. A third effect, *responses,* connotes those performances which appear in response to immediate stimulation or experience. In contrast to behaviors, they are not a function of role experience or long-term training, but appear in reply to immediate experiences.

The fourth effect, *scores,* is comprised of those behaviors which are observed, measured, and recorded during psychological experiment or testing. If the experimental context is nested in the other contexts, then the scores may be representative of the responses, behaviors and achievements of the organism. If the experiment has ecological validity, then the scores will have behavioral validity.

Relationships can be traced between the environmental and effects elements across the model. The molar arc ["E–0–E arc" in Brunswik's (1957) terms] operates across the top of the model. It is concerned with the life situation (in physical, environmental, and cultural terms) of an organism and its accomplishments. At the second level, the learning arc is concerned with tying together recurrent independent variables in the experience of an individual with his characteristic behaviors. The third level, that of the performance arc, is interested in more specific acts as a function of immediate and current experience. And at the fourth level, the experimental arc is devoted to the laboratory or other systematic study of relationships between experimental problems and test scores.

A recurrent problem for general experimental psychology, in terms of this model, is to say anything of value about causal relationships (at the two middle levels) while working almost exclusively with the experimental arc. And to this Brunswik (1957) would add the further problem of saying anything meaningful on this basis about the molar arc as well. The problem facing cross-cultural psychology tends to be the reverse: rather than failing to ascend the reductionistic–holistic dimension to achieve ecological validity, cross-cultural psychology has failed to descend the dimension to achieve a specification of experiential performance and experimental context variables which are responsible for task performance and behavioral variation across natural habits. In Campbell's (1957) terms, there has been insufficient concern in these two branches of psychology for "external" and "internal" validity respectively.

The original analyses of Barker (1969), Brunswik (1957), and Lewin (1936) which have stimulated the model presented here appear to underlie other contemporary analyses. For example, Eckensberger and Kornadt (1977, pp. 222–223) distinguish between group and individual levels of ecological analyses. When groups are the focus, analyses tend to be at the holistic level, with cultural and behavioral achievements being considered as the dependent variable. When individuals are the focus, analyses tend to be at the lower levels, with individual behaviors and performances constituting the dependent variables.

With these models as a guide we can now proceed to a review of some empirical studies of variations in individual behavior as a function of ecocultural context. In the first of these two sections we will consider behavior in relatively stable contexts, but in the second we will turn to an examination of behavior under conditions of ecocultural change. In both cases, the intention will be to illustrate how individual behavior may, and indeed *must*, be seen in its total ecological and cultural context. The focal problem will be to demonstrate the specific linkages (at the lower arc levels) which psychologists pursue, while at the same time indicating the integrity of their nesting in the broader linkages (at the higher arc levels), which the social and environmental sciences demand.

COMPARATIVE STUDIES OF INDIVIDUAL ADAPTATION

The now classical study of group variation in illusion susceptibility (Segall, Campbell, & Herskovits, 1966) has demonstrated that perceptual learning in differing visual ecologies can lead to systematic variation in perceptual response. These authors, working with variations in susceptibility to a number of geometric illusions, isolated two experiential contexts which appeared to be important. One was the degree of "carpenteredness" in a group's visual ecology (such as right angles in houses, furniture), and the other was the availability of "open vistas" (across fields, deserts, or water) in contrast to "closed vistas" (in forest or valley settings). Although "cross-cultural," in the sense of comparing different cultural groups, the study can more accurately be termed "cross-ecological," since culture contributed to the ecological context rather than directly to the psychological development of individuals.

In this section we will orient ourselves more specifically toward the role of cultural variables in the development of behavior, but at the same time we will keep in focus the conception of culture as adaptive to its ecological context. Brief reviews of two areas of research will be presented: the first concerns evidence for culture-related variation in the development of cognitive style (Witkin, Dyk, Faterson, Goodenough, & Karp, 1962; Witkin & Berry, 1975; Witkin & Goodenough, 1977b), and the second outlines some research on social influence and conformity. Since the central studies to be reviewed are based upon samples from a common set of cultures, we will begin with a consideration of these samples, and of their relationship to the ecocultural model outlined in the last section. Then we will examine the psychological constructs of cognitive style and conformity, and evidence for their distribution across cultures in relation to their ecological and cultural contexts.

Ethnographic descriptions of the ten cultures listed in Table 1 can be found in Berry (1976). They range ecologically from sedentary and agriculture-based peoples in West Africa and highland New Guinea to nomadic hunters and gatherers in Arctic Canada and Central Australia. Within six of the cultures, two or more communities were selected which represented differing levels of acculturation to European lifestyle, yielding a total of seventeen samples at or near economic subsistence level. In addition, four European samples were included (two Scottish and two Canadian), which brings the total number of participants to about one thousand individuals.

The purpose of Table 1 is to present in succinct form the essential characteristics of the various cultures and samples. This is accomplished by developing four standardized indices which integrate the ecological, cultural, and acculturational features of each sample. The indices, which are standardized around a mean of zero, were assembled in the following way:

Ecological Index: Ratings of exploitive pattern, settlement pattern, and mean size of local community from Murdock (1957). This index, when standardized, ranges the samples from a nomadic hunting pole (+1.09 for the Eskimo) to a sedentary, agricultural pole (−1.98 for the Temne).

TABLE 1

CULTURES, SAMPLES AND THEIR CHARACTERISTICS[a]

Cultural group	Location	Sample name	N	Ecological index	Cultural index	Ecocultural index	Acculturation index
Temne	West Africa	Mayola	90	-1.98	-1.93	-1.96	-1.68
		Port Loko	32	-1.98	-1.48	-1.66	-0.02
Telefol	New Guinea Highlands	Telefomin	40	-1.53	-1.48	-1.51	-1.47
Tsimshian	Coastal British Columbia	Hartley Bay	56	-0.27	-0.37	-0.34	+0.74
		Port Simpson	59	-0.27	-0.37	-0.30	+1.42
Koonganji	Coastal Australia	Yarrabah	30	-0.27	-0.53	-0.45	-0.38
Motu	Coastal New Guinea	Hanuabada	30	-0.39	-0.53	-0.49	+0.68
Carrier	British Columbia mountain	Tachie	60	+0.18	-0.26	-0.11	+0.47
		Fort St. James	61	+0.18	+0.36	+0.30	+0.95
Arunta	Central Australia	Santa Teresa	30	+0.52	+0.80	+0.72	-1.26
Ojibway	Northern Ontario	Aroland	39	+0.64	+0.64	+0.64	+0.34
		Long Lac	37	+0.64	+0.25	+0.38	+0.80
		Sioux Lookout	31	+0.64	+0.41	+0.49	+1.48
Cree	Northern Quebec	Wemindji	61	+0.86	+0.75	+0.79	-0.69
		Fort George	60	+0.86	+0.64	+0.72	+0.26
Eskimo	Baffin Island	Pond Inlet	91	+1.09	+1.58	+1.43	-1.20
		Frobisher Bay	31	+1.09	+1.57	+1.36	-0.44

[a] From Berry (1976).

Cultural Index: Ratings of political stratification, social stratification, and family organization from Murdock (1957), and ratings of socialization compliance–assertion from Barry *et al.* (1959), supplemented by respondent self-ratings on the same dimension. This index, when standardized, ranges the samples from a pole indicating low stratification, and socialization emphasizing assertion (+1.58 for the Eskimo), to high stratification and compliant socialization (−1.93 for the Mayola Temne).

Ecocultural Index: A combination of the first two indices (which in fact intercorrelate +.84) to provide a more general input variable. This combined index ranges the samples from a pole characterized by a "nomadic style" (the Eskimo at +1.43) through to a "sedentary style" (the Temne at −1.96).

Acculturation Index: Ratings of experience of European education, combined with ratings of the degree of urbanization and wage employment in the communities. In this case, the samples range, not by culture, but by sample exposure to acculturation. The most acculturated are the traditionally nomadic, but now settled Sioux Lookout Ojibway (at +1.48), while the least acculturated pole is represented by the traditional Temne and Eskimo (at −1.68 and −1.20 respectively).

These indices essentially provide a quantification of the input for the ecocultural model which was outlined in the previous section (see Figure 1). To be useful, they should vary widely in order to constitute a quasi-manipulation of the independent (ecological and cultural contextual) variables; and ideally the two main inputs (the Ecocultural and the Acculturation Index) should be independent of each other. We may note here that ecocultural and cultural variation is rather large, and that these two main input variables are insignificantly correlated (+.16) in these samples. In contrast, there is a pattern of substantial interrelationships within the three elemental indices and between the ecological and cultural indices, permitting their amalgamation; this latter relationship is, of course, consistent with a view of culture as an adaptation to its ecological setting.

Turning to cross-cultural research on cognitive style, we should note that it has been an area of intensive activity in the past few years (Berry, 1976; Dawson, 1975; Okonji, in press; Serpell, 1976; Witkin & Berry, 1975), most of it related to the cognitive style of Field-Dependence–Field-Independence (Witkin *et al.*, 1962; Witkin & Goodenough 1977b). The concept of Field-Dependence–Independence is part of the broader concept of psychological differentiation. In general the notion of differentiation refers to a process of change in a system toward greater specialization; this change occurs over time and constitutes a development in the system. Relatively undifferentiated systems are global, not internally separated in structure or function; relatively differentiated systems have greater structural complexity—they have more parts, and they are more elaborately integrated. Differentiation is a feature of a system as a whole; it refers to the overall structure of, and within, all its component parts.

In cultural systems, the notion of differentiation is historically associated with the concept of evolution. For example, Spencer (1864; p. 216) has defined evolution as "a change from a state of relatively indefinite, incoherent homogeneity to a state of relatively definite coherent heterogeneity, through continuous differentiations and integrations." In this definition, the term differentiation refers to the separations and distinctions, while the term integration refers to their tying together.

In psychological systems, as the term is employed by Witkin, differentiation takes on a more inclusive meaning, and in addition to referring to separations it also implies a corresponding elaborate degree of integration. Furthermore, just as there is progressive change in cultural systems, there is development in psychological systems. And just as general differentiation pertains to the whole system, psychological differentiation is considered to characterize the total individual organism. That is, evidence for psychological differentiation may be sought in all areas of behavioral functioning—perceptual, cognitive, neurophysiological, social, and affective. This evidence should indicate roughly similar levels of differentiation in each behavioral domain.

Although the concept of differentiation is linked historically with a process of individual *development,* it has also been based upon the need to describe and comprehend individual *differences* in perceptual and cognitive functioning. It is within this latter (individual difference) framework, rather than in the developmental one, that this chapter's discussion is contained. A major reason for using this approach is that when researchers find that populations differ in their psychological characteristics they are able to treat these differences simply *qua* differences, rather than having to judge one population as more, or less, developed than another (Dasen, Berry, & Witkin, 1979).

One component of psychological differentiation is the Field-Dependent–Field-Independent cognitive style, which refers to the characteristic separation of the self from its environment or field. It focuses upon two areas of psychological functioning: perceptual–cognitive, and social. The first is termed "restructuring," and includes such behaviors as disembedding and analysis. For example, individuals vary in their ability to isolate a small figure from its background context (such as a camouflaged animal from its immediate setting), or analytically to take apart or break up an intellectual problem as a step in its solution. The second, "interpersonal competencies," includes such things as social sensitivity and attention to social cues. For example, individuals vary in their ability to judge social and emotional signals from other individuals, and they differ in other social behaviors, such as interpersonal distance or eye contact during social interaction. Taken together, these perceptual–cognitive and social components are designated by Witkin as a field-dependent to field-independent (FD-FID) cognitive style; those at the field-dependent end of the dimension tend to rely upon external referents, while those at the field-independent end rely upon internal referents. The field-independent (FID) cognitive style, then, refers to an approach which is analytic and based upon standards internal to the individual, while the field-dependent (FD) cognitive style refers to an approach which is more global and based upon the external environment (both physical and social). Across domains, those (the field-independent individuals) who are analytic in their perceptual and cognitive life tend to be distant in their social relations, while those (the field-dependent individuals) who are more global in perceptual characteristics tend to be more sensitive and close in their social interactions (Witkin & Goodenough, 1977a).

Within some Western societies, clear evidence is available to show that there is a developmental change, ontogenetically, in FD-FID, with younger children being more field-dependent (Witkin, Goodenough, & Karp, 1967). There is also evidence for socialization practices contributing to its development: those individuals raised with an emphasis on autonomy and achievement tend to be more field-independent, while those raised in a protective or conforming mileu tend to be more field-dependent (Witkin, 1969). Thus the dimension is useful in characterizing individual differences based upon at least two background factors.

Moving cross-culturally, it is important both to check the operation of these two factors and to search for other, perhaps novel, features of the cultural ecology for their possible contributions to the patterning of cognitive style. When we consider these latter possibilities, two major classes of variable immediately appear relevant. One is the ecological engagement of a group [originally termed "ecological demands" (Berry, 1966)], and the other is the "cultural supports" available in the group for acquiring a particular cognitive style.

With respect to the ecological factors, it is possible to predict that those peoples who engage the physical environment through hunting and gathering activities will be called upon to develop "restructuring" skills to a high degree: tracks, signs, odors, and sounds all need to be isolated from context in order to carry on this subsistence pattern. Furthermore, the nomadic settlement pattern associated with hunting and gathering requires a developed sense of space, complete with an awareness of topographical signs (e.g., streams, mountains, coasts) and angular orientation to other features (e.g., paths, sun and stars, prevailing winds). It is difficult to conceive of a successful hunter without skills to find game and to return again to camp. In contrast, these skills are unlikely to be of similar value to agriculturalists.

With respect to cultural factors, we have already noted that authority pressures generally are weak (social and political stratification are low), and socialization pressures are toward achievement, independence, and self-reliance in hunting and gathering societies. In contrast, social systems tend to be "tight" and socialization practices emphasize compliance in societies engaging in agricultural pursuits in sedentary settlements.

Both the ecological and cultural factors to be found cross-culturally among subsistence-level peoples are predictive of greater field-dependence among agriculturalists and greater field-independence among hunters and gatherers. The evidence presented by Berry (1976) for the samples listed in Table 1, and the bulk of the evidence reviewed by Witkin and Berry (1975), support this generalization. For example, in the 1976 monograph, cognitive style tasks (such as Kohs Blocks and the Embedded Figures Test) correlated with the combined ecocultural index .73 and .88 respectively across the seventeen samples, and .65 and .84 respectively across the almost 800 participants in that study. That is, those peoples toward the nomadic, "loose" end of the ecocultural dimension are more field-independent in cognitive style, while those toward the sedentary, "tight" end are more field-dependent. Whether analysed at the sample or individual level, ecocultural adaptation clearly accounts for a high proportion of group and individual differences in cognitive style development (Berry, 1976).

Influences stemming from acculturation also contribute to the distribution of scores on these tests. The acculturation index correlates .65 and .38 at the sample level, and .47 and .32 at the individual level. That is, the higher the exposure to Western education (and the new wage and settlement life), then the more field-independent the sample; conversely, the less acculturated the sample, the less they exhibit field-independence. In all cases, though, acculturation (mainly through a form of Westernization in these samples) is less strongly related than is ecocultural adaptation. Given this pattern of both factors contributing, it is worth noting that a combined (ecocultural plus acculturation) analysis pushes the correlations to the .8 range, and a multiple correlation, employing all the variables in a stepwise fashion, pushes the correlation to the .9 range.

Contributing evidence stems from the work of Dawson (1967, 1975), MacArthur (1973, 1975), Okonji (1969, in press), and others. The overall picture supports the generalization made here that individuals develop a cognitive style which is encouraged in their culture, and which is adaptive to their habitat. That this is so may appear to some to be tautological; nevertheless the analyses of these differences and the demonstration of covariation among behavioral, cultural, and environmental elements within an ecological system seems to be a necessary first step. A second step, of course, requires the more fine-grained analyses outlined in Figure 2. There must be a descent from the molar arc to the learning arc, where the acquisition and development of these behaviors come more clearly into focus. And similarly there must be further specification of the performance contexts which elicit the appropriate style, and more experimental analyses which can explain more of the score variance.

A second, but related, set of behaviors has also been explored cross-culturally. In the outline of the concept of cognitive style, mention was made of "social autonomy," being theoretically related to "restructuring" within the field-independent cognitive style, and of "interpersonal competencies," being related to the FD end of the dimension. Social behaviors may also thus be subsumed within the framework outlined in this chapter.

More specifically, it may be predicted that individuals who grow up in a "tight" stratified and densely populated society, such as those described in agriculturally based groups, will be more sensitive to group needs and more responsive to group requirements. For example, among the sedentary Temne, greater social and political stratification, and a stronger emphasis on socialization for compliance, is likely to inculcate a greater degree of acceptance of social authority and influence. In contrast, those developing in "loose" social units, such as the nomadic Eskimo, might be expected to be more independent of authority and less conforming to group pressure, as a result of lesser stratification and a greater emphasis on socialization for assertion. A first approach (Berry, 1967) to this prediction contrasted samples from two cultures (the Temne and the Eskimo, in Table 1) on a conformity task. This involved a situation similar to the one described by Asch (1956), where individuals are requested to judge the length of a line in the face of a false social norm. In field settings, using confederates is impossible for a variety of reasons, and so a group norm was suggested by the researcher as "the

one most often chosen by the ——— people." Differences between the
two groups were as expected: in the "tight" samples, judgments were
significantly closer to the suggested group norm than in the "loose"
samples.

At this group level of analysis, there was thus correspondence between two behavioral domains which are theoretically related in the
Field-Dependent–Field-Independent cognitive style. However, at the
individual level of analysis (that is, using individual difference correlations), relationships were not significant. A recent review by Witkin and
Goodenough (1977a) has shown that substantial relationships between
restructuring and interpersonal competencies appear only in live or real,
rather than simulated, social contexts. Thus the task employed appears
in retrospect to have been unsuitable for the analyses of individual differences in cognitive style; however, group and individual differences
appear to be highly predictable across cultures.

Evidence for this latter generalization has been assembled from the
samples listed in Table 1, and has been reported in Berry (1979a). Although not so strong as those reported for the "restructuring" tasks in
the last section, the correlation with the ecocultural index across the
seventeen samples is .70, and across 800 individuals is .51; and the multiple correlation achieved when all constituent factors are taken in
reaches .75 at the sample level, and .43 at the individual level. That is,
those peoples toward the "loose," nomadic end of the ecocultural dimension are more independent of the simulated group pressure, while
those toward the "tight" end are more accepting of this form of social
influence. Although, at the individual level, we cannot claim to be assessing the Field-Dependent–Field-Independent cognitive style, it is
clear that we can account for a substantial amount of the cross-cultural
variation in this social behavior when we focus on the ecological requirements and sociocultural pressures ("tightness") which characterize
these various societies.

In concluding this section, it is worthwhile to note again that more
detailed analyses of the learning and performance arcs are required before we can specify the nature of the development of these behaviors.
For example, if this kind of analysis had been available earlier, the social
features of the performance and experimental contexts might have been
altered to make them more suitable for the exploration of individual
variations in cognitive style. Clearly, other pitfalls may be avoided in the
future if such descent from the molar arc is made sooner, rather than
later, in the cross-cultural enterprise.

Nevertheless, we have been able to track down substantial evidence
for the systematic covariation between behavior and features of its cul-

tural and ecological setting. It is clear that analyses of adaptation, both of culture to habitat, and of behavior to its ecocultural context, permit us to delve into a system, to describe variations and linkages, and, most of all, to understand some of the cross-cultural patterning of human behavior.

INDIVIDUAL ADAPTATION TO ENVIRONMENTAL CHANGE

If, as we have argued, individuals are behaviorally adapted to their cultural and physical habitat, then we may legitimately ask: How do they deal with changes in their habitat? An approach to this question requires some analyses of the concept of adaptation.

One general usage of the term "adaptation" refers to the reduction of dissonance within a system—the increase of harmony among a set of interacting variables. At least three strategies may be distinguished for attaining such increased harmony: adaptation by adjustment, by reaction, or by withdrawal.

In the case of adjustment, behavioral changes are in a direction which reduces the conflict between the environment and the behavior by changing the behavior to bring it into harmony with the environment. In general, this variety is the one most often intended by the term "adaptation," and may indeed be the most common form of adaptation. In the case of reaction, behavioral changes are in a direction which retaliates against the environment; these may lead to environmental changes which, in effect, increase the congruence between the two, but not by way of behavioral adjustment. For example, a group may develop a technology to eliminate a medical threat or to improve agricultural production on existing lands. In essence, the major change is in the environment, permitting a continuation of the group's way of life in that location. In the case of withdrawal, behavior is in the direction which reduces the pressures from the environment; in a sense, it is a removal from the adaptive arena. For example, migration away from a noxious or difficult environment, or isolation of the group from a portion of it, leave the environment more or less intact. These three varieties of adaptation are similar to the distinctions in the psychological literature (Horney, 1955; Lewin, 1936) made between moving with or toward, moving against, and moving away from a stimulus.

When adaptation is made to the ecocultural setting, most often we observe among subsistence-level peoples that the adjustment mode is employed; that is, individual behavior develops in a way which is congruent with ecological press. However, the reaction and withdrawal modes have also sometimes been employed, resulting in the development of technology (used to change the habitat), or in group or individual migration. If reaction is successful, then the group may be classified out of the subsistence-level category, or if reaction is unsuccessful, major breakdown may occur; and if withdrawal is used, the group is no longer available for study in that particular habitat. Thus in either case they are removed from the adaptive framework outlined earlier in this chapter, so that we are left with a set of phenomena exemplifying the adjustment mode.

When adaptation is to ecocultural change, we are often in a better position to monitor all three adaptive modes at work. An example of continuing adjustment is the impact that acculturation has had upon cognitive style. The effect of formal education (as one factor in acculturation) was to make the test performance more similar to the norms found in Western technological-industrial societies; these have been "behavioral shifts" (Berry, 1979b).

Examples of the reaction and withdrawal modes can also be found in the literature; they usually appear in association with the phenomenon of "acculturative stress" (Berry, 1971; Berry & Annis, 1974). This concept has been used to refer to the cluster of behaviors which is personally and socially disruptive, and which often accompanies acculturation. Such a cluster has been variously defined as including psychosomatic stress, social deviance, feelings of marginality, loss of identity (or having identity conflict), and interpersonal and intergroup hostility (Berry, 1979b).

A number of studies of these phenomena have indicated that, although frequently present, they are not universal accompaniments of acculturation. The key would seem to be the degree of conflict which is generated by the contact, and the amount of change which is being required (Berry & Annis, 1974; Chance, 1965; Wintrob & Sindell, 1972). We may illustrate some of these features of individual adaptation to change by referring once again to some of the samples listed in Table 1. With the nine Amerindian samples (Cree, Ojibway, Carrier, and Tsimshian), scales were employed to assess psychosomatic stress, feelings of marginality, attitudes toward assimilating into the larger society, and toward rejecting the larger society. These last two variables reflect an adjustment mode, and a combined reaction–withdrawal mode respectively.

The central hypothesis (Berry, 1976) was that those societies which are traditionally more similar to the demands of change will experience less acculturative stress. These demands generally include an increase in sedentarization, in settlement size, and in social and political stratification; that is, the "tighter" the society, the less will be the stress. In such "tight" societies, individuals are attuned culturally and psychologically to high population density, to the social conflicts which often appear in such communities, and to the authority structures which are developed to meet these conflicts. In "loose" societies, it is argued, individuals generally are unprepared for such demographic conditions and the accompanying social controls. Thus, across the ecocultural range that we have been dealing with, the expectation is that adjustment will be less common and less easy among the "loose" societies, that reaction and/or withdrawal will be more in evidence, and that these two modes of adaptation will be accompanied by greater acculturative stress. Conversely, among "tight" societies, adjustment will be more common, and acculturative stress will be lower.

Evidence for this hypothesis has been reported in Berry (1976), and supporting material has been reviewed by Berry (1979b). For example, across the nine Amerindian samples listed in Table 1 with the ecocultural index, Stress and Marginality correlated +.44 and +.70 respectively, while attitudes toward Assimilation (adjustment) and toward Rejection (reaction/withdrawal) correlated −.69 and +.80 respectively. The four correlations at the individual level ($n = 453$) were +.45, +.43, −.50, and +.31 respectively. This pattern of interrelationships supports the hypothesis in a consistent way: the "tighter" the society the less the Stress, Marginality, and Rejection, but the greater the Assimilation (adjustment); conversely, the "looser" the society, the more the Stress, Marginality, and Rejection, but the less the Assimilation. To illustrate, the Cree, who are "loose" in social structure and the most nomadic of the samples, turn out to exhibit the greatest degree of acculturative stress; conversely, the Tsimshian, who are traditionally sedentary and "tight" in their social structure, tend to experience the least acculturative stress. Supportive evidence also exists in the pattern of correlations among these four variables: Stress and Marginality correlate +.80 and +.58 at the sample and individual levels respectively, while Assimilation and Rejection attitudes correlate − .87 and −.24. Between them, Stress and Marginality negatively correlate with Assimilation (−.84 and −.91 at the sample level; −.24 and −.27 at the individual level), while they correlate positively with Rejection (+.54 and +.72; and +.28 and +.26). That is, the four variables do tend to cluster into a meaningful array, supporting the general notion of acculturative stress; the adaptions which people make to change are interrelated in consistent ways. Moreover, the overall pattern is one which suggests that the traditional ecocultural adaptation of a society is a significant factor in its adaptation to change; all societies do not become disrupted with acculturation, but appear to adapt in modes predisposed by their earlier adaptation to their habitat.

A second proposal, which at first glance appears to contradict this generalization, is that regardless of a group's ecocultural adaptation, there will be individual differences in how persons adapt to change. Specifically, it has been hypothesized that those individuals who are more field-independent in cognitive style will be more independent of the pressures of change; that is, they will suffer less acculturative stress. Evidence for this prediction also derives from the nine Amerindian samples listed in Table 1, and from data reported in Berry (1976). At the individual difference level of analysis, Stress and Marginality correlate negatively (mean of $-.29$ and $-.19$) with Kohs Blocks; and negatively (mean of $-.57$ and $-.26$) with the Portable Rod and Frame Test. This pattern of data suggests that those who are relatively autonomous within a group undergoing acculturation will either experience the impact of change less, or will be able to resist its disruptive effects more. Clearly, more research is necessary to disentangle these two alternatives.

CONCLUSIONS AND FUTURE DIRECTIONS

The fundamental theme of this chapter has been that individuals develop differentially in response to their varying ecocultural contexts. We have been able to show that different individual and group characteristics are readily observable—that human variation is real. Some might argue, on social, political, or humanitarian grounds, that this focus on differences is dangerous; however, it is surely more astute to recognize these differences and build upon them, than to ignore them. The challenge which this reality presents to cross-cultural psychology is twofold: we must carry out finer-grained analyses which will permit more detailed specification of the causal linkages between ecocultural contexts and individual development; and we must be ready to interpret and apply these findings, so that change will constitute development rather than destruction.

As we outlined in Figure 2, there are at least four levels of analysis which should be taken into account in attempting to specify causal linkages between environments and individual development. Traditional testing or experimenting approaches, where the stimulus is fixed and controlled, and where scores are assigned according to some fixed chart, cannot give us much appreciation of the richness of human behavior or its habitat. Conversely, attention devoted exclusively at the level of the broad ecological context and the global achievements of human development cannot by itself reveal the intricacies in the causal pattern. Only with multilevel research, which starts with the cultural ecology and ends with individual behavior, can we hope to progress beyond the present stage of research and state of knowledge.

It is essential to discover, for example, which kinds of behavior—be they intellectual or social—tend to be present in which kinds of population. Undoubtedly, the behaviors associated with the notion of psychological differentiation represent only a small piece of the puzzle; many more theoretical approaches, incorporating many other behaviors, await innovative research. In my view, the general framework of adaptation—both to ecocultural settings and to changes in those settings—is sufficiently comprehensive to permit considerable and broad advance within this single integrative framework.

If we do achieve such a causal understanding of ecocultural and individual variation, how can it then be employed for the benefit of human groups and their individual members who are undergoing change? A first requirement would seem to be that we must take human diversity seriously; each adaptation is a legitimate expression of a solution to living in a particular ecological setting. This acceptance of diversity must be exhibited toward both the traditional life-style and behavior, and toward the aspirations which are seeking expression. Too many "development" programs ignore the cultural roots of a people, and assume that all are seeking some common goal (Berry, 1979b). A sequel to this requirement is that, armed with a knowledge of individual and cultural characteristics and their relationship to ecological context, programs of change should be tailor-made for each group. No longer would it be possible to mount programs as standard imports; diversity in habitats, behaviors, and goals demands diversity in developmental change strategies. Thus, for example, designs for housing, sedentarization programs for nomadic peoples, education, industrialization, and all other environmental manipulations must be based upon an acceptance of diversity and an understanding of its origins. Without such acceptance of diversity, our applications will miss the entire point of the perspective of cultural ecology—that the criterion of adaptive success, of both individuals and groups, must be relative to the environmental setting.

REFERENCES

Asch, S. E. Studies in independence and conformity 1; A minority of one against a unanimous majority. *Psychological Monographs*, 1956, 70 (No. 416).
Barker, R. G. *Ecological psychology*. Stanford, Calif.: Stanford University Press, 1969.
Barry, H. Cross-cultural research with matched pairs of societies. *Journal of Social Psychology*, 1969, 79, 25–34.

Barry, H., & Paxson, L. Infancy and early childhood: Cross-cultural codes. *Ethnology*, 1971, *10*, 466–508.

Barry, H., Child, I., & Bacon, M. Relation of child training to subsistence economy. *American Anthropologist*, 1959, *61*, 51–63.

Berry, J. W. Temne and Eskimo perceptual skills. *International Journal of Psychology*, 1966, *1*, 207–229.

Berry, J. W. Independence and conformity in subsistence-level societies. *Journal of Personality and Social Psychology*, 1967, *7*, 415–418.

Berry, J. W. Ecological and cultural factors in spatial perceptual development. *Canadian Journal of Behavioural Science*, 1971, *3*, 324–336.

Berry, J. W. An ecological approach to cross-cultural psychology. *Netherlands Tijdschrift voor de Psychologie*, 1975, *30*, 51–84.

Berry, J. W. *Human ecology and cognitive style: Comparative studies in cultural and psychological adaptation.* New York: Sage-Halsted, 1976.

Berry, J. W. A cultural ecology of social behavior. In L. Berkowitz (Ed.), *Advances in experimental social psychology* (Vol. 12). New York: Academic Press, 1979a.

Berry, J. W. Social and cultural change. In H. Triandis & R. Brislin (Eds.), *Handbook of cross-cultural psychology* (Vol. 5). Boston: Allyn & Bacon, 1979b.

Berry, J. W. Ecological analyses for cross-cultural psychology. In N. Warren (Ed.), *Studies in cross-cultural psychology* (Vol. 3). London: Academic Press, in press.

Berry, J. W., & Annis, R. Acculturative stress: The role of ecology, culture and differentiation. *Journal of Cross-Cultural Psychology*, 1974, *5*, 382–406.

Bronfenbrenner, U. Toward an experimental ecology of human development. *American Psychologist*, 1977, *32*, 513–531.

Brunswik, E. Scope and aspects of the cognitive problem. In A. Gruber (Ed.), *Cognition: The Colorado symposium.* Cambridge: Harvard University Press, 1957, pp. 5–31.

Campbell, D. T. Factors relevant to the validity of experiments in social settings. *Psychological Bulletin*, 1957, *54*, 297–312.

Chance, N. A. Acculturation, self-identification and personal adjustment. *American Anthropologist*, 1965, *67*, 372–393.

Cohen, Y., (Ed.). *Man in adaptation.* Chicago: Aldine, 1968.

Dasen, P., Berry, J. W., & Witkin, H. A. The use of developmental theories across cultures. In L. Eckensberger (Ed.), *Cross-cultural contributions to psychology.* Amsterdam: Swets & Zeitlinger, 1979.

Dawson, J. L. M. Cultural and physiological influences upon spatial perceptual processes in West Africa. *International Journal of Psychology*, 1967, *2*, 115–128, 171–185.

Dawson, J. L. M. *Psychological effects of social change in West Africa.* New Haven, Conn.: HRAF Press, 1975.

Eckensberger, L., & Kornadt, H. The mutual relevance of the cross-cultural and the ecological prespective in psychology. In H. McGurk (Ed.), *Ecological factors in human development.* Amsterdam: North Holland, 1977, pp. 219–227.

Edgerton, R. B. *The individual in cultural adaptation.* Berkeley: University of California Press, 1971.

Feldman, D. A. The history of the relationship between environment and culture in ethnological thought: An overview. *Journal of the History of the Behavioral Sciences*, 1975, *11*, 67–81.

Forde, D. *Habitat, economy and society*, London: Methuen, 1934.

Hammond, K. R. (Ed.). *The psychology of Egon Brunswik.* New York: Holt, Rinehart & Winston, 1966.

Horney, K. In R. Munroe, *Schools of psychoanalytic thought.* New York: Holt, 1955.

Lewin, K. *Principles of topological psychology*. New York: McGraw-Hill, 1936.

MacArthur, R. S. Some ability patterns: Central Eskimos and Nsenga Africans. *International Journal of Psychology*, 1973, *8*, 239–247.

MacArthur, R. S. Differential ability patterns: Inuit, Nsenga and Canadian Whites. In J. W. Berry & W. J. Lonner (Eds.), *Applied cross-cultural psychology*. Amsterdam: Swets & Zeitlinger, 1975, pp. 237–241.

Murdock, G. P. World ethnographic sample. *American Anthropologist*, 1957, *59*, 664–687.

Murdock, G. P. Correlations of subsistence patterns. In D. Damas (Ed.), *Ecological Essays National Museum of Canada Bulletin No. 230* (Anthropological Series No. 86), 1969, pp. 129–146.

Nimkoff, M. F., & Middleton, R. Types of family and types of economy. *American Journal of Sociology*, 1960, *66*, 215–225.

Okonji, M. O. Differential effects of rural and urban upbringing on the development of cognitive style. *International Journal of Psychology*, 1969, *4*, 293–305.

Okonii, M. O. Cognitive styles across culture. In N. Warren (Ed.), *Studies in cross-cultural psychology* (Vol. 2). London: Academic Press, in press.

Pelto, P. The difference between "tight" and "loose" societies. *Transaction*, 1968, (April), 37–40.

Postman, L., & Tolman, E. Brunswik's probabalistic functionalism. In S. Koch (Ed.), *Psychology: A study of a science* (Vol. 1). New York: McGraw-Hill, 1959. pp. 502–564.

Segall, M., Campbell, D. T., & Herskovits, M. *The influence of culture on visual perception*. Indianapolis: Bobbs-Merrill, 1966.

Serpell, R. *Culture's influence on behaviour*. London: Methuen, 1976.

Spencer, H. *First principles*. New York: Appleton, 1864.

Vayda, A. P. (Ed.). *Environment and cultural behavior*. Garden City, N.Y.: Natural History Press, 1969.

Wintrob, R., & Sindell, P. Culture change and psychopathology: The case of Cree adolescent students in Quebec. In J. W. Berry & G. J. S. Wilde (Eds.), *Social psychology: The Canadian context*. Toronto: McClelland & Stewart, 1972, pp. 259–271.

Witkin, H. A. Social influences on the development of cognitive style. In D. A. Goslin (Ed.), *Handbook of socialization theory and research*. Chicago: Rand-McNally, 1969, pp. 687–706.

Witkin, H. A., & Berry, J. W. Psychological differentiation in cross-cultural perspective. *Journal of Cross-Cultural Psychology*, 1975, *6*, 4–87.

Witkin, H. A., Dyk, R. B., Faterson, H. F., Goodenough, D. R., & Karp, S. A. *Psychological differentiation*. New York: Wiley, 1962.

Witkin, H. A., & Goodenough, D. R. Field dependence and interpersonal behavior. *Psychological Bulletin*, 1977a, *84*, 661–689.

Witkin, H. A., & Goodenough, D. Field dependence revisited. *Educational Testing Service Research Bulletin*, 1977b, No. 77–17.

Witkin, H. A., Goodenough, D., & Karp, S. Stability of cognitive style from childhood to young adulthood. *Journal of Personality and Social Psychology*, 1967, *7*, 291–300.

4

Personal Space, Crowding, and Spatial Behavior in a Cultural Context

JOHN R. AIELLO
AND
DONNA E. THOMPSON

INTRODUCTION

Research interest in the topics of personal space, crowding, and spatial behavior has increased exponentially over the past fifteen years. This growing literature has indicated that the two primary functions served by the use of space are regulation or control and communication. One of the first systematic treatments of this domain was E. T. Hall's *The Hidden Dimension*. In his book, Hall (1966) proposed that individuals from various ethnic and cultural backgrounds differ with regard to their spatial behavior, and suggested that these differences were reflective of different cultural norms governing the use of space within different societies. During the last decade, Hall's ideas have stimulated a considerable amount of research and writing on the description and comparison of differences in the structuring and use of space. Unfortunately, only a small proportion of this research has examined spatial behavior within a

JOHN R. AIELLO • Department of Psychology, Rutgers—The State University, New Brunswick, New Jersey 08903. DONNA E. THOMPSON • Department of Psychology, George Peabody College, Vanderbilt University, Nashville, Tennessee 37203.

cultural context. Nevertheless, this growing body of research has generally been rather supportive of Hall's qualitative observations.

This chapter examines cross-cultural differences in how people ac-
tively use space and shape the physical environment in order to regulate
social interaction. The effects of crowding on behavior will be examined
across various cultural groups as well. Although the concept of environment refers to the total aggregate of physical, social, and cultural
forces surrounding an individual, the emphasis in the present chapter
will be on the physical features. Culture is viewed here as representing
the accumulation of norms, customary beliefs, and socialization patterns
which are used in the transmission of knowledge from one generation to
another.

The relationship between culture and the environment is complex.
A functional interdependence often exists among multiple cultural and
environmental elements. As a result, it is usually not possible to de-
lineate simple unidirectional causal relationships between a single cultural and a single environmental variable. The natural environment
(e.g., landscape or geographical features like mountains or rivers)
often influences the development of cultural practices within any given
society. In adjusting to the environment, people adopt certain patterns
of living which allow for their successful adaptation. The worshiping of
objects in nature by people in less technologically developed societies
(e.g., Egyptians and the Nile River), and the wandering by certain
people from place to place within a defined geographical region in order
to secure a food supply (e.g., nomadic tribes in Arabia), illustrate the
tremendous impact that the natural environment can have in the shaping of culture. On the other hand, cultural practices often result in
modifications of the environment. In adapting to the natural environment, people attempt to control or alter the physical setting by constructing man-made or built environments (e.g., homes, offices, cities, towns,
or villages). These built environments are constantly being modified to
meet human needs and to reflect the prevailing attitudes, life-styles, and
customs. Thus, cultural values influence people's perceptions and views
about the environment, which in turn affect environmental design.
Since the built environment is a product of culture, it helps shape future
generations by serving as a medium for the transmission of norms,
customs, and values. For example, the use of very heavy wooden doors
in England aids in communicating to later generations the high regard
for privacy, which is a salient characteristic of English culture.

Hall's approach to the study of the use of space emphasized how
people make active use of, and manipulate, the physical environment in
order to achieve preferred degrees of closeness and attain desired levels

of involvement during interaction. (For a more complete description of Hall's proxemic framework, see Altman & Vinsel in Volume 2 of this series, 1977.) Hall presented qualitative but detailed descriptions of spatial usage in physical settings (e.g., architectural designs of homes and offices, arrangements of furniture, use of doors), and the more discrete uses of space during interaction (e.g., distancing behavior), which related cross-cultural differences and similarities in spatial usage among European (e.g., German, English, and French) and non-European (e.g., Arab and Japanese) cultures. Mediterranean, Arabic, and Latin American societies were described as highly sensory, "contact" cultures wherein people were more likely to live in close physical contact and exhibit close interaction distances. In contrast, northern European and Caucasian American societies were described as somewhat more reserved, "noncontact" cultures, which were more likely to display larger interaction distances, especially in public settings and with strangers. Inherent in these descriptions is the notion that proxemic patterns vary as a function of how people perceive space and use their senses. People from various cultures have been reported to inhabit different "sensory worlds," with interpersonal distance and gross, complex spatial usage serving to regulate sensory stimulation. As one illustration of this, Hall (1966) describes the introduction of Americans to the sensory world of the Arabs and indicates the kind of conflicting sensory messages that Americans confront. In public spaces, Americans are often "compressed and overwhelmed by smells, crowding, and high noise levels," whereas in private residential spaces, they often feel "exposed and inadequate because of too much space" (Hall, 1966, p. 154).

Different perceptions of space, therefore, may often lead to different definitions of what constitutes an inappropriate interaction distance, or crowded living conditions.[1] Consequently, miscommunication can occur when individuals from different cultures attempt to interpret each other's spatial behavior. As a reflection of how misinterpretation may result from different spatial and architectural needs, Hall (1966) contrasted English and American regulation patterns:

> When the American wants to be alone he goes into a room and shuts the door—he depends on architectural features for screening. For an American to refuse to talk to someone else present in the same room, to give them the "silent treatment," is the ultimate form of rejection and a sure sign of great

---

[1]Although we wish to acknowledge the important role of selective perception and cognition in the subjective evaluation of the environment (e.g., Carr, 1967; Ittelson, 1973), the primary emphasis of our review in this chapter will be on the actual usage of space and the effects of density. The reader is referred to Altman and Chemers (1979) for a discussion of cross-cultural factors in environmental perception.

> displeasure. The English, on the other hand, lacking rooms of their own
> since childhood, never developed the practice of using space as a refuge from
> others. They have in effect internalized a set of barriers, which they erect and
> which others are supposed to recognize. Therefore, the more the Englishman
> shuts himself off when he is with an American the more likely the American
> is to break in to assure himself that all is well. (Hall, 1966, p. 140)

A number of other descriptive accounts of life in various countries, which are primarily sociological and anthropological in focus, lend support to Hall's contention that cultures differ with regard to their use of space and the physical environment. For the most part, these descriptions are concerned with global spatial behaviors rather than the specific regulation of interpersonal distance during interaction by individuals within any given culture. Quite frequently, living environments are arranged systematically so as to allow for differential access to the various parts of the home by different people, depending upon their relationship with the family. For example, the living room, which typically contains expensive furniture or religious objects in a Puerto Rican home, is only made accessible to relatives or close friends of the family (Zeisel, 1973).

The "entire" home of certain low-income families in Peru has been described by Alexander (1969) as being subdivided in order to permit visitors to enter into different parts of the home. Usually, close friends are given access to the informal living room and kitchen areas, whereas strangers typically only have access to the door and a porch (if one exists). Similarly, Lewis (1961) describes how an area in Mexico City, the Casa Grande, is physically separated from the rest of the city by high cement walls and rows of shops. Of particular relevance, however, is the observation that people do not enter each other's homes very frequently even though the one-room windowless apartments are only twelve feet apart and a strong sense of communality exists in Casa Grande. According to Lewis (1961), people must knock and wait for permission before entering another's home, and usually visit only the homes of close friends and relatives.

In examining the proxemic patterns of the Japanese, a number of other writers have noted that, although homes in Japan are often surrounded by high walls on the outside, an unusually flexible usage of space occurs within the home (e.g., Canter & Canter, 1971; Michelson, 1970). Michelson (1970) describes the use of space in Japan as follows:

> The Japanese exemplify successful adjustment to very high densities. Faced
> with huge urban masses in a country with no room in which to expand, and
> without the precedents for high rise construction, the Japanese have made
> their dwellings small, and private open space is minimal. The Japanese have

reacted to this pressure by "turning inward." They strongly distinguish between what is private and what is public in physical as well as social terms. Interiors of homes are personal, and their lack of size is compensated for by an intensity of detail. Every inch is open for utilization through physically undifferentiated use of interior space. Every room may potentially be used like any other, with only the movement of portable partitions as prerequisite. Furniture is at a minimum, and ornamentation is in miniature—a flower setting, not a collection of antique ale jugs. Perhaps, the Japanese garden most exemplifies the intensive use of personal space; it portrays meaning and detail while occupying little space. (Michelson, 1970, p. 155)

Other writers have described the use of physical barriers (e.g., closed doors, fences, hedges) to regulate interpersonal contact within the Unites States. For example, Altman, Nelson, and Lett (1972), Kira (1966), and Schwartz (1968) have all noted how bathrooms are made inaccessible to others through the use of closed doors.

The relationship between culture and the physical environment in the regulation of interpersonal contact can also be viewed in a much broader context by examining studies of urban life in Western culture. These investigations have indicated that large cities are often divided into various subcultural regions (e.g., "Little Italy" or "Chinatown" in New York City), with streets serving as boundaries (e.g., Sommer, 1969; Thrasher, 1936; Zorbaugh, 1929). In an early sociological study of Chicago's "North Side," Zorbaugh (1929) notes how these various regions, each of which is inhabited by different types and classes of people, remain separate and distinct communities despite their nearness to one another:

Every great city has its bohemias and is hobohemias; its gold coast and little Sicilies; its rooming-house areas and its slums. In Chicago, and on the Lower North Side, they are in close physical proximity to one another. This gives one an interesting illustration of the situation in which the physical distances and the social distances do not coincide; a situation in which people who live side by side are not, and—because of the divergence of their interests and their heritages—cannot, even with the best of good will, become neighbors. (Zorbaugh, 1929, p. ix)

In another similar early account of gangs in the city of Chicago, Thrasher (1936) described how the area called "gangland" was divided into three large regions (i.e., "North Side jungles"; "West Side wilderness"; and "South Side badlands"), by rivers, canals, railroad tracks and streets. Each of these regions was further subdivided into smaller areas, with streets typically serving as boundary lines. For example, within the "North Side jungle" region, one finds "Little Sicily," a community of Southern Italians, and "Pojay Town," a Polish community.

The relationship between culture and the physical environment can also be seen in less technologically developed societies. In the Mehinacu culture of Brazil, Roberts and Gregor (1971) note that although several families usually live in a single house, each family maintains its own area and does not invade another family's territory. Similarly, in the Indonesian society of Bali, high stone walls surround the houseyards in which people live, and only relatives are allowed within the houseyard (Geertz, as cited in Westin, 1970).

In some cultures, a lack of space often leads to either geographic isolation or to subtle nonverbal cues, which become important in the regulation of interpersonal contact, rather than physical barriers. For example, the !Kung bushmen live under highly crowded living conditions where there are no architectural features (e.g., no rooms or walls) to regulate interaction. As a result, people are easily accessible to one another. However, as Draper (1973) describes, the culture of this less technologically developed society does make some provisions for people to regulate their contact with one another. For example, the people within this culture have the option of moving from one camp to another. In addition, contact with strangers is also regulated, since the "campsites," even though they are densely populated, are usually located quite some distance from one another, separated by uninhabited regions.

A similar situation exists in Java, where there are few regulations for controlling entrance into homes, with people walking in and out of each other's homes quite freely. However, as in the English culture (Hall, 1966), this Indonesian society has developed an interpersonal contact regulation system which entails the use of a complex etiquette system and an emphasis on emotional restraint and "speaking softly" (Geertz, as cited in Westin, 1970).

In sum, much of the work presented so far has been concerned with global spatial behaviors. As we have indicated, the use of space as a means of regulation/control or communication occurs on a number of different levels (e.g., subdivisions of a city or village, interiors of homes, or dyadic interactions). While these functions operate in each of the cultures discussed, their particular manifestations have been found to vary considerably from culture to culture. In view of these divergent patterns of spatial usage, the potential for miscommunications across cultures (or subcultures) is clearly of critical concern. The present chapter will deal more specifically with the use of space during social interaction and the responses to crowded settings found among the various cultural groups. However, as Altman and Vinsel (1977) have indicated, the relationship between culture and personal space has not been firmly established. To date, there are few cultural comparisons, and inconsistent findings exist in the research that has been reported. Moreover, since a range of different methodologies have been employed, it is difficult to integrate across methods and reach general conclusions. The existing status of cultural research on crowding is very similar.

In the present review of this literature, an attempt will be made to summarize the similarities and differences which exist in the use of space across cultures.[2] In order to accomplish this, it will often be necessary to generalize across different levels of analysis, because of the paucity of research in the area. In addition, because of the multidisciplinary nature of the research in this area, the present coverage may not be a *fully* comprehensive review of all the relevant literature.

In the next section of the chapter, a review of cultural and subcultural research in the area of personal space will be presented, with a particular emphasis on the various methodologies and approaches that have been employed. Following this section, the results of cross-cultural investigations of crowding will be considered within the context of the distinction between crowding and density (Stokols, 1972), the various levels of analyses employed in crowding research (Aiello, Epstein, & Karlin, 1974; 1975a), and the four setting-specific events that evoke the label "crowded" (Karlin, Epstein, and Aiello, 1978). Lastly, the general implications of the present analysis in the areas of personal space and crowding will be examined, emphasizing where future research is needed.

PERSONAL SPACE

DEFINITION AND FUNCTIONAL USES OF PERSONAL SPACE

The concept of personal space refers to the preferred distance from other people that an individual maintains within a given setting. It has been defined as "an area with an invisible boundary surrounding the person's body into which intruders may not come" (Sommer, 1969, p. 26). As such, personal space serves two primary functions: (1) It *protects* against possible psychologically and physically uncomfortable social encounters by regulating and controlling the amount and quality of sensory stimulation, and (2) it *communicates* information about the relationship between the interactants and the formality of the interaction by

---

[2]The criterion we employed for the inclusion of studies in this review was based on their use of either two or more cultural or subcultural groups of subjects, or two or more cultural or subcultural stimulus persons (confederates) or stimulus figures.

making available to others (as well as to the self) cues as to the preferred distance which has been chosen.

A number of of investigators have acknowledged the importance of space in social interaction, but some have utilized, while others have challenged, the analogy of personal space as a protective "bubble." For example, Hall (1960) has suggested that people "carry around a series of spatial spheres" wherein different types of interactions are allowed to occur. Others, however, (Deutsch, 1975; Goffman, 1971; Kendon, 1977; Scheflen, 1976) have argued that personal space is but one type of space that should be considered. We agree with Patterson (1975) and Knowles (1979), however, that spatial behavior should be viewed as a continuous variable and not a dichotomous one with discrete boundaries.

CONCEPTUAL MODELS

A number of conceptual models have been developed to explain the functional usage of personal space (for a more complete description of these models, see Bell, Fisher, & Loomis, 1978). Most of the cultural research has utilized the Communication Model as a conceptual explanation for the function of personal space. In this model, interpersonal distance is viewed both as communicating information and as determining the quantity and quality of information exchanged. The other conceptual models include: (a) the overstimulation models of stress and overload, which posit that an individual maintains a preferred interaction distance from others in order to avoid excessive stimulation; (b) the behavioral constraint models, which maintain that personal space serves to provide an optimal level of behavioral freedom; and (c) the ethological models, which hold that interpersonal distance functions to protect against threats of physical attack.

METHODS OF STUDYING PERSONAL SPACE

We have categorized all of the cultural and subcultural research examining the concept of personal space on the basis of their use of one of three methods: unstructured or structured interactive techniques, quasi-projective techniques, or projective techniques. Of the 41 cultural and subcultural studies of personal space reviewed in this chapter, 24 (7 cultural; 17 subcultural) were interactive studies. Twelve (2 cultural; 10 subcultural) of these were unstructured interactive investigations wherein unobtrusive observations of actual spatial behavior are gathered in natural settings that subjects have self-selected. An example of this type of study is the field study of the proxemic behavior of black, white, and Puerto Rican subcultures that the first author conducted along with Stanley E. Jones (Aiello & Jones, 1971). Interaction distance and directness of shoulder orientation were recorded for interacting pairs of first- and second-grade children from three subcultural groups, who were observed on school playgrounds.

Twelve (5 cultural; 7 subcultural) of the interactive studies to be described were structured. As with the unstructured interactive technique, unobtrusive observations of actual spatial behavior are made during interaction. However, unlike unstructured investigations, these observations are typically gathered in a laboratory setting or in a field setting that has been adapted by the experimenter. For example, in another study (Jones & Aiello, 1973), we observed the proxemic behavior of black and white first-, third-, and fifth-grade children in modified classroom settings of two elementary schools. An adaptation of Hall's (1963) distance scale, which allows for the comparison of different-sized persons by the use of a 14-point scale based on body potential (e.g., arms' length, reach) was used instead of absolute inches to measure interpersonal distance. Consistent with our call for observation of more than one proxemic behavior, body orientation was also recorded. In addition, since it had been previously suggested that topic of conversation is a determinant of the level of intimacy established during social interaction (e.g., Argyle & Dean, 1965; Hall, 1966), we developed a procedure which allowed for control of the conversation discussed by the interactants. In this procedure, which has been used both with children and adolescents (Aiello & Aiello, 1974; Aiello & Cooper, 1972; Aiello & Jones, 1978), a pair of students is introduced to an observer in the experimental room, who asks them to talk about their favorite television programs. While the pair is interacting, the observer proceeds to copy material from a book, but glances up at preestablished time intervals to record the interpersonal distance and body orientation of the dyad. This kind of semisurveillance activity on the part of teachers was familiar to the students, and proved to be highly unobtrusive as a method of observation.

Quasi-projective techniques have been used in four (0 cultural; 4 subcultural) of the studies reviewed. These investigations are typically conducted in a laboratory setting. Subjects approach target persons to a point where they begin to feel uncomfortable or are asked to respond to actual distances from others, thereby making the distance dimension particularly salient. For example, in Frankel and Barrett's (1971) investigation of variations in personal space, each subject was placed in the center of the experimental room and approached by white and black confederates in counterbalanced order. Subjects were instructed to say "now" when they began to feel uncomfortable; at that point the distance between the subject and confederate was recorded.

The remaining 13 (7 cultural; 6 subcultural) investigations have used projective methods. In these studies, figures or symbols representing people are presented to subjects, who are in turn asked to arrange them or make judgments about the distance between them. Although such techniques are easily administered and allow an investigator a great deal of control over the experimental situation, they are totally devoid of any proprioceptive cues that would be present in any situation wherein an individual would be an actual participant in an interaction. Instead, subjects are asked to "imagine" themselves in a situation, as compared with their actually being in it. Moreover, by simply asking subjects to position or make judgments regarding the position of objects, the distance dimension is (as with the quasi-projective techniques) made particularly salient. An example of this type of investigation is Engelbretson and Fullmer's (1970) study, which examined cultural differences among the interaction distance of native Japanese, Hawaiian Japanese, and American Caucasian students. An adaptation of Kuethe's (1962) free-placement *Felt Figure Technique* was used, wherein subjects were instructed to place six pairs of figures (e.g., father with male student, male professor with female student, female student with female friend), and then answer three questions for each of these pairs, regarding how the interaction ended and how the "interactants" were feeling.

CORRESPONDENCE AMONG PERSONAL SPACE MEASURES

Numerous measurement techniques have been devised and utilized in cross-cultural and other studies of personal space behavior. A relevant methodological issue which needs to be addressed concerns how these various methods relate to one another. In an early investigation, Little (1965) examined the relationship between cardboard figure placement and the arrangement of live actors, and found a correlation of .77. It should be noted, however, that this relatively high correlation was obtained between two indirect methods because in each of the measures, subjects were asked to *place* either the cardboard figures or "live" actors, rather than engage in any type of interaction themselves. Thus, these findings do not reflect any degree of association between actual measures of interpersonal distance and projective measures.

Studies that have been done since that time have generally yielded mixed results (e.g., Dosey & Meisels, 1969; Duke & Nowicki, 1972; Haase & Markey, 1973; Knowles & Johnsen, 1974; Pedersen, 1973; and

Rawls, Trego, & McGaffey, 1968). In general, most of these investigations have obtained moderate correlations among projective and quasi-projective methods, but not so high as those found by Little. For example, Rawls *et al.* (1968) found correlations ranging from .34 to .91 among a series of measures of interpersonal distance which included a staged approach to another individual, two paper and pencil measures in which subjects were instructed to draw a circle and a square around a self-figure to indicate the preferred interpersonal distance, figure placements, and judgments of preferred distances between figures. Duke and Nowicki (1972) intercorrelated their paper and pencil *Comfortable Interpersonal Distance Scale* and a number of staged approaches of subjects to other people, and obtained correlations ranging from .65 to .84. More recently, Cronjè and Möller (1976) compared three different measurement procedures in a South African investigation, and found that two projective measures (i.e., judgment of photographs and a model room technique) yielded similar findings, but that the model room technique predicted actual spatial behavior much more closely. However, the possibility that this latter finding may simply reflect a commitment on the part of subjects to replicate their actual spatial behavior must be considered, since the model room technique replicated the setting subjects experienced in the actual spatial behavior condition. In a more comprehensive study, Knowles and Johnsen (1974) found only a low to moderate degree of convergence among nine interpersonal distance measures, which included: (a) disguised approach distance; (b) disguised sitting distance; (c) silhouette placement; (d) mannequin placement; (3) experimenter's approach stopped; (f) approach mannequin; (g) approach coat; (h) approach experimenter; and (i) doll placement. Subject-related variables (i.e., subject awareness and type of subject participation) were found to differentiate among interpersonal distance measures, rather than any of the specific procedures, instructions, or materials. The procedure unfortunately required subjects to complete all nine measures in a single experimental session, which probably created a circumstance in which later measures were affected by earlier measures.

Research investigating the development of personal space is an example of how, in some cases, completely divergent patterns of results have been obtained with the various methodological approaches. Petri and Huggins (1975) used Duke and Nowicki's (1972) comfortable interpersonal distance scale to examine the "developmental pattern in the size and shape of personal space" for individuals ranging in age from nine through adulthood. Their results indicated that personal space *decreased* with age. In contrast, we have found interaction distance *increases* with age (until young adulthood), when observations of *actual* spatial behavior have been made (Aiello & Aiello, 1974). A number of other studies have also found this trend of increasing distance with age using direct observation, interactive procedures (Baxter, 1970; Lomranz, Shapiro, Choresh, & Gilat, 1975; Willis, 1966), and quasi-projective methods (Tennis & Dabbs, 1975).[3] Only one other study reported that older age children generally use less space than younger children—and it was another *projective* investigation, using a figure placement procedure (Meisels & Guardo, 1969).

The first author's interest in the correspondence of results obtained from different methods was aroused eight years ago when he included a number of projective and quasi-projective measures in a series of pilot studies of the personal space behavior of young children. Surprisingly, the pattern of association between actually observed interaction distances and the more indirect measures was very weak. At the time, we reasoned that very young children may have rather unstable personal space patterns. Nevertheless, our doubts about the relationship between projective and actual measures of interpersonal distance were raised.

That skepticism motivated the first author and his colleagues to carry out a program of seven other studies with children and adults during the five-year period from 1971 to 1976, in order to examine the relationship more fully (see Aiello, 1976). In an investigation conducted along with Stanley E. Jones, no relationship was found between either a felt figure board placement task or an approach measure and actual (observed) interpersonal distance behavior (this study will be described more fully later in the chapter). In a developmental study of mutual liking and disliking dyads conducted with Ralph E. Cooper, a comparison was made between actual proxemic observations and Guardo's (1969) projective silhouette task for children and adolescents ranging from 7 to 17. The investigation was conducted over a 3-week period. Sociometric rating scales were completed during the first week, proxemic observations were made in the second week, and Guardo's pro-

---

[3]It should be noted that, from what little data are currently available regarding spatial preferences of the elderly, it appears that they (like the very young) prefer to interact at closer distances. DeLong (1970) found that mentally impaired, hospitalized elderly patients interacted at smaller distances than younger adults. Further, in a study of short-term crowding involving close physical proximity, elderly subjects reported not being disturbed by bodily contact, and described the crowded room as "cozy" (Aiello, Headly, & Thompson, 1978). This would mean that a curve representing the development of personal space would actually be *curvilinear*, increasing in a linear fashion from about age four to about age twelve, leveling off through adolescence and adulthood, and then decreasing sharply with the elderly.

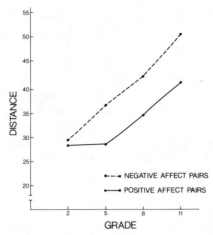

Figure 1.   Interaction distances of male and female, reciprocated positive and negative affect pairs at four grade levels.

jective task was administered during the third week. Once again, little or no relationship was found between the placements on the projective measure and observations of actual interpersonal distance behavior $\bar{r} = .15$, correlations ranged from $-.02$ to $+.20$). However, observed interaction distance was again found to increase with age, F (3, 112) = 18.61, $p < .001$ (see Figure 1). In the final study of this series, Kathlene D. Love and the first author (Love & Aiello, 1976) examined the relationship between three projective distance measures (approach distance, doll placement, and felt figure placement), and observed interaction distance. We purposely designed the procedure so that, following an interaction sequence, subjects were asked simply to *duplicate* their prior interaction distance behavior, using one of the more indirect measures of personal space. *None* of the projective or quasi-projective measures was found to be significantly related to the actual (observed) distance behavior. These results are particularly astonishing, since subjects were specifically requested to attend to and replicate their own behavior. Hall's observation on this problem would appear to be well-taken:

> proxemic patterns, once learned, are maintained largely out of conscious awareness and thus have to be investigated without resort to probing the conscious mind of one's subjects. (1963, p. 1003)

Since over half of the more than 200 studies of personal space have employed projective or quasi-projective measures (Altman & Vinsel, 1977), great caution must be used in extrapolating from this body of research.

In this section we have defined the concept, personal space, delineated its two primary functions: protection and communication, and briefly identified conceptual models which researchers have utilized. More importantly, we categorized the research on the basis of the type of method used: unstructured or structured interactive techniques, quasi-projective techniques, or projective techniques. Operational definitions and examples of these techniques were then offered, and the correspondence (or, more appropriately, the *lack* of correspondence!) among personal space measures was discussed. Serious note should be taken of the fact that, not only was there a minimal degree of convergence obtained among the measures, but studies investigating the development of personal space illustrate that, in some cases, opposite results have been found! Caution is therefore recommended in interpretations of investigations using projective and quasi-projective techniques.

Further systematic research using direct observation of spatial behaviors is needed in order to understand more fully the complex nature and various functions of personal space. The available research data indicate that the less direct, "more cognitive" measurement techniques need to be regarded and generalized with caution. Moreover, cross-cultural and subcultural studies examining the *development* of personal space are needed. Almost all of the normative data gathered to date have been obtained in the United States, with white, middle-class participants. Future research is necessary in order to determine the crosscultural comparability of findings regarding the development of personal space in countries other than the few which have been investigated, especially for older children and adolescents (who have only been studied in the United States), and for the elderly (who have not been studied at all).

CULTURAL INVESTIGATIONS OF PERSONAL SPACE

As described above, throughout *The Hidden Dimension* Hall (1966) proposed that cultures differ with regard to their use of space and the physical environment. In support of this proposition, he presented a series of qualitative but detailed anthropological observations of the manner in which various cultural groups utilize space in different ways. One of the best illustrations of this work is his detailed account of the disparate proxemic patterns of the Americans and the Japanese. The entire "experience of space" differs in the two cultures, as does their utilization of space. For example, in employing all of the senses in the perception of space, the Japanese attach meaning to spaces between objects, whereas Westerners perceive such spaces as empty.

Inherent in Hall's descriptive accounts is the distinction made between *contact* and *noncontact* cultures. Mediterranean, Arabic, and Latin American societies were described as highly sensory, "contact" cultures, wherein people maintained close interaction distances and exhibited a higher level of involvement in their communications with one another (e.g., touching, breathing in one another's face, direct body orientations). For example, according to Hall (1966), evidence of the high sensory involvement of the French can be seen in many aspects of their lives, ranging from their crowded living conditions or crowded spacing of cafe tables to their use of direct eye contact and close interaction distances during conversation. In contrast, Northern European and Western European cultures were described as somewhat more reserved, "noncontact" cultures, which were more likely to display larger interaction distances. Germans, for example, were described by Hall (1966) as very private people, relying on physical environmental features to preserve "their own space." Double doors are often used for soundproofing larger public buildings or offices. Similarly, yards tend to be well-fenced, so as to maintain visual privacy around homes.

The first author's own observations are, for the most part, in accord with those of Hall. Our informal photographic study of adult conversants on the streets of Europe, which was carried out several years ago, indicated that interaction distances used by both males and females in Southern European "contact" cultures (France, Italy, Greece, and Spain) were indeed closer than those of one of the Northern European "noncontact" cultures (England).

In this section, the small body of research which has attempted to find empirical evidence for Hall's (1966) contention that proxemic patterns differ as a function of culture will be reviewed. As indicated in Table 1, of the 14 cultural investigations examined, 7 were projective studies, 5 were structured interactive studies, and 2 were unstructured interactive studies. Further, all of these investigations used distance as a dependent variable.[4]

Most of these studies have focused on the more global distinction

---

[4]There are a number of studies, undertaken primarily in Great Britain and the United States, which have manipulated seating distance in a test of an affiliative-conflict theory. However, these investigations will not be reviewed in the present chapter (see Patterson, 1973 for a review of these studies). Future cross-cultural research needs to examine the regulation of interpersonal processes during social interactions which involves the manipulation of distance as well as other nonverbal behaviors (e.g., eye contact, body lean, smiling).

TABLE 1

CULTURAL INVESTIGATIONS OF PERSONAL SPACE

Investigator(s)/subjects	Age	Sex	Technique or distance measurement	Other variables	Results
Interactive-unstructured studies:					
1. Noesjirwan (1977) 147 Indonesian 139 Australian	Adults	107 females; 40 males 95 females; 44 males	Observed the number of seats a S sat from the nearest neighbor, ignoring the S's own companion.	Conversation initiation; verbal self-reports	Indonesian Ss were accompanied more, sat closer, and talked more to strangers in a doctor's waiting room than Australian Ss. Indonesian Ss reported that their seating position depended on the presence of others whereas Australian Ss reported that their seating position depended on the presence of some object in the room.
2. Mazur (1977) 26 Spanish 25 Moroccan 38 Americans from the West Coast	Adults	All males	Photographed bench position; sizes and shapes of the benches varied in the different countries.	None	No difference between Spanish and Moroccan "bench positions." Ss from San Francisco sat closer than Ss in either of the above two cultures.
Interactive-structured studies:					
1. Collett (1971) 10 Arabs 50 Englishmen	Adults	All males	Part I: Arab Ss were given a choice between an Englishman	Nodding and other head movements,	Arab Ss preferred Englishmen who exhibited "Arablike

No.	Study	Subjects	Sample	Procedure	Variables	Results
				employing "Arablike" nonverbal behavior and an Englishman employing "English" nonverbal behavior. Standing greeting and seated conversation between mixed ethnic dyads. Part II: Identical to the above with the exception that 10 Englishmen served as subjects.	smiling, eye contact, body orientation, and other body movements.	behavior." English Ss showed no preference.
2.	Forston & Larson (1968) 16 Latin Americans 16 Americans	Adults	Not specified	Seated conversation between homogeneous dyads. Interaction topic was the solution to the Middle East crisis.	Touch; body axis	No significant differences were found.
3.	Pagán & Aiello (1975) 77 Puerto Rican pairs in Puerto Rico 65 Puerto Rican pairs in the United States	1st, 6th, & 11th graders	69 male–male pairs 73 female–female pairs	Standing conversation between homogeneous sex and cultural dyads. Topic of conversation was the same for all dyads. Unobtrusive observations were made using an adaptation of Hall's (1963) system for the notation of proxemic behavior.	Body orientation	Puerto Rican students in both countries displayed similar proxemic patterns but older students in the United States tended to stand farther apart. Larger interaction distances and more direct body orientations were maintained at more advanced grade levels. Females stood more directly than males.

Continued

TABLE 1. (*Continued*)

	Investigator(s)/subjects	Age	Sex	Techniques or distance measurement	Other variables	Results
4.	Watson & Graves (1966) 16 Americans 16 Arabs	Adults	Males	Seated conversation between culturally homogeneous dyads. Interaction topic was anything that "came into their heads." Ss brought 3 other people from their subgroup to the laboratory. Distance was scored on the basis of Hall's (1963) system for the notation of proxemic behavior.	Axis, touching, eye contact, and voice loudness	Arab Ss interacted more directly, sat closer to one another, engaged in more eye contact, tended to touch each other more, and talked louder than the American Ss.
5.	Watson (1970) Contact cultures: 20 Arabs 20 Latin Americans 10 South Europeans Noncontact cultures: 12 Asians 12 Indian-Pakistanis 32 North Europeans	Adults	All males	Same as above	Same as above. A demographic questionnaire and proxemics research interview were also included.	Subjects from contact cultures faced each other more directly, touched more, and looked into each others eyes more than Ss from noncontact cultures. Arabs sat the closest together, significantly differing from all groups except the South Europeans and Indian-Pakistanis. North Europeans sat

farther apart than all the other groups except the Asians. South Europeans sat closer than North Europeans but did not differ from the other groups. Asians sat farther apart than Arabs and Indian-Pakistanis but did not differ from the other groups. No significant differences were found among cultures within the two contact/noncontact subcategories.

Quasi-projective studies:

None

Projective studies:

1. Cade (1972)
   21 American
   18 Philippino
   26 Japanese

Adults

Not specified

An adaptation of Kuethe's (1962) *Felt Figure Technique* was used with circle symbols instead of silhouettes. There were six placement conditions reflecting various nuclear family relationships.

None

Family relationship placements were similar for all three cultural groups.

Continued

125

TABLE 1. (*Continued*)

Investigator(s)/subjects	Age	Sex	Techniques or distance measurement	Other variables	Results
2. Engelbretson & Fullmer (1970) 56 Native Japanese 50 Hawaii Japanese 49 American Caucasian	Adults	32 males; 24 females 26 males; 24 females 24 males; 25 females	An adaptation of Kuethe's (1962) *Felt Figure Technique* was used. Dyadic silhouettes were placed according to instructional sets for six different interaction scenes which varied as a function of the relationship of the interactants and conversational content.	None	No difference between Hawaii Japanese and American Caucasian interfigure distance placements. Native Japanese had significantly larger distance placements than either of the above two groups. Across all groups, students with friend placements were closer than those involving student with father or student with professor. No sex differences were reported.
3. Engelbretson (1972) same as above	Same as above	Same as above	Same as above	*Perceived Cultural Influence Scale*	Perceived cultural influence was not related to interaction distance placements.
4. Graubert & Adler (1977) 77 South Australian 94 Great Britain	Adults	114 males; 266 females	Placement of colored round stickers.	None	Male figure placements were similar across all four countries whereas

96 South African 113 Eastern United States				female figure placements were only similar across all four countries on nonmental patient items. Across all responses, stimuli representing mental patients in hospitals received the furthest placement.
5. Little (1968) 106 Americans 85 Swedish 100 Scottish 70 Greek 71 Italians	Adults	53 males; 53 females	Doll placement technique was used with 4 gray plastic dolls. There were 10 different random orders of the 19 instructional sets used in the study.	Angle of placement	Ss from contact cultures (Greek & Italian) placed dolls closer together than subjects from noncontact cultures (Scottish & Swedish). The Greek Ss had the closest placements followed by the Italians and Americans, the Swedes, and the Scots respectively. All Ss, regardless of their cultural background, had similar ratings as to which interactions should require more intimate distances. No sex differences were reported.

Continued

127

TABLE 1. (*Continued*)

Investigator(s)/subjects	Age	Sex	Techniques or distance measurement	Other variables	Results
6. Lomranz (1976) 15 Argentinian 15 Iraqis 15 Russian	Adolescents	All males	Doll placement task wherein two dolls were arranged in a series of interaction situations which varied as a function of the nature of the relationship between the dolls.	None	Ss from all 3 cultures placed the dolls at the closest distance when the interaction situation involved a friend and at the farthest distance when the interaction situation involved a stranger. Argentinian students had the largest placement distance followed by the Russian and Iraqis students respectively.
7. Sommer (1968) 90 Americans 131 English 112 Swedes 98 Dutch 93 Pakistanis	Adults	Not specified	Rating of intimacy for seating arrangements.	None	No differences among the intimacy ratings for the English, American, and Swedish Ss. Dutch Ss rated the corner seating as less intimate than the above 3 groups while Pakistani Ss rated the "opposite-seating" arrangement as more distant than the other groups.

between contact and noncontact cultures, and have not systematically examined Hall's hypotheses concerning spatial usage by the people in a number of the specific countries (e.g., Germany) toward which Hall has directed his attention. In fact, in our sample, nine of the comparisons involved American subjects and other cultural groups. There were actually very few comparisons made between members of *different* cultural groups. It is also important to note here that even cultures that are assumed to be similar may actually have quite different spatial practices. For example, in a replication of Sommer's (1965) questionnaire study, Cook (1970) found that his English subjects chose to sit at greater distances than Sommer's American subjects for projected interactions involving cooperation and conversation.

Until recently, no evidence was available as to whether the developmental trend of increasing distance with age occurs in other cultures. One of the first author's graduate students, Gilberto Pagàn, and he extended the study of proxemic interaction patterns to Puerto Rican children at three grade levels (first, sixth and eleventh) in San Juan, Puerto Rico, and in New York City, using a methodology identical to that of Aiello and Aiello, 1974. Puerto Rican children in both countries showed very similar proxemic patterns (i.e., did not differ), and displayed increasing interaction distances $F (2, 130) = 18.03$, $p < .001$, and more direct body orientations $F (2, 130) = 8.91$, $p < .001$, as they increased in age. Only three other investigations have been conducted in other countries. Two of these studies (one in Canada: Bass & Weinstein, 1971, and one in Japan: Lerner, Iwawaki, & Chihara, 1976) used a projective, felt board technique, and found that for very young children (both studied 5- to 8-year-olds), less space was placed between figures by the youngest children tested. In the other investigation, Lomranz *et al.* (1975) found this same age trend for their Israeli subjects (ages 3 to 7), whose seating approach distance toward a same-sex, same-age mate was measured.

Unfortunately, the majority of cultural studies have also been performed with the participation of subjects who were in residence in a country outside of their own at the time of the investigation. Generalizing from data gathered with subjects of this category must, of course, be done with a good deal of caution. These subjects are not representative samples from the populations of their respective countries, since they are usually better educated and have traveled more extensively than the majority of their fellow countrymen. Furthermore, as Baldassare and Feller (1975) pointed out in their review of cultural differences in personal space, the spatial behavior of these subjects has been influenced by the proxemic patterns of the culture in which they have been residing for an undetermined length of time.

INTERACTIVE STUDIES

Support for Hall's notion that contact cultures use closer interpersonal distances than noncontact cultures is found in several structured and unstructured interactive investigations. In an early test of this idea, Watson and Graves (1966) examined the proxemic behavior patterns of Arab and American male students attending the University of Colorado. Subjects were observed in culturally homogeneous dyads during a five-minute interaction period, and their behavior was measured, using Hall's (1963) system for the notation of proxemic behavior. Overall, the results strongly supported Hall's earlier speculations concerning Arab–American differences in spatial behavior. Arab students interacted more directly, sat closer to one another, tended to touch each other more, engaged in more eye contact, and talked louder than the American students.

In a similar but more extensive investigation at the University of Colorado, Watson (1970) observed the proxemic behavior of male foreign students from a number of "contact" cultures (Arabs, Latin Americans, Southern Europeans) and "noncontact" cultures (North Americans, Northern Europeans, Asians). The observational method was similar to that employed in the preceding study. Subjects were also interviewed and completed a background questionnaire concerned with basic demographic and experiential information. The data from the 16 American male subjects from the preceding investigation by Watson and Graves (1966) were also included in this study. Foreign students from contact cultures generally faced each other more directly, touched more, and looked into each other's eyes more than students from noncontact cultures. Arab students sat closest together while Northern European students sat farthest apart. Also of interest were the questionnaire data which indicated that individuals from different cultures did not attach the *same meaning* to the same elements of proxemic behavior. Further, some indirect support for Hall's (1966) hypothesis, that the control of proxemic behavior is outside of the realm of conscious awareness, might be inferred from the fact that when interviewed, subjects could provide very little useful information about the rules of proxemic behavior.

In another investigation, Forston and Larson (1968) examined the spatial behavior of students from Latin America (contact culture) and North America (noncontact culture). Observations recorded during a five-minute discussion revealed no significant cultural differences. However, a number of methodological concerns regarding this study should be noted. First of all, obtrusive measures of distance were used. The floor of the experimental room was marked off in two-foot intervals. Moreover, the experimenter remained in the experimental room, noting the proxemic patterns and distances of the subjects. The subjects were photographed twice during the interaction, as well. Second, and perhaps more important, the intimacy of the conversation topic, the timing of the distance measures, and the sex of the members of each dyad were not controlled in this investigation.

Hall's (1966) contention that miscommunication can occur when individuals from contact and noncontact cultures attempt to *interpret* each other's spatial behavior has also received some attention. In the only study examining interaction between members of different cultural groups, Collett (1971) investigated the feasibility of training English students in "Arablike" nonverbal behaviors (which include interacting at closer distances), so that they could communicate more effectively with Arab students. In the first part of the study, Arab subjects talked about love with trained and untrained English subjects in two separate five-minute interaction periods. Following these two interactions, the Arab subjects completed a series of sociometric choices between the two Englishmen, and described the reasons for their choice in a few paragraphs. Results indicated that Arab subjects preferred the Englishman who had been trained to exhibit "Arablike" behavior. The same procedure was used in the second part of the experiment with ten Englishmen serving as subjects. Unlike the Arab subjects, however, the English subjects showed no preference between subjects who exhibited English behavior and those who exhibited Arab behavior.

Two recent interactive-unstructured studies have also examined the spatial behavior of contact and noncontact cultures. In a field survey study, Noesjirwan (1977) examined interpersonal seating distances between subjects and strangers in doctors' waiting rooms in Australia (noncontact culture) and Indonesia (contact culture). The number of seats a subject sat away from the nearest stranger was recorded. Results indicated that Indonesian subjects were accompanied more often by others, talked more, and sat closer (and more adjacent) to strangers, than Australian subjects. Moreover, when interviewed, Indonesian subjects reported that their seat selection was made with a specific intention to be close to or far from another patient. In contrast, Australian subjects usually selected their seat with reference to some desired object, not person. In another field study, Mazur (1977) examined seated interpersonal spacing between unacquainted male pairs on public benches in two contact cultures (Spain and Morocco), and one noncontact culture (United States). Contrary to Hall's contention, pairs of subjects in the United States usually sat closer than pairs of subjects in Spain and Morocco. However, when differences in the size and shape of the benches used in each country were taken into consideration, there were no apparent differences in spacing behavior across the three cultures.

PROJECTIVE STUDIES

While there have been no quasi-projective investigations, a number of cultural investigations exist which have used projective or simulation techniques. Two of these investigations, by Little (1968) and Sommer (1968), have been conducted at universities in different cultural settings. Using a doll placement technique, Little (1968) found that subjects from Mediterranean cultures (Southern Italy and Greece) placed dolls closer together than subjects from noncontact cultures (Scotland and Sweden). Subjects from all cultures had similar ratings as to which interactions should occur at more intimate distances than others. In an investigation of intimacy ratings of various seating arrangements, Sommer (1968) also found that there was a strong agreement among subjects from Holland, Pakistan, England, Sweden, and the United States. Subjects on campuses in their respective countries were presented with a series of 37 diagrams of dyads seated at all possible seating permutations around square, rectangular, and circular tables. Results indicated that the side-by-side seating arrangement was rated by all five cultural groups as most intimate, followed by corner-to-corner, and opposite-seating arrangements respectively. No differences were found among the intimacy ratings of the English, American, and Swedish samples. However, the Dutch students rated the corner seating as less intimate than the above three groups, while the Pakistani students rated the "opposite-seating" arrangement as more distant than the other groups.

Other projective investigations have also demonstrated similarities as well as differences among cultures in distancing behavior. For example, Cade (1972) found no differences in the figure placements which reflected various nuclear family relationships of American, Filipino, and Japanese subjects. In a series of two investigations, which also used a felt figure technique, Engelbretson (Engelbretson & Fullmer, 1970; Engelbretson, 1972) reported that native Japanese subjects had significantly larger interfigure distance placements than Hawaiian Japanese and American Caucasian subjects. However, no differences between the interfigure distance placements of the two latter cultural groups were found. Also of interest is the finding that, across all three subcultural groups, student-with-friend placements were closer than those involving a student figure with either a father or a professor figure. In another, somewhat less relevant, study, Graubert and Adler (1977) found that "Anglo" subjects in Australia, Great Britain, South Africa, and the United States all placed stimuli representing mental patients in hospitals at a far distance. Finally, similarities among cultures in projective placements were also reported in one other study by Lomranz (1976). Argentinian, Iraqi, and Russian students in an Israeli boarding school all placed dolls at the closest distance when the interaction situation involved a good friend, and at the farthest distance when the interaction situation involved a stranger. However, some cultural differences were found. Argentinian students had the largest placement distance, followed by the Russian and Iraqi students respectively.

We started this section on cultural investigations of personal space with a series of hypothesized divergencies in proxemic patterns among a number of cultural groups which has been advanced by Hall (1966). It is disappointing to report that, as of this writing, few of these hypotheses (particularly those involving the Japanese, the Germans, and the French), have been systematically tested. Future research is necessary to examine Hall's assertion that these cultures *"inhabit different sensory worlds."* Most of the research conducted to date has focused on the issue of whether members of contact cultures maintain closer interaction distance (reflecting higher levels of involvement) than members of noncontact cultures. Findings have been quite supportive of Hall's descriptive accounts of this difference. However, the scattered and unsystematic results from studies concerned with cultures not involved in this "contact/noncontact" distinction need to be integrated with further research efforts, and set into a more coherent framework.

Sorely needed are studies assessing transactions between members of *different* cultures. The fact that people of different cultures use space differently does not necessarily mean that *miscommunication* between them is inevitable. Miscommunication may occur, though, when individuals from different cultures attempt to *interpret* each other's spatial behavior. A fruitful direction for future studies might be an application of attribution theory processes (see Harvey, Ickes, & Kidd, 1976, 1978) to the investigation of mixed-cultural encounters. Attribution approaches focus attention directly upon the process through which people attempt to infer the motives, characteristics, and intentions of others from observation of their overt behavior.

SUBCULTURAL INVESTIGATIONS OF PERSONAL SPACE

Hall (1966) has stated that differences in spatial regulation patterns are basic not only to cultural groups but to subcultural groups as well, and has extended his distinction between "contact" and "noncontact" cultures to subcultural groups, particularly in the United States. Accordingly, he uses the term "American" to refer to the dominant noncontact group of Americans of Northern European ancestry. Hall (1966) posited that lower-income black and Spanish subcultures were "more highly involved" than white middle-class Americans, and, therefore, would use closer interaction distances. Moreover, he posited that black and Spanish subcultures may be particularly open to discomfort from misunderstandings, since these subcultures occupy different "sensory worlds" from that of the dominant North American Western culture.

It is apparent, therefore, that the cultural differences which have been found among the differing nations raise questions especially relevant for the United States, with its multiethnic, multiracial population.[5] As illustrated in Table 2, a considerable amount of research has examined ethnic and racial variations in proxemic behavior. Moreover, while 23 of these investigations comparing subgroups have been conducted in the United States, only two have been done in other countries.

Early evidence regarding preferred interaction distances of subcultural groups in this country was reported in studies by Efron (1941) and Watson and Graves (1966). Efron (1941), in a study primarily concerned with gesturing behavior, discovered that Eastern European Jews stood closer and touched more than did Southern Italians while conversing on New York City streets. In an investigation which examined the possibility of regional variations in proxemic behavior (described in the preceding section), Watson and Graves (1966) found that Midwesterners sat farther apart than subjects from the East and West coastal regions.

To date, there have been 8 unstructured interactive studies, 7 structured interactive studies, 4 quasi-projective studies, and 6 projective studies of ethnic and racial differences in spatial behavior. Several of these investigations have compared the proxemic behavior of Hispanic- and Anglo-Americans. With the exception of Jones (1971, who did not actually use an Anglo-American comparison group), all of these investi-

---

[5]It may be that subcultures (in terms of *life-styles*) may be independent of race or ethnic identification. All of the studies reported in this chapter have assumed *a priori* what cultures or subcultures existed (e.g., race, nationality, socioeconomic status). Another strategy for researchers would be to seek to discover (rather than assume) what the valid groups for comparison should actually be.

gations have found that Hispanic-American groups interact at closer distances than Anglo-Americans (e.g., Aiello & Jones, 1971; Baxter, 1970; Ford & Graves, 1977). For example, in an unstructured interactive field study, Baxter (1970) observed Mexican-American, black-, and Anglo-American pairs when they paused to look at indoor and outdoor exhibits at a zoo. Results indicated that Mexican-American subjects of all ages interacted at closer distances than Anglos and blacks. Informal observations indicated that Mexican-Americans also tended to touch and hold each other by the hand or arm more than did the other two subcultural groups. In addition, Mexican-Americans were found to cluster more closely when interacting outdoors than indoors. Baxter (1970) suggested that the greater clustering may be due to increased feelings of external threat. Although this latter finding has not been well replicated, the existence of wall-enclosed spaces in Hispanic architecture indicates that this may well be the case [see, for example, Lewis's (1961) description of Casa Grande]. Taken together, these findings are consistent with Hall's (1966) speculations. In addition, they are also in accord with Jourard's (1966) and Montagu's (1971) qualitative reports of greater use of touching in Latin American families.

Strong evidence supporting Hall's contention that "contact" and "noncontact" subcultures exist can be found in several other structured-interactive and unstructured-interactive studies. The proxemic behavior of interacting dyads of first-grade and second-grade children from Puerto Rican, black, and white subcultural groups in school playgrounds was examined in a field study that the first author conducted along with Stanley E. Jones (Aiello & Jones, 1971). Our results demonstrated that lower-class Puerto Rican and black children stood closer than middle-class white children. In another unstructured-interactive field study, Thompson and Baxter (1970) measured the regulation of distance (forward and backward moves) by black-Mexican, black-Anglo, and Mexican-American mixed pairs on the school grounds of two public schools, and in an automated food concession room of a general hospital. Results pertaining to Mexican-Americans indicated that the predominant direction of their interaction-distance moves with both black and Anglo-Americans was forward. Most recently, in a quasi-projective investigation, Ford and Graves (1977) examined the interpersonal distance and touching behavior of Mexican-American and white second-grade and eighth-grade children. Mexican-American second-graders were found to approach a confederate of his or her own age, race, and sex more closely than white second-graders. However, this ethnic difference disappeared by the eighth grade. Results also indi-

TABLE 2
SUBCULTURAL INVESTIGATIONS OF PERSONAL SPACE

Investigator(s)/subjects	Age	Sex	Techniques or distance measurement	Other variables	Results
Interactive-unstructured studies:					
1. Aiello & Jones (1971) 70 black pairs 70 Puerto Rican pairs 70 white pairs	Children	35 males; 35 females 35 males; 35 females 35 males; 35 females	Observations of homogeneous subculture-sex dyadic standing interaction were gathered during recess periods and during lunch hours in school yard using scales adapted from the proxemic notational system of Hall (1963).	Body orientation	Middle-class white children stood farther apart than lower-class black and Puerto Rican children. Sex difference was present only in white subculture. Black children faced each other less directly than white children.
2. Baxter (1970) 859 pairs of Anglo-, black, and Mexican-Americans	Children Adolescents Adults	Male–male pairs Male–female pairs Female–female pairs (Numbers of each not specified)	Observations of standing distance were made in indoor and outdoor settings when Ss paused to look at an exhibit in a zoo.	None	Blacks were found to stand farthest apart, Anglos were intermediate and Mexican-Americans stood closest together. Adults stood farthest apart, adolescents were intermediate, and children stood closest together. Male pairs were most distant, female pairs were

Continued

				Dependent variable	Results
					intermediate, and male–female pairs stood the closest together. Higher order interactions involving these variables and indoor–outdoor setting are also reported.
3. Jones (1971):Study I 22 black pairs 35 Puerto Rican pairs 19 Italian pairs	Adults	All males	Still photographs of standing dyadic interactions on the streets of New York City in Harlem, Lower-East Side, Spanish Harlem, and Little Italy. Photographs were scored using Hall's (1963) system for the notation of proxemic behavior.	Body orientation	No ethnic or sex differences were found for distance or body orientation.
Study II 100 black pairs 75 Puerto Rican pairs 51 Italian pairs 86 Chinese pairs	Adults	127 male–male pairs 92 male–female pairs 93 female–female pairs	Observation of standing dyadic interactions on the streets of New York City in Harlem, Bedford Stuyvesant, Spanish Harlem, Lower-East Side, Little Italy, and Chinatown using Hall's (1963) system for the notation of proxemic behavior.	Body orientation	Interaction distance of the four poverty subcultures studied were found to be quite similar. Regardless of subculture, women were found to be more direct in body orientation than men.

TABLE 2. (*Continued*)

	Investigator(s)/subjects	Age	Sex	Techniques or distance measurement	Other variables	Results
4.	Scherer (1974) Study I: 13 lower-class black pairs 20 lower-class white pairs	Children	Male–male pairs Female–female pairs (Numbers of each not specified)	Still photographs of standing interacting pairs of same-sex, same-race dyads. Photogrammetry technique used to determine proxemic distances.	None	No significant difference between subcultural groups in interaction distance although white children tended to stand farther apart than black children.
	Study II: 17 lower-class black pairs 14 middle-class black pairs 20 lower-class white pairs 17 middle-class white pairs	Children	Male–male pairs Female–female pairs (Numbers of each not specified)	Same as above. Observation sites were middle-class school playground and lower-class district playground.	None	Middle-class whites stood farther apart than lower-class whites. No difference existed between middle- and lower-class blacks although trend was the same as for whites.
5.	Schofield & Sagar (1977) 109 blacks 138 whites	7th & 8th graders	Males & females (Numbers of each not specified)	Observations of side-by-side and face-to-face seating patterns using gender and racial aggregation indices in an integrated school's cafeteria containing 32 rectangular (16 seat) tables.	None	Race was found to be an extremely important grouping criterion (even for students choosing to attend a desegregated school). Sex was found to be an even more important grouping criterion. Racial aggregation decreased over time in

Continued

No. Study	Age	Sex	Procedure		Results
					one grade but increased in another. In the grade in which aggregation decreased (7th grade) the increase in mixing occurred for side-by-side and not face-to-face seating.
6. Thayer & Alban (1972) 22 pedestrians in Little Italy 22 pedestrians in Greenwich Village	Adults	All males	E (male) wearing either a flag or peace button moved to within six inches of a S as he requested directions. Distance recorded for S was that assumed immediately after E's movement.	None	Interaction distance from E was smaller in Little Italy (the more conservative area) when E wore the traditional American flag button than when he wore the peace button. No difference was obtained in Greenwich Village (the more liberal area) although the results were in the opposite direction.
7. Thompson & Baxter (1970) 10 black–Mexican pairs 10 black–Anglo pairs 10 Mexican–Anglo pairs	Adolescents and adults	7 male–male pairs 7 male–female pairs 16 female–female pairs	Observations were made on the school grounds of two public high schools and in an automated food concession room of a general hospital. Identifiable moves, forward or backward, were recorded for each interaction.	None	In their interactions with both Mexicans and Anglos, blacks were found to move consistently backward. For Mexicans, the predominate direction of their moves with blacks and Anglos was forward.

TABLE 2. (*Continued*)

Investigator(s)/subjects	Age	Sex	Techniques or distance measurement	Other variables	Results
8. Willis (1966) Comparison I: 30 black pairs 30 white pairs	Groups matched for age and sex		Large number of *E*s recorded initial standing-speaking distance when approached using a cloth tape measurer. Field study was conducted in homes, places of business and in the halls of a university. Black/white comparisons formed a small part of the large sample of 755 *S*s studied.	None	Whites tended to stand closer than blacks.
Comparison II: 9 white–white pairs 9 black–white pairs		Same as above		None	Black–white pairs stood farther apart than white–white pairs.
Interactive-structured studies:					
1. Jones & Aiello (1973) 48 upper lower-class black pairs 48 middle middle-class white pairs	1st, 3rd, & 5th graders	24 male–male pairs 24 female–female pairs 24 male–male pairs 24 female–female pairs	Standing conversation between homogeneous sex and subcultural dyads. Topic of conversation was the same for all dyads. Unobtrusive observations were made using an adaptation of Hall's (1963) system for the	Body orientation	Black *S*s stood closer together than white *S*s at the first grade level but this difference disappeared by the third grade level and was reversed at the fifth grade level. Blacks faced one another less directly than whites. Males

			notation of proxemic behavior.		faced one another less directly than females.
2. Aiello & Jones (1978) 21 lower-class black pairs 28 middle-class black pairs 29 lower-class white pairs 36 middle-class white pairs	Adolescents	9 male–male pairs 12 female–female pairs 13 male–male pairs 15 female–female pairs 16 male–male pairs 13 female–female pairs 16 male–male pairs 20 female–female pairs	Same as above	Body orientation and head orientation. Following direct observations, two indirect procedures were administered. Half of the *S*s received approach technique and and half received the *Felt Figure Placement* technique.	Black *S*s stood farther apart than white *S*s. Lower class *S*s tended to stand farther apart than middle-class *S*s. Males stood farther than females. Black *S*s maintained more indirect body orientation and head orientation than white *S*s. No relationship was found to exist between actual interaction distances and approach distances or placement distances.
3. Hendricks & Bootzin (1976) 80 whites	Adults	All females	Three measures were used: (1) initial seating choice from black and and white confederates (*C*s); (2) reported level of discomfort at various approach distances; and (3) closest position to which *S* was willing to advance.	None	White *S*s maintained greater seating distance from black *C*s than white *C*s. Female *S*s approaching male *C*s reported greater discomfort than those approaching female *C*s. No significant effects were found on the measure of overt approach.

Continued

TABLE 2. (*Continued*)

Investigator(s)/subjects	Age	Sex	Techniques or distance measurement	Other variables	Results
4. Leibman (1970) 98 whites 18 blacks	Adults	All females	Observations of S's seated distance from white female C, white male C, black female C, or black male C on a six foot bench in a waiting area. In a second set of four conditions, Ss were given the choice between intrusive seats with white versus black females, white versus black males, male versus female whites, and male versus female blacks. In the third set of conditions, Ss were given a choice between an empty bench and a bench occupied by a white female confederate.	None	For both subcultural groups, interpersonal distance was not affected by the race of the C. Larger distances tended to be used when interacting with a male C than with a female C. When given a choice, Ss chose an empty bench over one that was occupied. Race of the Cs was not was not found to influence the Ss choice of intrusive seats.
5. Rosegrant & McCroskey (1975) 120 blacks 120 whites	Adults	60 males; 60 females 60 males; 60 females	Ss were requested to take the role of an interviewee and to take a chair and be seated with the confederate-	None	White Ss maintained larger initial interpersonal distances with black Cs. Black Ss showed no differential

			chair distance was recorded by the E.		function of the race of C. Males sat farthest from a male C, females sat closest with a female C, and mixed-sex seated distances were intermediate.
6. Watson & Graves (1966) 4 Ss each from 4 Arab regions and 4 United States regions	Adults	All males	Seated conversation between culturally homogeneous dyads. Interaction topic was anything that "came into their heads." Ss brought 3 other people from their subgroup to the laboratory. Distance was scored on the basis of Hall's (1963) system for the notation of proxemic behavior.	Axis, distance, touching, eye contact, and voice loudness	Arab regional groups did not differ on distance, touching, and eye contact variables and were relatively homogeneous on axis and voice loudness measures. American regional groups were somewhat more variable with some differences on all but the touching behavior. Midwesterners sat farther apart than Ss from East and West coast regions. Ss from the coastal regions maintained more eye contact and a less direct axis than Ss of internal regions. Midwesterners spoke louder than Ss from the three other United States regions.

Continued

143

TABLE 2. (*Continued*)

Investigator(s)/subjects	Age	Sex	Techniques or distance measurement	Other variables	Results
7. Zimmerman & Brody (1975) 38 blacks 40 whites	Children	All males	Ss were paired to form 10 white dyads, 9 black dyads, and 20 mixed-racial dyads. Children were observed for five-minute seated play session. Mixed-racial dyads additionally participated in a warm/ cold play interaction, video-taped modeling study. After watching friendly or indifferent mixed-race televised play sessions, their play (interaction) was observed for a second five-minute interval.	Eye contact, body axis, talking, and cooperation	Black Ss interacted at larger distances, talked less, and tended to face each other less directly. The interpersonal distance of mixed-ethnic dyads was intermediate between those of white and black dyads. Black Ss talked less and maintained less direct body axis with other black Ss than with white Ss. Boys exposed to the warm modeling episode looked at and talked more to the other member of their dyad and tended to face him more directly. In addition, they played closer to their dyad mates and were more cooperative with them.
Quasi-projective studies: 1. Bauer (1973) 30 blacks 30 whites	Adults	15 males; 15 females	An approach technique was used wherein Ss were asked to walk up to a C of his or her own	None	Approach distances to a C of black Ss were less than those of white Ss. No differences were

sex.

2.	Ford & Graves (1977) 40 whites 40 Mexican-Americans	2nd & 8th graders	20 males; 20 females 20 males; 20 females	An approach technique was used wherein Ss were asked to walk up to and greet a C of his or her own age, race, and sex.	Social touching	Mexican-Americans approached the C more closely than did males, the 2nd grade level but this ethnic difference disappeared by the 8th grade level. Females approached more closely than did males, and younger children approached more closely than older children.
3.	Frankel & Barrett (1971) 40 Caucasian native-born Americans	Adults	All males	Approach technique in which Ss were approached by white or black confederates in a counterbalanced order.	None	High-authoritarian and low self-esteem white Ss allowed closer approach distances for white than for black approacher.
4.	Tennis & Dabbs (1976) 28 blacks 28 whites	Adults	All females	Approach technique in which Ss approached and were approached by same-race partner.	*Comfortable Interpersonal Distance Scale*	White Ss allowed closer approach distance than did black Ss. Ss of both races preferred larger distances when in a corner than when in the center of a room. A significant but low correlation of .32 was found between the approach and *Comfortable Interpersonal Distance* scale measures.

Continued

145

TABLE 2. (*Continued*)

Investigator(s)/subjects	Age	Sex	Techniques or distance measurement	Other variables	Results
Projective studies:					
1. Cade (1972) 48 Hawaiian Orientals 24 Hawaiian Caucasians	Adults	Not specified	An adaptation of Kuethe's (1962) *Felt Figure Technique* was used. There were six placement conditions reflecting various nuclear family relationships.	None	The two Hawaiian subcultural groups differed in their interfigure distance placements.
2. Connolly (1974) 24 blacks 24 white Midwesterners	Children	38 males; 10 females	Four sets of photographs showing teacher-student dyads in spacings ranging from 12 to 84 inches were presented to subjects. Ss made three judgments choosing those which represented: (a) the most appropriate spacing; (b) enough forward movement to change the interaction; and (c) enough backward movement to change the interaction.	Ss were asked to explain their choices and rated the personalities of the models. Measurements of proxemic behavior were also correlated with their choices.	Black Ss placed less space between interactants than white Ss for all three choice conditions. They also appeared to use more spatial manipulation to mark different changes in content and context during a conversation. All Ss agreed that a a negative meaning was conveyed when the interactants were moved far enough apart. There was no agreement on the meaning of a close distance.

| 3. | Edwards (1973)
30 white students
Three South African
cultural groups:
30 Xhosa students
30 urban Xhosa laborers
30 rural Xhosa natives | Adults | All males | Doll placement technique wherein Ss placed two pairs of dolls (male–male and female–female) at three levels of acquaintance (friends, acquaintances, and strangers). | Angle of doll placement | Ss from all 4 cultural groups placed friends closer than acquaintances or strangers. Acquaintances were placed farther apart than strangers by the urban Xhosa Ss. The rural Xhosa Ss placed dolls at a greater angle in this condition. Both of these groups placed dolls less directly in this acquaintance condition than in any of the other conditions. In the male–female pairs, the man was usually placed by the Xhosa so that he faced more directly than the woman. Neither sex was placed more directly by the American Ss. |

Continued

TABLE 2. (*Continued*)

Investigator(s)/subjects	Age	Sex	Technique or distance measurement	Other variables	Results
4. Roger & Mjali (1976) 16 acculturated Xhosa South Africans 16 unacculturated Xhosa South Africans	Adults	All males	Doll placement technique wherein *S*s placed two dolls in three status conditions (chief, peer, or boy).	None	Acculturated Xhosa *S*s placed the doll representing themselves farther from the chief than from the peer. In contrast, the unacculturated Xhosa *S*s placed the doll representing themselves significantly farther from the boy than chief. This group had significantly greater mean distance and orientation scores for the peer and boy status conditions than the acculturated group.

5.	Tolor (1968) 9 emotionally disturbed blacks 11 emotionally disturbed whites 26 normal whites	Children	31 males; 15 females	An adaptation of Kuethe's (1962) *Felt Figure Technique* was used. There were four nonsocial stimuli (shapes) and four social stimuli (homogeneous and heterogeneous pairings of black and white boys and girls).	None	Interracial and male–female reconstructions were found to be made at greater distances than male–female pairings of the same ethnic background. No differences in replacement distance were obtained for emotionally disturbed children as compared to nondisturbed children but the disturbed children were less accurate in their placement of stimuli.
6.	Tolor & Orange (1969) 15 disadvantaged blacks 5 disadvantaged whites 20 advantaged whites	Children	20 males; 20 females	The *Psychological Distance Board*, a figure-placement technique was used.	*Make-A-Picture-Story* method	Disadvantaged Ss (primarily black children) consistently place farther apart all classes of social stimuli, regardless of whether they consisted of advantaged, disadvantaged, or mixed figures.

cated that the greatest touching behavior was observed for Mexican-American females.

Two unstructured-interactive studies reported by Jones (1971) fail to support Hall's notion of subcultural variations in proxemics. Observations of standing dyadic interactions of Puerto Rican, black, Italian, and Chinese subcultural groups were made on the streets of New York City, in Harlem, Bedford-Stuyvesant, Spanish Harlem, the Lower East Side, Little Italy, and Chinatown. The interaction distances and body orientations of the four subcultures were found to be quite similar. These results may reflect the influence of the dominant culture, particularly through television and movies, or, as Jones (1971) has suggested, the lack of differential findings may be due to physical environmental factors (e.g., noise level) present in the street settings. The cultural homogeneity of distance scenes may also reflect the existence of a "culture of poverty," or adaptation to generally overcrowded living conditions.

As can be seen in Table 2, the largest number of subcultural studies have examined similarities and differences in spatial usage by black and white Americans. The results of those comparisons have not been quite so clearcut as those involving Hispanic- and Anglo-Americans. In an early field study, Willis (1966) used an approach technique to measure the nose to nose, interpersonal distance between black and white college students. Preliminary evidence (a marginally significant difference between the groups) was obtained indicating that blacks prefer larger interaction distances than whites. In the study at the Houston zoo that was described above, Baxter (1970) found that blacks stood farthest apart at exhibits, whites were intermediate, and Mexican-Americans stood the closest. Distance was found to increase with age for all three subcultural groups. In addition, spatial behavior in different settings varied, with blacks interacting more closely in indoor settings than in outdoor settings (a result consistent with that of Baxter & Phelps, 1970), and whites interacting at approximately the same distance in both settings. Taken together, these findings are consistent with Willis's (1966) preliminary findings that blacks maintain greater distances than whites. Additional support for black and white differences in proxemic behavior can be found in the study conducted by Thompson and Baxter (1970). Blacks were found to move backward and away from their interaction partner to a greater extent during subculturally heterogeneous interactions, while Mexican-Americans tended to move forward, and whites maintained a balance between forward and backward movement.

In the study described earlier (Aiello & Jones, 1971), lower-class black and Puerto Rican children stood closer together than middle-class white children. Although black children showed less direct body orientations, there were no differences for this variable or distance between blacks and Puerto Ricans. In addition, while significant sex differences in distance scores were found among white children, there were no significant differences between male and female distance scores within either the black or the Puerto Rican subculture. Significant sex differences in axis were also found, such that females had greater mean axis scores than males in each subculture.

The data from the preceding investigations suggested that black and white subcultures do differ in proxemic behavior. Nevertheless, the possibility existed that the variations among the groups could have been a function of social class differences, and not subculture (race). Moreover, since this study, as well as those by Willis (1966) and Baxter (1970), involved naturalistic field observations, there was little control over the topic of conversation discussed by the interactants.

In an attempt to address these issues, we conducted a follow-up investigation (Jones & Aiello, 1973) which examined the use of space across three age levels, controlling for the topic of conversation discussed and the size of the interaction area. The proxemic behavior of middle middle-class white and upper lower-class black first-, third-, and fifth-grade children was observed in a free-discussion setting. A somewhat complicated pattern of results emerged which replicated the findings of Aiello and Jones (1971) and extended earlier reported findings. While black children were found to stand closer than whites in the first grade, this difference disappeared by the third grade, and showed signs of being reversed by the fifth grade. Black children of all grade-levels maintained less direct body orientations than white children.

Each of the preceding investigations had chosen to confound race with social class (including Jones & Aiello, 1973, since socioeconomic status [SES] differences were only minimized and not eliminated). They are, therefore, open to alternative explanations regarding the socioeconomic levels of the cultural groups studied. In an attempt to address this critical issue, Scherer (1974) conducted two field studies in school yards, wherein still photographs were taken of standing, interacting pairs of same-sex, same-race dyads of black and white children in grades one through four. In the first study, lower-class white children were found to stand farther apart than lower-class black children; but this difference was not statistically significant. In the second study, the spatial behaviors of black and white middle- and lower-class children were compared. Middle-class children were found to stand farther apart than lower-class children. This difference was only significant for the white children, however. No differences were found between white and black middle-class children, or between white and black lower-class children. Scherer suggested that the previously reported findings indicating differences between black and white proxemic behavior patterns may have been due to socioeconomic factors, and not subcultural background. However, the generalizability of these findings is somewhat limited, in that Scherer unfortunately confounded in his analyses the sex composition of the dyads he photographed, and had no way of assessing whether his groups differed in the topic of conversation which they had chosen to discuss. More importantly, the failure to replicate the racial differences in proxemic behavior found by Aiello and Jones (1971) may be accounted for by the larger age range selected by Scherer. As noted above, the development of personal space by blacks and whites appears to be somewhat different, and *while very young black children stand closer together than white children, the difference between these groups has been found to diminish at about age 8 or 9* (half of Scherer's sample) *and actually appears to be reversed by about age 10.* This study does however provide an important contribution, as it was the first study to uncover socioeconomic class differences in the use of space during interaction.

Recently, Stanley E. Jones and the first author conducted a subsequent investigation (Aiello & Jones, 1978), in order to address the issues considered above, and to attempt to resolve the apparent discrepancies in the existing proxemic literature. In this study, we observed interaction patterns of black and white, lower- and middle-class, male and female pairs of adolescents. Adolescents were selected to provide the "next step" in the development sequence. These observations were made under conditions which allowed for a similar environmental context (i.e., the same-sized interaction area, a partitioned classroom in their high schools) and for discussion to focus on the same topic of conversation (i.e., their favorite television programs). The procedure was the same as that used in our previous investigations (Aiello & Aiello, 1974; Aiello & Cooper, 1972; Jones and Aiello, 1973).

The results of this study indicated that blacks of this age group stood farther apart (27 inches) than did their white counterparts (22 inches), $F (1, 114) = 5.73$, $p < .05$, suggesting that the reversal trend for ten-year-olds found in Jones and Aiello (1973) had become more pronounced by the mid teens. There was in addition a marginally significant main effect for socioeconomic class. Unlike the results obtained for younger children in Scherer's (1974) study, lower-class children tended to stand farther apart while conversing (26 inches) than middle-class children (22 inches). There was no significant interaction between these variables for distance or the other two dependent measures of this study. Consistent with the results of our previous studies, blacks faced each other less directly, F (1, 114) = 8.81, $p < .01$, and looked in the direction of their partners less, F (1, 114) = 10.58, $p < .01$, than did white adolescents. Also, as consistent with previous results, females stood closer together, F (1, 114) = 7.25, $p < .01$, and looked in the direction of their partners more, F (1, 114) = 5.54, p $< .05$, than did their male counterparts.

We can conclude from these findings, therefore, that by adolescence (age 16 in this study), blacks have adopted an interaction style that places them farther apart than whites, a result that is consistent with the adult findings of previous investigators (e.g., Baxter, 1970; Willis, 1966). Since blacks also were found to be more indirect in their body and head orientations than whites, Hall's (1966, 1974) speculation that blacks have a "much higher involvement ratio" than whites does not receive support, and, at least for these variables, just the opposite appears to be the case.[6] His concern about blacks' and whites' "misreading" each other is, however, well taken, since differences between these groups appear early in life, and, after disappearing during pubescence, reappear (albeit in a reversed form) in adolescent and adult years.

A number of other studies have also addressed this issue of whether or not there are black-white differences in proxemic behavior.[7] With few exceptions (e.g., Jones, 1971; Leibman, 1970), these investigations have all reported racial variations in spatial usage. For example, consistent with the findings of Willis (1966), Baxter (1970), and Aiello and Jones (1978), Tennis and Dabbs (1976) found that, when approached by a same-race partner, adult white subjects tended to allow closer approach distances than did black subjects. Several other quasi-projective studies, which have examined interactions between members of black and white subcultural groups, have shown that white subjects prefer greater interpersonal distances from black confederates (e.g., Frankel & Barrett, 1971; Hendricks & Bootzin, 1976; Rosegrant & McCroskey, 1975). In contrast, one quasi-projective investigation (Bauer, 1973) found that

---

[6]Hall (1974) did find some support for his contention that blacks have a "much higher involvement ratio" in a photographic study that he did with working-class blacks and Hispanic-Americans interacting on the streets of Chicago, and with whites at an educators' convention. But, as Altman and Vinsel (1977) have indicated, "There were a number of results unique to different raters, making it difficult to draw firm conclusions. While Hall's monograph provides a comprehensive description of a methodology for proxemics analysis, his data are primarily illustrative and only in a pilot form, and it is difficult to draw conclusions about the spatial behavior of the various ethnic groups" (p. 247).

[7]The reader is referred to two descriptive accounts of nonverbal communication patterns in the black culture for detailed examples (Cooke, 1972; Johnson, 1972). Different patterns of gazing for blacks than have been found for whites are reported by Fehr and Exline (1978), LaFrance and Mayo (1973), and McKinzie and Hillabrant (1978).

white subjects preferred larger approach distances to confederates of their own sex and race than did black subjects. These inconsistent findings should be regarded with caution, however, since Bauer reports that many of the black subjects in his study either interpreted the "approach as close as comfortable" instruction as a challenge, or laughed and joked so much during the performance of the task as to indicate that they were not taking the experiment seriously.

Five other studies have focused on the spatial preferences of black and white children, using projective techniques. Connolly (1974) reported that black children placed less space between interactants, and appeared to use more spatial manipulation to mark different changes in content and context during a hypothetical conversation, than white children. However, while there was no agreement on the meaning of a close distance, children from both subcultural groups agreed that a negative meaning was conveyed when the interactants were moved far apart. A somewhat different pattern of results has been reported by Tolor (1968) and Tolor and Orange (1969). Interracial male–female reconstructions were found to be made at greater distances than male–female pairings of the same race (Tolor, 1968). Moreover, the disadvantaged children (75% of whom were black) studied by Tolor and Orange (1969) consistently placed social stimuli farther apart than did (white) nondisadvantaged children. Similar results were obtained by Schneider (1970), who used a social distance measure to study the conforming behavior of black and white children.

In a structured interactive investigation, Zimmerman and Brody (1975) found that, consistent with results reported in earlier studies, black male children interacted at larger distances, talked less, and tended to face each other less directly, than white male children. Also of considerable importance are the findings of "free-choice" studies, which have shown that race is an important grouping criterion. Black and white children tend not to choose to sit together, even when they have chosen to attend desegregated schools (e.g., Campbell, Kruskal, & Wallace, 1966; Schofield & Sagar, 1977).

Up to this point, all of the investigations discussed have examined personal space as a function of subculture or race in the United States. Subcultural variations in spatial behavior have also been studied in two investigations conducted in South Africa. In a projective investigation using a doll-placement task, Edwards (1973) compared the social orientation and distance schemata of white South African male students with those of three black subcultural male groups (Xhosa urban, rural, and student samples), by examining placements for three levels of acquaintance. Results indicated that shorter distances were used by subjects from all four subcultural groups when the interaction task involved friends than when it consisted of acquaintances or strangers. A number of other differences were found among the placements of the subjects from the three Xhosa groups. Both urban Xhosan subjects and rural Xhosan subjects placed dolls less directly in the acquaintance condition than in the friend or stranger conditions. Also, in the male–female pairs, the man was usually placed by the Xhosa subjects so that he faced more directly than the woman.

Roger and Majali (1976) investigated the effects of adapting to a new culture on two projective measures, interfigure distance and angle of placement, also using South African Xhosa males. A doll-placement task was used in which subjects were instructed to place a "self" figure with another figure representing a chief, boy, and peer. While no differences were obtained for orientation, significant changes in distance preferences, particularly for interactions involving individuals of different status levels, were found between African males acculturated to Western standards, and those who were not so acculturated. Acculturated subjects placed the dolls farthest apart when the interaction was said to involve a boy.

It is unfortunate that only two subcultural studies of personal space have been conducted in countries outside of the United States, and both of these on one cultural group, and with projective measures. Clearly, an important task of future researchers in this area will be to identify differences, as well as similarities, for subgroups in other countries. Are each of the national groups that Hall (1966) has described homogeneous as to their spatial behaviors and preferences? Or might these cultures vary as a function of some relevant subgrouping, given the preponderance of larger units of people subdividing into smaller units and growing more isolated from the whole as their different allegiances solidify? Do members of the various castes in India share common Indian proxemic patterns? Do Catholics and Protestants in Northern Ireland have similar expectations regarding appropriate levels of involvement? Do East and West Germans still show similar patterns of spatial usage, despite their separation of more than a generation?

In summary, while twice as many subcultural as cultural studies have been conducted, our knowledge in this area is still quite meager. Fairly consistent evidence has been obtained to support Hall's observation that Hispanic-Americans are more spatially involved than Anglo-Americans, but his contention that "Negroes have a much higher involvement ratio" (Hall, 1966, p. 172) has not been supported, except with young children. In fact, available evidence runs contrary to this position. Further research is necessary, and should seek to control or systematically vary such variables as subjects' socioeconomic class, age, and sex grouping, all of which have been found to mediate differences in personal space between black and white subcultural groups. Research evidence to date indicates that, by adolescence, black Americans maintain larger interaction distances than do white Americans. Further, seven of the nine studies which compared mixed-racial interactions with same-race interactions found larger distances used by the mixed-race groups. As we have indicated, for future research directions in the cultural personal space area, investigations of the dynamics involved in mixed-subcultural interactions, particularly concerning interpretations and attributions made by participants of heterogeneous encounters involving different proxemic patterns, are essential to our understanding, and would appear to be a prerequisite for our being able to ameliorate misunderstandings and miscommunications in cross-subcultural interactions. Additional research is obviously very much needed with other ethnic groups (e.g., American Indians) in the United States as well. We recommend that these investigations seek to uncover common proxemic patterns in addition to disparate ones, so that our understanding of the factors which may make intergroup communication more difficult will be enhanced.

CROWDING AND CULTURE

During the last decade, researchers have directed ever greater attention to the process and products of human crowding. The literature in this area has grown tenfold over this period of time. After an early consideration of the distinctions between the physical concept "density" and the psychological experience "crowding" (Stokols, 1972), studies (conducted primarily in the United States) have uncovered a great many antecedent conditions, psychological responses, and consequences of crowding (see Sundstrom, 1978 for a comprehensive review of this research).

We have suggested (Aiello et al., 1974, 1975a) that crowding may be assessed across several different observational levels: demographic, normative, phenomenological, nonverbal, and physiological. Most of the research that will be reported in this section of our chapter has been conducted at the demographic level.[8] At this level of observation,

[8]The studies that will be included in this section are primarily those conducted *outside* of the United States, and those involving comparisons of subcultures within the United States. Given the presence of so few cross-cultural or cross-subcultural investigations in this literature, comparisons for the most part must be made by implication rather than directly.

little attention is paid to specific characteristics of individuals or settings. Correlational studies assessing the effects of population density using aggregates (e.g., Schmitt's 1966 study of census tract data from Honolulu) comprise the bulk of studies at this level of observation. Investigations at the normative level introduce past learning histories and preferences of individuals in groups into the consideration of crowding. While none of the cultural studies of crowding conducted to date has been performed at this level, one of our studies done in the United States (Aiello, DeRisi, Epstein, & Karlin, 1977), which looked at reactions to crowding by individuals with close and far personal space preferences, is representative of research at this level. About half of the cultural work done in the crowding area has been performed at the phenomenological level; that is, when do people use the label "crowded" in their reaction to an environment (based at least in part on the nature of others in that setting). Mitchell's (1971) interview study of the individual reactions of Hong Kong residents to differentially crowded living conditions is a good example of this approach. Only one cultural study, Draper (1973), has utilized the nonverbal level of observation. Draper's observations of the !Kung bushmen's degree of touching and other nonverbal behavior is representative of a method that might be used in other crowding research. Although a number of cultural investigations have reported indirect evidence at the physiological level of observation (e.g., Booth & Cowell's 1974 Toronto study of the effects of crowding upon health), only Draper's (1973) investigation, and Singer, Lundberg, and Frankenhaeuser's (1978) study of reactions to urban commuting in Stockholm, are truly representative of studies conducted outside of the United States that have been performed at this level. A number of our own studies, conducted in the northeastern United States, have included observations at the physiological level (skin conductance level), and have indicated that children (Aiello, Nicosia, & Thompson, 1979), young adults (e.g., Aiello et al., 1977; Aiello et al., 1975a; Nicosia, Hymen, Karlin, Epstein, & Aiello, 1979), and the elderly (Aiello, Headly, & Thompson, 1978), do not adapt to short-term, episodic conditions of crowding involving close physical proximity.

Moreover, we have suggested that any of three events can evoke the label "crowded": congestion with resource scarcity; an inability to control interpersonal interaction; and extremely close physical proximity to others (Karlin et al., 1978). We further suggest here that the presence of large numbers of others be added to this set of events, as this factor is most often associated with the label "crowding." These events are differentially present in any particular setting. With rare exceptions (e.g.,

Singer *et al.*, 1978), the cultural studies of crowding that will be reported below focus on residential settings, and not on other settings in which crowding often occurs.

The difficulties associated with defining and measuring population density cross-nationally have been examined by Day and Day (1973). These authors have emphasized the need to consider factors such as geographical features of population distribution (e.g., pattern of settlement, proportion of the population living in areas of different sizes), transportation systems, and residential commercial mixes of functions. They point out the problems which are encountered when only a person to land ratio is used as a measure of density. For example, the reason countries of low average density (e.g., Australia) have many of the environmental problems (e.g., smog, water pollution, traffic jams) typically associated with countries of higher density (e.g., United States), is their population *distribution*, and not their population size *per se*. In short, these authors call for a need to investigate density as both a static and dynamic process, and in the social context and cultural setting within which it occurs, so that conclusive statements may be made about the effects of population density on human behavior.

Based on the differences in spatial behavior in the various countries, regions, and subcultural groups cited earlier in this chapter, we would expect that reactions to high density conditions would be different for these different groups. Unfortunately, there are few direct cultural comparisons available to test this expectation, so our consideration of this more slowly growing subarea of crowding research will focus on descriptions of the studies that have been conducted, and will provide some qualitative comparisons among these studies.

Early studies investigating the effects of crowding in residential areas indicated that density was related to such pathologies as mental illness (e.g., Hollingshead & Redlich, 1958; Lantz, 1953; Pollock & Furbush, 1921) and crime rate (e.g., Lottier, 1938; Schmitt, 1957; Watts, 1931). More recent correlational investigations of residential crowding have considered such important factors as socioeconomic class, education, and culture, when interpreting the relationship between density and social pathology.

In an early correlational study conducted in Honolulu, Hawaii, by Schmitt (1957), two measures of overall population density, persons per net acre and percent of units with 1.51 or more persons per room, were related to juvenile delinquency and adult offender rates. While household size was positively correlated with juvenile delinquency, it was not related to prison admission rates. In contrast, multiunit housing was negatively related to juvenile delinquency, with lower rates of delinquency found in apartment house districts than in single-unit housing areas, but was also not related to adult criminality. In a second study conducted in Honolulu, Schmitt (1966) found that the number of persons per acre was related to juvenile delinquency. He discovered that density was associated with several other types of social pathology as well (i.e., the incidence of mental hospitalization). More importantly, when the effects of income and education were statistically removed, these patterns of association still existed. Similar results have been reported in a demographic survey of mental health trends in Hong Kong. Lo (1976) found that the incidence of mental illness had increased, particularly for males, over a twenty-five year period of expanding population and urbanization. Lo interpreted these findings as indicating that people do not learn to adapt to high-density living conditions. In contrast, Schmitt (1963) and Mitchell (1971) found few pathological results when they looked at high density in Hong Kong households. Survey data were collected from 3,966 individuals by Mitchell in order to examine the effects of household density on emotional health, family relations, and attitudes toward housing. The only significant findings were that the number of nonfamily members within a household and in apartments on upper floors was related to poor attitudes about housing. On the basis of these results, Mitchell concluded that people are able to adapt to high-density living conditions. A similar view is explicated by Sommer (1969) in his brief description of cultural differences in spatial usage:

> Reports from Hong Kong where three million people are crowded into 12 square miles indicate that the population has adapted to the crowding reasonably well. The Hong Kong Housing Authority, now in its tenth year of operation, builds and manages low-cost apartments for families that provide approximately 35 square feet per person for living-sleeping accommodations. When the construction supervisor of one Hong Kong project was asked what the effects of doubling the amount of floor area would be upon the living patterns, he replied, "with 60 square feet per person, the tenants would sublet!" [American Institute of Planners Newsletter, January 1967, p. 2, as cited by Sommer (1969), p. 27]

This position is also consistent with that of Freedman (1975), who (in collaboration with S. Heska and A. Levy) examined the relationship between population density and social pathology, using data taken from 97 standard metropolitan statistical areas in the United States and 334 "health areas" of New York City.

   Anderson (1972) has suggested that special adaptation strategies, consisting of highly developed ways to manage time, space, and people, exist within the Chinese culture. This permits individuals to cope with overcrowding in the home. Of particular interest is his observation that, for the most part, the Chinese voluntarily choose to live in extremely crowded communities. High ratios of people per household are desired for traditional Chinese ideological and economic reasons. Moreover, there are a number of unspoken social codes which appear to permit successful coping with crowding. For example, space is allocated so that different rooms serve different functions, time management is extremely flexible, and noise (which is often regarded as stressful in other densely populated countries) is looked upon as a "sign of life and action." Most importantly, status and role allocation is straightforward, and a low level of emotional involvement in interaction is expected. Failures of recent attempts in the United States to develop and maintain communal living environments may be due to unrealistic expectations regarding high and continuous levels of emotional involvement.

Similar successful coping strategies have been noted in Japan by Canter and Canter (1971). Despite the fact that there are (approximately) more than 20,000 people per square mile in the city of Tokyo, there are relatively low crime rates. The authors suggest that this low frequency of social pathology may be accounted for by the emphasis placed on privacy within the culture, and the existence of small communities within the city.[9] Other methods for coping with high population density, employed by families in the urban slums of Colombia and Peru, have been described by Rogler (1967).

The effects of crowded living conditions on the !Kung bushmen hunter-gatherers of Southwest Africa were examined in a field study by Draper (1973). Although observations revealed that these people lived in camp settlements which typically provided less than 200 square feet per person, no signs of psychological or physical pathology were found. Moreover, it appeared as though the !Kung enjoyed being in close physical contact with one another, touching and engaging in a great deal of social interaction. On the basis of her observations, Draper concluded that norms allowing for easy departure exist, however. These norms allow for the regulation of social interaction because individuals are free to leave a tribal group at any time in order to join another group, or establish a new group whenever they desire.

In a study conducted in the Philippine islands by Marsella, Escudero,

---

[9]It should be noted, however, that alcoholism in Japan is much higher than in other Asian countries. The *form* of the environment (e.g., the role of the dwelling, garden, walls) may be most important. Recent reports have indicated that in the new highrises (*danchi*), there are some rather severe negative consequences of high density (Rapoport, personal communication).

and Gordon (1971), high population density was found to be related to social pathology. Specifically, inside density was related to self-reports of physical symptoms, independent of social class. Similar findings have also been reported in two East African studies (Munroe & Munroe, 1972, 1973). The effects of long-term population density on the affective relationships and attitudes of students from three East African societies, which differed in their rates of population increase, were examined in the first study. Results indicated that affiliative behavior (e.g., self-reported frequency of handholding with friends), short-term memory for affiliative words, and positive evaluations of "self" and family roles, decreased as population density increased. The authors suggested that these findings could be accounted for by an increase in competition for existing environmental resources in the higher-density East African societies, and, furthermore, that individuals within these environments may decrease their display of affiliative behavior in order to regulate or maintain positive interpersonal affect at a comfortable level.

Munroe and Munroe (1973) in a second investigation examined the relationship between population density and references to movements of the body through space in folktales. The most crowded societies were found to have the highest movement scores. Munroe and Munroe (1973) concluded that psychological concern with freedom of physical mobility exists in higher-density societies. Freely available space, measured in terms of unused land around the town, was perceived by individuals within the most densely populated societies in increasingly confining terms. Specifically, it was viewed as restricting opportunities for individuals to find some personal privacy (e.g., to be alone, to pick berries), and, therefore, as placing specific constraints on behavior.

In order to avoid some of the many problems involved in ecological correlation, investigators have used interview techniques to study the effects of residential crowding. A series of interview studies by Booth and his colleagues (Booth, 1974; Booth & Cowell, 1974; Booth & Edwards, 1976; Booth & Johnson, 1974; Johnson, Booth, & Duvall, 1974; Booth & Welch, 1974) investigated responses to residential crowding among inhabitants of Toronto, Canada. These studies produced a number of interesting results. There seems in general to be a greater effect for subjective crowding than for objective crowding (i.e., density). That is, in the main, the most potent effects were seen in the differing responses of those who felt and perceived themselves as crowded, and those who did not. The objective criteria used to identify crowded individuals did not produce the clear results seen when the subjective variable is used. These data are in accord with Stokols's (1972) distinction between density and crowding.

John R. Aiello and Donna E. Thompson

Booth and his colleagues found that, in general, crowding was unrelated to the social participation of the Toronto sample (Booth, 1974). However, like the earlier work of Chombart de Lauwe (1959, as cited in Hall, 1966), which found a relationship between a measure of space/person within the home and crime and illness rates, they do report some effects of density on family relations. Parents living in more densely populated dwelling units use more physical punishment to discipline their children. These investigators also report that dwelling-unit density adversely affects physical and intellectual development of children (Booth & Johnson, 1974). Booth and his colleagues note the importance of the distinction between density (a physical variable) and crowding (a psychological variable, related to the perception of spatial restriction). Their data reveal that, with respect to aggression, crowding, rather than density, is the more important determinant (cf. Booth & Welch, 1974). In a different study, using archival data from 65 countries, Booth and Welch (1973) found that increasing room density was related to a greater incidence of homicide. The authors continued to explore this relationship in a second study (Booth & Welch, 1974), conducted in over 600 cities in the United States. They found the relationship to be especially strong in those cities with populations exceeding 100,000.

As indicated earlier, Canter and Canter (1971) described the Japanese as being able successfully to adapt to crowded conditions. Dixon, Roper, and Ahern (1975) conducted a study to assess the effects of population density on the personality-need structures of Sansei (third generation Japanese-Americans), and Cosmopolitan (mixture of more than one ethnic group) high school students in Hawaiian and Japanese national high schools. Population density was measured by the number of persons per square kilometer. Results indicated that urban environments fostered a greater need for achievement and independence, and low-density rural environments (including those in Hawaii) produced much lower personality-need patterns. The authors suggest that need satisfaction may be relatively easier to obtain in rural environments. A series of laboratory investigations of the effects of crowding has been conducted by Iwata in Hawaii and Japan (it should be noted that this is one of the few programs of crowding research conducted in laboratory settings outside of the United States). In one of these investigations, the effects of density upon altruistic behavior were examined (Iwata, 1976). Japanese female junior college students were given a questionnaire containing 11 pairs of items representing different situations in which subjects were expected to help someone in need of assistance. The two questions differed with regard to their perceived density. Results indicated that in each of the 11 hypothetical situations, less altruistic behavior was indicated for higher perceived density situations than lower perceived density.

His other studies have all been concerned with the determinants of perceived crowding. For example, in one questionnaire study, Iwata (1974a) examined factors involved in the perception of crowding by Japanese-American and Caucasian-American students of the University of Hawaii. Subjects completed a questionnaire which assessed the effects of familiarity, ethnicity, sex, age, and social status of other individuals with whom an individual would share a high-density room. Results indicated that, for all subjects, the perception of crowding was influenced by familiarity and social status (professor–student), with subjects perceiving greater crowding if they were to be placed in a room with unfamiliar adults than with familiar adults. These findings are consistent with those of Engelbretson and Fullmer (1970), who found that greater interpersonal distances were maintained from professors than from friends by native Japanese and Hawaiian-Japanese students. Ethnicity was also a significant variable for all subjects except female Caucasian students, with individuals perceiving less crowding if they were to share a room with people from their own ethnic backgrounds. Additional findings were that the sex of others with whom a space is shared was a more important factor in the perception of crowding for females than for males of both cultural groups, and that age was also considered a significant factor in the perception of crowding by female Caucasians.

In another investigation, Iwata (1974b) examined the effects of three levels of density (low, medium, high) on the perceptions of density and crowding of male and female Caucasian and Japanese-American students at the University of Hawaii. Subjects were placed in rooms varying in density level for eight minutes, where they stood with their backs to the wall, and were instructed not to talk or move around. Following this activity, the subjects completed a questionnaire which assessed perceived density and perceived crowding (measured by amount of discomfort). Results indicated that the higher-density conditions resulted in greater feelings of perceived crowding and density for both cultural groups. However, Japanese-American students reported more discomfort in high-density conditions than the Caucasian students. While no sex differences were found for the Caucasian students, the Japanese-American males were more sensitive than the Japanese-American females.

In a comparative study on the perceptions of crowding, Iwata (1974c) found a negative relationship between minimum interpersonal distance and a measure of perceived crowding only for the Japanese students in his sample. No relationship was found for the Caucasian-American and Pacific Islanders also studied. Perceived crowding and discomfort were related to population density for each of the three ethnic groups, with the Japanese students being more sensitive to crowding than the Caucasian-American students. On the basis of these findings, Iwata suggested that, regardless of ethnicity, interpersonal distance was not an influential determinant for the perception of crowding. It should be noted, however, that both the interpersonal distance and the perceived crowding measures were obtained by questionnaire responses of subjects relating to distances and social densities which they thought they might prefer, and not by observations of their behavior or reports of their actual experience. In studies conducted in the United States, directly observed interpersonal distance preferences have been found to predict successfully reactions to crowded conditions (Aiello *et al.*, 1977; Dooley, 1974; and Rawls, Trego, McGaffey, & Rawls, 1972).

Most recently, in a subsequent investigation conducted in Japan, Iwata (1977) again found only a low, but significant, negative relationship between crowding and interpersonal distance preference. An approach method was used to measure personal space wherein subjects were instructed to stop at the minimum distance on a tape measure where they felt uncomfortable. Perceived crowding was again measured through the use of a questionnaire. In a reversal of his previous (1974) position, Iwata now suggests that "personal space is a significant but not much [sic] influential determinant of crowding" (1977, p. 36). Two other findings of interest reported in this investigation were that ethnicity and social status were important factors in the perception of crowding. Significantly higher levels of crowding were reported to be experienced if subjects shared a given space with people of different ethnic backgrounds than with individuals of the same ethnicity, or if they shared the space with adults and professors rather than with peers.

Cultural investigations of crowding have also focused on the effects of varying levels of density on different ethnic groups in the United States. Most of the major cities and metropolitan areas in this country are characterized by excessively high concentrations of people, often from very different cultural backgrounds. Since these ethnic groups maintain their cultural identities for a number of generations, great ethnic differences exist (e.g., Glazer & Moynihan, 1963). Given that spatial needs vary as a function of culture, one would expect cultural variation in responses to high density conditions to exist as well. For example, in *The Hidden Dimension*, Hall (1966) posits:

> The degree to which peoples are sensorially involved with each other, and how they use time, determine not only at what point they are crowded but the methods for relieving crowding as well. Puerto Ricans and Negroes have a much higher involvement ratio than New Englanders and Americans of German or Scandinavian stock. Highly involved people apparently require more protection or screening from outsiders. (Hall, 1966, p. 172–173)

It is critical, therefore, that we learn more concerning the optimum density for living conditions of the various subcultural population groups. What one ethnic group experiences as crowding may not necessarily be perceived as crowding by other ethnic groups. Plans for urban renewal often involve the construction of high-rise apartment buildings with little consideration for the spatial needs and preferences of the inhabitants. Dissatisfaction often results, as is illustrated by Hall's (1966) account of black condemnation of high-rise buildings:

> "It's no place to raise a family. A mother can't look out for her kids if they are fifteen floors down in the playground. They get beaten up by the rough ones, the elevators are unsafe and full of filth (people in defiance against the buildings use them as toilets). They are slow and break down. When I want to go home I think twice because it may take me half an hour to get the elevator. Did you ever have to walk up fifteen floors when the elevator was broken? You don't do *that* too often." (Hall, 1966, p. 169–170)

McCarthy and Saegert (1979) conducted structured interviews with black, white, and Puerto Rican tenants of 3-story and 14-story buildings of a low-income housing project in New York City, to examine the effects of two levels of residential density. Their results provide us with perspective for the above tenant's description. The large numbers of others in high-rise buildings was associated with the experience of "social overload" and consequent greater social withdrawal by tenants. They perceived their residence as more crowded, expressed feelings of less control, safety, and privacy, and reported more alienation and dissatisfaction with the residential environment generally. Similar social withdrawal results have been obtained with other types of architecturally induced crowding (e.g., corridor vs. suite design) in college dormitories (e.g., Baum, Aiello, & Calesnick, 1978; Baum & Valins, 1977).

Most of the demographic-level investigations of the effects of crowding carried out prior to the 1960s contained a crucial common flaw—they confounded social class and ethnicity with density level (e.g., Schmitt, 1957). Galle, Gove, and McPherson's (1972) study of population density and pathology linkages in the city of Chicago represents a new generation of investigations. In addition to examining four different types of density (ranging in level from the number of persons per room

to the number of residential units per acre), this study statistically controlled for the usually confounded factors of ethnicity, socioeconomic
class, occupation, and educational level. More recently, Galle and Gove
(1979) have suggested using "percent Negro" as the only substitute
variable of social structure, since it is the most strongly related to the
pathologies of the ethnicity variables involved in their investigations.
We recommend caution in generalization of this strategy, however,
since different geographical regions and cultures are likely to vary on the
ethnic composition of their populations.

In a more recent correlational investigation, Schmidt, Goldman,
and Feimer (1976) used a survey technique to examine the perceptions of
crowding by black, white, and Chicano Americans. Results indicated
that the three ethnic groups perceived the experience of crowding in the
urban environment in subjectively different ways, with whites expressing greater perceived control over the urban environment in general
than the other subcultural groups. Two experiments reported by Rodin
(1976) have indicated that children (more than 80% of whom were black)
living under chronic high-density conditions suffer motivational deficits, and consequently are less apt to exert control over outcomes affecting them when given the opportunity to do so. Levy and Herzog (1974)
examined the association between density and pathology in 125 geographical regions in the Netherlands. Their results extend the body of
research findings indicating crowding to "nonpoverty" cultures, since
they found that density, after adjustment for other variables, had a large
and significant independent effect upon total death rates.

Although there have been over 100 investigations of crowding and
human behavior conducted to date, only a few have directly compared
cultural or subcultural groups. We introduced this section with a description of five levels of observation that have been employed by investigators in their research on crowding, and provided examples of studies
at each of these levels. It was noted that almost all of the studies which
would be cited in this section were performed at the demographic and
phenomenological levels. We view as quite unfortunate the fact that so
few cross-cultural or cross-subcultural studies (which by definition
would be performed at the normative level, since past learning histories
and preferences of individuals in groups are taken into account) have
been done. Three important exceptions to our lack of information in this
area are investigations by Galle and Gove (1979), Galle et al.. (1972), and
Schmidt et al. (1976). This area is ripe for investigations to be conducted,
because so little is known. Similarly, all but one study (Singer et al.,
1978) have focused on residential crowded settings (see also Aiello &
Baum, 1979). Much more information is needed about how people of

different cultures and subcultures respond to crowded conditions in *other* types of settings (e.g., markets, public transportation facilities, and work settings). A comprehensive understanding of how density affects human behavior can only be obtained through research efforts at multiple observation levels, with multiple measures, and in a variety of settings.

Our primary consideration in this section was of studies conducted outside of the United States. These investigations have indicated that under many circumstances and for many populations at least some detrimental consequences result as a function of high-density conditions. Poorer health, higher degrees of crime or aggression, and somewhat greater tendencies toward social withdrawal appear to be the three primary negative consequences of higher residential density conditions. The existence of apparently effective coping strategies by cultures such as the Japanese, Chinese, and !Kung bushmen, however, would seem to indicate that negative outcomes need not follow directly from highly dense, crowded conditions. Future research investigating more transient forms of coping with crowded environments, rather than those which have evolved over numerous generations in the various cultures, could prove to be quite valuable. A systematic evaluation of how contact and noncontact cultures respond to high-density conditions (research surprisingly absent from the literature) is also critically needed.

SPATIAL BEHAVIOR AND ENVIRONMENTAL DESIGN

Given the diversity in spatial behavior and reactions to high-density conditions among the cultures and subcultures which we have discussed in previous sections, it is not surprising to find that architectural forms vary considerably as well. As we indicated in our introduction to this chapter, the design of an environment not only influences the transactions that occur within it but is also itself a product of the culture from which it originates. Sommer (1974) has indicated that in smaller, more traditional societies, there is often a great deal of consensus regarding the architectural forms of most buildings. Architectural designs of buildings are evolved to match the climate and cultural traditions of those societies. In contrast, heterogeneous, multiethnic cultures like the United States are characterized by much less agreement regarding "appropriate" architecture. As a result, there is considerably more variation.

The relationship between spatial behavior and the built environment is quite complex. There are three possible forms of the functional relationship between human behavior and the physical environment, which have been differentiated by Wohlwill (1970). In the first kind of relationship, the environmental context limits the particular behavior or behavior patterns that can occur within it. The second type of relationship is one in which some of the qualities that characterize specific environments affect both the behavior and the personality of individuals residing within them. Last, in the third type of relationship, the environment serves as a motivating force which may result in either strong feelings or attitudes, approach or avoidance behavior, or adaption. Several contradictions between spatial preferences and constructed environments can be gleaned from our review. For example, Hispanic architecture and that of the Arab cultures emphasize interior spaces so large as to cause Americans to feel uncomfortable within them, and yet, individuals in both of these contact cultures prefer to interact at much closer distances than Americans. The design of these interior spaces may be a direct function of traditions in these cultures, which focus the primary attention of design on its aesthetic characteristics. Although there is no direct evidence as to the reason for the inconsistency between spatial and environmental preferences, it is possible that people within these two contact cultures have developed norms stressing greater involvement during interaction in order to *compensate* for their traditional emphasis on large open spaces. As Sommer (1969) has indicated, "Various conventions and rules have been developed to complement architectural forms" (p. 10). It is also possible, though less probable, that this environmental design was adopted to compensate for the established norms of interaction.

In contrast to the large interior spaces of the Arab and Hispanic cultures, the Japanese represent a culture which compensates for the small interiors of their homes by utilizing great intensity of detail. Alteration of the same environment for *multiple* needs or functions (e.g., sleeping, eating, and socializing) is accomplished with little effort. In the United States, people *shift* their location to meet different needs or function. For example, in most American homes, while people eat in the kitchen or dining room, they entertain in the living room. While this may be effective when sufficient space is available, it may cause serious difficulties when space is at a premium. Numerous behavioral scientists and designers (e.g., Altman, 1975; Sommer, 1969; Zeisel & Griffen, 1975) have advocated that designs are necessary which are more functional, so that multiple purposes might be served by the same space. This principle is applicable at a more molecular scale as well. Furniture groupings, for example, can be arranged rather easily to facilitate larger group interaction or small subgroup encounters. This strategy could be applied to most given environments, and would allow spatial behavior (e.g., personal space) to shift with changing circumstances.

On a more global level, the form of the environment (e.g., room sizes, use of walls, spacing of dwellings) often mediates or intensifies experiences within it. For example, McCarthy and Saegert (1979), and Holahan and Wilcox (1979), have shown the kinds of undesirable impact which may result from the greater social overload conditions associated with high-rise as compared with low-rise residential conditions. In like manner, Baum, Davis, and Aiello (1978) have shown how the positioning of stores in an urban neighborhood interferes with residents' ability to regulate contact outside of their homes. Newman's (1972) work in urban housing developments has also demonstrated that *how* secondary and public territories (e.g., hallways) are designed influences residents' feelings of safety, as well as the actual rate of crime. More research is needed in order to determine how the form of environments in various cultures affects the residents.

Architectural design can greatly influence the degree of privacy of its occupants. Investigations indicate rather clearly how architectural factors influence social experience, and, as Davis (1978) has noted, "play an important role in the formation of qualitatively different affiliation patterns and social networks" (p. 366). Sommer (1969) described how one state university saved a good deal of money by remodeling a dormitory so that a third occupant could be added to each double room. He remarked, however, "I have no objection to the idea in theory but it would be nice to know how this affected the students" (p. 4). Two recent studies (Aiello, Epstein, & Karlin, 1975b; Baron, Mandel, Adams, & Griffin, 1976) have demonstrated quite clearly the types of negative consequences which result from such an environmental modification. We need to learn a great deal more about how environmental design is both a product of respective cultures and an influence on the spatial behavior of individuals within these cultures.

SUMMARY AND FUTURE DIRECTIONS OF RESEARCH

In this chapter, we have examined approximately 150 cultural and subcultural studies and accounts of personal space, crowding, and spatial behavior. Since these reports have summarized data gathered using a wide variety of methodologies, we have attempted to identify categories of these approaches with descriptions of the particular methods represented.

The two areas on which we have focused the bulk of our attention, personal space and crowding, have undergone very rapid growth during the past fifteen years. In 1963, there were fewer than a dozen studies of personal space. We now have identified over 300 studies of personal space conducted to date (less than half of which involved "real" interaction). Prior to 1970, only about a dozen or so investigations of human crowding had been reported (virtually all correlational–sociological studies). As of this writing, we have come across more than 140 studies of human crowding (almost half of which were conducted in the laboratory). Unfortunately, investigations involving cross-cultural or cross-subcultural comparisons have not increased at anywhere near the same rate. Much future research is needed to unravel the complexities involved in understanding similarities and differences in the use of space by, and the effects of space on, various cultural and subcultural groups.

In our consideration of literature pertaining to personal space, we found that considerable support was available for the proposition that contact and noncontract cultures use space differently. Studies on the effect of crowding, however, have not yet systematically addressed the question of whether contact and noncontact cultures are differentially affected by constructed space and high social density conditions.

Research on questions concerned with the more significant issues of *how* and *why* people use space differently, rather than simply describing elements within spatial behavior patterns, is needed. Such information would seem to be crucial to our ability to guard against the potential *miscommunication* that may occur in cross-cultural and cross-subcultural encounters. Investigators have begun the process of specifying spatial norms for various cultural and subcultural groups, but we have barely scratched the surface of an information pool containing the effects of mismatches among the divergent normative patterns. We have recommended research on the attributional processes which accompany these interactions. Since, under most conditions, space is but one of the defenses used to control unwanted interaction (or one of the mechanisms available to enhance the probability of desired interaction), we need to learn more about how people of different backgrounds *regulate and control* interactions through the use of space. Could differences in spatial preferences be compensated for by other (conscious or unconscious) interaction processes? This area affords a fertile field for future investigation.

One of the most important questions deserving attention in future work concerns the *basis* for the cultural and subcultural differences in personal space, spatial behavior, and reactions to crowding. Montagu (1971) provides a series of descriptions of early socialization practices relating to tactile behavior between parents and children of various cultural, subcultural, and socioeconomic class groups. He advances the rather convincing argument that

> from the moment of birth every society has evolved its own unique ways of dealing with the child. It is on the basis of repeated sensory experiences of the culturally prescribed stimulations that the child learns how to behave according to the requirements of his culture. (Montagu, 1971, p. 224)

He sharply contrasts the impersonal child-rearing practices of the English, Germans, and Americans with those of the more tactilely involved Latins, Russians, Jews, Japanese, and many nonliterate peoples, so as clearly to imply the greater eventual preference due to these practices that children of these former cultures will have for larger distances (spatial and psychological) from other people than will children of the latter cultures later in life. The present authors believe that it is rather a combination of these early experiences *and* continued reinforcement of these experiences through interaction with the social and physical environment within one's culture that influences cultural differences in spatial preference. Research is definitely needed on this question.

In closing, we might note that since we have accumulated at least some information about spatial-interaction norms for a number of cultures and subcultures, it would appear that another fruitful direction for future research would be a consideration of various *training* methods to increase participants' effectiveness in cross-cultural and cross-subcultural interactions. Collett's (1971) study provided a useful springboard for this type of endeavor. We would expect that, as our research base on the topics of personal space, crowding, and spatial behavior (within a cultural context) continues to expand, training programs designed to protect against miscommunication and misinterpretation should become more widely available as well as more effective.

REFERENCES

Aiello, J. R. *Development of spatial behavior.* Paper prepared for presentation at the American Association for the Advancement of Science, Boston, 1976.

Aiello, J. R., & Aiello, T. D. The development of personal space: Proxemic behavior of children 6 through 16. *Human Ecology,* 1974, *2,* 177–189.

Aiello, J. R., & Baum, A. (Eds.). *Residential crowding and design.* New York: Plenum Press, 1979.

Aiello, J. R., & Cooper, R. E. Use of personal space as a function of social affect. *Proceedings, 80th annual convention, APA,* 1972, 207–208.

Aiello, J. R., & Jones, S. E. Field study of the proxemic behavior of young school children in three subcultural groups. *Journal of Personality and Social Psychology,* 1971, *19,* 351–356.

Aiello, J. R., & Jones, S. E. *Proxemic behavior of black and white adolescents of two socioeconomic class levels.* Unpublished manuscript, 1978.

Aiello, J. R., Epstein, Y. M., & Karlin, R. A. *Methodological and conceptual issues in crowding.* Paper presented at the meetings of the Western Psychological Association, San Francisco, 1974.

Aiello, J. R., Epstein, Y. M., & Karlin, R. A. Effects of crowding on electrodermal activity. *Sociological Symposium,* 1975a, 43–57.

Aiello, J. R., Epstein, Y. M., & Karlin, R. A. *Field experimental research on human crowding.* Paper presented at the annual convention of the Eastern Psychological Association, New York City, 1975b.

Aiello, J. R., DeRisi, D. T., Epstein, Y. M., & Karlin, R. A. Crowding and the role of interpersonal distance preference. *Sociometry,* 1977, *40,* 271–282.

Aiello, J. R., Headly, L. A., & Thompson, D. E. Effects of crowding on the elderly: A preliminary investigation. *Journal of Population,* 1978, *1,* 283–297.

Aiello, J. R., Nicosia, G., & Thompson, D. E. Physiological, social, and behavioral consequences of crowding on children and adolescents. *Child Development,* 1979, *50,* 195–202.

Alexander, C. *Houses generated by patterns.* Berkeley, Calif.: Center for Environmental Structure, 1969.

Altman, I. *The environment and social behavior.* Monterey, Calif.: Brooks/Cole, 1975.

Altman, I., & Chemers, M. Cultural aspects of environment–behavior relationships. In H. Triandis (Ed.), *Handbook of cross-cultural psychology,* New York: Allyn & Bacon, 1979.

Altman, I., & Vinsel, A. Personal space: An analysis of E. T. Hall's proxemics framework. In I. Altman & J. F. Wohlwill (Eds.), *Human behavior and environment* (Vol. 2). New York: Plenum Press, 1977, pp. 181–259.

Altman, I., Nelson, P. A., & Lett, E. E. The ecology of home environments. *Catalog of selected documents in psychology.* Washington, D. C., American Psychological Association, Spring, 1972.

Anderson, E. N. Some Chinese methods of dealing with crowding. *Urban Anthropology,* 1972, *1,* 141–150.

Argyle, M., & Dean, J. Eye-contact, distance, and affiliation. *Sociometry,* 1965, *28,* 289–304.

Baldassare, M., & Feller, S. Cultural variations in personal space: Theory, methods and evidence. *Ethos,* 1975, *3,* 481–504.

Baron, R. M., Mandel, D. R., Adams, C. A., & Griffin, L. M. Effects of social density in university residential environments. *Journal of Personality and Social Psychology,* 1976, *34,* 434–446.

Bass, N., & Weinstein, M. Early development of interpersonal distance in children. *Canadian Journal of Behavior Science,* 1971, *3,* 368–372.

Bauer, E. Personal space: A study of blacks and whites. *Sociometry,* 1973, *36,* 402–408.

Baum, A., Aiello, J. R., & Calesnick, L. E. Crowding and personal control: Social density and the development of learned helplessness. *Journal of Personality and Social Psychology,* 1978, *36,* 1000–1011.

Baum, A., Davis, G. E., & Aiello, J. R. Crowding and neighborhood mediation of urban density. *Journal of Population,* 1978, *1,* 266–279.

Baum, A., & Vallins, S. *Architecture and social behavior: Psychological studies of social density.* Hillsdale, N. J.: Erlbaum, 1977.

Baxter, J. C. Interpersonal spacing in natural settings. *Sociometry,* 1970, *33,* 444–456.

Baxter, J. C., & Phelps, A. T. *Space utilization in pre-school children.* Unpublished manuscript, 1970.

Bell, P., Fisher, J. D., & Loomis, R. J. *Environmental psychology*. Philadelphia: Saunders, 1978.

Booth, A. *Crowding and social participation*. Unpublished manuscript, 1974.

Booth, A., & Cowell, J. *The effects of crowding upon health*. Unpublished manuscript, 1974.

Booth, A., & Edwards, J. N. Crowding and family relations. *American Sociological Review*, 1976, *41*, 308–321.

Booth, A., & Johnson, D. *The effect of crowding on child health and development*. Unpublished manuscript, 1974.

Booth, A., & Welch, S. *The effects of crowding: A cross-national study*. Unpublished manuscript, Ministry of State for Urban Affairs, Ottawa, Canada, 1973.

Booth, A., & Welch, S. *Crowding and urban crime rates*. Paper presented at the Meeting of the Midwest Sociological Association, Omaha, 1974.

Cade, T. M. A cross-cultural study of personal space in the family. *Dissertation Abstracts International*, 1972, *33*, 2759.

Campbell, D., Kruskal, W., & Wallace, W. Seating aggregation as an index of attitude. *Sociometry*, 1966, *29*, 1–15.

Canter, D., & Canter, S. Close together in Tokyo. *Design and Environment*, 1971, *2*, 60–63.

Carr, S. The city of the mind. In W. R. Ewald, Jr. (Ed.), *Environment for man: The next fifty years*. Bloomington: Indiana University Press, 1967, pp. 197–226.

Chombart de Lauwe, P. *Famille et habitation*. Paris: Editions du Centre National de la Recherche Scientifique, 1959. (Cited in E. T. Hall, *The hidden dimension*. New York: Doubleday, 1966. p. 172.)

Collett, D. Training Englishmen in the nonverbal behavior of Arabs. *International Journal of Psychology*, 1971, *6*, 209–215.

Connolly, P. R. An investigation of the perception of personal space and its meaning among black and white Americans. *Dissertation Abstracts International*, 1974, *34*, 4689.

Cook, M. Experiments on orientations and proxemics. *Human Relations*, 1970, *23*, 61–76.

Cooke, B. G. Nonverbal communication among Afro-Americans: An initial classification. In T. Kachman (Ed.), *Rappin' and stylin' out: Communication in urban black America*. Urbana: University of Illinois Press, 1972, pp. 32–64.

Cronjè, F. J., & Möller, A. T. Comparison of different procedures to assess personal space. *Perceptual and Motor Skills*, 1976, *43*, 959–962.

Davis, G. E. Designing for residential environments. In A. Baum and Y. M. Epstein (Eds.), *Human responses to crowding*. Hillsdale, N.J.: Erlbaum, 1978, pp. 353–369.

Day, A. T., & Day, L. H. Cross-cultural comparison of population density. *Science*, 1973, *181*, 1016–1023.

DeLong, A. J. The micro-spatial structure of the older person: Some implications of planning the social and spatial environment. In L. A. Pastalan & D. H. Carson (Eds.), *Spatial behavior of older people*. Ann Arbor: University of Michigan Press, 1970, pp. 68–87.

Deutsch, R. D. Personal space considered from an interactional point of view. Letter to the editor. *Man-Environment Systems*, 1975, *5*, 211.

Dixon, P. W., Roper, R. E., & Ahern, E. H. Comparison of rural and urban high school students in Japan using EPPS. *Psychologia*, 1975, *18*, 63–71.

Dooley, B. B. *Crowding stress: The effects on social density on men with close or far personal space*. Ph.D. dissertation, University of California, Los Angeles, 1974.

Dosey, M., & Meisels, M. Personal space and self protection. *Journal of Personality and Social Psychology*, 1969, *11*, 93–97.

Draper, P. Crowding among hunter–gatherers: The !Kung Bushmen. *Science*, 1973, *182*, 301–303.

Duke, M. P., & Nowicki, S. A new measure and social-learning model for interpersonal distance. *Journal of Experimental Research in Personality*, 1972, *6*, 119-132.

Edwards, D. J. A cross-cultural study of social orientation and distance schemata by its method of doll placement. *Journal of Social Psychology*, 1973, *89*, 165-173.

Efron, D. *Gesture and environment*. New York: Kings Crown Press, 1941.

Engelbretson, D. Relationship of perceived cultural influence to informally learned cultural behaviors, interaction distances among Sansei Japanese and Caucasians in Hawaii: A study of acculturation. *Psychologia*, 1972, *15*, 101-109.

Engelbretson, D., & Fullmer, D. Cross-cultural differences in territoriality: Interaction distances of native Japanese, Hawaii Japanese, and American Caucasians. *Journal of Cross-Cultural Psychology*, 1970, *1*, 261-269.

Fehr, B. J., & Exline, R. V. *Visual interaction in same and interracial dyads*. Paper presented at the meetings of the Eastern Psychological Association, Washington, D.C., 1978.

Ford, J. G., & Graves, J. R. Differences between Mexican-American and white children in interpersonal distance and social touching. *Perceptual and Motor Skills*, 1977, *45*, 779-785.

Forston, R. F., & Larson, C. U. The dynamics of space. *Journal of Communication*, 1968, *18*, 190-116.

Frankel, A. S., & Barrett, J. Variations in personal space as a function of authoritarianism, self-esteem, and racial characteristics of a stimulus situation. *Journal of Consulting and Clinical Psychology*, 1971, *37*, 95-98.

Freedman, J. L. *Crowding and behavior*. San Francisco: Freeman, 1975.

Fry, A. M., & Willis, F. N. Invasion of personal space as a function of the age of the invader. *Psychological Record*, 1971, *21*, 385-389.

Galle, O. R., & Gove, W. R. Crowding and behavior in Chicago, 1940-1970. In J. R. Aiello & A. Baum (Eds.), *Residential crowding and design*. New York: Plenum Press, 1979.

Galle, O. R., Gove, W. R., & McPherson, J. Population density and pathology: What are the relationships for man. *Science*, 1972, *176*, 23-30.

Glazer, N., & Moynihan, D. *Beyond the melting pot*. Cambridge: M.I.T. Press and Harvard University Press, 1963.

Goffman, E. *Relations in public*. New York: Basic Books, 1971.

Graubert, J. G., & Adler, L. L. Cross-national comparisons of projected social distances from mental patient related stimuli. *Perceptual & Motor Skills*, 1977, *44*, 881-882.

Guardo, C. Personal space in children. *Child Development*, 1969, *40*, 143-151.

Haase, R. F., & Markey, M. J. A methodological note on the study of personal space. *Journal of Consulting and Clinical Psychology*, 1973, *40*, 122-125.

Hall, E. T. The language of space. *Landscape*, Autumn, 1960, 41-45.

Hall, E. T. A system for the notation of proxemic behavior. *American Anthropologist*, 1963, *65*, 1003-1026.

Hall, E. T. *The hidden dimension*. New York: Doubleday, 1966.

Hall, E. T. *Handbook of proxemics research*. Washington, D.C.: Society for the Anthropology of Visual Communication, 1974.

Harvey, J. H., Ickes, W. J., & Kidd, R. F. *New directions in attribution research* (Vols. 1-2). Hillsdale, N.J.: Erlbaum, 1976, 1978.

Hendricks, M., & Bootzin, R. Race and sex as stimuli for negative affect and physical avoidance. *Journal of Social Psychology*, 1976, *98*, 111-120.

Holahan, C. J., & Wilcox, B. L. Environmental satisfaction in high- and low-rise residential settings: A Lewinian perspective. In J. R. Aiello & A. Baum (Eds.), *Residential crowding and design*. New York: Plenum Press, 1979.

Hollingshead, A. B., & Redlich, F. C. *Social class and mental illness*. New York: Wiley, 1958.

Ittelson, W. H. Environment perception and contemporary perceptual theory. In W. H. Ittelson (Ed.), *Environment and cognition*. New York: Seminar Press, 1973, pp. 1–19.

Iwata, O. Factors in the perception of crowding. *Japanese Psychological Research*, 1974a, *16*, 65–70.

Iwata, O. Empirical examination of the perception of density and crowding. *Japanese Psychological Research*, 1974b, *16*, 117–125.

Iwata, O. A comparative study on the perception of crowding. *Bulletin of Shikoku Women's University*, 1974c, *16*, 25–34.

Iwata, O. Effect of bystander population density upon altruistic behavior. *Journal of Gakigei Tokushima University* (Educational Science), 1976, *25*, 7–12.

Iwata, O. Factors in the perception of crowding and the relationship of crowding to personal space. *Psychologia*, 1977, *20*, 33–37.

Johnson, K. R. Black kinesics: Some non-verbal communication patterns in the black culture. In L. A. Samovar & R. E. Porter (Eds.), *Intercultural communication: A reader*. Belmont, Calif.: Wadsworth, 1972, pp. 181–189.

Johnson, R. J., Booth, A., & Duvall, D. *Social determinants of human crowding*. Unpublished manuscript, 1974.

Jones, S. E. A comparative proxemics analysis of dyadic interaction in selected subcultures in New York City. *Journal of Social Psychology*, 1971, *84*, 35–44.

Jones, S. E., & Aiello, J. R. Proxemic behavior of black and white first, third, and fifth grade children. *Journal of Personality and Social Psychology*, 1973, *25*, 21–27.

Jourard, S. M. An exploratory study of body-accessibility. *British Journal of Social and Clinical Psychology*, 1966, *5*, 221–231.

Karlin, R. A., Epstein, Y. M., & Aiello, J. R. A setting specific analysis of crowding. In A. Baum & Y. M. Epstein (Eds.), *Human responses to crowding*. Hillsdale, N.J.: Erlbaum, 1978, pp. 165–179.

Kendon, A. *Studies in the behavior of social interaction*. New York: Humanities Press, 1977.

Kira, A. *The bathroom*. Ithaca, N.Y.: Cornell University Center for Housing and Environmental Studies, 1966.

Knowles, E. S. An affiliative conflict theory of personal and group spatial behavior. In P. B. Paulus (Ed.), *Psychology of group influence*. Hillsdale, N.J.: Erlbaum, 1979.

Knowles, E. S., & Johnsen, P. K. Intrapersonal consistency in interpersonal distance. *Journal Supplement Abstract Service Catalog of Selected Documents in Psychology*, 1974, *4*, 124.

Kuethe, J. L. Social schemas. *Journal of Abnormal and Social Psychology*, 1962, *64*, 31–38.

LaFrance, M., & Mayo, C. *Gaze direction in interracial dyadic communication*. Paper presented at the meetings of the Eastern Psychological Association, Washington, D.C., 1973.

Lantz, H. R. Population density and psychiatric diagnosis. *Sociology and Social Research*, 1953, *37*, 322–326.

Leibman, M. The effects of sex and race norms on personal space. *Environment and Behavior*, 1970, *2*, 208–246.

Lerner, R. N., Iwawaki, S., & Chihara, T. Development of personal space schemata among Japanese children. *Developmental Psychology*, 1976, *12*, 466–467.

Levy, L., & Herzog, A. N. Effects of population density and crowding on health and social adaptation in the Netherlands. *Journal of Health and Social Behavior*, 1974, *15*, 228–240.

Lewis, O. *The children of Sanchez*. New York: Random House, 1961.

Little, K. B. Personal space. *Journal of Experimental Social Psychology*, 1965, *1*, 237–247.

Little, K. B. Cultural variations in social schemata. *Journal of Personality and Social Psychology*, 1968, *10*, 1–7.

Lo, W. H. Urbanization and psychiatric disorders: The Hong Kong scene. *Acta Psychiatrica Scandinavia*, 1976, *54*, 174–183.

Lomranz, J. Cultural variations in personal space. *Journal of Social Psychology*, 1976, *99*, 21–27.

Lomranz, J., Shapira, A., Choresh, N., & Gilat, Y. Children's personal space as a function of age and sex. *Developmental Psychology*, 1975, *11*, 541–545.

Lottier, S. Distribution of criminal offenses in metropolitan regions. *Journal of Criminal Law and Criminology*, 1938, *29*, 39–45.

Love, K. D., & Aiello, J. R. *Relationship between observed interaction distance and projective distance measures.* Paper presented at the meetings of the American Psychological Association, Washington, D.C., 1976.

Marsella, A. J., Escudero, M., & Gordon, P. The effects of dwelling density on mental disorders in Filipino men. *Journal of Health and Social Behavior*, 1971, *11*, 288–294.

Mazur, A. Interpersonal spacing on public benches in "contact" and "noncontact" cultures. *Journal of Social Psychology*, 1977, *101*, 53–58.

McCarthy, D., & Saegert, S. Residential density, social overload, and social withdrawal. In J. R. Aiello & A. Baum (Eds.), *Residential crowding and design.* New York: Plenum Press, 1979.

McKinzie, R., & Hillabrant, W. *The effects of gaze direction and interpersonal distance on impression formation in dyadic interaction.* Paper presented at the meetings of the Eastern Psychological Association, Washington, D.C., 1978.

Meisels, M., & Guardo, C. Development of personal space schemata. *Child Development*, 1969, *40*, 1167.

Michelson, W. *Man and his urban environment: A sociological approach.* Reading, Mass.: Addison–Wesley, 1970.

Mitchell, R. E. Some social implications of high density housing. *American Sociological Review*, 1971, *36*, 18–29.

Montagu, A. *Touching: The human significance of the skin.* New York: Columbia University Press, 1971.

Munroe, R. H., & Munroe, R. L. Population density and movement in folktales. *Journal of Social Psychology*, 1973, *9*, 339–340.

Munroe, R. L., & Munroe, R. H. Population density and affective relationships in three East African societies. *Journal of Social Psychology*, 1972, *88*, 15–20.

Newman, O. *Defensible space.* New York: Macmillan, 1972.

Nicosia, G., Hymen, D., Karlin, R. A., Epstein, Y. M., & Aiello, J. R. Effects of bodily contact on reactions to crowding. *Journal of Applied Social Psychology*, 1979.

Noesjirwan, J. Contrasting cultural patterns of interpersonal closeness in doctors' waiting rooms in Sidney and Jakarta. *Journal of Cross-Cultural Psychology*, 1977, *8*, 357–368.

Pagan, G., Jr., & Aiello, J. R. *Development of personal space among Puerto Ricans.* Unpublished manuscript, Rutgers—The State University, 1979.

Patterson, M. L. Compensation in nonverbal immediacy behaviors: A review. *Sociometry*, 1973, *36*, 237–252.

Patterson, M. L. Personal space—Time to burst the bubble? *Man-Environment Systems*, 1975, *5*, 67.

Pederson, D. M. Developmental trends in personal space. *Journal of Psychology*, 1973, *83*, 3–9.

Petri, H. L., & Huggins, R. G. *Some developmental characteristics of personal space.* Paper presented at the meetings of the Eastern Psychological Association, New York City, 1975.

Pollock, H. M., & Furbush, A. M. Mental disease in 12 states, 1919. *Mental Hygiene*, 1921, *5*, 353–389.

Rawls, J., Trego, R., & McGaffey, C. *A comparison of personal space measures and correlates of personal space*. Institute of Behavioral Research, Texas Christian University, 1968, NASA Grant Report.

Rawls, J. R., Trego, R. E., McGaffey, C. N., & Rawls, D. J. Personal space as a predictor of performance under close working conditions. *Journal of Social Psychology*, 1972, *86*, 261–267.

Roberts, J. M., & Gregor, T. Privacy: A cultural view. In J. R. Pennock & J. W. Chapman (Eds.), *Privacy*. New York: Atherton Press, 1971, pp. 189–225.

Rodin, J. Crowding, perceived choice, and response to controllable and uncontrollable outcomes. *Journal of Experimental Social Psychology*, 1976, *12*, 564–578.

Roger, D. B., & Mjali, Q. T. Personal space and acculturation. *Journal of Social Psychology*, 1976, *100*, 3–10.

Rogler, L. H. Slum neighborhoods in Latin America. *Journal of Inter-American Studies*, 1967, *9*, 507–528.

Rosegrant, T. S., & McCroskey, J. C. The effects of race and sex on proxemic behavior in an interview setting. *The Southern Speech Communication Journal*, 1975, *40*, 408–420.

Scheflen, A. E. *Human territories: How we behave in space-time*. Englewood Cliffs, N.J.: Prentice-Hall, 1976.

Scherer, S. E. Proxemic behavior of primary school children as a function of their socioeconomic class and subculture. *Journal of Personality and Social Psychology*, 1974, *29*, 800–805.

Schmidt, D. E., Goldman, R. D., & Feimer, N. R. Physical and psychological factors associated with perceptions of crowding: An analysis of subcultural differences. *Journal of Applied Psychology*, 1976, *61*, 279–289.

Schmitt, R. C. Density, delinquency, and crime in Honolulu. *Sociology and Social Research*, 1957, *41*, 274–276.

Schmitt, R. C. Implications of density in Hong Kong. *American Institute of Planners Journal*, 1963, *29*, 210–217.

Schmitt, R. C. Density, health, and social disorganization. *American Institute of Planners Journal*, 1966, *32*, 38–40.

Schneider, F. W. Conforming behavior of black and white children. *Journal of Personality and Social Psychology*, 1970, *16*, 446–471.

Schofield, J. W., & Sagar, H. A. Peer interaction patterns in an integrated middle school. *Sociometry*, 1977, *40*, 130–138.

Schwartz, B. The social psychology of privacy. *American Journal of Sociology*, 1968, *73*, 741–752.

Singer, J. E., Lundberg, U., & Frankenhaeuser, M. Stress on the train: A study of urban commuting. In A. Baum, S. Valins, & J. Singer (Eds.), *Advances in environmental psychology* (Vol. 1). Hillsdale, N.J.: Erlbaum, 1978, pp. 41–56.

Sommer, R. Further studies of small group ecology. *Sociometry*, 1965, *28*, 337–348.

Sommer, R. Intimacy ratings in five countries. *International Journal of Psychology*, 1968, *3*, 109–114.

Sommer, R. *Personal space*. Englewood Cliffs, N.J.: Prentice-Hall, 1969.

Sommer, R. *Tight spaces: Hard architecture and how to humanize it*. Englewood Cliffs, N.J.: Prentice-Hall, 1974.

Stokols, D. On the distinction between density and crowding: Some implications for future research. *Psychological Review*, 1972, *79*, 275–277.

Sundstrom, E. Crowding as a sequential process: Review of research on the effects of population density on humans. In A. Baum & Y. M. Epstein (Eds.), *Human responses to crowding.* Hillsdale, N.J.: Erlbaum, 1978, pp. 31–116.

Tennis, G. H., & Dabbs, J. M. Sex, setting, and personal space: First grade through college. *Sociometry,* 1975, *38,* 385–394.

Tennis, G. H., & Dabbs, J. M. Race, setting, and actor-target differences in personal space. *Social Behavior and Personality,* 1976, *4,* 49–55.

Thayer, S., & Alban, L. A field experiment on the effect of political and cultural factors on the use of personal space. *Journal of Social Psychology,* 1972, *88,* 267–272.

Thompson, D. J., & Baxter, J. C. *Interpersonal spacing in two-person cross-cultural interactions.* Unpublished manuscript, University of Houston, 1970.

Thrasher, F. M. *The gang.* Chicago: University of Chicago Press, 1936.

Tolor, A. Psychological distance in disturbed and normal children. *Psychological Reports,* 1968, *23,* 695–701.

Tolor, A., & Orange, S. An attempt to measure psychological distance in advantaged and disadvantaged children. *Child Development,* 1969, *40,* 407–420.

Watson, O. *Proxemic behavior: A cross-cultural study.* The Hague and Paris: Mouton, 1970.

Watson, O., & Graves, T. D. Quantitative research in proxemic behavior. *American Anthropologist,* 1966, *68,* 971–985.

Watts, R. E. Influence of population density on crime. *Journal of American Statistical Association,* 1931, *26,* 11–21.

Westin, A. *Privacy and freedom.* New York: Atheneum, 1970.

Willis, F. N. Initial speaking distance as a function of the speaker's relationship. *Psychonomic Science,* 1966, *5,* 221–222.

Wohlwill, J. F. The emerging discipline of environmental psychology. *American Psychologist,* 1970, *25,* 303–312.

Zeisel, J. Symbolic meaning of space and the physical dimension of social relations: A case study of sociological research as the basis of architectural planning. In J. Walton & D. Carns (Eds.), *Cities in change: Studies on the urban condition.* Boston: Allyn & Bacon, 1973, pp. 252–263.

Zeisel, J., & Griffen, M. *Charlesview housing: A diagnostic evaluation.* Cambridge, Mass.: Architecture Research Office Graduate School of Design, 1975.

Zimmerman, B. J., & Brody, G. H. Race and modeling influences on the interpersonal play patterns of boys. *Journal of Educational Psychology,* 1975, *67,* 591–598.

Zorbaugh, H. W. *The gold coast and the slum.* Chicago: University of Chicago Press, 1929.

5

Territory in Urban Settings

SIDNEY N. BROWER

INTRODUCTION

In any occupied place, separate spaces serve as cues for separate behavioral performances. We distinguish between spaces where one can
walk around in one's undershirt, and others where formal dress is required. We distinguish between spaces where one enters as a right,
others where one requests entry, and still others where one enters only
if invited to do so. Some spaces are meant to be seen and are regularly
cleaned and decorated, others are treated as if they are invisible and are
used to store surplus and waste. Just to be seen in some spaces can be an
honor, in others it can mean instant disgrace. To be removed from some
spaces can be a blessing, from others a cause for grief. While the degree
of spatial division and differentiation is more complex and sophisticated
in some settlements than in others, the use of space to guide behavior is
as characteristic of a village as it is of a city. It is so pervasive that some
believe it to be deeply rooted in man's biological and psychological
makeup. This paper is concerned with a particular aspect of spatial
behavior, known as territoriality. After defining the nature and purpose
of territoriality, a model will be used to show how certain features of the
physical environment, in the context of certain social relationships, are
associated with certain types of territorial behavior.

The word "territoriality" was first used in connection with spatial
behavior in birds, and subsequently in fish, rodents, deer, and primates.
It referred particularly to the act of laying claim to a geographic area,

---

SIDNEY N. BROWER • Planning Commission, Department of Planning, City of Baltimore, 222 East Saratoga Street, Baltimore, Maryland 21202.

marking it for identification, and defending it when necessary against others of the same kind. Territorial behavior was usually associated with mating, safeguarding the nest, and protecting the food supply, functions that are basic to the survival of the organism and the perpetuation of the species. Frustrating natural territorial tendencies, by overcrowding, for example, could lead to disruption of the natural social order.

Territorial behavior in man is far more varied, less consistent, and less predictable than it is in animals. This is due in no small part to the fact that human behavior is modified by cultural training to such an extent that territorial forms may be used to achieve purely symbolic purposes. The Code of Jewish Law (Ganzfried, 1927), for example, recognizes four classes of territory with regard to the observance of Sabbath laws: private territory, public territory, territory which is neither public nor private, and territory which is exempt. There are very precise prohibitions against transporting any articles (other than necessary items of clothing and specified adornments) from one territory to another on the Sabbath. It is possible, however, by means of an "eruv" (a symbolic act by which the legal fiction of a community is established), to extend that which is permitted from one domain into another, and an eruv can be created around an entire settled district by means of a continuous wall made up of solid partitions and a series of symbolic doors. These doors may consist of posts connected by poles or wires whose heights, widths, and methods of attachment conform to certain specifications. Such a wall has been constructed in Baltimore. According to *The Baltimore Sun* newspaper (June 8, 1978), it is 16 miles long and consists of an unbroken chain of fences and telephone wires, linked with stretches of fish line and wire, and surrounding the entire northwest quadrant of the city. Every Friday the entire wall is checked for breaks. If breaks cannot be repaired in time, special radio alerts are broadcast, warning orthodox Jews that they may not carry outside the borders of their homes.

The variety and complexity of human behavior makes classification difficult. One does not find the consistency of form and pattern that delimits the concept of territoriality in animals. In the absence of a commonly agreed upon definition of human territoriality, we will define it as the relationship between an individual or group and a particular physical setting, that is characterized by a feeling of possessiveness, and by attempts to control the appearance and use of the space.

The concept of territoriality should be distinguished from other spatial concepts, such as personal space, jurisdiction, and home range. *Personal space* refers to the mechanism for achieving a desirable spacing between one person and another, that which is appropriate being estab-.

lished by cultural norms and by the intimacy of the relationship. An American in a Latin country, for example, is inclined to feel that people in conversation stand uncomfortably close to one another, while he himself will tend to stand closer to his wife than to his boss. Personal space can be compared to a bubble that surrounds an individual and moves with him as he moves from place to place. Unlike territoriality, it is not tied to a particular geographic location. Jurisdiction and home range, on the other hand, are both concepts that are tied to particular geographic locations. *Jurisdiction* refers to the temporary control of a space where the origin and limits of authority are role-related. An actor, for example, may have jurisdiction over the stage during a performance, but jurisdiction may shift to the stage manager during the intermission, and to the security guard after the show. The concept of jurisdiction is, then, more limited than that of territoriality. *Home range* refers to the network of spaces that a person uses regularly. These are spaces that one is familiar with and feels at home in. The home range of some people is very small. Children, for example, may be limited to the spaces in and around the house or the neighborhood. The home range of other people may extend to include spaces in other parts of the city or of the world. Unlike territoriality, home range does not imply the active control of space.

A MODEL OF TERRITORIAL BEHAVIOR

Although human territorial behavior cannot be said to be directly tied to survival as it is in animals, the fact that it is so widespread suggests that it must serve an elemental purpose. It is generally agreed that its purpose is to regulate social interaction (Altman, 1975). Spatial separation makes it possible to create different settings for different uses, and so to reduce opportunities for conflict. Compare, for example, the activities and behaviors suitable at a religious service with those suitable at a ball game. Place-differentiation makes it possible to create separate stages for separate social roles. A setting can indicate whether one's host is to be addressed as "Sir," "Mr. Jones," "Jack," or "Darling." Territorial control makes it possible to achieve different degrees of privacy and intimacy, from high in a bedroom to low at a rock concert. In this way, territorial behavior narrows the range of encounters in various spaces, in order to create predictable environments with an accompanying sense of order and security.

Territoriality is not the sole mechanism for regulating social interaction. Interactions can also be controlled by introducing protocol and ritual. In Samoa, for example, it is not uncommon for people to achieve privacy by going into a trance (Rapoport, 1977, p. 341). Yagua Indians achieve similar results by turning away from the center of a room (Rapoport, 1977, p. 201). The English use a number of subtle hints to discourage interaction among strangers, to indicate that they do not want to be disturbed, and to terminate conversation (Hall, 1966, p. 131). In Rhodesia, families of black servants live in huts within white residential areas, and yet, because of the highly structured society, the two groups achieve almost complete social separation. Rules and customs can then serve the same purpose as—and, therefore, provide an alternative to—spatial separation. A culture that relies heavily upon rules and customs to regulate social interaction will depend that much less on territorial behavior. Whatever the balance, the combined effect of both rules and customs and territorial behavior is to mitigate the threat (real or imagined) of unregulated interaction. This threat may be directed to personal security (interactions that lead to conflict), to self-esteem (interactions that involve a loss of face or status), or to self-identity (interactions that involve challenge to one's values or life-style). The greater the threat (that is to say, the greater the need to regulate unpredictable or unwanted interactions), the stronger will be the tendency toward territorial behavior. As the threat diminishes, territorial behavior becomes more relaxed. This relationship between territorial behavior and threat is supported by the findings of a study by Altman, Taylor, and Wheeler (1971), in which pairs of men were shut up in isolated quarters for an extended period of time, and a number of aspects of their behavior, including territorial behavior, were observed. It was found that, as anxiety, stress, and nervousness increased, there was an increased tendency for individuals to become territorial with respect to their own beds, chairs, and spaces at the table. On the other hand, as levels of stress and anxiety decreased, territorial behavior became less evident.

This model of territoriality is represented in Figure 1.

The model represents territorial behavior as one of two interacting forces, one spatial and the other nonspatial, both guarding against the threat of unregulated interaction. (As detailed analysis of the nonspatial element is beyond the scope of this paper, we will assume in the following discussion that rules and customs generally remain constant, and that any change in threat must be balanced by change in territorial behavior alone.) If the protection is inadequate, there is an imbalance in the system. An imbalance is associated with increased aggression and mental anguish, and with disruption of social order. It also has direct implications for the entire system of land management, because territoriality insures that parcels of land are divided among many individuals

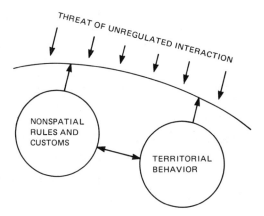

Figure 1.   Model of territorial behavior.

and groups, who accept responsibility, not only for their control, but also for their maintenance. The importance of this function is easily overlooked, but it becomes apparent when the system breaks down. This was illustrated in a study of small parks in an inner-city neighborhood in Baltimore (Brower & Williamson, 1974). These parks were designed to serve the recreational needs of local residents, and the city, with a tight operating budget, expected that local residents would play a major management role. However, the residents, divided among themselves and greatly afraid of the crime and violence that were prevalent in their community, did not assume a territorial attitude towards the parks. They saw them as city property, and when city management proved to be inadequate, many residents simply stopped recreating there. The parks became, in essence, a no-man's-land. They were used as a hangout by antisocial and fringe groups, and became a dumping ground for trash and garbage.

The concept of territoriality deals, then, with behavior that directly affects the security and maintenance of the physical environment. Because of this, it has much to offer city planners and urban designers, who are increasingly being faced with the dilemma of having their carefully designed spaces rendered virtually unusable because users apparently do nothing to protect them or care for them. In discussing the model of territorial behavior, especial emphasis will be placed upon its application to this particular problem.

Figure 2 shows a development of the model in which territorial behavior is divided into a number of component parts. The act of exercising control over a particular physical setting is referred to as the *appro-*

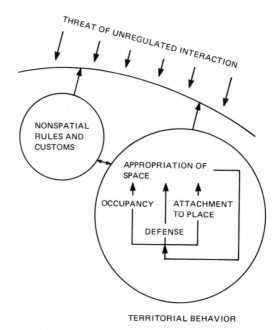

Figure 2.   Expanded model of territorial behavior.

priation of space. [1] There are three elements that contribute to appropriation: occupancy, defense, and attachment.

OCCUPANCY OF SPACE

Appropriation of space will be affected by the ability of an individual or group to establish a suitable type of occupancy. The typology of occupancy that will be presented here is an elaboration of one that was first used in a discussion of territorial signs (Brower, 1965). Other typologies have been proposed by other writers, but they derive in the main from sociological concepts, and do not suit the practical needs and the information resources of planners and urban designers. Altman (1975), for example, whose three-part typology has many points of similarity with the one discussed here, suggests a classification of primary, secondary, and public territories. Primary territories are those where one spends most of one's time and interacts with one's primary refer-

[1]For a broad development of this theme, see *Appropriation of Space,* Proceedings of the Third International Architectural Psychology Conference, Strasbourg, 1976. Brussels: Neuf, 1978.

ence group; secondary territories are those where one spends less time and interacts with one's secondary reference group, and public territories are those where one spends least time and interacts mainly with strangers. The major dimensions of this typology are centrality (the importance of the territory to the everyday life of a person or group), and the duration of use. This means that, in order to classify a space, an assessment must be made of the significance or quality of the interaction that takes place there. Such an assessment cannot be made by planners or urban designers. The four-fold typology presented here, by contrast, uses as a major dimension the controls that operate in a space. These are generally expressed in visual motifs and physical arrangements, such as boundary definitions and entrances, or in visible expressions of use, such as maintenance, embellishment, intensity of use, and activity of users.

Before discussing the occupancy types, it is necessary to define a number of terms. An attempt on the part of an individual or group to appropriate a space will be referred to as a *territorial claim*. The presence of a territorial claim will be referred to as an *occupancy*, and the claimant will be referred to as an *occupant*. Occupancy is usually accompanied by a display of *territorial signs*, which are objects associated with the occupancy (such as walls, hedges, fences, doors, flower boxes, name plates), and announce the existence, nature and extent of the territorial claim. Although signs are usually thought of as objects that are present, they are also found in the conspicuous absence of objects (such as dust, litter, and weeds) that one normally expects to find in the absence of a territorial claim. There are four types of occupancy, each one associated with a particular range of controls, a particular kind of occupant, and distinctive territorial signs that serve as cues for behavior. These occupancy types are: personal occupancy, community occupancy, occupancy by society, and free occupancy.

Personal Occupancy

Personal occupancy territories are controlled by individuals and groups whose members have clear and lasting relationships, and whose primary ties and loyalties are to one another. The most common examples are groups in which members are bound by marriage or blood relationship. The restrictive qualifications for personal occupancy are illustrated by a U. S. Supreme Court judgment that unrelated individuals may not occupy a house in a single family zoning district. The single-family house, and within the house the private bedroom, are the most common prototypes of personal occupancies.

Territories in personal occupancy are accorded the greatest freedom of any occupancy type to restrict admission and to control use. Regulations will be accepted even if they appear to be selfish, whimsical, or illogical, and without demanding justification, consistency, or advance notice, as long as they are not unduly antisocial. The rights of occupants are strongly supported by law, as demonstrated by the U. S. Supreme Court decision that government may prohibit the broadcasting of offensive words, because they could constitute an unwanted invasion of the home.

The signs of personal occupancy have private rather than general significance, and are strongest if they are directly associated with the identity of the occupants themselves, such as their visible presence, family photographs, diplomas. Personal occupancies seldom cater to the convenience of strangers, but they are usually very solicitous of guests.

Community Occupancy

Community-occupancy territories are controlled by groups whose composition may change, but whose members have undergone a common screening process, and, frequently, initiation rites. These serve to establish a clear and consistent distinction between group members and "outsiders." Claims of community occupancy are generally made by club members, church congregations, school faculty and student bodies, office co-workers, etc. Eligibility as a member of a community occupancy may depend upon sharing a physical setting (a neighborhood group), a system of values or beliefs (a church group), a climate of benefit and risk (a university group), or, as is frequently the case, upon a combination of these things. The organization of a group may be based largely on informal understandings, but a structured relationship will be more effective in dealing with outsiders.

Territories in community occupancy are allowed less freedom than those in personal occupancy. While a wide range of restrictions and controls are acceptable, they must fall clearly within the framework of the community purpose, and must conform to the common practices and established traditions of the larger society.

The signs of community occupancy derive from the practical and symbolic needs of its members. They frequently have strong esoteric overtones (for example, signs, badges, logos) that serve to impress upon outsiders the exclusionary nature of the occupancy.

Occupancy by Society

Territories occupied by society are controlled by the general public, and are open as a right to all. They may include some publicly owned places (a street), but not others (the mayor's office), and they may include many places that are not publicly owned (a movie theater, or a waiting room at the bus terminal).

Territories occupied by society are accorded less freedom to restrict admission and control use than either personal or community occupancies. They do not, however, have to be equally accessible to all members of the public, so long as the restrictions conform to the prevailing customs of the particular society. In this way, there may be differences based upon sex (as in many Eastern countries, where women, but not men, have to be veiled in public places), age (as in Baltimore, where unattended minors may not be in public places between 11 P.M. and 6 A.M. on weekdays), or race (as in South Africa, where separate public spaces are provided for different racial groups). Both the nature of controls and the measures for the enforcement of controls will vary from one society to another. Enforcement is frequently entrusted to officials who wear uniforms or badges.

The signs used to identify occupancy by society are explicit, clear, legible, and standardized. They are designed to serve as guides for the uninitiated.

Free Occupancy

Free-occupancy territories have no permanent occupants, and are subject to the rules and restrictions of no particular person or group. The rules that guide behavior are self-imposed, or else attributed to supernatural forces or to "common decency." Free-occupancy territories are characterized by the absence of territorial signs, and for this reason they invite exploration and excite the imagination. They can be exhilarating. They can also be terrifying. Deserted beaches and wilderness areas are generally examples of this type of occupancy.

In urban areas, all spaces are assigned. While some spaces may assume the character of free occupancy, it is usually for a limited time period (during a festival, for example), or because people ignore the controlling signs (in the case of squatters). These are not true examples of free occupancy, but indicative rather of relaxed or ineffective territorial control.

Use of the Typology

Each occupancy type has three basic elements: a range of control over the use of space, a person or group who wants to appropriate the space, and a display of signs announcing the appropriation. If one or more of these elements is absent or ineffective, territorial capability is diminished. Occupancy types are not intended as categories for the general classification of physical settings. Any place—a house, a cave, or a railway station—can be, say, a personal occupancy, if it satisfies the appropriate criteria. A common set of cultural norms may ensure that most caves are seen as free territory and most railway stations are seen as occupancies by society, but a different culture may produce quite a different classification of settings. In the United States, for example, hotels are generally classified as occupancies by society, because they are places where all visitors, whether they are strangers or regular guests, can expect to receive equal and impersonal treatment. In Japan, on the other hand, hotels tend to be community occupancies, where an occasional guest can expect to be inconvenienced if this should be necessary to satisfy members of the hotel's regular "family" (Hall, 1977). In the same way, we feel that strangers in town have as much right as we do to walk the public streets, but this is not a universal view. Visitors to the camp of Australian aborigines, for example, were required to recognize certain forms and ceremonies. These might have included a formal announcement (to show that there were no secret intentions), handing out credentials, receiving an invitation to enter, and engaging in certain welcoming gestures (Wheeler, 1910). The camp was clearly seen as a community occupancy, and not as an occupancy by society. Even within a single culture, there will be instances where a physical setting will appear in an unusual form of occupancy. In an army camp, for example, one's home can be a community occupancy; and there are communities where the public sidewalk serves as an extension of home, and is treated much like a personal occupancy.

The form of occupancy in any one setting may fluctuate over time. Sometimes a single space will be appropriated by several different people or groups at the same time, creating a potentially volatile situation. Such was the case in Delhi, India, in the mid-1970s, when the municipal government undertook to clear the streets of hawkers and the sidewalks of unauthorized structures and store displays. The brutal manner in which this was accomplished serves as a reminder that interactions associated with territorial behavior are as capable of excesses as the behaviors they seek to regulate. In New York, a case was reported ("Man, 30, Is Arrested," 1978) in which three men attacked a pair of paddle-ball players in a crowded park in Lower Manhattan, killing one and injuring the other, because they "didn't like the fact that two guys from outside the neighborhood were playing in the park."

Nor is a single physical element always a sign of the same type of occupancy. A fence may be used to keep people out of a space, and so create an area of seclusion (in the case of a private garden), but the same fence can equally well be used to contain people within a space, and so reinforce the sense of community (in the case of a day care center). A family photograph may signify personal occupancy in a living room, but in a restaurant it simply means that a customer will receive a level of personal attention that is usually reserved for a guest in a private house (a claim that may well prove to be false). In this way, territorial associations enter into our visual language, and are used to express design intent (family photographs at Jack's Place, signed team pictures at the Ball and Bat Grill, painted portraits of the presidents in the Congressional Restaurant).

Signs associated with occupancy can do more than announce the existence of territorial claims; they can also be seen as visible evidence of caring. They can represent a feeling of attachment between the occupant and the physical setting, and as such they will be felt to add "warmth" or "intimacy" to a setting, which, in the absence of such signs, would be too "monumental" or "sterile" or "inhuman." This response to objects associated with occupancy is fully recognized by urban designers. Cullen (1961) shows how designers can use "the furniture of possession" to accentuate the impression of occupancy. He writes: "Although the amount of possession is small, yet its perpetuation in the furniture gives the town humanity and intricacy in just the same way that louvres on windows give texture and scale to a building even when the sun is not shining" (Cullen, 1961, p. 23). This use of territorial signs may be convincing, but it is important for designers to recognize that they are only convincing as long as they are supported by evidence of continuing use and care. Seats must be used, flowerbeds must be watered, grass cut, paving repaired. It is not enough to introduce "furniture of possession" in the absence of conditions in which appropriation will take place and a suitable occupancy will be established.

The four types of occupancy are, of course, points on a continuous scale of social regulation that runs from strict control to no control. The location of these points on a scale may vary between one culture and another and, within a single culture, between the life-style of one group and that of another. Figure 3 illustrates this point.

Line A on Figure 3 represents a suburban neighborhood similar, say, to Whyte's Park Forest (Whyte, 1956), where the population is highly conforming, and where residents are in and out of one another's houses in a casual and informal way, but where outsiders are viewed with suspicion. Because there are virtually no territories that are completely open to those who live outside the community, and none that are completely closed to community members, the total range of controls is relatively small, and both personal occupancy and occupancy by society verge on community occupancy.

Line B in Figure 3 represents a cosmopolitan urban neighborhood

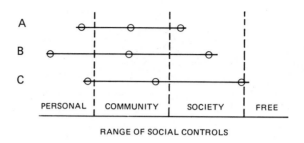

Figure 3.   The range of occupancy types varies with life-style.

similar to, say, the Georgetown area in Washington, D. C., where the privacy of the house and yard is absolute and closely guarded, and where the commercial area caters primarily to tourists. In this example, the range of controls extends from rigid exclusiveness in the home, through cautious parochialism in the local churches, schools, and play-grounds, to cosmopolitan openness in the shopping streets.

Line C on Figure 3 represents a typical inner city neighborhood, where a great deal of family life happens out on the sidewalk, where living room windows open onto the street, where everyone knows everyone else's business, and where public spaces are so lightly con-trolled that they verge on free territory. Here there are virtually no territories that are highly exclusive, few local facilities that are not also used by "outsiders" from another neighborhood, and many public spaces that are virtually free of controls. While the range of controls is wide, each occupancy verges on the low-intimacy end of the scale.

DEFENSE OF SPACE

As threat or the perception of threat increases, territorial behavior tends to become more defensive. Defense may take various forms: in-creased surveillance, clearer delineation of boundaries, erection of bar-riers, tightening of rules governing admission and use, more blatant display of territorial signs. There are several different ways of handling increased threat. One is to defend all claims more aggressively (see Figure 4A). Another is to shrink the boundaries of one's claims, falling back to the territories that are most defensible—much like retreating to one's bedroom to avoid having to face unwelcome guests in the living room (see Figure 4B). Yet another strategy is to renounce, or at least not to press, one's claims to ineffective types of occupancy (for example, resigning oneself to the litter in one's neighborhood, while remaining particular about the cleanliness of one's apartment). The last two strategies may well result in the abandonment of territorial claims in some spaces, leaving them undefended and effectively unappropriated. The readiness with which a physical space lends itself to territorial defense will have an effect on the chances that it will be appropriated. An understanding of the relationship between defensible space and appropriation is especially important in urban areas, where all spaces are essentially man-made, and many of their physical characteristics are affected through public policy.

Oscar Newman (1972), following up on early propositions by Jane Jacobs (1961), and using the premise that defensive behavior associated with appropriation of space will not only increase the occupant's feeling of security, but will also discourage criminal activity, has developed a set of criteria for the design of defensible spaces. He has argued that a space will be defended if it has clearly defined geographic boundaries, and if it provides good opportunities for surveillance. Other writers have criticized this concept, pointing out that designing a space to be defensible would not necessarily make people more defensive of it (Taylor, Gottfredson, & Brower, 1978). There are also examples of defensive behavior occurring in spaces that violate Newman's defensible space criteria (Banham, 1974). The viewpoint that is presented in this paper, and incorporated into the model, is that improvements in site design that make a space more defensible will increase the likelihood of appropriation, but only to the extent that suitable occupancy conditions exist (space that is well suited for community occupancy may not be easily defended as a personal occupancy, and it will not be appropriated at all in the absence of a community), and that occupants have a feeling of attachment for the place. (Occupants will not be strongly driven to defend a space, no matter how defensible the design, if the space is inconvenient, or unpleasant, or without personal or social significance.)

In order to increase the likelihood that the space they design will be

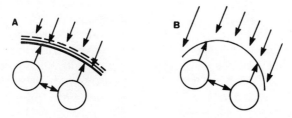

Figure 4.   Alternative strategies for dealing with increased threat. A: More aggressive defense. B: Fallback to more defensible position

appropriated by their users, designers must go beyond the concept of defensible space. It may be necessary, for example, to design spaces with a view toward strengthening the management capability of a particular occupancy type, or of developing a greater sense of attachment between the space and its occupants. In this way, a design objective for community spaces might well be to encourage collective effort and to foster group identity. The solution may include involving the users in the design and management of the facility, making the settings malleable and adaptable to local conditions, encouraging the display of territorial signs, promoting community events in the space, and developing ways of maintaining a visible record of these events to serve as affirmation of group continuity, achievement, and values.

Defensive behavior, as a feature of appropriation, is most urgent under threatening conditions. In a community with high mobility and high cultural and social diversity, especially where crime is a concern, one would expect that much importance would be attached to opportunities for clear definition and defense of territories. In low-threat situations, however, unassertive signs may be all that are necessary for the regulation of interaction. Walter (1978) notes that in the socially homogeneous and spatially distinct Malay *kampong*, for example, there is no obvious delineation between public and private space; residents maintain a common claim to the whole area.

ATTACHMENT TO PLACE

Attachment to place refers to the feeling of possessiveness that an occupant has toward a particular territory because of its associations with self-image or social identity. Attachment is associated with appropriation in two ways. First, the likelihood that place will be appropriated is greatest where potential occupants have a strong sense of identification with it. Secondly, a strong sense of personal identification is frequently a consequence of an act of appropriation, and it is those territories that reflect a sense of personal or community worth that will, in the face of a challenge, be most tenaciously defended.

Proshansky (1978) suggests that one's self-identity is composed of a number of subidentities, one of which is derived from the physical environment that has been a part of one's socialization experience. This means that people who grow up in similar kinds of physical settings (urban as opposed to rural, say, or single-family houses rather than apartments) will develop common ways of coping with their physical environment. Different settings will produce different demands, create different challenges, and provide different levels of satisfaction. They may well lead to different patterns of attachment (city people, for example, preferring environments that are differentiated, stimulating, choiceful, and changeable).

Attachment should not be equated with ownership. It is true that a sense of attachment frequently accompanies the acquisition of legal title to a place, but it does not necessarily come with it. On the other hand, lack of ownership may exclude or hamper certain forms of appropriation, but people often appropriate places they do not own.

Attachment to place is associated largely with the symbolic qualities of a site, with relationships between the space and objects in it, and the experiences, aspirations, and condition of the occupants. These relationships will usually derive from real-life events, but they could be based upon myth. Mutwa (no date), for example, writes of two African tribes who were notified by the government of Northern Rhodesia (as it was then called) that they would have to evacuate their traditional home for the construction of the Kariba Dam. The area was poor agricultural land and disease ridden, and the government, in offering to move the tribes, felt they were doing them a favor. The tribes, however, refused to leave. They opened fire on the police, and five tribesmen were killed before the remainder could be forcibly removed. In their new location, many of the people died for no apparent reason. Mutwa attributes this attachment to the Kariba site to the fact that it was a tribal burial ground, and that custom forbade tribes, under pain of death, from leaving their traditional burial grounds. This injunction was all the more serious in this particular instance because the Kariba gorge had special significance as a burial place, having been established by local custom as the gateway to the underworld.

When people identify strongly with a space, they tend to personalize it, and frequently the same objects used as indications of the personality (real or desired) of the occupants also serve as signs of occupancy. This is especially true at points of real and symbolic penetration, such as doors, windows, and approachways. In territories that are occupied by society, strong personalization of territorial signs can have the effect of making strangers feel like outsiders—and of adding considerably to the charm of foreign travel.

Summary

It may be useful to repeat some of the points that have been made about the nature of territorial behavior.

1. The effect of territorial behavior is to mitigate the threat (real or imagined) of unregulated interaction. The greater the threat, the

stronger will be the tendency toward territorial behavior, and the more important it will be to satisfy criteria for the design of defensible space.

2. A culture or life-style that relies heavily upon nonspatial rules and customs to regulate social interactions will depend that much less upon territorial behavior.

3. There are three territorial strategies for dealing with increased threat: increase the defense of existing territorial claims; narrow the field by shifting or shrinking territorial boundaries to a more defensible position; renounce one's territorial claims.

4. Territorial behavior has direct implications for land management, because it insures that parcels of land are divided among many individuals and groups who accept responsibility for their maintenance.

5. The ability to establish a territorial claim will be affected by the ability of the prospective occupant (individual or group) to establish an appropriate type of occupancy.

6. Occupancy is usually accompanied by a display of territorial signs that announce the existence, nature, and extent of the claim. Weak territorial signs do not necessarily mean, however, that a space has not been appropriated.

7. A place where potential occupants have a strong sense of identification is most likely to be appropriated, and, once appropriated, is likely to be defended most tenaciously against challenge.

8. A strong sense of attachment is not only a cause, but is frequently a consequence, of the act of appropriation.

9. Improvements in site design that make a space more defensible will increase the likelihood of appropriation to the extent that suitable occupancy conditions exist, and that occupants have a feeling of attachment for the place.

APPLICATION OF THE MODEL: A CASE STUDY

The model of territorial behavior that has been described was first developed as a general framework against which to view findings of a study that dealt with neighborhood parks in Baltimore. The application of the model to analyze these findings cannot, then, serve as test of the validity of the model, but it can serve to illustrate its usefulness, both in explaining existing behavior and in suggesting intervention strategies.

STUDY DESCRIPTION

Fourteen parks in Baltimore were included in detailed studies of residents' use of and attitudes toward various outdoor spaces in their neighborhood (Brower, 1977b; Brower & Williamson, 1974). Twelve of the parks were in a black lower-income area, and two were in a contiguous white middle-income area. Both areas had undergone renewal, which had resulted in the creation of over 30 new, small (less than one acre) parks. Most of these parks were situated in the center of blocks surrounded by the back yards of homes that fronted onto the surrounding streets. Both areas consisted predominantly of row houses (see Figure 5). In the low-income area, the population density was higher, both in terms of persons per acre and of persons per room.

Data-collection methods included a walking census, to record, in a systematic way, what spaces were used for what purpose and by whom; resident diaries, to record individual outdoor use; interviews, to identify attitudes and neighboring patterns; perceptual tests, to find the symbolic value attached to objects and spaces; doll play with elementary-age children, to discover the location and nature of children's play spaces; and systematic observations of use and condition of various urban spaces.

In the lower-income area, people represented a wide range of circumstances, with behavior norms that ranged from those of a retired school teacher with an old-fashioned sense of propriety to those of a teen-age mother on welfare. A high percentage of residents were renters, who moved too often to form a real attachment to any one place; others were place-bound homeowners. There were all the personal

Figure 5.   A typical block with an inner-block park.

problems and frustrations of a low-income life-style, and there was a high rate of crime. The overall result was that people tended to be mistrustful of one another. Churches and special clubs which employed screening procedures and a strict behavior code were popular associations. Outdoor recreation (including sitting out) was an important activity for all age–sex groups, and most people in all groups recreated on the sidewalks in front of their homes, despite heavy automobile traffic in the street, rather than in the parks at the back. The parks were popular hangouts for winos, drug users, and teen-age groups, and many residents were afraid to use them or to let their children play there. They complained of frequent fights, of gambling, and the use of bad language. Residents were also concerned over the daily accumulation of trash in the parks that included litter, household garbage, broken glass, old refrigerators, and abandoned cars.

Conditions in the middle-income area were different. People had a more uniform code of behavior and a past history of structured social organization. There were far fewer people outdoors. The parks were used, although not intensively, and were cared for by local residents. Very little active recreational use was made of the street front, even in the case of one street that has been closed and turned into a park. The most intensively used outdoor spaces were the private backyards.

OCCUPANCY

The major outdoor spaces that were used by residents were rear yards, sidewalks, and parks. In both middle- and lower-income areas, the yards were recognized as personal occupancy. They were generally fenced in, and were considered to be an extension of the house. The parks, however, clearly represented a form of shared occupancy. The city, in building them, had expected that they would become community occupancies, with local residents assuming a major responsibility for their use and care. This expectation was justified in the middle-income area, where abutting residents saw a park as a common concern, and, acting as a social unit, made a collective appropriation of the space. They tended the plants, opened new windows onto the view, and kept a watchful eye for intruders. Residents in the surrounding blocks recognized (some resented but accepted as legitimate) this possessive attitude on the part of the occupying community.

In the low-income community, however, because of the diversity of the population and the high degree of mistrust and fear that existed among neighbors, associations based primarily on proximity were cautious and fragile. Bound by weak ties and faced with strong and constant challenge to their territorial claims, any community organization that did attempt to control a park had little chance of success. There was, however, an alternate space where collective appropriation could be accomplished without strong commitment to a communal cause. This space was the sidewalk, where, the study showed, a community occupancy

Figure 6.   Residents exercise territorial claims over the sidewalk.

could develop incrementally with only the most casual agreement among neighbors, and with very little strain upon social ties, by relying upon parallel and largely independent acts on the part of individual householders.

Community occupancy of the sidewalk was established in the following manner. Each householder appropriated the stretch of sidewalk in front of the house: washed it, swept it, furnished it with chairs, plants, and tables, and used it for sitting out (see Figure 6). The combined effect was to create a clear and visible distinction between residents sitting out on the sidewalk and passersby who, if they hung around, could be charged with loitering. This distinction, and the rights associated with it, was generally recognized in the community. It established the difference between insiders and outsiders which is the essence of community occupancy.

As for the parks in the lower-income area, residents regarded them as an occupancy by society, and held the city solely responsible for their condition. The city was, however, not equipped to assume a heavy management responsibility. There were no full-time representatives to watch over the space and to defend the many challenges to its regulations (such as "no dumping" and "no ball playing" signs; see Figure 7). As a result, the space was not effectively appropriated by anybody, and it became the temporary territory of any occupant whose demands were insistent enough and forceful enough.

Figure 7.   A challenge to occupancy by society in the parks.

In terms of the general territorial model, these findings suggest that different spaces, if they are to be appropriated, require different forms of occupancy, and that some forms of occupancy are more readily achieved in some communities than in others. Where occupancy is weak, the physical design of the space can have a strong influence on territorial behavior.

DEFENSE OF SPACE

People in the study area had an overriding concern for personal security. Doors were kept locked, and people were unwilling to allow strangers into their homes. Many residents were afraid to venture away from home after dark. Their attitude toward the use of shared spaces was revealed in an interview, in which residents in a number of sample blocks were shown eight three-dimensional models, each model representing an arrangement of four rows of houses (see Figure 8). The arrangements differed so that four models showed outdoor spaces in the front of the houses, the other four in the back; four of these spaces provided a connection between two streets, the other four were dead ended; four spaces were streets and alleys, the other four were parks. The eight models represented all possible variations of these three variables. Subjects were asked to select the arrangement that they felt would be the safest. They were asked to give reasons for their choices. In addition, they were asked to make selections based upon likelihood of littering, suitability for children's play, and general desirability.

Several interesting things emerged (Brower, 1977a). The first was that residents, in response to the "danger" question, took a strong territorial position. They made a clear distinction between imaginary users who would have territorial rights over a space (the abutting residents), and those who did not (commonly referred to as "outsiders"). Danger was associated with the presence of outsiders; consequently, spaces were most dangerous that could not be adequately defended against outsiders. This insider/outsider dichotomy did not appear as a strong rationale in response to the other, less threatening questions.

Another interesting finding was that there were two essentially different defense strategies for dealing with outsiders. The first was to keep an eye on outsiders. In evaluating alternative spaces, subjects used the following line of reasoning. Most outsiders would be on the street front. The safest place would, therefore, be an active street with many residents sitting around, because they would serve as street-watchers, would discourage troublemakers, and would provide help and support in case of need. In addition, a street front would have patrolling police

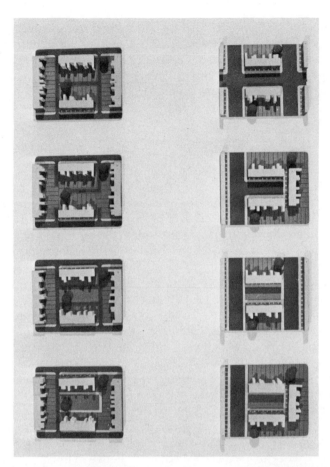

Figure 8A.   The eight models of housing arrangements used in interviews.

and street lights at night. Views up and down the street were not obstructed; this contrasted with the back spaces, where views were obstructed by fences and planting, and where night lighting was so poor that outsiders could hide undetected. The most dangerous of all back spaces were those that were dead ended, because there one could be trapped with no way of escape. The second strategy was to retire to a place that was free of outsiders. It followed that the street front, as a public-access way catering to outsiders, was the most dangerous place. It was especially dangerous in the case of a through street, because troublemakers had multiple escape routes, and there would be fast au-

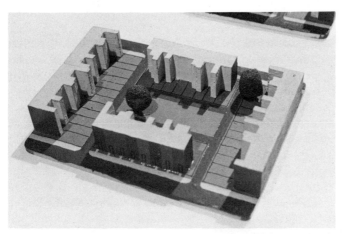

Figure 8B.   A close-up of one of the models.

tomobile traffic. The safest place was somewhere removed from the street front, preferably a dead-end space, because there would be less reason for outsiders to be there, and because troublemakers would be less likely to go where they might be trapped. Such a back space would then be for the exclusive use of the local community.

It should be noted that the space that was chosen as most secure under the first strategy was chosen as the most dangerous under the second strategy, and vice versa. It should also be noted that one strategy provides, in essence, a rationale for front use, and the other a rationale for back use. It would have made an elegant argument if the responses of subjects in the lower-income area had favored the first strategy, and the responses of middle-income subjects had favored the second; but this was not the case. Subjects were divided about evenly in each area. This suggests that the particular territorial behavior that characterized each of the two areas cannot be attributed to the fact that residents were unaware of an alternative strategy, but rather to other considerations that influenced the choice in different directions. These considerations, I believe, were based upon an assessment of the territorial claims that could most effectively be established and defended in their community.

In terms of the general territoriality model, these findings illustrate the importance of territorial defense in conditions with high threat. They illustrate also that physical design features can influence the pattern of territorial behavior, and that features most suitable for one type of occupancy may make a space less suitable for defense by a different occupancy type.

Attachment to Place

To all residents of the study area, the street was the public face of the house, and a clean, attractive front was a sign of respectability and care. But residents of middle- and lower-income neighborhoods had very different attitudes with respect to the use of front and back spaces.

In the middle-income neighborhood, the street front was the setting for the house, but sitting on the front was considered to be "not nice," and a lower-class thing to do. When people sat out, they did so in the back yard, which was screened for privacy, and when they socialized (this usually took the form of entertaining preselected persons at prearranged times), they frequently did so in the back yard. People tended to see themselves as living on a block that they shared with their neighbors at the back, so that a park in the interior of the block fell within their neighborhood space.

In the lower-income neighborhood, however, people knew and associated mainly with people who lived on their street. People who lived at the back were thought of as being in a different neighborhood, and so houses that backed into a park belonged to four different neighborhoods, and the park in the middle was not clearly in any one of them. This was illustrated by the fact that a park had a different name, depending on where you lived. To one resident, the park behind his house might be described as behind the 1100 block of Harlem Avenue; to another resident, who lived around the corner, the same park would be behind the 1600 block of Arlington Avenue. Thus, the front space, rather than the back space, was the focus of group identity, and was more likely to invite collective appropriation.

Most residents in the lower-income area did not have a strong sense of personal identification with their back yards. The back was generally associated with the service side of the house. It was where one stored one's garbage cans, hung the wash, kept the dog, or planted a garden. For most people, the appearance of the yard was as important as the appearance of the basement. It should be neat, clean, and secure. The street front was where one put one's flower pots. Nor were the yards considered to be really secure. Even if they were fenced, children out to retrieve a stray ball could find a way in get in. Any screening that would have provided visual privacy would also have afforded criminals a hiding place, and so, when using the yard, one was exposed to the full range of uses, some unsightly and some objectionable, that were relegated to back spaces. As a result, few people sat out in their back yards, and the fact that the yards were seldom used contributed to the feeling that back spaces were dangerous. When residents in the lower-income areas sat out, they sat out on the street front. This was very much tied to the predominant form of socializing in the area, which was informal, and included chatting to one's neighbors and to people passing by.

In the light of their preference for the front spaces, it was interesting that most residents of the lower-income area, when shown a set of sketches of street fronts, identified those with people on the front as representing lower-status neighborhoods than similar drawings without people (Taylor, Brower, & Stough, 1976). Perhaps it is because of its lower-class connotations that sitting in the front is generally treated as if it were a temporary and undesirable condition, one to be corrected rather than accommodated in any long-range program of neighborhood improvement. In Baltimore, for example, a group of apartment buildings was built to accommodate lower-income families. As a condition of their lease, tenants were forbidden from sitting out on the front steps, because, as the manager explained, "it looks bad." Instead, they were encouraged to use the interior courtyard or the adjacent park. In spite of the restriction, however, tenants did sit out on the front, but it was a point of conflict with management. Besides, the steps had been designed to be so narrow that there were complaints both about having to weave one's way through step sitters to get in and out of the building, and about being constantly disturbed by the passing traffic when sitting out front.

In terms of the general territoriality model, these findings suggest that the tendency to appropriate a space will be stronger if the space is associated with the identity of the occupants. It illustrates also the importance of context in establishing attachment to place: one may be attracted to appropriate a certain place, even if it is not felt to be desirable in itself, because it fits into a larger pattern of behavior that has proven to be effective in coping with threatening conditions. Under these circumstances, sitting in front is not likely to be eliminated simply by making alternative spaces available elsewhere.

APPLICATION OF THE MODEL

The territoriality model provides a framework for organizing complex behavioral data. It can be useful to planners and urban designers, because it lends conceptual clarification to the relationship between physical aspects of the environment and the actions and attitudes of people who use it. For example, the finding that there is a positive relationship between an active street front and a feeling of security can be misapplied. Unless interpreted in a territorial context, it could lead to design decisions that have costly consequences. A current renewal plan in Baltimore seeks to create a heightened sense of security in the back spaces by building connected, inner-block parks in adjacent blocks, with provision for continuous pedestrian movement through them. This kind of activity in the back spaces, it is felt, will create the same kind of security conditions that presently exist on the street front. The occupancy model suggests, however, that security on the street front depends, not upon its use by passing pedestrians (who are felt to be a dangerous element), but rather upon its use by local residents who appropriate the space and create a community occupancy. Without major changes in the physical environment (like reversing the houses so that access is provided from the inner-block spaces only), residents are likely to continue to recreate on the street fronts, and the introduction of pedestrian movement in the back spaces is likely to make them seem more dangerous. The design objective should be, instead, to generate increased use of the back spaces by abutting residents, and so to create a community occupancy. To further this objective, the space should be designed to promote and support collective action by a resident group. The first thing one might do is restrict all access to nonresidents, so as to establish the claim to occupancy clearly, and make the space more defensible. To increase the sense of identification, residents should be involved in the planning, design, and management of the facility. (It should be noted that involvement does not necessarily lead to appropriation. Residents were involved in the design of all the parks in the Baltimore study area. A measure of success of community involvement must be the extent to which it develops a sense of attachment by members of the planning group.) Community identification with the park could be constantly reaffirmed if the park is designed so that the occupants can continually make their mark upon it. This may be done inexpensively by allowing the community to plant in the flower beds, move the equipment, control the night lighting, operate the spray pool, be responsible for paint-up, etc.

Interpreting the need for children's play space provides another example of the practical usefulness of the model. The study found, for example, that most children in the lower-income area played on the street front, and that automobile traffic represented an ever-present danger. A logical conclusion would seem to be that, whenever possible, streets should be closed to traffic and turned into play streets. (This was the recommendation in the case of several other studies of urban streets. See, for example, Appleyard, Gerson, & Lintell, 1976; Reiss, 1975.) Before implementing such a plan, however, consideration should be given to the implications it may have for territorial control. Closing the street to traffic and introducing items of public furniture and play equipment, if done on a permanent basis, is sure to attract children (and adults also) from adjoining areas, and thus by intensifying use by outsiders, may blur the distinction between outsiders and residents. This may result in a shift from community occupancy to occupancy by society, and a consequent increase in the demand for public services—a demand the city may be unprepared to meet. An alternative approach would be to institute a traffic management plan that will reduce the speed and volume of automobile traffic, to widen the sidewalks so that they are more suitable for recreation, and to encourage residents to bring out their own seats and play equipment. (These are clearly private items, and residents' rights over them are not likely to be challenged.)

DIRECTIONS OF FUTURE STUDY

While the model illustrates the dynamic nature of territorial behavior and the strong interrelationship of social, cultural, and physical influences, it also poses a great many questions about the way in which changes are introduced into the system, and about the effects of intervention.

We need to know more about the sensitivity of the system in responding to an addition or reduction in the level of threat. One suspects that the reaction to reduced threat can be very sluggish, because secondary purposes served by an established behavior often sustain the behavior even when the original purpose no longer exists. It may well be, as Jackson (1969) indicates, that the law requiring farmers to fence in their cattle, introduced into the United States toward the latter part of the 19th century, led to the removal of protective fences fron innumerable yards and gardens in towns and suburbs across the country; but the reduced fear of trespass might not have sparked so dramatic a reaction, had it not been accompanied by a shift in fashion, which decreed that fences were unneighborly. Certainly the fence is still regarded as an essential element in any English garden, although the conditions that caused the fences to be erected in the first place have, no doubt, disappeared long ago.

The literature contains many examples of behavior patterns that are similar to those found in the Baltimore study, but it is not clear whether these are responses to similar conditions. Remy (1976), for example, in a study of Belgian working-class neighborhoods, found the same sharp differentiation between front and back spaces, the back spaces generally being more disorderly than the front spaces, and the street being the focus of collective life. This is very similar to the lower-income neighborhood in Baltimore. Remy found, however, that in Belgium, unlike Baltimore, the back spaces were used for private, family occasions. Rapoport (1977, p. 293) also noted the use of the front for interaction, and the back for withdrawal. Kandiyoti (1977), in a study of self-built housing settlements in the vicinity of Izmit, in Turkey, noted the absence of community-occupancy territories. Instances of children playing on the street front have been recorded in many places around the world (Appleyard et al., 1976; Department of the Environment, Great Britain, 1973; Lynch, 1977; Zerner, 1977). While these all have certain similarities with the Baltimore findings, we need to know whether similar forms of behavior are responses to similar conditions, and whether similar intervention strategies are likely to have similar effects. We also need to know to what extent culture and life-style provide a context for territorial behavior, and to what extent changes in territorial behavior bring about changes in life-style. Studies of present territorial patterns will explain how space is being used and how it is likely to be used under the prevailing circumstances. But some of these circumstances will change. Design improvements will themselves create new opportunities. This is especially true in low-income areas, where the difference between old and new environments can be so dramatic. If new housing narrows the difference between low- and middle-income settings, will it have the effect of shifting low-income people toward a middle-income life-style? If this is the case, should new environments be designed to satisfy present-day behavior?

We need more information about those cultural and environmental factors that, once experienced, have a lasting influence on behavior, and those that only operate if they are experienced on a day-to-day basis. We need to be able to separate out the effect on life-style of changing income, changing density, changing role models, and so on. The dynamics of change provide a fruitful area for future research in developing our understanding of territory in urban settings.

REFERENCES

Altman, I. The environment and social behavior. Monterey, Calif.: Brooks/Cole, 1975.
Altman, I., Taylor, D., & Wheeler, L. Ecological aspects of group behavior in social isolation. Journal of Applied Social Psychology, 1971, 1, 76–100.
Appleyard, D., Gerson, S., & Lintell, M. Livable urban streets: Managing auto traffic in neighborhoods. Washington, D. C.: U. S. Government Printing Office, 1976.
Banham, R. Parkhill revisited: English public housing that broke the rules but worked anyway. Architecture Plus, 1974, 2, 109–115.
Brower, S. The signs we learn to read. Landscape, 1965, 15(1), 9–12.

Brower, S. *Streetfronts and backyards: Two ways of looking at neighborhood open spaces.* Baltimore, Md.: Department of Planning, 1977a.
Brower, S. *The design of neighborhood parks.* Baltimore, Md.: Department of Planning, 1977b.
Brower, S., & Williamson, P. Outdoor recreation as a function of the urban housing environment. *Environment and Behavior,* 1974, *6*, 295–345.
Cullen, G. *The concise townscape.* New York: Van Nostrand Reinhold, 1961.
Ganzfried, S. *Code of Jewish law* (Rev. ed.). New York: Hebrew Publishing Co., 1927.
Great Britain, Department of the Environment. *Children at play.* London: Her Majesty's Stationery Office, 1973.
Hall, E. *The hidden dimension.* Garden City, N.Y.: Doubleday, 1966.
Hall, E. *Beyond culture.* Garden City, N. Y.: Doubleday, 1977.
Jackson, J. B. A new kind of space. *Landscape,* 1969, *18* (1), 33–35.
Jacobs, J. *The death and life of great American cities.* New York: Random House, 1961.
Kandiyoti, D. *The effects of social change on housing patterns: Its implications for crowding.* Paper presented at symposium on Human Consequences of Crowding, Antalya, Turkey, 1977.
Lynch, K. *Growing up in cities.* Cambridge, Mass.: M.I.T. Press & UNESCO, 1977.
Man, 30, is arrested on charges of beating 2 with baseball bat. *New York Times,* July 13, 1978.
Mutwa, C. *My people.* Johannesburg: Blue Crane, no date.
Newman, O. *Defensible space: Crime prevention through urban design.* New York: Macmillan, 1972.
Proshansky, H. The city and self-identity. *Environment and Behavior,* 1978, *10,* 147–169.
Rapoport, A. *Human aspects of urban form.* New York: Pergamon, 1977.
Reiss, M. Guidelines for the creation and operation of urban play streets. In *School trip safety and urban play areas,* 2. Washington, D. C.: Federal Highway Administration, 1975.
Remy, J. *Spatial appropriation and intergroup relationships: Open region and closed interactional networks.* Paper presented at the Third International Architectural Psychology Conference, Strasbourg, France, 1976.
Taylor, R., Brower, S., & Stough, R. User-generated visual features as signs in the urban residential environment. In P. Suedfeld & J. A. Russell (Eds.), *The behavioral basis of design* (Book 1). Stroudsberg, Pa.: Dowden, Hutchinson, & Ross, 1976, pp. 94–101.
Taylor, R., Gottfredson, S., & Brower, S. N. *Territoriality, defensible space, informal social control mechanisms and community crime prevention.* Baltimore: The Johns Hopkins University, Center for Metropolitan Planning and Research, unpublished manuscript, 1978.
Walter, M. A. H. B. The territorial and the social: Perspectives on the lack of community in high-rise/high-density living in Singapore. *Ekistics,* 1978, *45* (270), 236–242.
Wheeler, G. C. *The tribe and intertribal relations in Australia.* London: Murray, 1910.
Whyte, W. *The organization man.* New York: Simon & Schuster, 1956.
Zerner, C. The street hearth of play. *Landscape,* 1977, *22* (1), 19–30.

6

Culture and the Urban Stage

THE NEXUS OF SETTING, BEHAVIOR, AND IMAGE IN URBAN PLACES

MILES RICHARDSON

INTRODUCTION

Although a product of the same impersonal, natural process that brought forth the earthworm and the eagle, the amoeba and the dinosaur, man moves about within a personal, artificial world that he himself has built. The paradox of nature's giving birth to a *supra*natural creature is central to our lives, and the constant search for its meaning a characteristic of our species (Becker, 1973, 1975; Eiseley, 1969). On the one hand, we view nature ambiguously. Are we in nature, or out of it? Are the animals our brothers, or are we their keepers, indeed their masters? Is our natural body, with its noises, smells, and impulses, a part of our highest aspirations, or is it something to be covered up, kept from view, and excused when it indelicately intrudes into our conversations? Is death nature's ultimate reality? Or can we construct a self that is tough enough to transcend this biological event? On the other hand, we find ourselves in a similar ambiguous state when we seek to relate to our fellow humans. Unhooked from many of the genetically keyed responses that form the natural, social world of other creatures, we respond to each other through the medium of arbitrary symbols. Through this medium we communicate in a way no other animal can. We can, in a literal sense, talk about our *selves*. At the same time, the symbolic

MILES RICHARDSON • Department of Geography and Anthropology, Louisiana State University, Baton Rouge, Louisiana 70803.

character of our conversation, by its very reflexive nature, full of the mist of misinterpretation and misunderstanding, isolates us from one another. For all of our intimate words about our secret selves—and perhaps because of those very words—we struggle to touch each other, and to feel the warmth of the primate response through the cold communion of words.

The argument of this chapter is that the two questions of our location with respect to nature and of our location with respect to one another intersect in the material environment that we build around us. In bald form, each culture defines its relation to nature through the creation of a cultural landscape upon a physical one. This same cultural landscape becomes a series of behavioral settings or stages that provide cues for people to read as they seek to relate to each other in the construction of everyday life.

The argument begins with a sketch of the evolutionary interplay between human-constructed objects and the emerging consciousness of a self apart from nature; then, using core ideas from symbolic interactionist theory, the presentation attempts to conceptualize the process whereby people transform the material environment into dramaturgical stages; next, the conceptualization of this process and the notion of a self apart from nature are used to interpret the cultural landscapes of small urban places in Spanish America and the American South; and, in the final section, the argument is reviewed, and lines indicated for future work.

THE HEROIC SELF

The debate between those who propose that late Pliocene–early Pleistocene man was a single species evolving through time (for example, Wolpoff, 1971), and those who hold that there were two or more species existing contemporaneously (Leakey, 1973), waxes and wanes with each new fossil find. However, both sides appear to agree that bipedalism (McHenry, 1975) and tool making (Butzer, 1977) preceded the expansion of the brain. One variety of early man was walking erect and working stone (and no doubt other, more perishable materials) prior to the enlargement of the brain noted in later forms. The tantalizing evolutionary reciprocity between walking erect and manipulating the environment with tools has yet to be agreed on; but a single, dramatic fact seems clear: man's construction of objects has played a crucial role in his mental evolution. The record of the Pleistocene, from its beginning, nearly 2 million years ago, to its ending, some 10 thousand years ago, is the record of man's biological and social adaptation to a world that he himself was creating.

The importance of tool manufacturing in human evolution is not solely a matter of technological efficiency—the better the tool, the more food in the stomach—but it is also the case that tool manufacturing may relate to word manufacturing. Bronowski and Bellugi (1970), for example, suggest that the process of reification of human experience that produces language, and allows us to talk about concepts as if they were objects, is the same reification process that leads to the construction of artifacts. Holloway (1969), in a longer and more detailed article, argues that the cognitive reorganization of the brain and the development of the motor activities that produced a recognizable tool tradition—as opposed to random banging of rock upon rock—may have also produced the beginnings of language. Furthermore, Holloway continues, just as the imposition of an arbitrary form upon the environment is characteristic of human tool making, so the acceptance of arbitrary rules by society's members is characteristic of human social life. So, when Australopithecus, or some larger-brained variant, chipped out a pebble tool in Olduvai Gorge, perhaps he was also constructing a social self.

Following the appearance of *Homo erectus*, roughly 700,000 years ago, with his expanded tool kit and larger brain, the Neanderthals, who lived about 100,000 to 35,000 years ago, present us with the first glimpse of humans coping with death. Recognized now as our subspecific cousins, and possessing a brain slightly larger than our own, the Neanderthal people placed their dead in shallow graves (Rowlett & Schneider, 1974). These intentional burials, many of them containing grave goods—flint tools, food offering, flowers, bones of other animals—suggest that at least by Neanderthal times human capacity for self-reflection had reached the point where the survivors were struggling to affirm a continued social existence in the face of biological death.

With the evolution of anatomically modern man in the closing millennia of the Pleistocene, we have our first unequivocal evidence of human selfhood: the cave paintings of the Upper Paleolithic. As Hallowell (1960) pointed out nearly twenty years ago, Upper Paleolithic art reveals the ability of the artist to discriminate himself from other objects and display attitudes toward himself. An overriding characteristic of this art is the naturalistic, dynamic depiction of the ice-age mammals, bison, reindeer, mammoths, and the stylistic, often grotesque presentation of humans. As the artists painted the delicate-hoofed animals, leaping along the cave walls with gracefully controlled energy, and then drew the animal–human "sorcerer" of *Les Trois Frères*, his head sprouting antlers, his humanoid face turned as if in fright to confront the viewer, and his body crouched midway between the upright stature of a man and the four-footed gait of an animal, surely the artists were speculating on the magnificent simplicity of animals and the cumbersome complexity of humans. They must have wondered, there in the caves beneath the flickering light of their unsteady torches, who was the master, animal or man.

With the close of the Pleistocene, however, the age of the megafauna and their hunters ended, and the domestication of animals and plants began. With domestication, the balance between animals and humans tilted, perhaps irrevocably, toward humans. The primitive world view of man and nature bounded together in a single, moral system was changing to a stratified, civilized one (Redfield, 1957, pp. 103–110).

The enormous literature on the nature of civilization notwithstanding (succinctly reviewed in Fairservis, 1975), the civilizational world view seemed dominated by the figure of an individual, a separate self, completely differentiated from nature, confronting an open-ended universe (King, 1972). Torn from his earlier egalitarian matrix, the individual sought to close in his reality, to "fetishize" it (Becker, 1975, p. 153), to pit himself against it (or to compare himself with it), so that he could define himself. Robert Bellah, in his classical article on religious evolution (1964), notes that during the first millenium B.C., the religions of the Old World centers of high culture counterposed man against an ultimate reality that lay beyond the empirical world. These religions promised that the individual, as an active agent, could reach out and grasp the nature of ultimate meaning and become a part of it. He could also, again as an active agent, fail to grasp it and become condemned to agonizing isolation. So, man in the civilized world had much to gain, and much to lose. Even in the New World, where at times cultural evolution departed from the pattern of the Old, the Aztec thinkers in the imperial city of Tenochtitlan sought a reality beyond that of the daily sacrifice of victims in the great temples that towered above the populace. They posed the paradoxical question of human freedom and divine omnipotence:

> Our Master, the Lord of Close Vicinity,
> thinks and does what he wishes;
> He determines, He amuses himself.
> As he wishes, so will it be.
> In the palm of His Hand He has us;
> At His will He shifts us around.
> We shift around, like marbles we roll;
> He rolls us around endlessly.
> We are but toys to him; He laughs at us.
>
> (León-Portilla, 1963, pp. 121–123)

Thus, with the emergence of civilization, the theme of man's separation from, or, better, rejection of, nature, and the theme of man's heightened sense of isolation, come sharply into focus. One might well speculate that both themes arose out of the material and social construction of the civilized landscape. The increasing urbanization that accompanied most early civilizations literally built walls between the urban specialist and the countryside. The densely packed houses, the occupational diversification, the hierarchical society, and the temple-palace thrusting into the sky produced empirically observable boundaries between citizens and nature, and between citizens. As they watched these boundaries grow, as they saw their king, magnificent in his apparel, seemingly invincible before his enemies, fall dead like the meanest beggar, they must have pondered, as we do today, its significance. That they did is told in the story of Gilgamesh (Richardson, 1972; Sandars, 1960).

Foreshadowing the trends that Bellah noted, the epic of Gilgamesh was widely known throughout ancient Mesopotamia, and around 2000 B.C. the Semitic scribes composed their version from earlier Sumerian fragments. A recent narrative verse interpretation by Herbert Mason begins:

> Gilgamesh was king of Uruk,
> A city set between the Tigris
> And Euphrates rivers
> In ancient Babylonia.
> Enkidu was born on the Steppe
> Where he grew up among the animals.
> Gilgamesh was called a god and a man;
> Enkidu was an animal and a man.
> It is the story
> Of their becoming human together.
>   (Mason, 1972, p. 15)

Like all heroes, Gilgamesh was restless, bent upon going on a strange journey, determined to do a great deed; but his longing for significance was greater than that of other heroes, for he was two-thirds god. Because of the god part, he had to see everything, learn everything, and understand everything. He was a tyrant, and the people of Uruk groaned under his demands. They pleaded with the gods for relief, and in response the gods made Enkidu. Enkidu lived with the animals and spoke with them, but a temple harlot taught him the pleasures of men. Hearing from her about Gilgamesh and his strength, Enkidu traveled to Uruk to see for himself. The two fought in a battle that wrecked a considerable part of Uruk, but Enkidu recognized that Gilgamesh was the stronger, and they became close friends. Together, they performed great feats. They killed the Monster of the Forest, and they slaughtered the Bull of Heaven. As they performed these acts together, Gilgamesh became less brash and capricious. He began to care. Then after a series of foreboding dreams, Enkidu died. Racked by grief and now fearful that he too might die, Gilgamesh set off to find the secret of immortality. He encountered great difficulties, but driven by the fear of a man who was two-thirds god, he eventually found Utnapistim, the one whom the gods had saved from the great flood. Utnapistim told him of a plant that renewed the strength of those who ate it. Gilgamesh secured the plant, but on his way back to Uruk he became careless, and a snake stole the plant. Wearily, Gilgamesh walked on toward Uruk, his great strength wasted, his bright vision now murky and dull. As the outlines of his city penetrated his fatigue, the pride of a builder straightened his walk. He turned to a companion to exclaim to him that if he will but look he will see how strong is the wall and how glorious is the city that it guards.

In the epic we clearly see the emergence of the isolated self heroically confronting the universe and demanding its secret. The epic is a "revolt against death" (Jacobsen, 1949, p. 223), but a revolt that inevitably fails. Denied immortality because he is one-third human, but cursed with the desire for lasting significance because he is two-thirds god, Gilgamesh can only turn to the city that he has built. The material city, its strong walls, its prosperous precincts, its beautiful gardens, is a sign for all to see and a testimony to his greatness; yet within Gilgamesh an "inner turmoil is left to rage on, a vital question finds no answer" (Jacobsen, 1949, p. 227).

The image of man as represented by Gilgamesh in turn represents the end of a sequence that began back at the beginning of the Pleistocene. The sequence started with early man's construction of material objects. Early toolmaking led to, or was concordant with, the beginnings of self-reflexivity. Subsequent adaptation to the world that man himself was creating led to an enlargement of the brain and an expanded tool inventory. With the appearance of anatomically modern man, humans had become aware of death and of their ambiguous place in nature. With the emergence of civilization, and paralleling the construction of cities and hierarchical societies, people became increasingly conscious of themselves as isolated individuals confronting an open-ended universe. Gilgamesh is the prototype of this heroic self.

This self, seeking significance in a world that may have none, continues to characterize, I would suggest, much of what we do. Ernest Becker, in two brilliant, honest books (1973, 1975), argues that each human society is a heroic denial of death fashioned by man's desire to matter. The fear of insignificance, of impotence, of loneliness drives man to create meaning, to produce proof to himself and to others that he counts. Since man first began to symbolize, first began to bury his dead, first began to paint in a cave, and especially since he first began to erect a wall around his society, a large measure of that proof has been the material environment that he has created out of nature.

THE INTERPRETATION OF PLACES

The figure of the heroic self sets the theoretical, philosophical mood for the investigation of the cultural landscape of urban places. The task of this section is to tie that mood, elusive though it may be, to the hard, empirical data the fieldworker observes. The concepts of symbolic interactionism are an appropriate beginning point. As a competing paradigm to the positivistic, normative position characteristic of contemporary social science, symbolic interactionism confronts directly the question of how humans, living within a world of symbols, construct reality; and its account of the emergence of human reflexivity is, in short, a synchronic interpretation of the Pleistocene. Symbolic interactionism is principally associated with Herbert Blumer (1969), who in turn draws upon George Herbert Mead. Blumer, himself, has influenced a whole generation of students, and all have added their modifications (Meltzer & Petras, 1970). Consequently, what follows only underscores, as I understand them, the key concerns of this broad stance.

According to symbolic interactionism, humans construct reality through the objectification of social experience. The process begins with the interpretation of one's acts in terms of another's response. In order to understand the significance of what one is doing, one has to look at other people's reactions to his actions. This is accomplished when the individual steps outside of his subjective shell and takes on the role of the other person. Once outside of himself, he turns, looks back, and conceives of himself as an object, as a "me." The meaning of that object, of that "me," is located in one's interpretation of other people's responses to it. In the same manner, the meaning of their "me" is located in their interpretation of his responses to their acts. So, social interaction is a constant reciprocal process of objectification and interpretation (Scheff, 1967).

To phrase the matter slightly differently, a person reacts to objects—physical things, people, or abstract principles—on the basis of what those objects mean to the individual. However, the meaning is not located solely within the mind of any individual, but it arises out of the joint process of action and reaction. The process of action and reaction becomes conceptualized, labeled, talked about, and responded to. That bit of action and reaction becomes a segment of human reality; it becomes a situation defined as possessing meaning.

Once a situation is defined as being meaningful, people respond to it; however, characteristically, the symbolic interactionist approach insists that the situation must be continually redefined; human reality is symbolic, *and therefore fluid*. In contrast to the prevailing normative paradigm, which stresses that human behavior is rule-governed, the interactionist (interpretive) paradigm warns that "the tentative character of the individual's own role definition is never wholly suspended" (Wilson, 1970, p. 700). "Life may not be much of a gamble," Erving Goffman observes, "but interaction is" (1959, p. 243).

Social scientists writing from an interactionist stance often find common ground with those scholars writing from a more humanistic position, such as Peter Berger (1963), Kenneth Burke (1966), and Hugh Duncan (1968). Both emphasize the tenuous, fragile quality of human social life, and both use the metaphor of the theater. Material settings, behavior, and norms are often described as stages, performances, and scripts. Opinions vary, of course, as to the usefulness of this theatrical language (Messinger, Sampson, & Towne, 1962). Even Goffman, the foremost exponent of the dramaturgical perspective, ambiguously refers to the language as "scaffolds," useful but temporary platforms for building other things (1959, p. 254). Yet, as metaphor, this dramaturgical language shares the same ontological status as other social science models—such as society as an organic whole in functionalism, or society as a cybernetic machine in the systems approach—and has the advantage of bringing out the constructed artificiality of human life. Indeed, Perinbanayagam (1974) argues vigorously that human social reality is in fact dramatical. In order to make sense out of nonsense, people *must* present themselves, not as molecules in a vacuum, but as actors in appropriate settings. Only through responding to the performances of others do people define their situation, that is, they create order and endow it with meaning.

To amplify the discussion, symbolic interactionism argues that a person can become an object to himself, a "me." He takes the role of the other, and sees himself as a performer. Likewise, other people are taking *his* role and looking at *themselves*; from their view, he becomes an observer of their acts. The result is that we become both actor and audience to each other. This dichotomy of a person between an actor, a "doer," and an audience, a "watcher," appears closely related to the familiar dichotomy of participant–observer. Although commonly applied to the ethnographer in the field doing qualitative research, participant-observer seems equally descriptive of everyday life (Lingenfelter, 1977; Scheff, 1977). This is especially true if we consider the expression, not as a dichotomy, but as a continuum. We are all more or less participants and all more or less observers, and our position on the continuum determines our reaction to the events occurring around us. As we approach the participant end of the continuum and become engrossed (or even lost) in the nitty-gritty, taken-for-granted everyday life, human action ceases to amaze us. When we reverse ourselves and put distance between ourselves and the behavior of others, human action becomes wonderfully strange, mysterious, and, as we near the observer end, slightly insane. When we are participants, life becomes mundane; when we are observers, it becomes theatrical.

Yet, the question of whether or not human life is, in fact, dramatical is not so easily resolved. From the view of the ethnographer and other marginal and ill-at-ease people, the goings-on of humans will always appear peculiar. The essential point is that reality for humans is fluid. For that reality to be sensible, people have to make sense out of it. They have to construct it, and they use material objects to locate it, to bound it, and to shape it into meaningful forms.

Making continual sense out of the slippery reality of everyday life is a process that integrates the material setting which surrounds a place, the behavior which occurs within that surrounding, and the image which the place presents, into a single segment, a social place, which contrasts with other segments that make up a people's social universe.

The process begins with people scanning the material setting. The material setting, the *built* environment constructed by man as opposed to the *natural* environment produced by nature, represents the end point of the objectification of social experience. The ability of humans to step outside of their subjective beings and to treat themselves as objects, thereby transforming a biological organism into a social person, seems closely related to, or identical with, the ability to transform natural substance into material objects and to endow these objects with meaning. People look at social interaction, they reflect on it, they talk about it, and eventually they treat it as if it were a thing apart from their own individual actions (Berger & Pullberg, 1965). They may mystify their own social experience until it becomes a repressive force, as in "I fought the law, and the law won"; or they may deify it until it takes on a life of its own, as in "the word becomes flesh." Such objectifications, and probably even the mystification, are necessary for social life. Hugh Duncan expresses it succinctly: "Men create symbols in dialogue [in order] to name things, events, and relationships so they can act together" (1968, p. 104). In the same manner that people name relationships so they can act together, they carve, mold, and hammer natural material into human objects so that the objects express and contain social experience. The objects become communication devices for signaling social interaction, or, in dramaturgical language, they make up a stage upon which people act out their performances.

For the material setting, which may be starkly utilitarian, like a prison cell, or splendidly ornate, as in the case of a baroque church, to become a social stage, it must be incorporated into the actors' definition of the situation. To be sure, the "meaning of an object resides not in the object itself but in the definitions brought to it, and hence must be located in the interaction process" (Denzin, 1969, p. 923). Yet, the argument here and expressed elsewhere (Rapoport, 1977; Richardson, 1974, 1978) is that the material setting, having been constructed by man, already contains a preliminary definition of the situation. The meaning of interaction has already been located in it, at least in a provisional sense. Thus, when we look at a prison cell, although it may be empty, we are prepared to expect a certain type of behavior, and a type of behavior considerably different from that which we would expect to see in a baroque church. The cell and the church are stages set for certain performances, and evoke distinct images. Certainly, settings are not always used for the purpose intended, as any college librarian can attest; and the final use of a material setting, such as retirees "colonizing" a bus station and turning it into a home territory (Lofland, 1973), is an intriguing subject for study. However, these cases take on significance only against the backdrop of the original stage set. Heavy necking between the stacks strikes the librarian as inappropriate because the behavior is literally *out of place.*

Thus, the material setting of a social place becomes a stage that people scan for cues as to what acts they should select from their behavioral repertoire. How they read the setting is the subject of considerable speculation. Several geographers and psychologists have suggested that people carry around in their heads of spatial schema, a mental or cognitive map, that they use to locate themselves in space (Downs & Stea, 1973). These schemata are more than simple perception of physical attributes, as they involve the individual's assessment of his surroundings and his conceptualization of what is important in the environment. Since these schemata are, for the most part, in the unconscious, they are extremely difficult to tap (as noted in Rapoport, 1977, pp. 118–129; see also Tuan, 1975).

The work of cognitive anthropologists (Tyler, 1969), which draws heavily upon linguistic models of the organization of language into complementary distinctive units of sounds, or phonemes, strongly implies that people think in terms of contrast sets; they organize their reality into conceptual domains based on features that contrast with one another. Applied to social place, this means that when people are scanning the material setting for behavioral cues, they concentrate on the manner in which one social place contrasts with others. This in turn seems plausible, when we realize that a single social place seldom exists in isolation.

Even in primitive society, as among the aborigines of Australia, there are a number of places having behavioral significance (Rapoport, 1975). In complex, hierarchical, urban society, because of the social diversity that demands the staging of numerous performances, and because of the technological resources that permit the construction of relatively elaborate stages, social places abound. In this society, an individual has to be prepared to switch roles. In one long day, he has to present himself as loving husband, gentle father, compassionate friend, inspiring teacher, brilliant intellectual, and during the middle of the night, when something deep inside of him threatens to break out, as a person with a bad dream. To play these roles, he cues on the contrast among the stages as he enters into one performance and exits from another. The stage that he is on takes on meaning as he compares it with the one he just left and the one that he will enter. In the same manner that the material setting of a social place provides a preliminary definition of the situation for acts occurring within its context, so the wider setting of other social places aids in the definition of a single social place (Rapoport, 1977, pp. 298–305).

People scan the material setting of a social place, they note how one place contrasts with others, they fit, perhaps, the contrasts into an underlying schema, and as they do this, they select from their behavioral repertoire acts that will call forth, they hope, appropriate responses from other players. The responses may range from the nonverbal lift of the eyebrows or the touch of a hand to conversations loud or soft, and their subjects from the grossly public to the gently private. Some of the more semiconscious nonverbal acts, such as smiling whimsically and frowning slightly, and the more self-indulgent movements, scratching the head and picking the nose, no doubt are performed in a number of different places; while the more explicit motions, kneeling in prayer or bargaining over a price, are more place-specific. Based on the works of Birdwhistell (1970) and Hall (1959, 1969, 1977), one strongly suspects that the nonverbal and verbal responses the actors make in front of each other's presence form an overall pattern peculiar to a social place. As a practical matter, keeping track of the full range of behavioral responses occurring even in the most placid social place is extremely difficult, and the ethnographer can only record certain responses. Parenthetically, it may well be that the native actors do the same thing for the same reason. Overwhelmed by all the data he is seeing, the actor cues only on certain acts, and as a knowledgeable performer he relies on the material setting to provide the information he needs to select the acts to cue on.

Critical to the understanding of the behavior patterns associated with a social place are the characteristics of the actor. Fortunately, these characteristics are more easily recorded than are the behavioral responses. Both the more obvious, external features of sex, race, and age, and the more subtle, internal attributes of status, religion, and kinship are among the factors that determine the presence of an actor at different social places. Some places admit only those of a certain sex, race, or age, or of a certain social status, religious affiliation, or kinship tie, while others are more inclusive. It is these latter places that are ideal for ethnographic study, for here, on the public stage, the ethnographer can see the old and the young, the rich and the poor, the brother and the stranger, the believer and the heretic, act out the themes and contradictions of their society.

If the material surrounding is a stage, and if the behavioral pattern is a play, then the image that people have of a place is a script. However, unlike the script of a playwright, the script of everyday action emerges out of the play. It explains more than it dictates; it interprets more than it regulates (Falk & Pinhey, 1978). People look at the material setting, they respond to each other's behavior, and *then* they formulate an image of what they are doing. This use of image differs from that often encountered in the literature about the built environment (Downs & Stea, 1973; Gould & White, 1974), where image becomes the organizing schema mentioned earlier, and thus presumably is antecedent to the behavior it organizes. In a strictly empirical sense, however, the image of a social place is the response that the investigator gets when he asks a participant, in one form or another, subtly or directly, what is his view of a place. As Ashcraft and Scheflen argue (1976, pp. 172–73), this response may or may not accurately report why a participant behaves the way he does at a particular place. In fact, if we agree with the dramaturgical assumption that humans, when talking about themselves, are "consciously rationalizing, not consciously rational" (Brisset & Edgley, 1975, p. 7), then the response is not so much a cause as it is an explanation, a verbal picture, a word image, of a social place.

For the native participant in a social place, his image of that place provides him with a sense of comprehending the events that are occurring around him; for the ethnographic observer of social places, *his* image becomes his analysis. The procedure for studying social places is the same as that for acting in them. The ethnographer first scans the material setting for cues as to the preliminary statement of what is occurring. Through contrasting the features of one social place with another, he determines its definition of the situation. He records (and in a special sense, responds to) as much of the behavior flowing around him as he can. He listens to the explanations that participants offer, and then formulates his own image as to the kind of reality that is being constructed. In the formulation of his image he asks himself: What segments of the society's reality are being presented? How are people using the material setting as a stage? What societal plays are they acting out? What are the plays' themes and contradictions? Finally, back in the recesses of his mind, behind the conventional questions of the social scientist, he asks in a whisper, almost as if he were afraid: What does it mean?

THE CULTURAL IDIOM

Although symbolic interactionists speak eloquently about the symbolic nature of human communication and the slippery universe of everyday life, they rarely talk about cultures. They seem content, as does Goffman, to explain that they are limiting themselves to Western, American, middle-class styles of living. In a sense, they are holding the cultural variable constant as they investigate the social psychological processes of the emergence of the self, the performance of roles, and the construction of a meaningful reality. Yet, as Clifford Geertz (1965) insists, a human does not become human through learning to be a generalized abstraction; he first becomes a specific member of a specific culture. Only after he becomes Billy Jack Hargrove from Mt. Olive, Texas, does he begin to think of himself as a *Homo sapiens*. In other words, the process of assigning and interpreting meaning is always phrased in the idiom of a particular culture. To get at that process, we need to understand its cultural expression.

Any discussion of culture soon runs into the old but still thorny question of how to talk about it. Can one speak of it as a superorganic determinant of people's actions, or is it best to consider it as an anthropological abstraction residing only in the ethnographer's head? The position here is similar to that of Peter Berger (expressed in Berger, 1963; Berger & Luckmann, 1967; and Berger & Pullberg, 1965), that is, culture—or society, in his terminology—is both a historical continuum that we are born into, and an object that we create. Culture makes us, and we make culture. This seemingly impossible feat of self-creation, of one part of ourselves making a second part and that part creating the first, is precisely what materialized in the Pleistocene; the evolutionary record of that period is the adaptation of a primate to the use of culture as a means of exploiting the natural environment. The feat of self-creation also occurs today, synchronically. We become human as we become members of a particular culture; that particular culture continues because of us. We become culture, and culture becomes us. The answer to the question of how this transpires, *how culture, as a historical continuum, achieves empirical reality, lies somewhere, I am convinced, in the cultural landscape*—more precisely, in the ways in which people use material settings to present themselves to each other and thereby recast anew their reality.

Coming down from this flight of conviction, I turn to two distinct urban places: the smaller cities of Spanish America and of the southern United States. Smaller urban places are especially suited for the ethnography of social places, because they contain considerable variety, yet are sufficiently small that the ethnographer can at least walk around the entire community and note how the different social places interrelate and complement each other. Also, the natural environment is not the distant, nebulous realm that it is in the megapolis, but it is there, right at the outskirts, a visual counterpoise to urban life. Similarly, the cultures of Spanish America and of the southern United States are sufficiently distinct that a comparison highlights the similarities they do possess, and in so doing provides insight into both. In the comparison, I will, of course, be making gross generalizations about both regions and about their traditional small towns. For Spanish America, I have in mind the small towns in interior Colombia, Costa Rica, and Mexico; for the South, I am considering towns of the upland South, as opposed to the lowland, or Tidewater South (Newton, 1974a,b).

I will proceed by first describing how Spanish-American culture achieves empirical existence through the expression of itself in two distinct but complementary social places, the plaza and the market. The emphasis here is on the question of symbolic isolation, that is, how do people, separated from each other by the mist of human symbolizing, locate one another within the diversity of a single culture. Next, through the broader perspective of two cultures in juxtaposition, I will describe how the two, in their settlement patterns and particularly in their religious settings, define themselves through their attitude toward nature. The emphasis here is on the question of human controntation with nature, that is, how people, on the stages of these two small town cultures, act out their heroic quest for significance.

DIVERSITY WITHIN A CULTURE

Throughout Spanish America, urban communities are laid out in a grid pattern of perfect squares. The esthetic focal point of the grid is the plaza (Figure 1). Larger communities may have several, but all have a principal one, located at or near the geographical center of the town. Fronting the plaza on one side is the principal church of the community, and on an adjacent side is the main branch of the local government. Nearby are shops and stores, and also, traditionally, the large homes of the local elite. Only a few blocks from the plaza is the market place. In early days, in the last century, the plaza doubled as a market place, and still today in smaller, isolated communities, the merchants set up their stalls in the plaza (Gade, 1976; Richardson, 1978). For the most part, however, the plaza is a garden–park; as a material stage it is nature carefully manicured into submission. The soft green of its grass and trees softens the strident noise of the street, and the curve of its walks relaxes the grid's rectangularity. Frequently centered in the plaza is a fountain, and its water currents shoot upward to gather in the sun's glare as it bounces off the sterile walls of the surrounding buildings. Sometimes, instead of a fountain, the center is a bandstand; and, even in these days of television, people come to hear an evening concert of

Figure 1.   The plaza, a proper place, where nature is transformed into an ornament.

stirring martial music played by the town's brass band. Interspersed among the grass and flowers are statues and plaques commemorating the great men and events of the past. In some communities one may even see the bronze likeness of a conquistador, or that of a hero in the battle against Spain, seated on a rearing stallion, his arm raised to urge us on into the fray. Near the hero is a more modern expression of civic pride: the wheel of the International Rotarians, embedded in a grassy knoll.

Only late in the night is the plaza empty. During weekdays, workmen, housewives, and children all pause there for a moment's rest; but it is on Sundays and holidays that people congregate within its green confines. Brightly dressed, they stroll around the center and sit on the benches under the trees: father, mother, and their children; two women chatting, their kids eyeing each other; a father and his daughter, hand in hand; a recently married couple, close together and far away; adolescent boys and girls, traditional values still lingering in their separate promenades; and kids, dashing, whirling, and returning. In one corner of the plaza, a man is selling cones of flavored ice that he grates off a large block resting on top of his cart. Nearby, a lottery vender offers favorite numbers from a sheaf of papers that he waves about. In another corner, a shoe-shine boy kneels in token homage at the foot of a customer, who, seated on a makeshift throne, gazes impassively at the crowd.

In contrast to the curves of the plaza place and the soft green of its grass and trees, the market place is starkly square. It may be a slab of concrete, or, in smaller, poorer communities, a rectangle of packed earth. Usually it is a large, barnlike structure with an interior that is crisscrossed with lines of small booths and narrow passageways. Appropriately to an economic place, it is a minimal structure, devoid of ornamentation.

Although the physical structure of the market is plain and nearly barren, as a place the market is full of color, supplied by the people who shop there and the produce they bring to sell. Pyramids of red tomatoes, bunches of yellow bananas, sacks of brown potatoes, and trays of tropical fruit of many different shapes and hues transform the stark setting into a stage full of people shouting, pushing, selling, and buying (Figure 2).

Although markets in larger communities may be open all week, even their activity peaks on a special day, a weekday, a Saturday, or even a Sunday. At that time people from the small communities and from the rural areas arrive on battered buses and dilapidated trucks that grind slowly through the crowd, their exhausts pouring out oily smoke, their brakes screeching. People from the city also come to take advan-

Figure 2. The market, a smart place, where nature becomes a commodity.

tage of the larger selection of bargains, and their numbers swell the crowd. Both sexes, all ages, different economic levels, and several ethnic groups are represented in the population. A local matron, followed by a small boy staggering under a heavy basket, makes her way from buyer to buyer. A thin, brown man, dressed in freshly pressed pants, chats with a neighbor from the country. Depending on the location of the city, Indians from the highlands or blacks from the coasts intermingle with the local population. In addition to the people who are at the market to buy or to sell food, clothing, or hardware, there are those who live off the crowd. Small restaurants offer plain dishes served on uneven tables, and cantinas sell cheap rum across scarred counters. Around their edges cluster those who are down and out, begging for a peso, for a drink, or for the food left over from a customer's plate. A brightly dressed woman leads a hesitant, shy man across the street to a dilapidated structure called a hotel.

As distinct social places situated within the context of an urban environment, the plaza and the market bound, separate, and define their respective realities.

As material stages, the plaza is cultivated nature, curvilinearly centered around a fountain or a bandstand; whereas the market is rectangular, and starkly utilitarian. The plaza makes nature into an ornament, while the market transforms natural products—tomatoes, bananas, potatoes, and fruit—into commodities to be bought and sold.

Through the location of benches, the plaza distributes clusters of people across its space. On the other hand, the market uses its arrangement of booths and passageways to create a solid flow of people circulating through its aisles. The plaza is a relatively quiet spot circled by noise, whereas the market is a loud, raucous place surrounded by a zone of less intense activity.

As behavioral patterns, the two contrast both in gross differences and in finer details: the plaza has fewer people; they mainly come from a broad middle sector; they move about in units, frequently familial; their kids play in the plaza while other kids work in the market; their individual personal space is greater, as is the space between clusters; their eye contact is longer and body contact is frequently sought after rather than avoided; the tempo of their walk is slower and their voices less shrill; and their conversation is more general, their faces more public, and their thoughts, perhaps, more idle. Finally, their behavior is within the acceptable range, that is, they do not drink excessively, smoke marijuana, or solicit for prostitution.

After scanning the two stages, after observing the everyday microdramas performed on the two stages, after gathering in through informal conversation people's images of the two places, in fact, after many hours of ethnographically responding to what he has seen, felt, and heard, the ethnographer constructs the following images of the two places.

In general, the plaza and the market present two distinct, but complementary faces: the market is the intense face of a Spanish-American town; the plaza is that face in repose. The terms, *cultura* (culture) and *progreso* (progress), which appear frequently in the conversations of people talking about the qualities of life in small Spanish-American towns, come close to expressing the contrast. *Cultura* is the victory of Spanish-American civilization over nature and over the bestial aspects of human behavior; it stresses the thoughtful, contemplative life of reason, of unhurried decision making. The plaza, by its very greenery and by its behavior, leisurely strolling under the trees, epitomizes *cultura.* On the other hand, *progreso* also is a quality of urban life; it stresses the dynamic, bustling life of monetary achievement, of crafty, almost ruthless exploitation of opportunities. The market, as a vortex of behavior swirling in and out of a minimal, barren structure, is the hard and fast expression of *progreso.*

This contrast between plaza and market, between *cultura* and *progreso*, is, in Morris Freilich's words, a contrast between being proper and being smart (1975). Being proper is complying with the rules; being smart is getting ahead. Being proper is moral; being smart is exploitation. Being proper assures us that the world is sane and has meaning; being smart allows us to cut corners and to show a profit. In dramaturgical terms, in the plaza, utilizing its backdrop of trimmed grass, tilled flower beds, and pruned bushes, people present themselves as persons of *cultura*, of correct dress, and of proper deportment. In the market, against its stage of material goods, the freshly caught fish, the recently slaughtered pig, the potatoes brought down from the mountains, the buyer and seller act out their mutual smartness. The plaza, then, is the proper side of Spanish-American small-town culture, and the market is its smart side. The dichotomy, according to Freilich, reflects the basic dualism of human existence, of sanity and survival; and the two often conflict. There is smart behavior in the plaza, such as selling snow cones and shining shoes. Indeed, the shoe shiner is often the prototype of the smart operator, ears tuned, eyes alert, fingers nimble, seeking to turn every outcome to his advantage: the *pícaro* of the plaza. There is also proper behavior in the market, such as the patron–client relationship between an established vender and his permanent customers. Yet, the smart behavior in the plaza and the proper behavior in the market occur against the dominant display of the opposite behavior; and, if pursued too vigorously, the behaviors will become blatantly out of place, and their actors will suffer: the shoe shiner may be run off, and the vender may go broke.

A third contrast between the image of the plaza and that of the market comes directly from Erving Goffman (1959). He distinguishes between front regions and back regions of a social establishment, such as the dining room of a restaurant and its kitchen. Waitresses present a decorous self while serving customers and a sarcastic self back in the kitchen, occasionally aping the manners of a particularly antagonistic customer. Similar terms that Goffman uses for this division are, frontstage and backstage for the settings, and on stage and off stage for the behaviors of the actors. In a manner analogous to Rapoport's application of these contrasts to the front and back yards of houses and the front and back areas of settlements (1977, pp. 290–293), they can be used to designate the difference between the plaza and the market. The plaza is the front region of the town, people are self-consciously on stage, particularly on Sundays and holidays, while the market is more like a back region, where people drop the mask of leisured politeness and don the one of hard negotiation. Although the contrast can be pushed too far, to a certain degree the smart behavior in the market can be said to ridicule the proper behavior of the plaza. The theme of the market play, with its emphasis on the nitty-gritty matter of making the best deal, hints that the plaza performance of social decorum is an overstuffed production. This, however, is an interpretation of Spanish-American ritual politeness by an Anglo-American ethnographic critic.

A final contrast between the plaza image and the market one is between observation and participation. As mentioned earlier, people in everyday settings, like ethnographers in the field, are more or less observers and more or less participants. Social places differ in the degree to which they stage for observation or participation. The plaza is the front region for on-stage, proper, *cultura* behavior, because it cues, through its statuary, benches, and park, for observation. People watch each other, and because they know that they are each other's audience, they perform the role of being proper. While a stroll around the fountain places them "away" from the obligations of earning a living (Goffman, 1963, pp. 69–75), and lets them relax from the pressures of being smart, it locates them on the observer end of the continuum. They are ready to see life as theatrical, and they present themselves as good actors. Conversely, the utilitarian-constructed market cues for participation. People are engaged; they are meshed with society. They are in the matter-of-fact back regions and off stage; they are being smart and full of *progreso*.

The plaza and the market are two complementary social places in a single culture. As the Spanish American townsmen move through their small but diversified universe, they search the material setting for information as to what acts will be successful, that is, what kind of performance do they need to present so that others may appropriately respond. Their efforts result in the construction of the everyday reality of plaza and of market. These two realities take the shape of:

cultura	vs.	*progreso*
proper	vs.	smart
front	vs.	back
observation	vs.	participation

In the same manner that people construct and present different realities within a single culture, so people of different cultures construct and present their cultural heritage. They do this, that is, transform a historical continuum into observable data, through producing an image of how man relates to nature.

CONFRONTATION WITH NATURE

The two cultural landscapes of Spanish America and of the southern United States define their attitude toward nature abruptly. They both implant the grid pattern of perfect right angles on nature's irregular, curvilinear surface, and they both assign largely negative values to life outside the grid. This is especially true for Spanish America. According to its interpretation—expressed both by everyday life and by literature (Fuentes, 1972, pp. 9–14; León Hazera, 1971)—within the comforting, reassuring confines of the grid lives urban man, the man of education, of correct speech, of proper behavior—in brief, the man of *cultura*. Even if this man farms for a living, and in Spanish America farmers often are urbanites, he separates himself from those who live away from the grid and next to nature, people who resemble the beasts that surround them, unlettered, ignorant, and potentially savage. The South often expresses the same sentiments. In its everyday life and in its literary fiction (as in the works of William Faulkner), the southern townsman is a man of letters, familiar with the classics, at home with the scholarly discussions of law and religion, civilized even in his prejudice, and opposed to the crude violence of the poor white trash, the red-neck, who threatens to displace the townsman and to turn civilization into demagoguery.

Yet, as Tuan (1973) reminds us, cultural views of the environment are ambiguous. In Spanish America, the squared landscape of the grid, instead of liberating people from nature, may become oppressive; as it did in the words of the Argentinian poet, Alfonsina Storni, who wrote that living in a right-angled universe makes people's souls rectangular, and

> Yesterday, I myself spilled a tear.
> My God, squared.
> (Storni, 1974, pp. 130–131, my translation)

In the South, conversation among men often turns to guns, dogs, camps, and bass boats; and the love of the outdoors, that is, drinking good whisky on a cold night by a big fire, becomes part of the southern male mystique (Gibson, 1976). This ambiguity, Tuan suggests, is an emotional reaction to the mind's penchant for binary symmetry that has been mentioned earlier; and one might even speculate that expressing ambiguity may be related to the human ability to take the role of the other, and to view things conversely. In any case, both cultures insist that life within the grid of a small town is superior to living next to nature's chaos.

The grid pattern of perfect squares is eminently egalitarian; one block is exactly like another. However, both societies are strongly hierarchical; since colonial times both have had people at the top and people (and slaves) at the bottom. The intersection of the binary value of civilization over nature with the hierarchical structure of society transforms the egalitarian, rectangular grid into a circle, with civilization at the center and nature at the peripheries. Both societies have traditionally designated the center of the grid, where paved streets form neat squares, as the focal point of their cultures, and they have assigned the grid's peripheries, where dirt streets fade into curving paths, to the social edges of their universes.

In Spanish America, the center is defined by the plaza, flanked on one side by the Catholic church and on another by the secular establishment. In the South, it is set apart by the courthouse, the pillared symbol of ordered authority in a hierarchical society, located in the middle of the central square and bounded by lawns and trees (Price, 1968). Placed at a strategic corner is the war memorial. In the more prosperous communities the memorial may be, as in Spanish America, a man on horseback, or in other communities it may be a soldier standing guard; but, in either case, on the base are engraved the words, "Lest we forget." The memorial, of course, is not to the heroes in the struggle for independence from England, but to the Confederacy.

Only a block or two from the square are the major churches of southern towns—Methodist, Presbyterian, Episcopalian, and, especially, Baptist—with the First Baptist Church a close rival to the courthouse in size and splendor.

Around the plaza in Spanish America, and near the courthouse square in the South, are the older homes of the established elite. In Spanish America, the homes are solid castles with plain walls that rise immediately from the street, leaving no grassy yard where intruders might dare linger and envy the occupants' happiness (Foster, 1972). The walls, one room deep, block off the interior patio or courtyard, which, in some curious way, resembles the plaza. In the South, the older homes are ornate structures, with cupolas, gingerbread, large windows, and porches. Surrounded by yards dotted with flower beds and trees, these domestic places are much more outwardly oriented than the impregnable fortresses of Spanish America. In both societies, these homes mark the end of the center of their cultures. Between this point and the peripheries are the houses of the less well-to-do. In Spanish America, the houses are often modest versions of the courtyard house; in the South, the small yards of the more simple structures of the white working class are cluttered with dogs and junk cars. Somewhere in this nebulous region, away from the center but not in the peripheries, is, in the South, the Catholic chapel, whose priest comes once a month to hold mass. In Spanish America and much closer to the grid's edge is a Protestant church, where, on Sundays, you can hear, "When The Roll Is Called Up Yonder," sung in Spanish.

At the edge of the Spanish-American town, the structures that line the dirt streets and trails are nearly styleless—four walls of split bamboo, perhaps, and a roof of thatch or rusting bits of corrugated metal. In colonial times the work force of the city lived here, Indians for the most part, particularly in the highlands, but also Negroes, mulattoes, and mestizoes. Today, the racial and ethnic divisions are less sharply drawn, but the work force is still here, their skin, colored by genes and by sun, considerably darker than that of the people who live near the plaza. In the South, the heritage of the caste system expresses itself in continual vigor. At the edges of the grid, where they have been since slavery, live the blacks. Here, in the "Quarters," are the crowded rental structures of the poor; the larger, more spacious houses of the black middle class; the numerous Baptist churches; the elitist African Methodist Episcopal church; and the small black businesses.

In their settlement patterns, both distinctive and similar, these two New World societies have constructed a definition of themselves as differentiated from and higher than nature. As hierarchical societies they have reshaped the grid pattern into a vertical continuum that ranges from center to edge, from civilization to nature. They imply related continua that go from religion to amoralism, authority to lawlessness, wealth to poverty, and white to dark. Because of the dominance of Catholicism and the absence of the caste system (at least since independence), the continuum is purest in Spanish America. In the South, competition among the Christian denominations, the caste system, and the internal rankings within the black half of the society obtrudes into the symmetry. However, both societies are clear in their harsh assessment of color: white is at the center, near civilization; dark is at the edge, near nature.

At the civilized center, surrounded by all that separates them from nature and that elevates them from their animal heritage, the two societies act out their heroic quest for significance in the struggle against death.

In Spanish America, the quest takes place in the parish church, appropriately the most imposing structure in town. Ornate and massive, it presents its face to the plaza. Above its large entrance is frequently a pediment, a heritage from classical times, its triangular lines often obscured by scrolls, whorls, and protuberances of one kind or another. Centered in the pediment is a large window, a clock, or a niche sheltering the image of the town's patron saint. On one side of the pediment, frequently on both, rises a tower, with windows and niches, and a real bell that peals forth at numerous intervals (Figure 3).

Inside the church, plaques depicting the scenes of Jesus' path to the

Figure 3.   The Spanish-American church, with steeple and saint.

cross line the dark walls. Between the plaques stand the holy men, the saints, staring out at the congregation—St. Paul, St. Peter, St. Martin of Porres—their lacquered eyes shining in the light of candles that the faithful have placed at their feet. In the corner by the altar rail is the Mother of God. Dressed in pure white and delicate blue she holds the Christ Child in her hands, and the sorrow on her gentle face betrays her knowledge of the future. Over the altar, high above the priest, hangs the figure of Christ. Nailed to the cross and crowned with a ring of thorns, Christ looks at the congregation as if to plead with them to release him from his crucifixion and bring an end to his perpetual agony.

With this setting as a stage, the townspeople come together to construct a collective self. It is during Easter, during Holy Week, that their efforts are most explicitly dramatical. From Palm Sunday through Holy Wednesday, processions leave the church to march around town in commemoration of events in Jesus' life. On Thursday normal business activity stops, and the town is strangly silent. A special procession commemorates the first communion, and then Friday dawns. The priest leads a solemn procession out of the church and down the steps. He murmurs a prayer, and the townspeople, principally women in somber black with their heads covered with mantillas, follow his prayer with a low and mournful chant. Above the procession and standing in a platform carried by men is the Christ figure, his head bleeding from the crown of thorns and his shoulders bent under the weight of the cross.

As the procession moves slowly through the streets, it periodically pauses. Each pause is a station of the cross, an event that took place when Christ made the original journey to Calvary—where he fell the first time, where he was lashed by the Roman soldier, where Veronica wiped his face with a cloth—and at each stop, the participants kneel, pray, and then continue on, the sound of their chanting rising above the silent town. After the completion of the symbolic journey and the return to the church, the Friday services continue with a special sermon delivered at 3 P.M., the hour of Christ's death. Saturday is a quiet day, and the mass at midnight to commemorate the resurrection is an anticlimax to the drama of Friday. Easter Sunday resembles the other Sundays of the year, and is a quiet epilogue to the eventful week (Richardson, Bode, & Pardo, 1971).

The principal religious structure in the upland South, the First Baptist Church, is conspicuously plain (Figure 4). In contrast to the sinuous lines of Spanish-American Catholicism, the southern First Baptist is sharp rectangles and pointed angles. The only curves are the white columns that support the large pediment that may run across the entire front. In its triangular shape, the pediment is a prominent reminder of the classical heritage of both cultures, but in the Baptist expression its austere lines are free of scrolls and whorls. The structure may not even have a steeple. Inside, the walls are light and plain. Not one saint and

Figure 4.   The upland South First Baptist Church, with pediment and columns (photo courtesy of Dr. Sam Hilliard).

not one Virgin, in statue or picture, adorn the sides. The only color is the light coming through the stained glass windows and the flowers placed on the table in front of the pulpit. From this table is served, not Holy Communion, but the Lord's Supper, and as they sip the grape juice and taste the cracker, the congregation is reminded that they do this only in *remembrance* of Christ. Behind the pulpit is the choir, and above the choir, where in Spanish America Christ hangs in perpetual agony, there is the baptistry, where those who have accepted Jesus as their personal savior are fully immersed, to rise reborn in Christ.

The differences between the two structures are matched by the differences in behavior: the Baptists never kneel and the Catholics rarely sit still, the Baptists sing and the Catholics chant, and the minister preaches salvation for those who are lost while the priest offers communion to those who have confessed. Highlighting these differences and counterposed to the Catholic Christ is the collective self that the Baptists construct on Easter.

For the Baptists of the South, Easter is Sunday, the day Christ arose. It is an important day, but perhaps not as important as December 25, the day Jesus was born. In any case, Easter is an occasion for a full church at the 11 o'clock morning service, the women sparkling in their newly purchased finery, the men glad-handing each other at the church door. Some churches may hold a sunrise service and gather at a convenient outdoor location, such as the high school football field, but, regardless, the emphasis of the ritual is on Christ's resurrection.

In both sermon and song, the words ring out. The minister shouts, "Why do you seek the living among the dead? The stone that covered the tomb has been rolled away. Christ has arisen! He is with his Father, who is in Heaven, and he has gone there to prepare a place for you. 'For God so loved the world that He gave his only son, that whosoever believed in him should not perish, but have eternal life.' He suffered. He died. And on the third day, He arose!"

The choir sings,

> Up from the grave He arose (He arose).
> With a mighty triumph o'er His foes (He arose).
> He arose a victor from the dark domain,
> And He lives forever with His saints to reign.
> He arose! (He arose) He arose! (He arose)
> Hallelujah! Christ arose!

> (Sims, 1956, p. 113)

The interpretation of these two complex, culturally rich social places, the Spanish-American Catholic church and the southern-American Baptist church, will, of necessity, be brief and incomplete. It begins with underscoring the view that the two peoples are using their respective material settings to stage a definition of a situation. The situation they are defining, through their joint, congregational behavior, is the heroic triumph of civilization over nature. Like Gilgamesh, these two cultures are revolting against death. They are denying impotence through the construction of a self that tests the nature of death. The self they construct, the Christ image, conquers death, and likewise so will they—until they die. But even as they die individually, the collective self they have jointly shaped continues on through the acts of others. As in the general case of culture, they become Christ, and Christ becomes them.

This reciprocity materializes through the idiom of the two cultures; they speak the Christian language with different accents. Both talk of Christ, his death, and his resurrection; but, in Spanish-American culture, Christ is God who *died*, and then arose to be God once more. In the culture of the Baptist South, Christ is God who died and then *arose* to become God once more.

The Spanish-American accent on the death of Christ is depicted in both setting and behavior. Both stage and performance are explicitly dramatic. Carved figures and costumed people represent the holy figures of the faith both in church and in procession, and the pain and the sorrow that death calls forth are clearly portrayed in their postures and in their faces. On Holy Friday, as the townspeople carry Christ to his cross, they symbolically walk toward their own individual deaths. In dramatic rehearsal, they exaggerate the emotions of death, so that Christ's victorious struggle—to die continually, and still remain God—becomes their own achievement and their own immortality.

The southern accent on the resurrection of Christ also is expressed in setting and behavior. The complete absence of statuary and processions, no doubt, reflects the history of the Protestant reaction to Catholicism; it is also the Baptist construction of the risen Christ. The Baptist stage and performance conveys the message that Christ does not appear materially on earth; he may be felt with the heart, but not with the fingers. The baptistry, located above the minister, replaces the crucified Jesus, located above the priest, as the dominant symbol of the group. Baptism by full immersion "is a dramatic re-enactment of the death, burial, and resurrection of Jesus" (Smith, 1958, p. 108), so the baptistry becomes a symbolic tomb, empty, with the stone rolled away. In the Easter service, both sermon and song celebrate, not a Christ engaged in a victorious struggle, but a Christ who has already won the battle; and so death is transformed into a temporary transition, a prelude, to a new existence that has no end.

In the grid-stamped landscape of two New World cultures, the historical continuum that stretches back to Mesopotamia and beyond, past the cave paintings, past the burials, past a million years and more, extending, perhaps, back to the first pebble tools in Olduvai gorge, this continuum achieves reality once more. The confrontation with nature has been staged and performed once again, and already the players are preparing for the next act; for, as with Gilgamesh, an inner turmoil is left raging, a vital question still unanswered, and a paradox unresolved.

SUMMARY, UNCERTAINTIES, AND FUTURE WORK

This chapter argues that people use their built environment as ways of locating themselves with respect to nature and with respect to each other. This summary will review the main steps of the argument, indicate major points that are not clear, and suggest areas for additional work. First, the human paradox, man's mystery, is that man is a product of natural processes, yet he lives within a self-created world. This means that the boundaries between nature and man, and between the "I" he is and the "me" others see, are not stable. They have to be reconstructed continually; thus, identity becomes central to our existence (Altman, 1975, p. 50).

The emergence of human self-reflexivity occurred in the Pleistocene. Exciting interpretations of that epochal time will continue to stir our imagination (for example, Johanson & White, 1979); in the meantime, the record is one of human adaptation to a world that humans themselves were creating. Delaying the emergence of a completely differentiated self trying to wrestle meaning out of an open-ended universe until the emergence of civilization may recall Paul Radin's attack on Lucien Lévy-Bruhl for the latter's conclusion that the primitive mind was prelogical (Radin, 1957). In suggesting a relationship between a type of self and civilization, I am not implying any difference between the intellectual capabilities of contemporary primitives and of civilized man. Likewise, I do not mean to imply that all early civilizations were "highly carpentered"; as Arensberg mentions (1968), there are the "green cities" of Yucatan, south India, and west Africa south of the Sudan. Nor do I mean to suggest that the only civilized self is the heroic one; there is, I am sure, a contemplative self; but the heroic self seems more descriptive of what we do, as opposed to what we wish. What I do mean to propose is a relationship between a material differentiation from nature, and a conceptual one: the more we build, the more isolated we become, both from the natural environment and from our primate sociality; the more isolated we become, the more heroic is our quest for significance.

Second, in trying to tie the notion of an heroic self to everyday life in small urban places, I have used the ideas of symbolic interaction in a way the specialist may see as crudely incomplete. Nonetheless, the symbolic interactionist consideration of how a bipedal primate treats himself as an object, is both a synchronic interpretation of the Pleistocene hominid record and a statement on the communications function of the built environment. Because of the powerful insight of this position, social scientists in other fields will, in due course, make increasing use of its concepts; the symposium on geographical perspectives in symbolic interactionism at the 1978 meeting of American Sociological Association indicates this growing trend.

Third, a noticeable gap in the argument is the one between symbolic interaction as a social psychological process and specific cultural idioms. Crossing the gap between nomothetic processes and idiographic forms has long challenged anthropologists. They have thought of the gap as being the distance between form and meaning, or history and function, and most have gone from one side to the other via the "leap of faith" presented here. Geertz's discussion (1975) of ethnography as a dialectic between the experience-near world of the informant and the experience-far abstractions of the ethnographer, may be the foundation upon which can be constructed a more sturdy traverse.

The stereotype of the volatile Latin very much aside, the cultural idiom of Spanish America is more explicitly dramatical than that of the South. I am not certain how to handle that idiom within the framework of the basic premise that all human action is dramaturgical. In distinguishing between the plaza and the market, I said that plaza behavior is proper, on stage, and observational, and that market behavior is smart, off stage, and participative. This dichotomy does not distinguish between Spanish-American and southern religious behavior, because both are proper, on stage, and observational. One could suggest that Spanish-American religious behavior is more observational, and therefore more theatrical, than Southern Baptist; but that is hardly an explanation. Parenthetically, probably no culture can be smart, off stage, and participative in its confrontation with death.

Fourth, both Spanish-American and southern towns, caught up in the surges of modernization, are redefining the grid. In the larger communities in Spanish America, the plaza, curvilinear and green, is now a paved parking lot (Gade, 1976). But the conquistador is still there, still seated on his rearing stallion, his arm still raised to urge us on into the fray, as the cars screech, honk, and blow oily black smoke about him. In the South, as part of a country where the surges of modernization crest higher and fall with greater force, the redefinition proceeds apace. The construction of white-, middle- and upper-class homes on the outskirts of town, and the construction of shopping centers to serve that population, have turned the downtown area dark. The observer cannot help but grin and shrug at the unconscious irony of black men leisurely passing the time of day beneath the cold stare of the Confederate soldier, the words, "Lest we forget," almost hidden by the coarse weeds sprouting rankly around the base. In this new, fluid arrangement, perhaps the suburbs become the center, with nature on one side and downtown on the other. Perhaps the society no longer has a center, but only a series of circles, occasionally touching, frequently colliding, and somehow continuing.

Finally, reflecting the restless quality of human endeavor, social places take shape, change, and break apart, only to be replaced by others of similar fate. The material surroundings take new forms and cue for new acts. New acts may use old stages to present evocative images, which in time may grow stale and lose their meaning. Social places are to be discovered, comprehended, and presented, not as things in themselves, to be counted up, cataloged, and forgotten, but for what they reveal about the dramaturgical process by which people present themselves as unique individuals, as members of particular cultures, and as spokesmen for the species.

In the presentation of social places, the social science investigator, as Buttimer (1976) and Wagner (1975) have thoughtfully explored in other contexts, has a crucial, if inconspicuous role. His procedure for investigating a social place duplicates that of the people he is attempting to understand. He scans the material surroundings, observes the behavior as it flows about him, gathers in local explanations, and then formulates his own image. Articulated and refined, his image becomes his analysis. Grasping about for concrete expressions, he transforms the analysis into a prose that, if he is successful, evokes both a cerebral and a visceral response. At his best, at his very best, the social science trappings slip away, and the investigator becomes a teller (Richardson, 1975). As a teller, he talks of places where humans, caught in nature's uncaring paradox, move through the mist of their own minds as it swirls about them in ever-thickening spirals. Haunted by a reality they cannot forget, and cursed with a determination they cannot lay down, they search through the mist for those delicate seconds when laughter is spontaneous, when tears are unashamed, and when a friend's hand reaches out.

ACKNOWLEDGMENTS

The observations on Spanish America draw upon fieldwork done in Colombia, 1962–1963, and work in Costa Rica, and travel in Mexico during the summers of 1967 and 1972 through 1976. The observations on the upland South draw upon my personal experience, and upon fieldwork in northern Louisiana during the summer of 1978. The International Center for Medical Research and Training, Tulane University, and Universidad del Valle, Cali, Colombia, funded the work in Colombia, and the Graduate Council, Louisiana State University, supported a portion of the work in Costa Rica. Several of the points made about symbolic interactionism and the built environment as sets of behavioral cues parallel those in Rapoport (1977). I thank the editors of this volume for their most helpful comments on a first draft of this chapter, and I am especially grateful for Professor Rapoport's encouragement.

REFERENCES

Altman, I. *The environment and social behavior.* Monterey, Calif.: Brooks/Cole, 1975.
Arensberg, C. The urban in crosscultural perspective. In E. Eddy (Ed.), *Urban anthropology: Research perspectives and strategies.* Proceedings of the Southern Anthropological Society, 1968, 2, 3–15.
Ashcraft, N., & Scheflen, A. *People space.* Garden City, N. Y.: Anchor, 1976.
Becker, E. *The denial of death.* New York: Free Press, 1973.
Becker, E. *Escape from evil.* New York: Free Press, 1975.
Bellah, R. Religious evolution. *American Sociological Review*, 1964, 24, 358–374.
Berger, P. *Invitation to sociology.* Garden City, N. Y.: Anchor, 1963.
Berger, P., & Luckmann, T. *The social construction of reality.* Garden City, N. Y.: Anchor, 1967.
Berger, P., & Pullberg, S. Reification and the sociological critique of consciousness. *History and Theory*, 1965, 4, 196–211.
Birdwhistell, R. *Kinesics and context.* Philadelphia: University of Pennsylvania Press, 1970.
Blumer, H. *Symbolic interactionism.* Englewood Cliffs, N. J.: Prentice-Hall, 1969.
Brisset, D., & Edgley, C. (Eds.). *Life as theater.* Chicago: Aldine, 1975.
Bronowski, J., & Bellugi, U. Language, name, and concept. *Science*, 1970, 168, 669–673.
Burke, K. *Language as symbolic action.* Berkeley: University of California Press, 1966.
Buttimer, A. Grasping the dynamism of lifeworld. *Annals of the Association of American Geographers*, 1976, 66, 277–292.
Butzer, K. Environment, culture, and human evolution. *American Scientist*, 1977, 65, 572–584.
Denzin, N. Symbolic interactionism and ethnomethodology: A proposed synthesis. *American Sociological Review*, 1969, 34, 922–934.
Downs, R., & Stea, D. (Eds.). *Image and environment.* Chicago: Aldine, 1973.
Duncan, H. *Symbols in society.* New York: Oxford University Press, 1968.
Eiseley, L. *The unexpected universe.* New York: Harcourt, Brace & World, 1969.
Fairservis, W., Jr. *The threshold of civilization.* New York: Scribner, 1975.

Falk, W., & Pinhey, T. Making sense of the concept rural and doing rural sociology: An interpretative perspective. *Rural Sociology*, 1978, *43*, 547–558.

Foster, G. The anatomy of envy: A study in symbolic behavior. *Current Anthropology*, 1972, *13*, 165–202.

Freilich, M. Myth, method, and madness. *Current Anthropology*, 1975, *16*, 207–226.

Fuentes, C. *La nueva novela hispanoamericana*. México: Editorial Joaquín Mortiz, 1972.

Gade, D. The Latin American central plaza as functional space. *Proceedings of the Conference of Latin Americanist Geographers*, 1976, *5*, 16–23.

Geertz, C. The impact of the concept of culture on the concept of man. In J. Platt (Ed.), *New views on the nature of man*. Chicago: University of Chicago Press, 1965, pp. 93–118.

Geertz, C. On the nature of anthropological understanding. *American Scientist*, 1975, *63*, 47–53.

Gibson, H. *Deer hunting clubs in Concordia Parish*. Unpublished master's thesis, Louisiana State University Press, 1976.

Goffman, E. *The presentation of self in everyday life*. Garden City, N. Y.: Anchor, 1959.

Goffman, E. *Behavior in public places*. New York: Macmillan, 1963.

Gould, P., & White, R. *Mental maps*. London: Pelican, 1974.

Hall, E. *The silent language*. Garden City, N. Y.: Anchor, 1959.

Hall, E. *The hidden dimension*. Garden City, N. Y.: Anchor, 1969.

Hall, E. *Beyond culture*. Garden City, N. Y.: Anchor, 1977.

Hallowell, I. Self, society, and culture in phylogenetic perspective. In S. Tax (Ed.), *The evolution of man*. Chicago: University of Chicago Press, 1960, pp. 309–371.

Holloway, R. Culture: A *human* domain. *Current Anthropology*, 1969, *10*, 395–412.

Jacobsen, T. Mesopotamia. In H. Frankfort, H. A. Frankfort, J. Wilson, & T. Jacobsen (Eds.), *Before philosophy*. Harmondsworth, England: Penguin Books, 1949, pp. 137–237.

Johanson, D., & White, T. A systematic assessment of early African hominids. *Science*, 1979, *203*, 321–330.

King, A. The five-thousand-year challenge. In J. Aceves (Ed.), *Aspects of cultural change*. Proceedings of the Southern Anthropological Society, 1972, *6*, 7–19.

Leakey, R. Australopithecines and hominines: A summary of the evidence from the early Pleistocene of eastern Africa. *Symposia of the Zoological Society of London*, 1973, *33*, 53–69.

León Hazera, L. de. *La novela de la selva hispanoamericana*. Bogotá: Instituto Caro y Cuervo, 1971.

León-Portilla, M. *Aztec thought and culture* (J. Davis, trans.). Norman: University of Oklahoma Press, 1963.

Lingenfelter, S. Emic structure and decision making. *Ethnology*, 1977, *16*, 331–352.

Lofland, L. *A world of strangers*. New York: Basic Books, 1973.

Mason, H. *Gilgamesh: A verse narrative*. New York: New American Library, 1972.

McHenry, H. Fossils and the mosaic nature of human evolution. *Science*, 1975, *190*, 425–431.

Meltzer, B., & Petras, J. The Chicago and Iowa schools of symbolic interactionism. In T. Shibutani (Ed.), *Human nature and collective behavior*. Englewood Cliffs, N. J.: Prentice-Hall, 1970, pp. 3–17.

Messinger, S., Sampson, H., & Towne, R. Life as theater: Some notes on the dramaturgic approach to social reality. *Sociometry*, 1962, *25*, 98–110.

Newton, M., Jr. Settlement patterns as artifacts of social structure. In M. Richardson (Ed.), *The human mirror*. Baton Rouge: Louisiana State University Press, 1974a, pp. 339–362.

Newton, M., Jr. Cultural preadaptation and the Upland South. In J. Walker & W. Haag (Eds.), *Man and cultural heritage. Geoscience and man*, 1974b, *5*, pp. 143–154.

Perinbanayagam, R. The definition of the situation: An analysis of the ethnomethodological and dramaturgical view. *The Sociological Quarterly*, 1974, *15*, 521–541.

Price, E. The central courthouse square in the American county seat. *The Geographical Review*, 1968, *58*, 31–60.

Radin, P. Primitive man as philosopher (rev. ed.). New York: Dover, 1957.

Rapoport, A. Australian aborigines and the definition of place. In P. Oliver (Ed.), *Shelter, sign, and symbol*. London: Barrie & Jenkins, 1975, pp. 38–51.

Rapoport, A. *Human aspects of urban form*. Oxford: Pergamon Press, 1977.

Redfield, R. *Primitive world and its transformations*. Ithaca, N.Y.: Cornell University Press, 1957.

Richardson, M. Gilgamesh and Christ: Two contradictory models of man in search of a better world. In J. Aceves (Ed.), *Aspects of cultural change*. Proceedings of the Southern Anthropological Society, 1972, *6*, pp. 7–19.

Richardson, M. The Spanish American (Colombian) settlement pattern as a societal expression and as a behavioral cause. In J. Walker & W. Haag (Eds.), *Man and cultural heritage. Geoscience and man*, 1974, *5*, pp. 35–52.

Richardson, M. Anthropologist: The myth teller. *American Ethnologist*, 1975, *2*, 517–534.

Richardson, M. La plaza como lugar social: El papel del lugar en el encuentro humano. *Vínculos: Revista de Antropología del Museo Nacional de Costa Rica*, 1978, *4*, 1–20.

Richardson, M., Bode, B., & Pardo, M. The image of Christ in Spanish America as a model for suffering. *Journal of Inter-American Studies*, 1971, *13*, 246–257.

Rowlett, R., & Schneider, M. The material expression of Neanderthal child care. In M. Richardson (Ed.), *The human mirror*. Baton Rouge: Louisiana State University Press, 1974, pp. 41–58.

Sandars, N. *The epic of Gilgamesh*. London: Penguin, 1960.

Scheff, T. Toward a sociological model of consensus. *American Sociological Review*, 1967, *32*, 32–46.

Scheff, T. The distancing of emotion in ritual. *Current Anthropology*, 1977, *18*, 483–505.

Sims, W. *Baptist hymnal*. Nashville: Convention Press, 1956.

Smith, T. Baptism. *Encyclopedia of Southern Baptists*. Nashville: Broadman, 1958.

Storni, A. Cuadrados y ángulos. *Obra poética completa*. Buenos Aires: Sociedad Editora Latino Americana, 1964.

Tuan, Y. Ambiguity in attitudes toward the environment. *Annals of the Association of American Geographers*, 1973, *63*, 411–423.

Tuan, Y. Images and mental maps. *Annals of the Association of American Geographers*, 1975, *65*, 205–213.

Tyler, S. (Ed.). *Cognitive anthropology*. New York: Holt, Rinehart, & Winston, 1969.

Wagner, R. *The invention of culture*. Englewood Cliffs, N. J.: Prentice-Hall, 1975.

Wilson, T. Conceptions of interaction and forms of sociological explanation. *American Sociological Review*, 1970, *35*, 697–710.

Wolpoff, M. Competitive exclusion among lower Pleistocene hominids: The single species hypothesis. *Man*, 1971, *6*, 601–614.

7

Human Ecology as Human Behavior

A NORMATIVE ANTHROPOLOGY OF RESOURCE USE AND ABUSE

JOHN W. BENNETT

INTRODUCTION

Since the term "anthropology" appears in the title, and since anthropology is intimately associated with the concept of culture, it is necessary at the outset to describe the writer's views on the use and meaning of the concept. I consider that "culture" is an abstract generalization made from observing behavior, and, as such, it cannot be a cause of that same behavior.[1] However, some of the various phenomena included in the catchall conception of culture are undeniably influential in shaping concepts and practices related to the physical environment. But these phenomena have differing roles to play in this complex process, and therefore must be treated separately. For example, while ideology may influence conceptions of the conservation of resources for posterity,

[1] The view is developed in Bennett, 1976b. The present paper is an attempt at synthesizing various aspects of a theoretical argument appearing in the former, and in other publications, particularly Bennett, 1968, 1976a, 1978a. The title of the paper is borrowed from a lecture presented by the writer to the Institute of Ecology, University of California (Davis), in 1976.

JOHN W. BENNETT • Department of Anthropology, Washington University, St. Louis, Missouri 63130.

consumer desires may work in the opposite direction. To say that "culture" shapes or determines our use of the environment thus has little meaning. It is necessary to specify what components of culture, in what circumstances, at what times. Moreover, it is necessary to translate these cultural elements into active behavioral tendencies: responses and adaptations made by real people in real-life contexts.

Anthropologists also use the term "culture" to refer to particular historical entities: groups of people who presumably possess a distinctive life-style. This usage grew out of the ethnological style of research: making field studies of discrete communities or "tribes," each of which was treated as if it were a social isolate. In this usage, each culture would have its own pattern of adaptation to the physical environment. Evolutionary considerations entered the picture as anthropologists attempted to develop a typology of levels or stages of adaptation, based on major subsistence patterns: hunting and gathering, pastoralism, settled agriculture, and so on. The approach received its modern treatment by Julian Steward (1955), who called it "cultural ecology."[2]

The association of ecological adaptations to environment with a typology of cultures and culture stages contributed important knowledge, but it was not capable of analyzing adaptation as a process which takes place in human behavior, and possesses regularities which may be independent of cultures and stages of development. Lacking the capacity to view adaptation and use of the physical environment (and social phenomena *qua* environment) as a dynamic process, it was not possible for cultural ecologists to provide answers to the difficult question of why humans do what they do to the environment (and to each other). That is, causal inquiries into the reasons and cures for particular forms of environmental abuse were not easily accomplished in the absence of a behavioral theory of purposive use of the environment.

Thus, in order to acquire solutions to the problems of environmental use and abuse, it is necessary to translate "culture," however defined, into relevant behavioral tendencies and activities. A "normative anthropology" of environmental use thus is defined as an inquiry into the social and behavioral context of human intervention in the physical environment, or of the "resources" which they conceptually analyze out of the physical context. Meaningful theory in this sphere must have its takeoff in real issues and practical concerns. These are generalized in this paper as a proposition that the human use of the environment is out

---

[2]See Steward, 1955 for basic papers. Bennett, 1976a, Chapter 7, contains a critique of Steward's work and the cultural ecology tradition. Moran, 1979, adds material.

of control, and that there is danger in this situation, both for the state of the environment, and for human welfare, health, and survival.

The human use of the physical environment is a multidimensional affair. No one scholarly discipline can attempt to comprehend it in totality, and attempts to unify the disciplines to create a synthetic human ecology have mostly failed.[3] Consequently, the problem of the human use of the environment is divided between the social and physical sciences, and between the theoretical and applied branches of each. In the social sciences alone, one can distinguish psychological, cultural, institutional, and behavioral dimensions: the first of these concerns possible underlying neural processes and capacities; the second, the precedents, values, and symbols which define the meaning of the environment, and resources; the third, the configurated sets of rules and expected decisions and responses in key fields like economics and law; and the last, the spontaneous, adaptive or adjustive behavioral responses made by individual humans to the physical, and also to the cultural and institutional dimensions—which together might be called the "social environment" (with technology, or the "built" environment, a subclass). The behavioral component is the one of key importance for this paper, since it is considered to be primarily responsible for the constant dynamism of modern approaches to environment and resource use. In contemporary society, constraints against behavior designed to satisfy wants are weak; hence, there are few reliable controls. The ethnological literature, on the other hand, provides us with examples of human groups which occasionally have achieved strict institutional control over environmental use. The significance of these differences will be discussed later.

In societies with weak institutional controls, one also finds disjunction between the various social dimensions. A society with a well-publicized ideological respect for nature can nevertheless ruthlessly exploit and degrade its resources, if there are segmental institutional forces which can safely ignore the ideology. Japan is a case: economic growth was considered to be more important, by the government and the business–industrial oligarchy, than the nature-respecting values in the aesthetic culture. But tribal cultures have similar problems: in the Sahel, pastoralists who had achieved a stable balance between their population, herds, and vegetation cover for centuries, began abusing their pasturage under the influence of economic development programs and the drawing of political boundaries which prevented normal transhum-

---

[3]See Bennett, 1976a, Chapter 3, for discussions of the various disciplinary approaches to human ecology.

ant movement.[4] In this case, the forces accelerating degradational use of the habitat came from the outside; in the Japanese case, the source of the impetus is probably mainly internal. But from the viewpoint of this paper, the source may be less important than the behavioral patterns concerning perseverance of habits, survival anxieties, and accumulating wants.

Whether it is possible to achieve a resource ecology that can create a general theory uniting the psychological, institutional, and cultural components remains to be seen. We can only experiment with the ideas, as we do in this paper, and design particular research projects that attempt to bring into alignment two or more of the component dimensions. There is great need for adequate models of behavior here: models which emphasize the key processes of want satisfaction, task accomplishment, and the like. We suggest one or two in this paper.

A normative psychology of environmental use should carry the assumption that humans are multipotential organisms, whose varying capacities emerge and change as they deal with wants and survival necessities. This is a temporal process since it requires various degrees of anticipation, desire, foresight, and planning. As humans deal with the contexts of existence (which include social and mental milieus, as already suggested, in addition to the social, the built, and the physical environments, they create new problems, so that living becomes a matter of solutions to a chain of problems, each solution involving a combination of past precedents and present innovations.

From this it follows that to understand behavior one must view it both as a set of psychological processes which are probably universal or nearly so, and as a set of novel behavioral responses adapted to particular times and situations. One must, therefore, know about institutions and precedents, in order to determine why people do what they do in particular places and times. But this knowledge can never answer all questions. One must always allow for some emergent novelty in the situation, or simply a certain basic unpredictability as to which of the many possible or logical responses that humans are capable of are likely to make their appearance. There are some generalizations at the cultural and institutional levels about the causes of the human abuse of the physical environment, but they do not work for all societies at all times. While the problem of abuse is very much a behavioral problem, it is also a problem of how behavior is shaped by current institutions. Thus, the

[4]For the Japanese case, see Bennett and Levine, 1976; for the Sahelian case, and the general problem of "desertification, see Schechter, 1977; Sheets and Morris, 1974.

problem has both unpredictable and predictable aspects, and it is often difficult to know which is which.

A basic empirical process of human behavior, in the context of how and why humans abuse resources, concerns what may be called the tilt toward gratification, or more generally, toward cumulative processes which often result in exponential growth curves. This process suggests that human behavior lacks a set of physiological or neural controls over gratification or goal accomplishment (these are the same thing ecologically—the distinction has purely social significance). If humans are to control their wants or needs, they must do so by responses to situations; or they must be constrained by available technology at given levels of development; by scarcity which is either natural or induced by humans; or finally, by moral or legal controls residing in precedents in the institutions. However one classifies these control measures, the point to be emphasized is that none of them can be assumed to operate automatically. Humans are not broadly subject (as are animals) to automatically operating controlling processes based on systemic relationships and feedbacks, since humans can manipulate and change the systemic processes. However, the fact that human systems can be subject to governing forces *to a degree*—as, for example, in the case of tribal groups who lived by hunting and the gathering of vegetable foods—does not modify the fact that, over time, humans overcome such forces, and bend the physical environment in desired directions to serve gratification. In other words, no useful public purpose, or policy objective, can be served, it seems to me, by emphasizing the existence of homeostatic processes in human ecology, even though they may appear from time to time. They are too easily overridden, as the exponential curves of population growth and energy use indicate.

Another important issue is the distinction between the control function at individual and at group or societal levels. An individual who has learned to control his wants is not necessarily the prototype of the group which uses fewer resources or abuses them least. That is, individual want control can be irrelevant[5] for group resource use control, since, in

[5]I use the term "resources" here not as a purely physical phenomenon, but as a cultural one. That is, I obviously assume that humans define or create resources. However, once defined, they can be viewed as physical components which can be used, husbanded, etc. The tendency to forget that humans create the concept of resource is one of the behaviors leading toward exploitative abuse. Consequently, we need to externalize the process of resource creation and subject it to control. In the ideal–typical isolated tribal society (probably always nonexistent, and certainly so today), there was no need for conceptualization of resources, or their conservation.

the quest for control over the use of some resources, the group may abuse other resources. Moreover, low individual use can add up to high aggregate use by the group. A trivial example may be found in the cultural dropout or hippie communities which appeared in wilderness areas during the 1960s, as an attempt to live in tune with natural processes. Many of these communities were abusive of the environment. At a more imposing level, the quest for less-abusive mass energy sources may simply introduce alternatives which have even more serious impacts. Moreover, the finding of alternatives to abusive practices, while satisfying behaviorally or cognitively, may not alter the basic institutional fact of abuse in a larger sense.

THE PROCESS OF ADAPTATION

It seems to me that the adaptive potential in human behavior is the heart of the matter. That is, adaptation is a way of conceptualizing the process which unites the several levels or dimensions of the problem of resource use and abuse. The individual's capacity to cope with the environment can be defined as adaptation, and, likewise, the group's capacity to survive and change can be defined as adaptation. The use of the concept to refer to both individual and group processes is meaningful, but confusing, because the adaptive process is not identical for both—or for the third element, environment. The lack of identity is caused by absorption of the adaptive process into the normative perspective of human thought and action. The following distinctions therefore are necessary:

1. What may be adaptive—i.e., good—for the individual, may be maladaptive—bad—for the group, and *vice versa*. The individual's gratifications may be at the expense of group welfare or continuity, or the group's solidarity may require individual sacrifice.

2. What may be adaptive for the individual or group, may be maladaptive for the environment, and *vice versa*. This is the basic formula in the contemporary environmental situation: in order to protect our environmentally derived resources, or to shield ourselves and the environment against pollution, we must suffer deprivation, or even endanger survival of part of the human population.

Thus, while for scientific purposes it is possible to study the adaptive process objectively, without reference to values, for long-range solutions it is necessary to see it as a *normative*—really moral—process. On a practical level, it means that we solve problems of environmental use and abuse by juggling contradictions which emerge out of the normative intersections described above, and making trade-offs and compromises. As the conceptual and physical transformation of natural substances into resources expands, these contradictions become more numerous: hence, adaptation becomes, in fact, identical to the interplay between them—we increasingly adapt more to each other, in order to resolve human-made contradictions, than to the physical environment.

Adaptation as a general behavioral process[6] is based on the psychological factor of anticipation: foresight, memory, time binding, and so on. The ability to envisage complex sequences of behavior over indefinite spans of time is a fact, even though the capacity of humans to incorporate this institutionally as "planning" seems to be severely limited and subject to constraints of many kinds. The importance of anticipation means that *time* is an inherent factor in adaptive processes, and temporal aspects of adaptation always must be studied if the movements of the behavioral systems are to be thoroughly understood. Adaptive behavior or "strategies" by themselves cannot determine the overall adaptive consequences of a particular sequence of events and processes, as suggested previously. This is so because the time when the observation is made may be merely one point or phase of a complex process. Too many generalizations about human affairs, including the ecological, are made on the basis of incomplete understanding of the importance of temporal unfolding in adaptive processes.

The ability to envisage outcomes and anticipate gratification obviously facilitates the process of exponential accumulation. The corresponding vector in human behavior is suggested by the aphorism, "the more you have the more you want," a process which is not always operative, but which is frequent enough to contribute to generally rising aspirations and wants. The establishment of *precedents* (anthropologists generally use the word "tradition") means that there is always a stimulus available in past accomplishment which can feed present desire. As already noted, the only reliable way this stimulus to accumulative action can be overcome is to deliberately limit its function by moral, social, or physical constraints. The problem with precedents is that they become embodied in the institutional level as protocols, which are interrelated with other elements of the system, and are therefore extremely difficult to change. That is, the dynamic qualities of human existence are only one side of a complex system, the other being conservatism and

[6]The best current symposium on adaptive processes in behavior and psychology is Coelho, Hamburg, and Adams, 1974. For the most part, psychologists conceive of adaptation as coping behavior: manipulating the self and the milieu in order to achieve satisfaction. Usually this conception does not concern itself with temporal processes, or the impact of coping on the social and physical environments.

resistance to change. Or, more explicitly, one way to guarantee change is to preserve, conserve, the precedents for it; i.e., to resist changing them, so they are available to stimulate change. Thus, the behavioral and institutional levels of human action interrelate, and create paradoxes for the scholar who works within one dimension only.

Behaviorally, adaptation involves a contradiction: both tolerance of conditions, and also dissatisfaction. Thus, the term connotes both active and passive change in the individual. However, over the course of history, altered milieus have generally provided a stimulus to change— Toynbee's "challenge and response"—rather than the opposite. In any case, tolerance of conditions has never formed an absolute limit or stopping point to aspiration: sooner or later the movement toward bettering or changing conditions begins, usually in the form of political and economic movements. Adaptive tolerance merges with exploitation when vested interests utilize the ability of populations to "suffer in silence" in order to enhance their own wealth and power.

Embedded in adaptive tolerance is the process of comparative or relative choice: X may be bad, but one can tolerate it in order to obtain Y. In the environmental context, this frequently results in tolerance of pollution if employment or income is related to the conditions producing the pollution. The process leads toward the search for means of avoidance or retreat before the polluted conditions or resource, rather than elimination of the condition. An example is the filtering of impure air or water, instead of removing the source of industrial effluents which cause the impurity.

Adaptation when defined as behavioral coping becomes a general positive value in human existence. That is, there is a high value placed on coping or adjusting in all societies; it is, perhaps, one of the few "universal patterns" which anthropologists have spent so much effort searching for. Sometimes the concept of mastery over nature is linked to the normative process of coping, an especially common pattern in Western civilization since the Industrial Revolution and its increasingly ready transformation of physical substances into resources. In fact, the concept of "resource" is a recent one, and a product of the linkage between coping adaptation and optimistic superordination of humans among the natural species. Once the concept of resource appears, then the way is clear to using resources without limit, restraint being produced only by the artificial means already noted.[7]

The problem of the human relationship to nature is thus in one

---

[7]Cf. Simon's "Sciences of the Artificial" (1969): the mechanisms of quantitative construction of milieu required for planning, regulation, etc.

sense simply the quantitative accumulation of coping solutions—not solely to survival needs, but to the needs or wants which emerge in the process of social living without relationship to the state of physical nature or resources. This detachment or alienation of humans from the physical processes and feedback which control the behavior of other species, and maintain balanced (though changing) systems for those species, is the most general cause of our mounting ecological problems, and has given rise in recent years to a large literature which has attempted to reformulate a behavioral ethic more closely integrated with natural processes (e.g., Dubos, 1969; Hardin, 1972). As already mentioned, this is an essential preliminary step toward reasserting control, but by itself it cannot do the job. Values alone constitute only one of the several necessary modes of control over behavior and the institutions which stimulate this behavior.

A more analytic presentation of some of these concepts and processes is in order. This far, I have used the term "process" in a rather general way, referring to any sequential or continuous manifestation of behavior with cognitive unity; and the terms "coping" and "strategies" to refer loosely to detachable units of such processes. A more precise rendering might be as follows.

First of all, for reasons already presented, it is necessary to distinguish between individual and group levels of adaptation. Starting with the individual, we are concerned with behavioral processes, and the key term here is *coping*. That is, as previously noted, the individual simply deals with circumstances in order to obtain what he needs and/or wants, or to come to terms with the situation (active and passive changing). When his coping behavior takes on patterned and sequential character, and therefore is communicable to others, one may speak of *strategies*, or adaptive strategies. Coping and adaptive strategies are in essence ways of making means appropriate to the ends sought. In this sense, the underlying psychological dynamic is purpose, or goal orientation. Since not all human behavior is purposive, we deliberately restrict the behavioral context here: the topic of this paper is not *all* behavior, but only that crucial segment which relates means to ends. This is not a global social science approach or theory: this should be underlined. As a model of individual and group behavior, it is deliberately restricted to the cognitive–purposive, though, as we shall see in a moment, the linkage between this mode of behavior and other modes becomes a crucial issue.

This linkage is dominated conceptually by the concept of *culture*. As noted previously, in its classical form, culture was a global concept, and, like all such, eventually became nothing more than a descriptive rubric. For analytical purposes, it is necessary to separate culture into components with different causal significance. Among the important ones are the following: the *precedents* or traditions which provide rationalizations for action and the choice of strategies; the *moral precepts* which define the strength and purpose of the action; and the *styles* or routine behaviors which provide the content, themselves embodying all of the previous components. The origins of these components are not confined to the cognitive–purposive mode of behavior, but can be derived from any other mode, including the religious, aesthetic, and affective. Thus, the gods may sanction the attack on nature as the freedom or the right of the individual to achieve gratification. Or, in sociological jargon, the expressive aspects of behavior reinforce and give meaning to the instrumental.

At this point, the behavioral dimension merges into the institutional. The particular configurations of instrumental strategies and cultural sanctions become embodied in systems of action and purpose associated with the major activities of social life (the activity we are primarily concerned with here is, of course, the economic–technological). This institutional system does not exist in a vacuum, but is buttressed by all the others. The interconnections of institutions make change both possible and impossible: this is the heart of the problem. Consuming resources is not only profitable, but can become a definition of the human spirit.

When the element of time is considered, the analysis shifts to *process*. There is a useful distinction between *adjustive processes,* which define the continuity of strategic action at the level of the individual; and *adaptive processes,* at the level of the group. This conveys the idea that the individual, in his coping, does not respond directly to signals from the larger systems, but usually tries merely to achieve gratification in accordance with current styles and modes. The adaptive process level generalizes these individual actions and defines their cumulative effects for the group and for the environment. Examples of *adjustive* or individual-level processes are readily available in the vocabularies of all languages: manipulating, correcting, helping, making pleasurable, and so on. Adaptive processes are usually not rendered by folk lexicons, but are found in the jargon of the specialized fields of study and practical knowledge related to institutions. Social sciences speak of competition for resources; replacement of small-scale systems by large-scale; increasing specialization of technical or any cultural institution which has proven successful; escalation of wants and the escalation of particular technologies due to economic forces such as rising labor costs.[8] Adaptive

[8]See Bennett, 1976a, Chapter 9, for discussion of some of these processes.

processes promote gratification at the group level; the paradox is that as the systems become more complex, the gratification level begins to fall, and new constraints—and discontents—make their appearance.

All of the preceding pertains to the individual and group behavioral aspects of the problem of environmental use. Let us now reverse the coin, and view the situation from the standpoint of the environment. Most of the terms already presented can be used here, but with some changes and additions. If we are interested in the state of the material substances which have been transformed into resources, both for the sake of the social systems that depend on those resources, and also for the sake of the resources themselves, we become concerned with their state of being now and in the future. We are less concerned with the individual's or the group's desires for gratification. We view the problem as an interplay between the human desires and needs, and the conditions of the environment which must satisfy them. That is, a trade-off or bargaining process emerges.

From the standpoint of the environment, it is necessary to distinguish between the *techniques* used by the individual and group to satisfy their wants, and the *strategies* which these techniques make up. A strategy, in this sense, is a sequence or pattern of techniques for using material substances, stretching through time.[9] Secondly, we need to think of the concept of *conservation*, and distinguish it from *preservation*. That is, we acknowledge a domain of ambiguity in the condition of resources: human society could endure indefinitely without certain resources, if they should run out; but the environment might not be able to tolerate such deprivation, and then other changes would take place. Humans generally do not preserve things for the sake of preservation; they *con*serve them, which means that they (should) use them prudently, allowing for change, but at the same time avoiding irreparable or accelerating deterioration. (We hope.)

Finally, viewing the process of adaptation from the viewpoint of the environment, we perceive the individual and the group as performing a series of choices of alternative techniques and strategic patterns, which have varying consequences for the resources and the environment in general. This is the heart of the problem of resource use, and we shall now turn to an analysis of it.

[9]A convenient example may be found in the technique of fallowing in Great Plains grain agriculture. By keeping a certain proportion of the cultivated fields fallow in alternate years, moisture in a semi-arid environment is saved for future use, to be added to the marginal quantities available from precipitation. This generally works on a three-year cycle of moisture use and conservation (for a few more details, see Bennett, 1969/1976, pp. 234-235.

THE PROCESS OF RATIONAL CHOICE

The guiding principle of human behavior in the context of use and abuse of resources is the rational choice of alternative goals and the strategies to achieve them.[10] This process of choice is rooted in human psychology, and its indirect discovery by economists in the last half century is one of the milestones of social science. The economists, trying to make sense out of everyday action and purposive behavior in the real world, had an advantage over the psychologist, who by and large stayed in the laboratory. Rational choice becomes meaningful in relation to real issues and purposes, not vaguely defined or artificial categories. One must be concerned with what humans strive to accomplish; there must be sensitivity to the intrinsic nature of the goals which shape the direction and intensity of the behavior. Thus, choice theory was developed initially in studies of the economic consumption function: humans want things; this is the guiding force in society, and a force which has become more significant as control over the transformation of material substance into resources has progressed.

The basis of rational choice is the aspect connoted by the term "rational." This is not the concept of rationality which is equivalent to common sense, or efficiency, but describes a distinctive feature of thought: the comparison of two or more goals in order to choose among them, and to effect a compromise of some kind. Usually an intervening third factor will influence the choice or trade-off. Undoubtedly animals make such choices, although the mental processes probably do not involve cognition in the human sense. The human endows rational choice with a temporal dimension called *anticipation;* that is, the choice between two or more possible goals and wants is made partly on the basis of differences in the future gains or losses to be expected, as influenced by other factors. Error is, of course, possible and quite common (errors, that is, in choosing as a result of misassessment of value). The classical paradigm of rational choice is represented as a right-angled diagram with desired phenomena on the two axes; for more than two choices, one must construct more complex diagrams, or break the thought process paradigm into two or more two-valued sequences (e.g., if x, y, and z are wanted; then paradigmatically, the chooser must decide between x and y; x and z; y and z). The advantage of this paradigm is that the diagrammatic logic apparently closely matches the actual sequences and patterns of thought. There is probably no other analytical scheme in the social sciences which comes so close to actual mental process. If it were

[10]For a critical introduction to rational choice theory in the social sciences, see Heath, 1976.

possible to discover the choice and decision processes that characterized large-scale movement and precedental configurations (institutions) in societies, one would have a way of linking psychological, behavioral, and institutional components, and thus approximate the needed cross-disciplinary synthesis mentioned in the Introduction.

Whether that is possible I cannot say, but I believe that the process of rational choice is one important tool for the analysis of the behavioral components of resource use and abuse.

To begin, it is necessary to consider that rational choice takes place in a social field, not a vacuum. The resource user receives signals from many sources: his associates, neighbors, competitors, government, the economic marketplace, and the media. The rationality of the choices and decisions made is thus always substantive, which means that allowance has been made for contrasting or conflicting demands, and therefore the choices are vectorial compromises. This means that pure quantitative rationality—e.g., maximization of profits, or the most at the least cost—is an ideal type, and rarely found in real life. Its ideal typicality is useful in creating models and criteria for analysis, but there is always a danger that people will confuse the real with the ideal, as has been done repeatedly with the "economic man" concept. The fact that choice is made in a social milieu does not infringe the degree of rationality involved: the thought process of comparative choice is the same, whether the choice is made in a theoretically pure uninfluenced self-interested vacuum, or whether it is made in a complex milieu, with winds blowing from every direction.

The element of *time* is represented in the process by the anticipation of future gains. That is, the choice between the phenomena in the two-valued model is made on the basis of which of the two will produce the most satisfaction in the future ("expected utility"). In the more elementary applications in economics, this element of time is not really measured, but taken as a given. In more sophisticated sociological versions, either or both of the axes may represent not only quantities to be gained by choices, but also the *change* in these quantities over time. This will become clearer in a moment. The process of decision or choice culminates in a *trade-off* in the type case: a gain along one value or choice axis usually implies a loss along some other, and the ideal solution is, of course, a choice point where exactly the same amount of satisfaction can be gained for both, in relationship to third factors. In such a case no trade-off is involved. Whether a trade-off must occur, or an equalization of gain can be achieved, depends on the phenomena themselves.

In any case, it is important to underline the substantive nature of the whole affair: the outcome depends on situational factors, including behavior patterns and cultural definitions. In real situations of choice, this can become extremely complex, since each phenomenon is accompanied by many other factors. In some situations, the choice will be governed by single, powerful elements which themselves may represent needs; e.g., a choice between two phenomena, say profit and social influence, may be resolved by another valued phenomenon, say the adherence to some ritual behavior pattern which confers prestige. Thus, the chooser may decide to take less profit in order to gain influence over others by behavior in prescribed ways.

The abstract example suggests the dynamics of resource use and abuse. The choice of a particular line of action or goal can be influenced by factors emanating from the social milieu or process, and not only by the condition of the resource itself. As social systems become more complex, the likelihood of a decision on environmental matters being made on purely conservationist grounds is lessened, and the risk of abuse accordingly increases. Thus, humans can abuse their resources even though they know they are doing so, since other values have emerged which dictate abusive exploitation, and these values cannot be resisted. This is not an abnormal situation, but is the rule, because it is a reflection of the institutions emerging out of behavior, which then feed back to channel subsequent behavior.

These ideas give rise to a rather simplified paradigm of resource use (perhaps especially biased toward agriculture and extractive resources), which can be represented by the diagrams in Figure 1A and 1B.[11] Figure 1A shows the rate of resource depletion varying in accordance with particular strategies used; and Figure 1B a particular variable strategy, which includes the three idealized possibilities in Figure 1A represented as alternative choices made over a time period. Taking Figure 1A first:

Resource depletion is deliberately simplified here as a function of desired yield. The higher the yield, the more rapid the rate of depletion. Obviously, many factors affect depletion other than desired yield alone. However, "desired yield" is used here as a kind of central or summary factor to suggest that in the long run, the human use of resources—the demand placed upon them—will result in change or depletion. All use curves thus should be convex to the point of origin of the diagram: over time, any use of a physical resource will serve to deplete it. What is called "sustained yield use" is simply a time function: ultimately, the use will

[11]The discussion to follow is a revised version of Bennett, 1978a. In particular, the figure has been revised to separate the choice function from the temporal resource-depletion process—a considerable improvement.

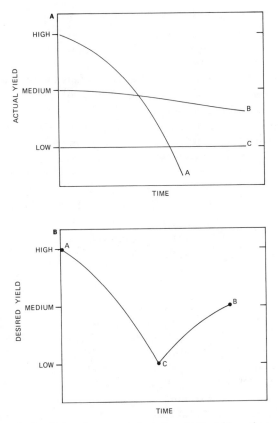

Figure 1. A: Rates of resource depletion. B: Variable soil use strategy.

change the resource beyond recovery. However, there are degrees of this; time is a variable; alternative resources can be found; and so on through a number of qualifying possibilities.

In any case, Figure 1A shows three idealized possibilities: *A, B,* and *C. A* is the high-yield, rapid-depletion case; *C* the low-yield, low-depletion case; and *B* the moderate-yield, moderate-depletion case. Relating these to existing strategies in agriculture, *A* represents the "hit hard and get out," or "get rich quick" strategy, in which no thought is given to the condition of the resource in the future. *C* is the classic low-population, low-energy utilization strategy characteristic of tribal environmental use. However, in modern terms, it might be considered equivalent to the careful underutilization strategies followed by conservative ranchers, whose grazing acreage is large enough to permit income satisfaction from the beef produced with a minimal use of pasture. One of the key problems of human resource ecology is to determine just which factors of economic scale, population size, and income demand may influence the choice of a strategy of resource use. One suspects that this cuts through the classic culturally defined levels of socioeconomic complexity. If this is true, it is clear that the classification impedes construction of an adequate theory of resource ecology in human societies. The classification perpetuates disciplinary boundaries which make it extremely difficult for students, say, of tribal–peasant society to communicate effectively with economists, agronomists, and resource management specialists concerned with contemporary societies.

Depletion curve B is a medium-use or medium-yield curve, which like A will eventually deplete the resource, but at a moderate rate. To know if the rate is moderate implies the existence of specific information on the quick degradational effect of a higher yield; and the extreme caution, or ignorance, implied by curve C. That is, B represents in some respects a more sophisticated type of strategy than either of the others; perhaps behaviorally a very different approach, not just a midpoint of some kind. This, if true, is extremely important. It suggests that, while yield and resource depletion are continuous quantitative functions, the behavioral strategies expressing them are qualitatively different. This suggests the importance of understanding the behavioral and institutional bases of particular resource use strategies, and the reason for not reducing them to quantitative least common denominators, at least if interventional change is attempted. The crux of the issue is the nature of the knowledge, and the attitudes, which permit the exact location of curve B with respect to a particular resource use pattern. Such knowledge is, of course, relative to the general cognitive milieu; there is always a degree of uncertainty because of incomplete information or research. However, if incentive exists to locate such a strategy curve, B may become easier to locate.

Now let us turn to Figure 1B. This figure suggests a typical pattern of variable resource use as it might be found in an agricultural producer's environment like the Great Plains, where there are known risks of serious abuse of resources, but, at the same time, variable pressures, emanating from the market and consumer culture, for income. The V-shaped curve shown in Figure 1B is that of a producer who varies his strategies, moving from A to C, then to B; i.e., he risks resource abuse one year by choosing a high yield (going for broke), then compensates (overcompensates?) by moving down to a very safe choice, C; then attempts to regain a balanced strategy by proceeding to B. While this type of mixed strategy is typical for agriculturalists in high-risk and marginal-resource environments, something like it is characteristic of most production regimes, and the problem it presents is the necessity to take account of strategy choices over extended periods of time, in order to be certain just which average or vector is being followed. For example, if the producers whose choices for three time points follow the pattern in Figure 1B, and if the amount of abuse is proportionate to the concepts of high, medium, and low, then the descent to C and the return to B at regular intervals compensates for the abuse displayed by the recurrent choice at A. However, once again the complexities of the situation make this logic doubtful of application in all cases. Nature may "bounce back" only in particular types of resources. As already suggested, the resource situation in nature is a kind of zero sum game: once used, never returned, or only partly returned. This finite function is, of course, qualified by stretch-out of the depletion rate in more conservationist strategies, which, as previously suggested, may allow sufficient time for finding substitutes or accumulating better information about strategies. However, where the mixed strategy course illustrated in Figure 1B does work, we may consider it an optimal one, since both reasonable yield and reasonable protection of the resource are achieved, over time.

Another common phenomenon in contemporary resource utilization systems is the location of curve B at some level higher than the one shown on the diagrams as medium. That is, a high or abusive strategy may be *culturally defined* as medium. This contingency has already been suggested as a function of defective information, but it also commonly occurs deliberately, even in the face of available knowledge to the contrary. Such strategies are then "sold," or urged upon producers for various reasons, and they may become established as a kind of delusion of conservation. We see this behavior currently in the attractive advertisements of extractive industries like oil and timber, designed to give the impression that they are following sustained-yield practices, whereas in fact they probably are not.

Embedded in this situation are the basic ethical and moral questions of contemporary ecological relations. Why do people abuse resources, thereby jeopardizing posterity, when they know, or at least suspect, they are doing so? How can people value present gain over future losses or disaster? The answers to these questions do not lie wholly within the domain of psychology, but perhaps more importantly in institutions which free the individual from group responsibilities, since present gratification is considered a right rather than a privilege. Perhaps the gratification orientation which seems to be fundamental in human behavior will give rise to these hedonistic institutions eventually in all cases, but this does not mean we are powerless to control them.

Perhaps a simple example of the applicability of this extremely elementary model will be useful. One may be found in livestock production [recalling that Garret Hardin's (1968) classic "tragedy of the commons" behavioral paradigm was also based on cattle and their pasturage]. Such an example serves to remind us that the strategy choices and their effects on yield depletion or sustainment will vary depending on the particular set of opportunities and constraints peculiar to the resource itself—in this example, pasture. In livestock production, the basic constraint–opportunity ratio is expressed as carrying capacity, or the maximum number of animals that can be supported at a given level of nutrition by the forage produced with a particular technique, e.g., the native vegetation managed as a resource. If the present carrying capacity of a pasture is 5 animals to the acre for a grazing year, and there are 10 acres available, then a yield of 50 animals can be achieved with, presumably, a resource sustained-yield condition, i.e., the choice of technique represented by curve B. Let us also say that this sustained-yield (year-after-year) condition can be obtained on the 10 acres *only* if the land is grazed in yearly rotation on several adjoining 10-acre plots, so that overuse of any one plot is avoided. Thus, the particular technique chosen becomes a crucial factor.

Now, if this defines the conservationist strategy at the existing B, the resource user can also visualize several other possible alternatives. He can, first, move up to A in years when rainfall is exceptional, so that he can produce more animals at relatively little risk of abuse of his grass. But if he increases his herd *without* a corresponding increase in resource capacity, he endangers his grass. However, this may be possible if he falls back, on the third year, to C, thereby allowing his pasturage to recover. This type of strategy is facilitated, in this example, by the rotational grazing system. In other words, the optimal movement between strategies is assisted by the particular resource use technique. Obviously, not all resource use situations have this feature. In fact, each one is unique. An entirely different strategy pattern must be followed, for example, if the user decides to supplement his grass by irrigated forage production.

Let us consider this case, because it could involve the "delusions" mentioned earlier. That is, it suggests that, under human manipulation, B is not fixed, but can move, depending on technology and knowledge. Such movement is extremely common, and is a capsulized definition of the overall grand strategy of North American and other resource economies which have been influenced by it. The question that arises, however, is whether the move to higher production levels is really yield- or resource-sustaining. Fertilizer use is a case in point: it has been assumed that by putting fertilizer on the soil one achieves higher yield without harming the soil. However, it is now known that many artificial fertilization techniques are harmful in various ways, and may gradually reduce the capacity of the soil to sustain plant growth.

One additional dimension needs discussion. This is the problem of *uncertainty* and *risk*. [12] The definitions used here view risk as the assessment of the degree of uncertainty. How much risk is perceived or measured will certainly influence the choice of technique or strategy, but it would appear that there is no simple relationship. That is, the relationship between the state of the resources, the goals sought, and the techniques chosen depends on combinations of these factors, and on other factors not mentioned, particularly those related to conditions in the marketplace which will help set the intensity of the goals. If the goal of financial gain is strong, and the pressures from the market such as to make satisfaction of that goal advisable or urgent, then risks will be minimized and resource abuse becomes highly probable. If the risk is still great, resource practices are still likely to tend toward the abusive, because the goal system is powerful; hence, the folklore has it, the user is in a mood to "take risks."

When goals are moderate to weak—that is, not particularly pressing—and risk perception high, then resource use is likely to be conservationist. There is little doubt that economic depressions have generally resulted in a letup in abusive practices, and prosperity and growth the opposite. However, there are exceptions, particularly in resource contexts where poverty or the small scale of operations result in practices which are abusive because the capital available to make them less so, through technological means, is not available. In other words, technology is another variable which has its effects on the equations; as it evolves, the relationship between risk and resource use also varies. But, in general, and over a period of time, a fall in economic values or a rise in prices (same thing) tends to result in overall lessening of resource abuse.

There are related considerations pertaining to economic scale. In some production regimes, large scale may result in resource protection. Examples can be found in some of the large ranches in the North American West, where land and water supplies are large enough to permit income satisfaction at lower levels of livestock yield, or in the case of large timber companies, where capital is sufficient to finance reforestation and other conservationist practices. On the other hand, large scale

---

[12]Most of our practical knowledge of behavior in the contexts of uncertainty and risk is derived from economics. For a classical statement, see Knight, 1921.

can lead to severe resource abuse where the economic goals are rapa-
cious, or where production is controlled by external ownership which is
concerned only with "making a quick buck and getting out."

In these considerations, as in all others, it is important to remember
that the configurations of resource use vary greatly from resource to
resource, and from situation to situation: there are few across-the-board
generalizations other than the basic behavioral processes we have been
describing. The overall quotient of resource abuse must be determined
from empirical studies of many significant contexts; it cannot be determined on theoretical grounds or limited-factor observations. The system
of resource use is governed by an unfolding and changing matrix of
comparative choices which vary sensitively to changing circumstances;
and while we know, in general, the processes which guide these
choices, we cannot determine their vectors without empirical study.

ADAPTIVE STYLES AND THE PROBLEM OF CONTROL

In the preceding sections, we mentioned the case of tribal societies
that appear to maintain, for relatively long periods at any rate, styles of
adaptation which underuse, or preserve, resources (point C in Figure
1A). This section will examine this problem with the help of some recent
anthropological research.

The underlying premise is that the scale of resource use and abuse is
influenced by situation, levels of economic–technological development,
and various cultural elements. The interrelationships of these factors is
so complex that it has been only recently that we have begun to understand how adaptive styles are established and maintained. The policy
issue here is whether the fact that some human societies have been able
to avoid progressive or exponential resource exploitation may provide
some hope that the present situation can be brought under control.

The story can begin with the ecologically simplest societies known:
the nomadic bands of hunters and gatherers which have populated refuge areas like deserts and rain forests in recent times, but were much
more widespread before food producing began.[13] In fact, the longest
span of Homo sapiens history—roughly from about 100,000 years ago to
about 4,000 years ago, when food producing spread rapidly—was lived
out in the context of the nomadic food-collecting style. Given the
dynamic qualities of the intelligence and behavior of Homo sapiens,

[13]For a general symposium on hunting–gathering economies and cultures, see Lee and
DeVore, 1968.

there has always been a problem of why this period lasted so long. Various answers have been given: one is biological—that the prevailing hominoid varieties were less evolved intellectually, and the thrust toward a more sophisticated style required the presence of *Homo sapiens*. Then, there is the challenge and response theory: archeological evidence which suggests that such factors as climatic change, increasing population, thinning of game, or migrations provided the necessary stimulus for more intensive adaptations. Other approaches emphasize fortuitous factors: accidental dropping of plants which could grow in human loci, or the gradual association of animal species with human groups—both of these processes leading eventually to genetic change, and the emergence of tame varieties of plants and animals.

The precise sequence of events will probably never be known in full, and perhaps the problem of origins is mainly an academic or scholarly one. Obviously, more intensive uses of resources did appear; this has led to the progressive tendencies already described, and it is the cumulative results of this process which create our present problems. So we can turn to the living remnants of the earlier, simpler styles to see how the controls were exercised—or, whether the concept of control over resource use really applies to such cases.

The first issue to be dealt with is that of the relatively static populations of these bands of hunters and gatherers. Obviously, their populations did increase slowly, since eventually this style of adaptation covered the earth. However, when these people retreated into refuge areas, their populations appear to have become more stable, so that natural increase seems to have maintained that number which could subsist on the resources made available by the simple subsistence techniques. There is evidence which suggests that hunting and gathering peoples were capable of dynamic and expansionistic styles: the Plains Indians of North America were in such an episode when the Europeans found them, and the evidence from the art in the case of the postglacial European *Homo sapiens* population suggests another vigorous episode. Hunter–gatherer populations of this type can exert considerable pressure on resources: the effect of Indian firing of grass on the Great Plains in the course of bison herding and hunting is a case in point. And there is a theory which suggests that the extinction of some of the great Pleistocene mammals may have been due to human hunting pressure.

So we are really examining a particular case of hunting and gathering populations: those who were restricted to bounded territories, and who therefore had to work out some kind of control system which restrained resource use and population growth. Most of the available research comes from two sources: the !Kung Bushmen of the Kalahari

Desert in Africa, studied by Richard Lee (1972a), and an East Africa forest group, the Hadza, studied by James Woodburn (1972). Additional data for Central African pygmy bands were supplied by Colin Turnbull (1972). In these studies, an effort was made to locate unspoiled or aboriginal populations; but these are becoming rare or nonexistent in the modern world, and questions have been raised as to the validity of some of the findings as referring to truly aboriginal groups. Moreover, as I have suggested, the refuge character of these populations probably is mainly responsible for their extraordinary stability; i.e., their static character is itself an adaptation to circumstances thrust upon them, and not necessarily an inherent feature of their mode of subsistence.

As for slow population growth, Lee (1972b) has proposed that the nomadic existence is disadvantageous for childbirth. Women must carry infants on their backs, and this would tend to lengthen birth intervals, since they cannot carry more than one—although the older children are usually pressed into service on this score, so that the argument does not carry conviction. But there are other factors: the need for women to perform much work connected with plant food gathering; the physical stress of the general way of life. Lee feels that all these factors combine to reduce birth rates, and his findings seem to be reinforced by his studies of Bushman groups which have become sedentary and are supported by wage labor and agriculture. These groups have shortened birth intervals and higher fertility rates.

Woodburn's data on the Hadza suggest a different set of factors: the interrelationship of various social components to produce restraint in fertility and also resource use and development (1972). The key factor is what he calls the threat of conflict, which increases when group size becomes larger. This tends to reinforce small band size, which in turn creates a distinctive social world into which people are socialized: one of extreme intimacy with a very small number of people, all relatives. Once this exists, the adult individual finds it extremely difficult to adjust or adapt to a more heterogeneous and larger social situation.

A third major factor, which has been cited by both Lee and Woodburn and by several other anthropologists, is the influence of nomadic life and its connection with subsistence intake. There are several facets here, some of them partially contradictory. One is the fact that the hunter–gatherer adaptation can, when resources are abundant, be a remarkably easy life, since only a short time is needed to collect enough food to satisfy basic needs. This case of subsistence can be attractive in comparison with tribal agriculture, which presumably requires more labor; hence, hunting and gathering groups on the margins of agricultural populations would tend to persist in their ways. Another factor is the lack of food storage facilities, and the corresponding emphasis on short-term accumulations—a pattern called by Marshall Sahlins (1972) an orientation toward survival, rather than toward wealth or property accumulation. This orientation in turn produces an emphasis on cooperative sharing of all food and other possessions, such as they are, and hoarding or storage of food, or personal acquisition of anything, tends to be negatively valued. Again, once this orientation becomes established, the argument goes, it tends to be self-reinforcing, and conscious administration or regulations need not be used.

Well, this might be. There is, of course, an element of tautology in all such explanations, but they are the best we can do at this point, and in any case they do throw light on the issue of stability. What is important is what they tell us about the conditions which permit or direct human populations to live in a static or homeostatic relationship to nature ("homeostatic" is the appropriate term, since it allows for fluctuation around various points—e.g., it should be assumed that population probably fluctuated with resource availabilities, droughts, etc., rather than remained absolutely static). Such conditions are, quite simply, extraordinary. Rather than supply us with models we might copy today, these cases tell us that control over resource use can become automatic or systemic—i.e., built into the social system—only under very special and remote circumstances. The key factor is isolation and spacial boundedness. Humans under such conditions sooner or later learn to control their population and their wants. I think we can also assume that this state was not reached quickly, and if some of these groups were required to adapt quickly, due to hostile pressure from sedentary agriculturalists or pastoral nomads with a military organization, they may well have suffered overpopulation and other disasters before they learned how to cope. No human group adapts quickly or easily if the change is considerable, but adapt they will, sooner or later. It is only a question of time and costs.

Nomadic food collectors are not the only adaptational mode which possesses control over use of resources. Another is the sectarian agricultural societies associated with various cultural traditions. Most of them are found in the Western world, where they represent an alternative interpretation of Christian principles. There are analogical traditional groups, principally monastic, in Asia. All these groups have perhaps four major features: an emphasis on humility before God and sometimes Nature; a conscious taboo on personal wealth and excessive consumption generally (i.e., an austerity ethic); economic institutions based on the idea that most property and wealth belongs to the group, not the individual; and decision-making procedures requiring maximum participation of the group membership. The groups vary with respect to their attitude toward population growth; their use of technology; and their degree of contact with the outside world and the institutions of growth economics.[14]

In this mixture of characteristics there exist the seeds of care in dealing with resources and the environment in general: humility tends to reinforce the idea that humans must respect Nature because she is powerful, and the source of sustenance; communal property means that the entire group has a collective responsibility for resources, which tends to guarantee care and conservation; the austerity ethic means that consumption pressures tend to be low, removing one major stimulus to resource abuse. And, since these groups believe they have a special mission in the world (as true of the secular versions, like the kibbutz, as for the religious, like the Hutterites), they tend to believe they will last forever and therefore their resources are a sacred trust which must be husbanded for future generations; i.e., the "posterity ethic." Conservationism is rarely an explicit philosophy: the optimal conservationist practices are *de facto* results of these views and practices.

This set of institutions and cultural elements differs from case to case, and not all factors lead to conservationism in all groups. In addition, the external forces of the market may force such groups to abuse their resources out of sheer survival necessity, or out of needs to maintain solidarity with each other, or with neighbors. And some of the factors are not completely determinative of conservation, but only tend to be—for example, consumption austerity does not preclude the possibility, as represented by some kibbutzim, of the establishment of a high *collective* level of consumption, which can exert as much pressure on income, and accordingly on resources, as a high *individual* level. But the conservationist tendencies are very strong; the mix for factors does produce more respect and care for physical resources than individualistic entrepreneuring behavior.

The collective agrarian societies show that it is possible for a modern group to develop controls over environmental use on the basis of a self-conscious and articulate philosophy or theology, implemented, of course, by specific institutional practices and forms of decision making which keep the controls operative. Moreover, controls are built into the social system and beliefs in an effective way: they have clear "sacred" rationale. In individualistic or entrepreneuring systems of resource use,

---

[14]For the Hutterites, see Bennett, 1967; Bennett (cited in Dorner, 1977); Hostetler, 1974; Ryan, 1977. For the kibbutz and other Israeli forms of communal and cooperative settlement, see Weintraub, Lissak, and Azmon, 1969.

controls have to be levied *against* the group by external agencies and forces, and this is always difficult. There is too much room for the individual to manipulate or cheat the system, and the institution breeds dislike and resentment.

In the late 1950s, Walter Firey (1957) was concerned with the problem of individualistic resource strategies in his studies of the behavior of agriculturalists and other groups in West Texas in their use of groundwater for irrigation. He examined a variety of documents—newspaper editorials, policy statements, farm organization literature, and so on, in an effort to discover the logic and rationale for control of the practice of well drilling, which was beginning to endanger the water table (it still does). He found that the language of the statements dealing with the situation always included references to government *regulation* of well drilling and water use, if conservation of water was seen to be important to the welfare of the community. There were few appeals to some higher morality of conservation, or to individual integrity or caution. The materials carried an implicit assumption that Texas farmers and industrial water users would not voluntarily curtail their use of water in the interest of conservation alone; they would have to be required or compelled to do so. Firey also noted that the literature which defined the way water was to be used as a resource always assumed that the individual had a right to use all of the water he needed, at the moment he needed it, without waiting for a group consensus on use strategies: e.g., asking the permission of his neighbors who also depended on the water; or writing for information on the state of the supply. This is, of course, an extreme "Texas" version of entrepreneuring individualism, and in recent years Texas water users, helped by those regulations, have developed more cooperative and cautious strategies, although the problem of abuse remains serious. But the example makes a sharp contrast to the cases of the communal societies just presented, where it is inconceivable that government regulation would be required to curtail abuses of the community's own water supply.

This does not quite end the story, however. The communal societies must function within a larger system of entrepreneurial market economics, and their participation in this system may well unleash abusive and competitive grasping. In fact, this has happened with respect to land purchases in the case of Hutterite colonies in the northern Great Plains. This does not, of course, result in abuse of the soil, since Hutterites are remarkably conservationist farmers, but if and when it should be carried out over water, or some other resource, it could have some of the same effects as in the Texas case. That is, the Hutterite colony, as a community, is forced into the institutional mold of entrepreneur because that is the

nature of the larger system, and in this role, the colony may begin to
move into Garret Hardin's tragedy of the commons process (Hardin,
1968).

We should return to the issue of social isolation. This appears in the
case of the sectarians, although their isolation is due to the erection of
mental or social boundaries, and not geography. But both sets of cases
suggest that the common factor is the detachment from outside contacts,
with their influences and inducements. One might venture a broad
generalization: that resource overuse and abuse is a function of the
progressive enlargement of scale and communication within the human
community. Left to themselves, small populations may be likely to develop stable or homeostatic systems of resource use because there are
few alternatives, and in the absence of alternatives they become
habituated—adapted—to what they have.

But this similarity between the hunter–gatherer bands and the
modern sectarian groups does not explain everything, because there are
important differences. The hunting and gathering bands had a low-
energy technology to begin with, and undoubtedly this was a reinforcing factor in fixing a simple subsistence economy with its minimal pressures on the environment. Most of the modern sectarian groups accept
modern technology and scientific techniques for using resources; in fact,
the Hutterites and the kibbutzim, the most communal and possibly the
most conservationist of all these groups, utilize the most modern high-
energy machinery. Thus they combine what in the world at large has
become dangerous for the environment—production for the market
with powered machinery—with a markedly conservationist use of their
own resources. They are able to do this because the deleterious consequences of their technology is not felt locally, but is part of larger systems. For example, the use of fossil fuels to plant and harvest grain has a
number of serious consequences for the environment, but it does not
affect the producer who uses the technique along with safeguards for his
own premises and resources. This is an example of how the enlargement
of scale and the broadening of systemic interconnections can result in
resource abuse and pollution.

The functions of scale are, however, quite complex. In another
paper (Bennett, 1978b), dealing with the effects of livestock and grain
production on land degradational processes in the Great Plains, the
writer has concluded that enlargements of scale can work in the opposite
direction, when scale is sufficient to provide funds to pay the high costs
of the use of certain techniques and machinery which safeguard pasturage and soil. One key factor here is sufficient income to cover the costs of
taking unsuitable and vulnerable resources out of production to prevent

degradation. But the problem of trade-offs continues: the use of expensive powered machinery in grain production can facilitate conservationist use of soils, by permitting adequate and more careful fallowing and tillage, but this is done at the cost of high consumption of fossil fuels. The scale–conservation relationship is extremely complex, and deserves more careful analysis than it has received to date by agricultural specialists. There are similar problems, of course, with respect to pollution-avoiding techniques in other contexts: corrective measures used to lessen industrial pollutants often carry very high energy costs.

To return to the comparisons of these sectarian agriculturalists, we can consider the Amish. These people, religious cousins of the Hutterites, maintain an individualistic entrepreneuring mode of production and resource use, but do so with minimal powered technology and "horse and buggy" techniques generally. A recent article by a team of researchers (Johnson, Stoltzfus, & Craumer, 1977) outlines their technology in terms of its low energy consumption, and shows that, despite their avoidance of escalating production, they are able to survive in a competitive market-oriented economy.[15] The Amish use natural methods on the whole, avoiding chemical fertilizer, excessive tillage, and other techniques which are known to abuse soil and water.

However, what the paper does not point out is that the Amish are apparently not able to support their entire natural increase, since the out-migration rate is very high—perhaps as high as 15%. Their young people leave for many reasons, but there seems little doubt that most of them add up to an inability to provide sufficient income or land to maintain the entire population. In addition, the research was not concerned with the condition of their basic resource: soil. There is evidence that Amish yields in most of the Midwestern settlements have been slowly falling, as soil fertility, after two or three generations of cropping, has gradually diminished. However careful the techniques, as mentioned in the previous section, ultimately resources will begin to fail. In other words, conservationist and low-energy-utilization farming are only two factors among many which must be taken into consideration when assessing the ecological significance of a particular method of using renewable resources.

In contrast, the Hutterites, with their conservationist techniques, and their high-energy technology (incidentally they use chemical fertilizer, but cautiously), are able to support their entire rapidly growing population. This is the case not only because their production is high, and its efficiency also, but because they live in the northern Great

[15]Stolzfus, 1973 is an earlier paper containing a general description of Amish farming.

Plains, where land is still relatively abundant, allowing for expansion. And their productivity means good returns, which gives them the money for resource enhancement and purchase. But cultural factors continue to operate: the consumption austerity of the Hutterites adds a very substantial amount to their capital savings. Hutterites eventually can begin to experience some of the Amish problems as their resources begin to wear out, but their large-scale and impressive capital reserves suggest that they will be in a position to enter alternative occupations, or to engage in expensive resource renewal schemes, which the Amish are prevented from doing because of their limited income.

THE "SOCIAL LIMITS TO GROWTH"

But this is not the end of the story. These ethnic styles of production and consumption contain important lessons and implications for our problem, but they do not focus on the modern dilemma in its pure form: how to control our use and abuse of resources in a world society that is increasingly committed to the proposition of high growth rates and their apparent promise of prosperity and gratification for all.

The setting of this problem is familiar enough: we all live off each other's backs: what we consume is no longer our own affair, but depends on, and influences, the consumption of everyone. This is true not only for the nations, taken as consumers, but for the individual: it is a micro–macro problem. It means, as Fred Hirsch (1977)[16] notes, that the distinctions cherished by economists between public and private goods no longer make much sense, just as the belief that resources are there for the taking by the entrepreneur no longer makes sense, when dependence on resources, wherever they are found, becomes ever more dispersed across the world. Out of this problem comes collectivism, political or social, acknowledged or covert, since it means that to meet the demand for equity there is need for control. It means that the simple necessities of life, like air and water, are no longer "free public goods," but are rapidly becoming resources which need to be husbanded and protected. It means that the more insistent the demand, and the more attempts there are to meet these demands, the greater the scarcity value of the resource, and therefore the greater the need to move that resource into the domain of social control.

In the previous discussions I focused on the producer and his decisions to use, conserve, or overuse the supply. But in this section we

[16]Also see Barkley and Seckler, 1972; Ophuls, 1977.

shift our emphasis to the consumer. We are concerned with his demands on the system, and how these demands limit the supply and require its control. The proposition to be examined is whether these demands constitute a limiting process, a form of automatic control. In previous passages we have been pessimistic about the possibility of automatic or systemic controls, since our argument was based on a series of behavioral processes which can produce insatiable wants, and which cannot easily be brought under control because of institutional reinforcements. Here we speculate that because of the magnitude of the wants, and their attempted satisfaction by a growth-oriented production system, the institutional system itself may eventually have to develop its own constraints. This does not necessarily lend itself to optimism, because institutional constraints in this case are equivalent to political challenge and upheaval. The problems are those not only of the hyper-developed countries, but also of the developing world, where rising expectations have created insistent demands on an unprecedented scale.

Although the argument emphasizes institutions, it is underlain by behavioral considerations. We are still confronted with the proclivity of humans to want things, to require that material substances and social arrangements be reorganized to supply defined needs. The engine continues to be driven by the human desire for gratification and the adaptive behavioral process as we have defined it. But once these demands create institutions for their satisfaction, these arrangements give rise to new constraints and opportunities, and these forces begin to generate their own consequences. The process begins to assume the characteristics of a self-generating but also degenerative system, but its automatic qualities are ambiguous, since there is widespread knowledge of its workings among the experts. What the experts cannot do is modify the political process to take account of the impending disasters. The political system generally lags behind the operations of the economic—or the general want-satisfying and resource-creating institutional system.

Reverting for the moment to the arguments in the section The Process of Rational Choice, we proposed that the root of the problem is to be found in the choices made by the individual in the process of satisfying his wants. We also observed that from the standpoint of the individual, his wants are either satisfied or not, and that this is the foundation of modern economic theory. The possibility that these satisfactions may result in deprivation for all, or in the loss of resource capacity, is not included as a normal or anticipated possibility. The basic issue is one of scarcity: if my wants are satisfied, it may be at the expense of yours. This possibility was remote in a world where most people got along on less, or where population was small in proportion to the supply of resources. But in a world of increasing population, and increasing demands for gratification, it becomes a real and ever-present possibility. Moreover, it is not merely a problem of spreading deprivation, but also of environmental abuse. The demands tend to become insatiable, and there can be no stable satisfaction level or plateau so long as the culture lacks moral controls over wants.

We should all give more attention to the concept of scarcity. Economists focus on material scarcities: shortages of particular commodities or objects which can be produced in larger quantities when the demand exists. As we have already noted, there seem to be finite limits to this: just how many automobiles can our streets hold, or the petroleum supply afford? The assumption that scarcities are simply material is the necessary assumption behind the concept of economic growth; growth, as noted, is an attempt to alleviate scarcities.

This is too simple a view of scarcity, which is a matter of values and cultural definitions and not merely a one-to-one reflection of quantity. First, scarcity is always relative to something: I may have lots of something until I see that you have more, and then I have little. Scarcity, like feelings of deprivation, is on a sliding scale; it is basically subjective. Therefore, without definitions, there is no end to it; in modern populations, the relativity of scarcity tends to work toward an ever-rising scale of wants.

Second, scarcity is not based solely on material phenomena. There are several classes of scarce phenomena which do not depend on quantity, but wholly on social judgments and the distribution of nonmaterial phenomena in social organization. The classic case is, of course, leadership: only a few can lead, or rise to positions of power and prestige, because the social meaning of leadership is based on an unequal distribution of roles in a population. The best one can do is try to guarantee a rotation or circulation of such roles, something that is successful only in small communities where the number of people is not much greater than the number of elite positions. Or, in a nutshell, scarcity which is rooted in unequal distributions of social phenomena is in a sense not scarcity: it is simply a way to create the meaning or value of something. Another example is fads, and the small hobby or participation groups that form around them. They gain their value from the fact that *relatively* few people follow them. Without this snob appeal, they lose meaning and are abandoned.

Another class of social judgments involving a concept of scarcity is the desire to maintain or attain states of being which become increasingly scarce or hard to obtain, because of the very attempt to satisfy them. Solitude and peace of mind become increasingly scarce in an ever more crowded society; as ski slopes become more crowded with skiers, it becomes increasingly difficult or frustrating to indulge in the sport. Automobiles for a time became ever more powerful, until, and only just recently, the possibility of using that power on increasingly crowded roads and at reasonable levels of accident, diminished to the point where a rollback in the power vector commenced (but was really caused by manufacturing costs and constraints in petroleum supply—i.e., social constraints).

As these patterns emerge, people exhibit a curious *desire* for scarcity—the opposite of the classical economic theory of the desire to alleviate shortages. That is, while the individual may perceive that something is scarce because more and more people seeking it deprive him of the chance of getting it, he also begins to seek out things which are rare—scarce—in order to find substitute gratifications. No better example of the subjective-social aspect of scarcity can be found. Scarcity turns out not to be based on absolute quantity, but on any quantity of anything which is perceived as rare, special, meaningful, etc. The individual is frustrated by scarcity, but attempts to alleviate his frustration by finding scarce goods.

This seemingly paradoxical situation is brought about by several forces, but the major factor is probably the fact that social scarcities do not usually have collective impact. That is, not all social scarcities affect all individuals. We select our scarcities, so to speak. The fact that I may be frustrated or deprived by heavy traffic, and therefore must take the bus, does not mean that I will lose my desire for going on weekend trips with the car. That is, I may use my car just as much as I would anyway, and thereby continue to contribute my share to the general disorder produced by automobiles. Or, I may discover that automobiles are a nuisance, and stop all traveling; or, if this all happens when I retire, I will stay home anyway, and then I will not suffer the frustrations associated with growth-induced scarcities. Since there is as yet no large-scale convergence of deprivations, there is no perception of the general need to reduce the scale of wants and to change the compulsion to constantly attempt to meet these wants, whatever they may be. Garrett Hardin's version of this process is so well known that one scarcely needs to quote it, and of course it is a version somewhat more relevant to our problem of resources. Hardin's concept of tragedy of the commons is that the resources may be consumed because individuals are concerned only with their particular share of a resource needed by everyone. When everyone comes to share this view of the right to a share, demand increases to the point of exhaustion of the resource.

This process generates economic growth, and of course increased consumption of resources. Sometimes these can be seen as socially beneficial, and also not harmful to the resource base. For example, dissatisfaction with processed foods in recent years gave rise to the natural foods movement, which supplies "old-fashioned" foodstuffs (at high prices) to those people who want them. In such an arena, the choice and relative abundance is maintained. But for every relatively benign case of this kind, there will be many more which generate undesirable consequences in overuse of resources, pollution, increased density, and so on.

Now, the central element in this process is the shift of the definition of value from intrinsic quality, or social morality, to individual gratification. That is, the meaning of consumption in the pre-growth age—which in general is all of human history up to the industrial revolution—was provided by either: (1) some intrinsic quality like aesthetic complexity or skill—another social scarcity; or (2) by the relationship of the phenomenon to some moral or social-consensus component of the culture. Fine art is an example of the former; the parlor recreations of the family group in the 19th century of the latter. These types of meaning or satisfaction are not dead, of course, but they have been transformed and overlain by purely material, individualistic-hedonistic, or status–prestige factors. It might be argued that the latter—prestige phenomena—represent the old type of social value, but the difference is that in true social morality, the activity or object is given meaning by how it helped or gratified *alter*; other people, the collectivity. Contemporary prestige value tends to be purely selfish, representing only the attainment by the *ego* of some positional badge or status.

For the time being, we therefore must find constraints in the form of government regulation and control, since there is no consensus in a pluralistic culture in which every desire, and every concept of scarcity, is equally valid. This introduces the familiar dilemma: while everyone admits that control is needed, the only form the system will tolerate is governmental; yet we consider government control a form of tyranny! We can recall Walter Firey's (1957) findings with regard to the Texas well-drilling farmers: the voices of the media and the establishment encouraged individualistic and self-interested use of the water on the one hand, and the desperate need for government regulation of this behavior on the other. The intermediate process—the need for a genuine cooperative consensus—is ignored. It may emerge, and sometimes it does when things get very bad, but there is no social guarantee, and the record, overall, is not promising.

We have then the following alternatives:

1. We can drift toward increasingly severe regulatory mechanisms

designed to control our personal consumption, our use of resources, and, eventually, our desires and needs. These regulations will contribute to the growth of huge impersonal bureaucracies—as they already do—which will use increasingly devious manipulatory methods, since the value system decries such control. This process is under way in all countries, regardless of political economy. The message we hear from some pundits to the effect that socialism will be an improvement over capitalism because it is more efficient, humane, or conservationist, is hardly realistic or useful. The control of wants and resource consumption is subject to the same behavioral forces in all societies, whatever their formal institutions, if and when they are committed to growth economics. This is currently true for every country except a small handful—like Burma—and perhaps including some institutional spheres in mainland China.

2. We can let things go along pretty much as they are—that is, permit the growth mechanism to continue operating with only moderate development of regulation—and allow for Hirsch's "social limits to growth" (1977) to manifest themselves. That is, on the basis of an assumption that in fact they will do so. However, perhaps the social limits to growth are simply the regulatory mechanisms and bureaucratic processes just described—I rather think they are. As crowding, deprivation, rising prices, and material shortages become increasingly severe, the social unrest they create inevitably gives rise to government intervention. The social limits to growth can escape this fate only if:

3. We conduct a search for a new moral definition of wants and the humane use of the earth and its substances. We *must* search for it—it will not spring ready-made on the lips of a prophet, and we may find what we are looking for only after disaster and deprivation have had their effects. Each country, like each individual, will have to experience privations and frustrations before growth is brought under control, and this will take a long time. Meanwhile, we debate the issues and inch forward toward humility, and toward reform of our resource policies and practices.

As this proceeds, we discover needs for information on alternative strategies and policies of environmental use and conservation. Here anthropological research can be of value. However, as noted earlier, such descriptive information on institutions and styles of adaptation cannot be used simplistically, because there are other dimensions of behavior which are not adequately rendered in the discrete portraits of particular cultural adaptations. The information, nevertheless, provides an abundance of illustrative examples of particular ways of handling resources, and particular ways of managing resources to provide for their continued yield. At other levels, anthropological research can provide detailed data on the symbol systems developed by various social groups—and individuals—to rationalize and explain their environmental policies.[17]

We have given a number of examples of such information in the preceding sections. However, we have had to qualify these cases, since historical changes have tended to drive all social groups toward a common frame of environmental exploitation, based on a universal ideology of high want gratification, and a drive toward equality of consumption styles at a relatively high level. While particular social groups will probably continue to develop their own distinctive patterns of resource definition and use, there would seem to be a general vector toward heavy exploitation associated with the international development movement. Consequently, we also need theoretical models with common human, or behavioral-process, generality.

REFERENCES

Barkley, P. W., & Seckler, D. W. *Economic growth and environmental decay.* New York: Harcourt Brace, 1972.

Bennett, J. W. *Hutterian brethren: The agricultural economy of a communal society.* Stanford, Calif.: Stanford University Press, 1967.

Bennett, J. W. The significance of the concept of adaptation for contemporary sociocultural anthropology. *Symposium 7: Proceedings, VIII, International Congress of Anthropological & Archeological Sciences.* Tokyo, Volume 3, 1968, pp. 237–241.

Bennett, J. W. *Northern plainsmen: Adaptive strategy and agrarian life.* Chicago: Aldine, 1969. (4th printing: AHM Publication Co, Arlington Heights, Ill., 1976.)

Bennett, J. W. *The ecological transition: Cultural anthropology & human adaptation.* New York: Pergamon, 1976a.

Bennett, J. W. Anticipation, adaptation, and the concept of culture in anthropology. *Science,* 1976b, *192,* 847–852.

Bennett, J. W. A rational-choice model of agricultural resource utilization and conservation. In N. L. Gonzales (Ed.), *Social and technological management in dry lands.* Selected Symposium No. 10, American Association for the Advancement of Science. Boulder, Colo.: Westview Press, 1978a, pp. 151–185.

Bennett, J. W. Social processes affecting desertification in developed societies. In P. Reining (Ed.), *Desertification papers.* Washington: American Association for the Advancement of Science, 1978b.

Bennett, J. W., & Levine, S. B. Industrialization and social deprivation: Welfare environment and the postindustrial society in Japan. In H. Patrick (Ed.), *Japanese industrialization and its social consequences.* Berkeley: University of California Press, 1976, pp. 439–492.

---

[17]The work of Mary Douglas is especially intriguing in this context. See Douglas, 1975, especially Part III.

Coelho, G. V., Hamburg, D. A., & Adams, J. E. (Eds.). *Coping and adaptation*. New York: Basic Books, 1974.

Dorner, P. (Ed.). *Cooperative and commune: Group farming in the economic development of agriculture*. (See chapter by J. W. Bennett, on Hutterites.) Madison: University of Wisconsin Press, 1977.

Douglas, M. *Implicit meanings*. London: Routledge & Kegan Paul, 1975.

Dubos, R. *A theology of the earth*. Washington: Smithsonian Institute, 1969. (Lecture printed as paperbound)

Firey, W. Patterns of choice and the conservation of resources. *Rural Sociology*, 1957, 22, 112–123.

Hardin, G. The tragedy of the commons. *Science*, 1968, *162*, 1243–1248.

Hardin, G. *Exploring new ethics for survival*. New York: Viking, 1972.

Heath, A. *Rational choice and social exchange: A critique of exchange theory*. Cambridge: Cambridge University Press, 1976.

Hirsch, F. *The social limits to growth*. Cambridge: Harvard University Press & Twentieth Century Fund, 1977.

Hostetler, J. A. *Hutterite society*. Baltimore: Johns Hopkins University Press, 1974.

Johnson, W. A., Stoltzfus, V., & Craumer, P. Energy conservation in Amish agriculture. *Science*, 1977, *198*, 373–378.

Knight, F. H. *Risk, uncertainty and profit*. Boston: Houghton Mifflin, 1921.

Lee, R. B. Work effort, group structure, and land use in contemporary hunter–gatherers. In P. J. Ucko, R. Tringham, & G. W. Dimbleby (Eds.), *Man, settlement and urbanism*. London: Duckworth, 1972a.

Lee, R. B. Population growth and the beginning of sedentary life among the !Kung Bushmen. In B. Spooner (Ed.), *Population growth: Anthropological perspectives*. Cambridge: M.I.T. Press, 1972b, pp. 329–342.

Lee, R. B., & DeVore, I. (Eds.). *Man the hunter*. Chicago: Aldine, 1968.

Moran, E. *Human adaptation*. North Scituate, Mass.: Duxbury Press, 1979.

Ophuls, W. *Ecology and the politics of scarcity*. San Francisco: Freeman, 1977.

Ryan, J. *The agricultural economy of manitoba hutterite colonies*. Carleton Library No. 101. Toronto: McClelland & Stewart, 1977.

Sahlins, M. *Stone age economics*. Chicago: Aldine, 1972.

Schechter, J. Desertification processes and the search for solutions. *Interdisciplinary Science Reviews*, 1977, 2, 38–54.

Sheets, H., & Morris, R. *Disaster in the desert: Failures of international relief in the West African drought*. Washington: Carnegie Endowment for International Peace, 1974.

Simon, H. A. *Sciences of the artificial*. Cambridge: M.I.T. Press, 1969.

Steward, J. A. *The theory of culture change*. (Especially chapter 2, The Method of Cultural Ecology.) Urbana: University of Illinois Press, 1955.

Stoltzfus, F. Amish agriculture: Adaptive strategies for economic survival of community life. *Rural Sociology*, 1973, *38*, 196–206.

Turnbull, C. M. Demography of small-scale societies. In G. A. Harrison & J. A. Boyce (Eds.), The structure of human populations. Oxford: Clarendon Press, 1972, pp. 283–312.

Weintraub, D., Lissak, M., & Azmon, Y. (Eds.). Moshava, kibbutz, and moshav: Jewish rural settlement and development. Ithaca, N. Y.: Cornell University Press, 1969.

Woodburn, J. Ecology, nomadic movement and the composition of the local group among hunters and gatherers. In P. J. Ucko, R. Tringham, & G. W. Dingleby (Eds.), *Man, settlement, and urbanism*. London: Duckworth, 1972.

Natural Hazards

A CROSS-CULTURAL PERSPECTIVE

JOHN H. SORENSEN
AND
GILBERT F. WHITE

CROSS-CULTURAL COMPARISON

A camper in the Big Thompson Canyon, Colorado, ignores the heavy rainfall, and his trailer is swept away during a flash flood. A family in coastal Bangladesh, not wanting to leave their home and possessions, are reported missing after a tropical cylone ravishes the area. A farmer in Tanzania shrugs his shoulder and watches the sky for rain to replenish his shriveled crops. Similarly, the occupants of a small wheat farm in Kansas pray that the next year will bring better weather. Small store owners in San Francisco, California, and Managua, Nicaragua, earning their livelihoods miles apart, laugh, saying that there is nothing you can do about earthquakes, for God is responsible.

Different hazardous events, different cultures, but a similar response: do nothing, and bear the loss imparted by natural events. On a global scale this is the most common form of human response to natural hazard.

Behavior is not, however, perfectly homogeneous. Big Thompson

JOHN H. SORENSEN • Department of Geography, University of Hawaii, Honolulu, Hawaii 96822. GILBERT F. WHITE • Institute of Behavioral Science, University of Colorado, Boulder, Colorado 80309.

Canyon occupants were warned to evacuate to higher ground. Coastal Bangladesh had a series of dikes and levees designed to protect small villages. In Tanzania, the farmer sold firewood to supplement his income. The Kansas farmer's cooperative could have hired a cloud seeder to augment precipitation. San Francisco city council members passed an ordinance requiring dangerous parapets to be removed from buildings. Managua has been involved in a massive effort to rebuild a safer city following disaster.

Such similarities and differences in human response to natural hazards may be sorted out in part by taking a cross-cultural perspective. The processes by which the Tanzanian farmers and the San Francisco store owners cope with environmental risk may be found to share certain features in common. Other hazard managers may show large deviances in their responses.

On reviewing the increasing geographical literature on natural hazard, it is possible to conclude quickly that little can be offered in the way of solid empirical findings about cross-cultural differences in human response. This may result from several general problems encountered in cross-cultural research (Goodman & Moore, no date). First, existing research has not focused on culture as the major variable under investigation. Thus it is impossible to distinguish the influence of culture on response from other possible factors. Second, existing studies lack a systematic definition of culture, making comparison of case studies difficult. Finally, the field methods employed may be inadequate to reveal the impact of culture, or can bias the study toward the researcher's cultural values (Saarinen, 1974; Whyte, 1977a).

On the other hand, it is possible to offer some conclusions about similarities in response, and a few instances where responses appear to be shaped by cultural factors. Second, unobtrusive measures or subtle indicators of response, such as differential death rates among countries, may point out the possibility that cultural differences exist. These findings are based on research which has focused on investigating how people perceive natural hazards, their awareness of possible means of coping with hazard events and loss reduction efforts, and the process by which individuals choose particular courses of action.

The Evolution of Geographic Research on Human Response to Hazard

The findings presented in this paper are best interpreted in the context of the evolution of geographic studies on natural hazards. More detailed reviews are also available (Burton, Kates, & White, 1978; Mitchell, 1974a; White, 1973) for the interested reader.[1]

The early work by White (1945) questioned why persons lived on floodplains in light of the annual risks presented, and why public coping action centered on flood-control engineering in preference to a wide range of actions or adjustments which could be taken to reduce losses from flooding. This work was largely ignored until 1958, when a more elaborate investigation sought to identify how human occupance of urban floodplains in the United States was changing, and showed that, notwithstanding massive investments in the flood-control projects, the annual national toll of flood losses was increasing (White, Calef, Hudson, Mayer, Scheaffer, & Volk, 1958). This spawned a series of investigations at the University of Chicago on human cognition and behavior in hazardous areas, and on public policies covering hazard loss reduction.

The earlier studies focused primarily on the flood hazard in a Western cultural context. Kates's (1962) study of individuals' "perceptions"[2] and choice in selected towns of the United States revealed that behavior was consistent with Simon's (1956) model of bounded rationality, in which floodplain adjustment decisions were made under satisfying conditions. Burton (1962) investigated response to floods in rural agricultural settings in the United States. Together with White's (1964) companion study of hazard adjustment in six cities, the theoretical basis for subsequent investigations was formed.

During the remainder of the 1960s, research expanded to cover additional hazards, employ new methodologies, seek broader conceptual frameworks, and initiate a program of collaborative cross-cultural research. In addition, the research diffused from the University of Chicago to Clark and Toronto Universities, and eventually to many universities in the United States and other nations.

Under the auspices of the International Geographical Union's Commission on Man and Environment, a series of comparative studies of selected hazards was launched in a variety of cultural settings. In total, human response to nine hazards was investigated at 26 sites. Included were avalanche (Peru), coastal erosion (U.S.A.), drought (Australia, Brazil, Kenya, Mexico, Nigeria, Tanzania), earthquake (U.S.A., Canada), flood (Sri Lanka, India, Malawi, U.S.A., England), snow (U.S.A.), hurricane or cyclone (U.S.A., 3 sites; Puerto Rico; Virgin Is-

[1]Reviews with other disciplinary perspectives are also available: economics (Cochrane, 1975; Dacey & Kunreuther, 1969); sociology (Dynes, 1970; Mileti, Drabek, & Haas, 1975); and geology (Bolt, Horn, Macdonald, & Scott, 1975).
[2]"Perception" as used in geographic study is closer to the psychological definition of cognition. See Schiff (1970) for a discussion of this point.

lands; Bangladesh), volcano (Costa Rica, U.S.A.), and wind (U.S.A.). A number of other studies which are not part of this effort have also been made (White, 1974).

These studies were based on a central framework and shared hypothesis. Differences in the interests and attributes of the wide range of researchers resulted in alternative types of analysis and points of emphasis. The base of geographic knowledge on human response to hazard is eclectic in nature. Certain researchers have emphasized social aspects, some have centered on psychological factors, others deal with economic aspects, and still others have researched politcal variables. Overall, they provide glimpses of the dynamic interaction of humans and extreme environments.

These studies provide the basis for the major observations made in this paper. Detailed case studies of individual sites are found in White (1974), and a synthesis is made by Burton et al. (1978). There have also been several methodological commentaries (Porter, 1978; Waddell, 1977; White, 1974).

The current research trend is broadening to include a wider range of environmental hazards (Whyte, 1977a), utilizing new methodologies and frameworks (Kates, 1978). Despite such progress, the systematic study of culture as a major underlying or causal factor is still largely ignored.

The majority of these studies are based on standard interview techniques (Saarinen, 1974). A variety of behavioral research instruments has also been utilized, including Thematic Apperception Tests (Mitchell, 1974b; Saarinen, 1966), Semantic Differentials (Golant & Burton, 1969), Modified Rosenzweig Picture Frustration Tests (Barker & Burton, 1969), Kelly Repertory Grid Tests (Barker, 1977), and Locus of Control (Baumann & Sims, 1974; Kirkby, 1972; Schiff, 1977; Sims & Baumann, 1972).

More recently, efforts of the Man and the Biosphere (MAB) program and of the Scientific Committee of Problems on the Environment (SCOPE) are aimed at developing standardized field techniques to investigate human response to a large array of environmental, natural, and social risks (Burton, 1977; Man and the Biosphere, 1973; Whyte, 1977b). This represents an ongoing step in geographic research, aimed at expanding knowledge of human behavior and processes of social change.

MODELS OF HUMAN RESPONSE TO NATURAL HAZARD

Two models have been found useful in explaining and discussing human response to natural hazard. First is a general systems model of

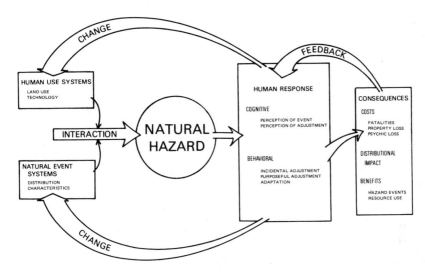

Figure 1.   Dynamics of response to natural hazards.

human adjustment to natural hazard (Figure 1), patterned after Kates (1971). The second model relates human response to hazard in terms of stages of economic development (Burton *et al.*, 1978).

Critical to understanding cross-cultural dimensions of human response is to grasp the concept that hazards are a product of an interaction between society and nature. Human occupance of the land always involves a resource utilization, with benefits and costs. And that use always runs the risk that some part of the resource base will be perturbed by an extreme event in a natural system. The land which produces bountiful yields of rice may be subject to severe flooding. Houses scenically perched on shoreline cliffs are vulnerable to earthquakes or landslides. Natural events become hazardous only when overlapped by human activity.

As depicted in Figure 1, humans are not a passive element in this model. They continually adjust to new sets of circumstance in the physical and social environment. To some the restraint to avoid this may mean no overt behavior, to others it may mean the construction of billion-dollar engineering schemes.

This interplay results in a set of costs and benefits from human occupance and response. The costs are frequently measured in fatalities and monetary damages, although a psychological set of consequences also exists. The benefits are most commonly measured in the net gains from land use.

The system is not static. New environmental conditions and changing human activities alter both the social and natural subsystems in the model. In communities of the United States floodplain regulations alter the pattern of residential construction. In drought-stricken Africa, new patterns of migration are established because of foreign aid. In a similar fashion, the construction of dams and levees alters the downstream character of flooding (Leopold, 1968). Additionally, agricultural adjustments to drought may partially alter climatic patterns (Glantz, 1976). New examples can be added yearly.

Natural events and human use systems provide the broad links between the social and natural environments. They give a context for guiding response. At the microlevel, individual behavior is also guided by perceptions and cognitive thought processes. Taken together, this model helps explain patterns of response on a global level.

The second model which is helpful in discussing human response segregates society into four configurations of economic and social development: (1) folk or preindustrial; (2) transitional; (3) industrial; and (4) postindustrial. These are viewed as types, and their definition does not imply that a nation progresses through them in an orderly fashion. Different areas within a country may closely resemble more than one type. The slopes of Kilauea in Hawaii resemble a transitional society, and not the industrial stage predominating in Oahu. Some general characteristics which help distinguish among these four types are found in Table 1.

Preindustrial nations are characterized by primarily rural agrarian land use, have low per capita incomes, are primarily self-sufficient, and display patterns of life in which people practice a mixed variety of adjustments in using natural resources.

Transitional societies are marked by rural to urban migration, new investment in industry, shifts from labor to capital-intensive land uses, possess a low to moderate per capita income, and have achieved a higher level of trade, often with a deficit balance, and subject their industrial activities to the risk of extreme natural events.

Industrial societies are typified by predominantly urban land use, are capital-intensive and heavily mechanized, have a moderately high per capita income, have complex political institutions, and rely heavily upon adjustments which seek to control extreme events.

Postindustrial societies possess highly developed social networks, rapid communication systems, and flexible political institutions. In addition, they make large investments in research and human development, have high per capita incomes, and have stabilized levels of population

TABLE 1
GENERAL FACTORS DISTINGUISHING TYPE OF DEVELOPMENT

Some distinguishing factors	Type			
	Folk	Transitional	Industrial	Postindustrial
Income	Low	Low	Moderate	High
Trade	Low level	Some, usually with deficit	High level	Moderate level, toward self-sufficiency
Land use	Primarily agricultural	Agricultural and rural	Urban and suburban	Urban
Literacy	Low level	Basic level	High level	Very high level
Communications	Poorly developed	Poorly developed	Highly developed	Sophisticated
Flexibility of social organizations	High	Low	Low	High
Orientation toward nature	Harmony	Dominated by nature	Dominant over nature	Harmony
Technology	Simple	Industrialization	Energy	Information
Time orientation	Cyclical	Linear; oriented to present	Linear; oriented to past and present	Linear; oriented to future

and economic growth, in which they employ mixed strategies in coping with extreme events.

This is not a classification based on culture; albeit it is possible to classify different cultural groups within this framework. Culture signifies a set of shared ideas, thought processes, and learning patterns (Keesing, 1976). These four types of societal development represent patterns of socioeconomic behavior. The two are, however, related. Culture, as a cognitive process, influences behavior, and is manifested in the artifacts and organization of society. This classification also avoids distinguishing between Eastern and Western nations, socialist and capitalist economies, or democratic and communist political systems. Those apparently are not the relevant variables which affect human response, and either side of those three dichotomies could theoretically apply to each type of socioeconomic development.

Severe dangers are associated with this generalization. In a strict sense it does not reveal cross-cultural differences, although it takes us closer to identifying possible cultural variance. Second, it is highly generalized. It does provide, however, one useful comparison and, hopefully, a stimulus for other researchers to sort out the finer points of differences in cross-cultural response.

When it is observed that two communities or two cultures cope with a given hazard differently, the question arises as to whether the difference is to be explained by the nature of the total level of natural risk, the type of resource use system, culture, the form of social and economic organization, or other factors. No single factor appears dominant in explaining behavior. It is also difficult to say which factors are more important; are perceived future losses more relevant than past damages? Therefore it is necessary to take a broad view of the relationship between hazard response and environment, and explore a variety of interrelated factors.

The remainder of this chapter is organized around the systems model in Figure 1. Differences in response are viewed, when feasible, within the context of the different types of socioeconomic development. Finally, culture, in a limited sense, is linked to similarities and differences in national experiences.

DIFFERENCES IN PHYSICAL EVENTS

The events of nature which produce hazards are not uniformly distributed over the earth's surface. Some events, such as earthquakes, are concentrated in certain locations (Nichols, 1974). Some arid areas are more susceptible to seasonal deficits in moisture, one determinant or measure of drought. Tropical cyclones have greatest impact on coastal areas. Flooding occurs in low-lying river basins.

Each region or place has a distinctive combination of natural systems, and, therefore, of the extreme events which perturb them. These combinations are in many instances associated with distinctive resource use systems, and the latter may or may not correspond to cultural groupings. The circumstances determine the total range-levels of risk from all possible natural events in one place. Only one study has comprehensively examined the magnitude of all hazards in one community (Hewitt & Burton, 1971). This study estimated the historical incidence of natural events and man-made disasters in London, Ontario. That Canadian city of 200,000 is faced with floods, heavy snowfall, ice storms, hurricanes, hailstorms, and tornadoes. Man-made disasters include fire, explosions, and accidents. Extrapolating from historical records, it is likely that Ontario will experience three natural and three man-made disasters at the community level during the next 50 years. For the individual, the risks are lower; for the region, the possibility exists for disaster of catastrophic proportions. Currently, the International Geographical Union Commission on Man and Environment's Working Group on Environmental Perception, is organizing cross-cultural investigations along these lines (Burton, 1977). Such research may begin to answer many of the unresolved questions which spring from this paper.

GLOBAL DISTRIBUTION OF HAZARDS

The geographical extent of some hazards, such as floods, volcanoes, or earthquakes, can be delimited with relative ease. Others, such as drought or cyclones, are more difficult to locate on a global scale. Most earthquakes occur in fairly well-defined zones (Figure 2), which conform to global tectonic boundaries, although some major earthquakes of the past have been exceptions. These zones run the gamut of countries falling within each type of socioeconomic development, and cover diverse cultural groups. In any given year, on the average there will occur in the world 120 earthquakes of a Richter Magnitude 6 and greater. All are capable of inflicting serious damage, but it is likely that only a few

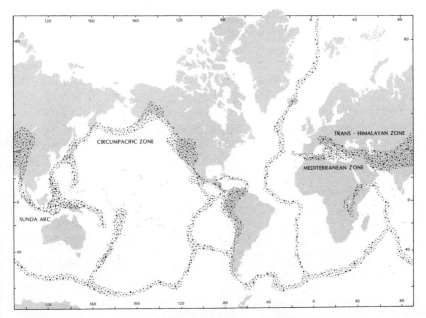

Figure 2. Global distribution of earthquake risk.

will take a heavy toll, and that toll will differ from country to country. In the past decade, countries of all four types have experienced a major disaster from earthquake; but because of other factors, the consequences will vary among world regions and cultures.

Consider the volcano hazard, which has a more specific areal distribution. Some regions of the world are affected by volcanic activities in a disproportionate manner (Figure 3). Of all currently active volcanoes which have historically caused property damage or fatalities, over 40% are located within Asia. Other regions, such as North America, or Africa and the Middle East, have been exposed to lower risks. The location in which society makes its livelihood is subject to varied degrees of environmental threats. The degree to which risk as a factor in locational choice either influences a culture or results because of it is unknown. Along socioeconomic lines, roughly two-thirds are found in countries in which the annual per capita income is less than $1,000. When compared to the world distribution of active volcanoes, the low income countries have a proportionately higher number of damaging volcanoes. Nature, without intent, discriminates against certain societies and world regions. But, in accordance with the interactive model, society can also create varying levels of risk.

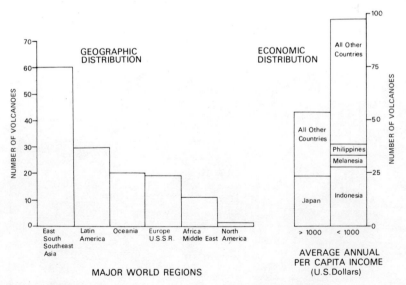

Figure 3.   Distribution of active volcanoes which have historically caused damage.

CHARACTERISTICS OF NATURAL EVENTS

Attributes of physical events, unaffected by society's intervention, influence human response (Burton *et al.*, 1978). Relevant factors include the magnitude, frequency, temporal spacing, predictability, speed of onset, duration, and areal extent of an event.

Events of large magnitude may foil most efforts to successfully prevent losses. The storm surge accompanying the 1972 cyclone in Bangladesh would have caused considerable damage regardless of a much greater level of protection from dikes. Events of low frequency may spawn complacency. Such appears to be the case with preparation for earthquakes in California. Those of high frequency may create "disaster cultures" (Barton, 1969). The inhabitants of Bangkok, Thailand, do little to stop floods from causing their nearly annual damages. Seasonal events are planned for differently than those random in time. The ability to predict reduces the uncertainty as to when and where a hazard event will occur, and creates more opportunities for adaptive response. For example, the ability to predict earthquakes will provide the potential for saving many lives, while continuing to utilize high-risk locations. Rapid onset of hazards reduces the number of adjustments theoretically available. More actions can be taken to mitigate flood losses than earthquake losses. The range of adjustments lessens for communities faced with flash flood problems, as opposed to the slow riverine variety. Events of long duration allow society to take mitigating actions in response to changing environmental circumstances. Gradually, scientific study of the Sahelian Drought led to policy revisions, which attempted to eliminate responses, such as digging new wells, which were linked to exacerbating drought conditions. Finally, events widespread over space may result in a variety of responses from diverse cultural origins.

In total, these multidimensional profiles define a rough scale of hazardous events, ranging from intensive to pervasive. Intensive events are of large magnitude, rare frequency, low predictability, rapid onset, short duration, and small areal extent. Pervasive events would rate opposite to the intensive on those six dimensions.

Some hazards fall on opposite ends of the intensive–pervasive continuum, while others have mixed characteristics. Earthquakes exemplify the intensive hazard; drought exemplifies the pervasive. Floods exemplify the events which will fall along a range between the two extremes.

The relationship between the characteristics described by the scale and response is well illustrated by historic and potential volcanic hazards in Hawaii and Martinique. The Hawaiian volcanic hazard is pervasive, while that of Martinique falls towards the intensive end of this scale. Since the Hawaiian event is slow in unfolding, relatively frequent, and is somewhat predictable, residents of the island have responded adaptively. Historically, few lives have been lost, and property damage has been minimized (MacDonald, 1972; Warrick, 1975a). In contrast, volcanic eruptions of a Peleean nature, as found in Martinique, are infrequent, of rapid onset, and thus far unpredictable. Such conditions make it difficult for persons to respond in a manner which minimizes adverse consequences (Francis, 1976), and catastrophic disaster can and has occurred. Similar comparison can be made of other situations where the physical event limits or influences response.

Thus, the physical dimensions of natural hazards are one of the important factors which shapes human response to extreme environments. Some areas are more prone to certain hazards. Overall levels of risk may also vary. Over time, certain hazards may become more frequent, and others less serious. There is a distinct need to investigate more fully the impact of different hazard types and risks on human decision-making processes.

DIFFERENCES IN HUMAN USE

Like physical events, human use of the land and human activities vary throughout the world. Inhabitants of the Big Thompson Canyon, Colorado, are chiefly engaged in recreational activity (Gruntfest, 1977). Ninety percent of the coastal Bangladesh residents make their occupation in agriculture (Islam, 1971). The farmer in Oaxaca, Mexico, hand tills a small field of five acres (Kirby, 1974), while the wheat farmer of Kansas runs his tractor over a 1,500 acre farm (Saarinen, 1966). The shopkeeper in San Francisco pays $1,000 a month for rent. In Managua, a shopowner may have only $1,000 invested in the shop he owns. Such factors also influence the character of natural hazards, as contrasted to the event and the manner in which individuals respond.

In general, two important factors describe human-use systems—the specific categories of land use, and the technologies employed to achieve that given use. Both factors may vary with type of socioeconomic development (Table 2), although they are not solely determined by it. Cultural processes may play extremely strong roles in guiding land use and technology, but comparisons among different cultural groups have not been well documented in geographic studies.

TABLE 2
HUMAN USE SYSTEMS

Land use		
Floodplain in	Development type	Use
Malawi	Folk	Predominantly shifting rural agriculture
Sri Lanka	Transitional	Rural, agricultural, some urban
Great Britain	Industrial	Urban, residential, industrial
?	Postindustrial	Recreational, open space

Technology		
Drought prone area	Development type	Cropping practice
Nigeria	Folk	Hand; small plots
Turkey	Transitional	Semimechanized; medium plots
Australia	Industrial	Machine; large plots, cooperatives
?	Postindustrial	Machine; corporate forming

Earthquake prone area	Development type	Predominant housing
Rural China	Folk	Adobe/mud
Urban Turkey	Transitional	Unreinforced concrete and frame
Urban Japan	Industrial	Mid- and high-rises
?	Postindustrial	Earthquake resistant

LAND USE

The type of resource utilization and human occupance of land often determines the degree to which human life and material goods are exposed to risk. Consider the predominant use of a stereotypical floodplain in four locations, each representing different types of development and cultural groups. In the Malawi floodplain, the land use is predominantly shifting rural agriculture. In the transitional society of Sri Lanka, family-owned farms may form the chief use. The major utilization in Shrewsbury, England, is urban residential, commercial, and industrial functions. A floodplain in a postindustrial country is ideally represented by mixed use, emphasizing open space and recreational activities. These uses are a product of a variety of factors, one of which is the conscious attempt to reduce flood risks.

The use of a floodplain determines vulnerability. The greater the value of property, the larger the damages from flooding. The more persons living on the floodplain, the higher the potential for fatalities. The farmer owning floodplain land has different risks than the urban villager, or an urban landlord.

Also of importance is the relationship between land use and response. The family practicing shifting agriculture can relocate quite easily, compared to apartment dwellers. A warning system suitable to a densely populated area may be unnecessary in a sparsely populated region.

TECHNOLOGY

A second consideration is the technology society applies and utilizes in a specific category of use (Table 2). The farmer in Nigeria, Turkey, and the United States may raise comparable crops, but the method each employs may vary drastically. The farmer in Nigeria plants sorghum and other grains on lands cleared with axe and fire, and cultivated by hoe in a shifting pattern (Dupree & Roder, 1974). The farmer in Turkey has integrated the use of the animal-pulled plow, and adopted soil conservation techniques, to raise barley and maize. The grain farmer of the midwest employs the latest mechanical equipment, cultivating a much larger area (Warrick, 1975b). The postindustrial farm would ideally utilize the latest agricultural innovations, within a corporate organization which has diversified geographical practices.

Similarly, it is suggested in Table 2 how the construction and architectural styles of different cultural regions can affect response. The resident of San Fernando, California, remains in his house during an earthquake, knowing it is safe. The urban villager in Haicheng, China, has little choice, because his dwelling is likely to collapse in an earthquake of similar magnitude. Numerous other factors which relate to technology may also be important.

HUMAN RESILIENCE TO HAZARD

Thus within the four types of socioeconomic development we find different patterns of land use, and different technologies aimed at carrying out the goal of each use. Along with other social and economic conditions, both help determine the vulnerability of society to hazard loss, and help shape the options society has to respond to environmental threats. On the basis of limited case studies, it is possible to make some observations on human resilience to hazard.

Folk societies in the study display a low level of resource use, low material wealth, and less exposure to hazard risks. The social systems of folk societies are least vulnerable to all but the most catastrophic natural events of large magnitude or areal extent. These social systems display resonance with the environment, seeking to harmonize land use and technology with natural systems. Thus, folk societies display great resiliency to most hazards.

Transitional societies have larger wealth and higher degrees of occupance in risk areas. Coupled with marginal economic status, which limits the ability to prevent and recover from loss, such areas are extremely vulnerable. A prime example is provided by rural Turkey and Iran, which have recently experienced devastating losses from earthquakes because of those factors. Thus, resilience is extremely low.

Industrial societies characterized by more intensive land use have increased their exposure to the extreme event. More sophisticated technologies and greater wealth reduces risk to life in the face of higher material damages. Resilience is also low, but of a different nature; the vulnerability to high-frequency events is decreased, while low-frequency events may have greater potential for catastrophe.

The postindustrial society cultivates a minimum sensitivity to conditions affecting fatalities and economic loss. Land uses are compatible with natural systems. Bolstered by sufficient resources, technology expands the availability of adjustments to reduce losses. Resilience to hazard is again restored.

Thus, we witness a cycle in which postindustrial society returns to a system of land use spawned by the philosophies of folk society. Humans are more harmonious with nature, and employ technologies commensurate with these cultural ideologies. In the middle lie two systems less resilient to hazard. As indicated by increasing tolls of life and property, it appears that the world as a whole is becoming less resilient to natural perturbations.

COGNITION, PERCEPTION, AND ADJUSTMENT

The environments which produce hazard events, and the socioeconomic systems which define human use, provide an important set of contexts which guide, force, and limit human behavior. They are not, however, the sole determinants of response to hazard. Processes of decision making, perceptions, and cognition of individuals and corporate groups within different societies or cultural groups play a central role.

Perception, cognition, and adjustment are by definition elements of culture, and are therefore culturally variable. On the other hand, they may drastically differ among persons in a single culture. For example, a farmer of the Sahel may view drought as punishment for some wrong deed, while a Kansas wheat-belt farmer perceives it as a cyclical fluctuation of climate. These differences may be erroneously attributed to culture when that same difference is observed between two other farmers residing in one of these areas. Research to date does not provide a firm basis for making such distinctions.

Models of Human Decisions

In the face of hazardous events, individuals and groups must choose among a theoretically immense number of alternative paths of behavior. Although the choice is often to do nothing, in most situations two or more alternative courses of actions are feasible. The nature of the decision varies in simplicity and breadth. To the inhabitant of the Shrewsbury, England, floodplain, his choice in response to a flood warning may be to evacuate or stay. To the Army Corps of Engineers hydrologist, it is how much storage capacity to allocate to flood control in a multipurpose dam. To the farmer in Tanzania, it may be to employ one or more of approximately 20 separate adjustments when drought conditions prevail. At the extreme, residents of the Sri Lanka floodplain face over 200 possible hazard adjustments.

The process by which such choices are made appears to be similar, despite the wide variety of decisional context and cultural conditions. A simple model suggests that the individual or group: (1) appraises the likelihood of natural events; (2) examines a range of alternative behaviors or adjustments; (3) evaluates the consequences of each perceived action; and (4) chooses one or more actions (Slovic, Kunreuther, & White, 1974).

Field study shows that this general process is modified by several factors. First, persons are not highly competent estimators of the likelihood and consequences of extreme events. Second, persons rarely are aware of a wide range of alternative adjustments. Third, information-processing bias limits the ability to compare alternatives. Finally, persons demonstrate a wide and diverse range of goals to be satisfied by the decision outcomes.

Such observations and more empirical studies lead us to believe that human response to natural hazards is described by a "bounded rationality" model of decisions (Simon, 1956). Responses are made to satisfy individually set goals, rather than to "maximize expected utility or gain." Such findings suggest that, unless carefully designed, hazard protection and relief policies on a global level, and particularly in transitional and industrial contexts, may promote, rather than alleviate, human loss.

In addition, evidence exists that information on alternatives is not simultaneously processed, but that alternative actions are considered in a sequential, ordered process (Kunreuther, 1974; White, Bradley, & White, 1972). For example, the occupant of a floodplain in the United States does not carefully weigh the probabilities and consequences of disaster against premium costs in arriving at a decision to purchase flood insurance. He does, however, tend to base his choice on whether a flood has been experienced, and whether a neighbor has purchased insurance (Kunreuther, 1978). Likewise, Tanzanian farmers base their crop-planting decisions on meeting the simple goals of survival, rather than attempting to maximize economic returns (Kunreuther, 1972).

RANGE OF HAZARD ADJUSTMENTS

Adjustment is the term used to describe behavioral response to a hazard either before, during, or following the occurrence of the physical event (White, 1945). Numerous typologies of adjustments have been offered (Burton et al., 1978; White & Haas, 1975), but only the most recent is briefly outlined (Burton et al., 1978).

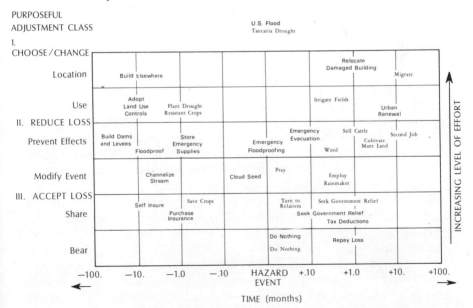

Figure 4.   Natural hazard adjustment: A time/effort perspective (the United States flood and Tanzania drought adjustments are distinguished by different type faces).

One way of viewing adjustments is through a typology along a discontinuous scale measuring in both economic and psychic terms the level of human effort expended in coping (Figure 4).

Two broad groupings of adjustments—incidental and purposeful—refer to individual intent. Incidental actions are made in the course of everyday life, and unconsciously reduce vulnerability or increase human capacity to absorb loss. For example, building codes made many structures less susceptible to earthquake damage, although it was ancillary to their purpose. Similarily, the extended family makes a social system less susceptible to loss.

Purposeful adjustments may be divided into three categories—(1) accept losses by either bearing or sharing, (2) reduce losses by either preventing effects or modifying the events, and (3) radical change of either land use or location. Figure 4 gives examples of adjustments for floods in the United States and for Tanzania drought.

COGNITION OF HAZARD EVENTS AND ADJUSTMENT

Within this model of decision making, individual perceptions or cognition act to shape the evaluation of these alternative actions. We can distinguish between two general types of stimuli. The first involves the physical event, and the second, hazard adjustments. Persons have perceptions of both physical hazard characteristics and the potential consequences of the disaster caused by the event. Adjustments are thought of in terms of their availability, providing they are viewed as a possible form of behavior, and, in terms of desirability, based on economic and social criteria.

It is generally accepted that some residents of hazardous areas view physical events with a different perspective than that of the expert or scientist (Kates, 1962; Mitchell, 1974b; White, 1964). For instance, residents of a floodplain in the United States may attach different meanings to the concept of the "100-year flood" than that of the hydrologist (Burton & Kates, 1964). Likewise, denizens of northern Nigeria may view drought in different terms than the climatologist (Dupree & Roder, 1974). The behavior of the individual who misinterprets scientific information will often differ from that of the person with the more acute understanding.

One important measure of perception is assessing how persons view the temporal nature of hazard. Are events random, clustered, cyclical, or nonrepeatable? Scientific evidence suggests that most hazards occur in a random fashion. Research shows that this view is shared by many residents of hazardous areas (Table 3) (Burton et al., 1978).

TABLE 3
PERCEPTIONS OF HAZARD EVENTS[a]

	Flood			Drought		
	Folk (Malawi)	Transitional (Sri Lanka)	Industrial (Shrewsbury)	Folk (Nigeria)	Transitional (Brazil)	Industrial (Australia)
Random	43	78	72	17	49	81
Clustered	23	8	2	4	22	6
Cyclical	22	14	5	3	6	11
Denial	5	0	14	75	17	0

[a] Numbers indicate percentages.

Individuals in a folk or transitional society are more likely to perceive events as cyclical or clustered than those in an industrial society. This is congruent with the cyclical outlook of time found in many primitive societies (Tuan, 1977).

In a more sophisticated manner, these perceptions relate to how persons subjectively evaluate probabilities of rare events. Studies have shown that, while people in general are poor probabilistic thinkers (Tversky & Kahneman, 1974), they are good at estimating the frequency of some hazards, and much less accurate at others (Hewitt & Burton, 1971). For example, the residents of London made better estimates of the objective frequency of tornadoes and hurricanes, and were less accurate for floods, ice storms, and blizzards.

More recent evidence shows that persons tend to overestimate small frequencies and underestimate larger frequencies of lethal events (Lichtenstein, Slovic, Fischoff, Layman, & Combs, 1978). In addition, these perceptions may change over short or long time periods. Adams (1973) demonstrates that beach-goers' perceptions of weather forecasts changed as the summer season drew to a close.

A person's image of loss or hazard consequences is a second important factor shaping human response. The floodplain resident who perceives that a flood will sweep away his home is likely to respond differently than the persons who see floods as "only high water" (Burton & Kates, 1964).

While variation is found among individuals, appraisals also differ among culture groups. In Shrewsbury, England, only 27% of those questioned felt that floods would cause substantial damage. This contrasts with Sri Lanka, where 90% of the floodplain residents expected a flood to be totally destructive if it occurred.

A third important factor influencing response is how persons perceive and evaluate possible adjustments to hazard. On a global scale, only a moderate number of risk-zone occupants are aware of actions they can take to prevent loss, and few are aware of more than one. Those with greater knowledge are likely to be members of a folk or a postindustrial society. Persons residing within transitional and industrial societies perceive a narrower range of possible actions.

The social and economic perception of adjustments may play an important role in influencing behavior. When actions are judged to be economic and efficacious, as in the case where residents of tornado-prone Illinois perceive emergency response to warning to be effective in preventing loss (Sims & Baumann, 1972), or community officials evaluate a levee system as economically efficient (White, 1964), adaptive and positive action is more likely to be taken.

Thus, it is demonstrated that persons vary in their appraisal of natural events, and view the range of possible adjustments in different manners. The final choice of adjustment is influenced by this, and by a broader set of circumstances, outlined below.

CHOICE OF ADJUSTMENTS

Individual adoption of adjustments has been found to be influenced by four main factors: experience, material wealth, resource use, and personality; however, when taken together, in most situations they have weak explanatory powers, and are not strong predictors of behavior. In a recent examination of positive action taken by people receiving information about their location in a flood plain, about 75% of the variance was associated with factors of experience (Waterstone, 1978).

Recent encounters with hazard have the most powerful influence on adjustment behavior in most industrialized locales, although this may not be true for folk and transitional society (Heijnen & Kates, 1974). Both number and type are affected (Burton et al., 1978). A recent study by Kunreuther (1976) shows experience as a principal factor in the decision to purchase flood and earthquake insurance. This can pose a problem for the planner: Is behavior influenced only by direct and often catastrophic circumstances? On the other hand, studies of response to hurricane warnings show that recent arrivals are more likely to follow instructions to evacuate vulnerable areas than are old-timers (Baker, 1977; Davenport, 1978; Windham, Posey, Ross, & Spencer, 1977).

Material wealth increases the theoretical range of adjustment options open to an individual, and may enable one to absorb greater losses, although it does not necessarily lead to a greater variety in response. For example, the wealthy farmer can afford to buy land in areas with favorable climates, while the poor farmer must locate on more marginal land. The wealthy nations can afford a sophisticated hurricane warning system, while poor nations lack money to employ a good monitoring system.

Personality traits may have a small impact on adjustment adoption. In a controversial study, Sims and Baumann (1972) attribute the higher death rate for tornadoes in the southern United States to a fatalistic locus of control. Recent studies dispute this finding (Kirkby, 1972; Schiff, 1977). Other variables, such as a risk-taking propensity, do not appear to be related to behavior (Schiff, 1977), although much work is needed to reveal the details of personality–behavior relationships.

The final factor in shaping behavior is the role the individual plays in society, coupled with type of resource utilization. The head of a large family, out of a sense of concern for the children, may build a tornado shelter, while the childless couple does nothing. Likewise, the owner of a small store along the San Andreas fault may purchase earthquake insurance, unlike the renter next door.

Few well-supported generalizations can be offered about cross-cultural differences in adjustment perception and behavior. In anecdotal fashion, it is possible to discern that residents of Nigeria evaluate the likelihood of drought differently than Australians. Similarly, the range of possible flood adjustments may vary from less than 10 in Shrewsbury, England, to over 200 in Sri Lanka. A multitude of other national comparisons have and can be made. Such information does not allow us to identify different behaviors attributable to culture. Along the lines of socioeconomic systems, observation has shown that folk societies are likely to embrace a wider range of adjustments, which are harmonious with nature, and operate at low costs and technology. Conversely, those areas within an industrial framework consider only a few options, and primarily ones which are dominant over nature, and operate at high costs and levels of technology (Kates, 1971, 1977).

CONSEQUENCES OF HAZARD

Each response to hazard has an associated set of costs and benefits, both real or perceived. These are important in the calculus of human response, because in the dynamic system framework they link behavior through time (Figure 1).

In discussing the consequences of hazard, it is important to dintinguish between benefits and costs, types of consequences, and their distribution within a region and between societies.

COSTS

Headlines read "600,000 killed in Chinese earthquake," or "Flash flood in South Dakota causes $100 million in damage." To many persons, gross figures about death and damage following an extreme event may be the most salient feature of a hazard. To others, the consequences are much different. The neighboring farmer's baby dies from malnutrition, or a newly constructed beach house is left destroyed by the forces of a storm surge.

The cost of natural hazards can be measured in a variety of ways: fatalities, injury, property loss, monetary loss from the hazard event, cost of adjustments, and psychic damage. It is impossible to convert all to a common denominator. Can the loss of one's family be equated to the loss of another's factory or farm? Or to the anxiety resulting from severe stress? Second, the accuracy of measurement decreases through the above sequence of costs. Deaths are more easily counted than injury, property loss is measured more accurately than mental health effects.

We can, nevertheless, make some specific cross-cultural comparisons of loss in terms of fatalities, per capita damages, impacts on gross national product, and the distribution of costs from specific hazard events. When we observe these types of differences, it provides some grounds for indicating that culture may influence behavior.

Deaths by hazard are disparately distributed between the rich and poor countries, paralleling the general trend for loss of life from all causes (Dworkin, 1974). All factors previously mentioned, such as resource use, perception, and adjustment, shape this distribution. In a simple fashion, the death rate is higher in the poor countries, because the folk and transitional societies are less likely to respond to a warning in a manner which saves lives. Often this is not by conscious choice, but because of a way of life, involving lack of warning and evacuation facilities.

Statistics (Figure 5) illustrate the degree of this gap. Of the 17 countries with a death rate greater than 200 annual deaths per million people (computed between 1947 and 1973), 16 had annual per capita mean incomes below $1,000. Stated in other terms, 94% of the high income countries (income > $1,000) had low death rates. Because records and data collection are more accurate in the developed countries, these are

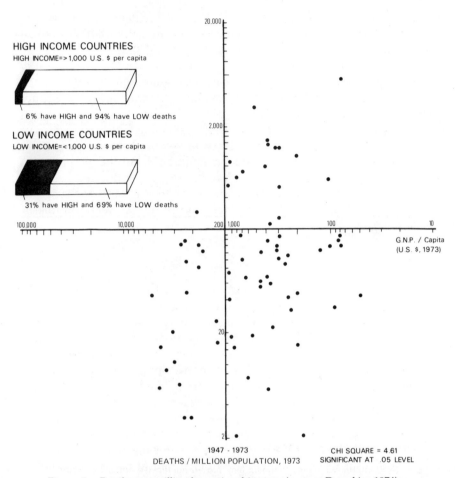

Figure 5.   Deaths per million by national income (source: Dworkin, 1974).

probably conservative estimates, and some of the lower income countries most likely have higher death rates.

The degree of human hardship created by natural events can be
measured partly in terms of gross national product (GNP). A general
relationship is that, as per capita loss of GNP mounts, the monetary
measure of social and economic disruptions also rises. We can view this
in average figures for different nations, or compare the impact of disasters from similar events.

Comparing the annual costs of floods, drought, and cyclones between a folk society and an industrialized society, we see that the gross

per capita losses are roughly two to five times greater in the industrial nation, yet per capita loss expressed as a percentage of GNP is 10 to 20 times greater in the folk society (Burton *et al.*, 1978).

The 1972 Managua earthquake caused losses which were three times the per capita GNP of the typical Nicaraguan. On the other hand, losses from the 1971 San Fernando quake, comparable in magnitude, inconvenienced the million residents of this South California valley in an average amount of five percent of a year's per capita GNP. The Sahelian drought of the 1970s caused monetary losses modest by comparison with those of the Great Plains grain farmer in 1977, but the disruption in social fabric was greater.

While total economic losses may be greater in industrialized nations, damages measured in more social terms are far greater in folk or developing nations.

DISTRIBUTIONAL IMPACT

In average or aggregate terms, the impact of the San Fernando earthquake was small; that in Managua was severe. But in daily life, the real world is not comprised of averages and aggregates. Some persons die, others are injured, more are dislocated, many damaged, and most are affected in small ways (Bowden & Kates, 1974). Hazard effects are distributed in an uneven fashion. The distributional impact differs among the folk, transitional, industrial, and postindustrial societies. Returning to the comparison of San Fernando and Managua, we can trace the cascading impact of hazard effects (Figure 6).

We see that the greatest costs are borne by a few—the dead and dislocated. The shape of the graph is similar for the two disasters; but the lives of a far greater number are interrupted in the less developed nation.

In comparing losses, we see that the average cost to the individual in Managua who is injured, disrupted or damaged is comparably four to five times greater than his or her counterpart in the United States. At both the national and the individual level, the toll of natural disaster is often more serious for the less advantaged.

DISTRIBUTIONAL BENEFITS

Three distinct societal benefits are linked with hazardous natural events: benefits of human occupance of hazardous areas, direct benefits of hazard events, and benefits of human response.

As stated earlier, human activity in hazardous areas may produce

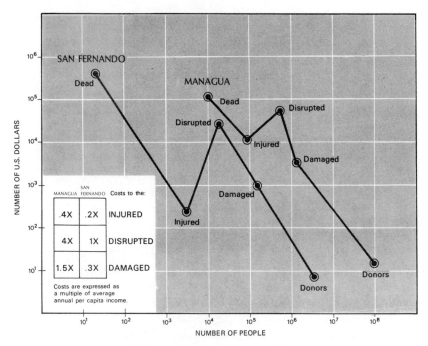

Figure 6.   Distribution of hazard costs.

immense benefits, as society utilizes land and other resources in a productive manner. Huge sums of income are generated and exchanged each day on the earthquake-prone sites of San Francisco or Tokyo. The Solomon Islanders raise coconuts as a cash crop on atolls which are occasionally ravaged by tropical storms. The list is nearly endless; few, if any, locations are totally free of natural hazards. Indeed, if a location were consistently to yield lower benefits than costs to its residents, counting social subsidy of occupance of the site as a benefit, it would likely be abandoned. Much of the public policy controversy about adjustment measures centers upon the justification for subsidized occupation of hazardous sites, as when dams are built to protect floodplain occupants, or public relief is given to residents of a town in an active seismic zone.

To the inhabitants of St. Thomas, and other Caribbean islands, tropical storms bring rains vital to crop production and domestic water supply (Bowden, 1974). They are important sources of moisture for crop growth in the United States (Hartman, Holland, & Giddings, 1969). The eruption of Kilauea, in Hawaii, gradually extends the shoreline in a seaward direction (MacDonald, 1972). Benefits of flooding can be traced back to ancient Egypt, where the flooding of the Nile brought nutrients and water to agricultural areas. The prevention of extreme events of nature may be welcome to some, but may also deprive others of valuable benefits.

Human adjustment has a set of associated benefits measurable in terms of fatalities prevented, property damage averted, and the human suffering avoided when disaster strikes. A Tennessee community finds new coherence in fighting a flood disaster. The farmer in Tanzania may avert the loss of life by taking a job in the village, and extend his employment base. The farmer in Colorado may prevent personal loss and keep the price of bread from rising by planting drought-resistant wheat. Each form of behavior has an economic benefit, some measurable in the market, others unquantifiable.

Benefit/Cost Relationships

Every human response with respect to hazard resource use, perception, and adjustment, results in a set of benefit/cost (B/C) relationships. These can only be socially meaningful when computed in terms of long-term averages and potential for catastrophic impact. Some forms of human behavior, for example the adoption of land use control regulating development in floodplains in the United States, may achieve a favorable B/C relationship, and reduce the possibilities of catastrophic loss. Conversely, other behavior, such as increased human occupance of the dike-protected lowlands of the Bangladesh coast, may result in a low B/C relationship, and create conditions of extreme catastrophic potential. In between, we witness a vast range of action which affects the yearly tolls of damages and the distributional character of fatalities and dollar loss.

At the individual level, a choice of adjustment which has a high probability of yielding net gains, as when a speculative builder constructs an apartment building in a floodplain where the probability of a 100-year flood's occurring before he resells it in the next ten years is .096, may spell eventual disaster for the community when the 1% event does occur.

TOWARD AN UNDERSTANDING OF HAZARD AND CULTURE

As demonstrated, human response to natural hazard encompasses a wide range of factors related to environments and human behavior. These factors are interrelated and dynamic. Environmental and social systems change over time, experience alters response, shifts in levels of hazard consequences may change cognitions and thus influence behavior. Culture provides an unknown medium to guide this change. In our concluding section, we seek to identify some common modes of coping with hazard, illustrate how change is discontinuous and difficult to predict, summarize what we know about culture in relation to behavior, and point out major lessons from hazard research in different cultural settings.

FOUR WAYS OF COPING WITH HAZARD

Aggregation of individual adjustments (Figure 4) found among the different study sites permits us to identify four general ways social systems respond when confronted by hazard. Research shows that these modes are fairly discrete, and limited evidence indicates that a given society may adopt one in response to a hazard such as flood, and another in response to a different hazard, say earthquake. Societies may shift from one mode to another over time, although not in an ordered fashion (Burton *et al.*, 1978).

We refer to these modes as: *loss absorption, loss acceptance, loss reduction,* and *radical change.* Transition is respectively promoted by crossing thresholds of *awareness, action,* and *intolerance.*

Pattern one, loss absorption, typified by residents of San Francisco or of the Virgin Islands, is exemplified by the view that hazard is not a problem. In such locations, persons frequently rely on their ability to absorb loss when disaster occurs. In a sense, hazard has been integrated into life-style or culture.

Crossing a threshold of awareness, into the second pattern, those making their livelihoods on the Malawi floodplain, or living on the flanks of Kilauea volcano, acknowledge loss, but remain content with bearing and sharing damage. The most frequent form of behavior is nonaction.

Pattern three, indicative of societies which cross an action threshold, is to take action to reduce and prevent loss in a consciously positive manner. This is well illustrated by United States flood hazard policies.

Finally, at the extreme, some societies reach a threshold of intolerance, and completely change land use or location in response to hazard. Such is the case of Brazilian farmers, who are quick to migrate from drought-stricken areas, or the residents of Tristan De Cunha, who evacuated many miles to England in the wake of a volcanic eruption.

No evidence suggests that a given nation, or a distinct cultural group, progressively shifts through these four behavioral patterns; nor are they readily placed into direct correspondence with the four developmental types. On the other hand, evidence suggests that individuals living in certain hazardous areas subconsciously scale their efforts in accordance with these four patterns (Sorensen, 1977).

Responses of individuals in eight of the comparative study sites on past adjustment behavior were analyzed, using a basic scalogram analysis. Results from five of those sites were statistically acceptable.[3] The analysis indicated that individuals in certain sites distinctly order their responses to hazard in a cumulative and orderly manner.

For example, the first anticipated response of the typical resident of San Francisco, when faced with an earthquake threat, is emergency evacuation after the disaster. Those who adopt only one adjustment are likely to adhere to that behavior. A second action would be prayer. This is subsequently followed by protecting one's home from fire and theft, structural modification of the house, and then, purchasing insurance. At the extreme of the scale are those persons who have considered or attempted other actions, and subsequently decide to relocate permanently. A time sequence of actions is not determined but is suggested by the adjustments themselves. Actual behavior is not predicted by the scale for any given individual. The results indicate a decision process which resembles an ordered choice or lexiographic model. From it, seven distinct modes of behavior emerge (Figure 7). Reflected in these modes is a movement from actions indicating loss acceptance to choices which reduce loss, and, in the extreme, radically change location. The extent to which this difference is shared along cultural lines is uncertain. Preliminary investigation suggests that not all locations follow this pattern. The reason behind this remains elusive.

Predicting Behavior: Adjustment Interaction

The ability to predict changes in social systems, and individual response to natural hazard, is limited by the complexity of the problem, and lack of data and empirical methods of analysis. It is possible to anticipate types of response in the wake of major catastrophe, but not under more routine circumstances. Kates's system model (Figure 1) is an initial attempt at viewing the dynamics of human response to hazard, but has not been rigorously tested. Ericksen (1975a,b) utilizes scenario

---

[3]These analyses produced coefficients of reproducibility above .85, and coefficients of scalability above .6.

ADJUSTMENT CLASSES:

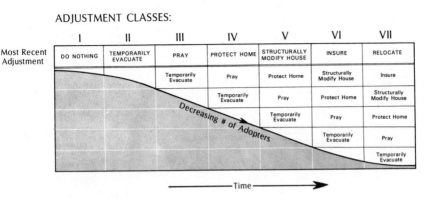

Most Recent Adjustment	I	II	III	IV	V	VI	VII
	DO NOTHING	TEMPORARILY EVACUATE	PRAY	PROTECT HOME	STRUCTURALLY MODIFY HOUSE	INSURE	RELOCATE
			Temporarily Evacuate	Pray	Protect Home	Structurally Modify House	Insure
				Temporarily Evacuate	Pray	Protect Home	Structurally Modify House
					Temporarily Evacuate	Pray	Protect Home
						Temporarily Evacuate	Pray
							Temporarily Evacuate

Decreasing # of Adopters

———— Time ————→

Figure 7. Scaling of earthquake adjustments.

methods to estimate future behavior given alternative sets of assumptions. This deserves further refinement and application. Another method is to examine relationships between adjustments, or adjustment interactions (Sorensen, 1977).

Adjustment interaction may be viewed as "how one adjustment encourages or inhibits (the adoption of) another" (White & Haas, 1975, p. 63). Expanding this concept, it is possible to describe several different ways in which adjustments interact.

First, one action may causally influence the selection of a second action. For example, studies indicate communities adopting flood control works often become reliant on federal relief and rehabilitation programs to cope with the effects of events exceeding the design magnitude.

Second, a single factor or set of factors may influence the simultaneous or sequential adoption of two adjustments. In the United States, the Flood Hazard Reduction Act of 1973 provides incentives to communities to enter a flood insurance program and adopt land-use ordinances. Likewise, certain factors may create sanctions against other hazard adjustments. Along the Bangladesh coast, social taboos against women meeting men outside their own families discourage the practice of evacuating to a common refuge on high ground, while encouraging individual investment in household improvements. Other studies suggest factors such as laws, regulations, bribes, hazard experience, education, resource level, hazard characteristics, technology, or taxes, to name a few (Burton et al., 1978; Sorensen, 1977).

Finally, adjustments may interact in a random manner, where no relationships exist between pairs or sets of actions. Such may be the case in Tanzania, where one farmer could employ a rainmaker because of

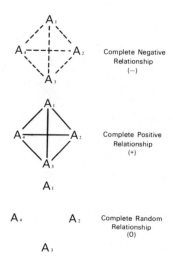

Figure 8.   Three extreme patterns of adjustment interaction (A_N = Adjustment).

religious beliefs, while cultivating larger land areas because of technological advantages.

Using this classification of interaction, a number of possible systems of adjustment with dynamic implications can be derived, and three hypothetical systems are considered in this paper (Figure 8). The first system is characterized by generally negative associations among all adjustments. Within this system, each individual or group would rely on a single mode of adjustment that does not encourage the adoption of others. Over time, single solution strategies, as in the case of United States flood policy in the 1940s, would be promoted. So long as the federal government under the policy established in the flood control acts of 1936 and 1938 directed its major efforts at constructing flood control dams, levees, and channel improvements, there was no encouragement to extend the flood-proofing of buildings, or land-use regulations, or flood insurance, as a means of promoting the other two types of measures.

The second system is characterized by positive associations among two or more adjustments. In this system, a broader range of adjustments would be practiced. The adoption of one action, given time, would lead to additional adjustment practices, as when the purchase of insurance motivates the purchaser to consider structural alterations in his dwelling, and to be more alert to warnings.

The third system is characterized by random associations among adjustments. Interactions would tend to promote behavior in a somewhat random and unpredictable fashion. This system is exemplified by farmers who purchase drought-resistant seeds in drought conditions, yet fail to employ soil conservation techniques. These three systems provide a means for comparing actual adjustment behavior in cross-cultural settings. There is some reason to think that the patterns of adjustment behavior are strongly influenced by the cultural context, but comparative studies of these differences are rare.

COMPARATIVE STUDY: NIGERIAN DROUGHT AND SAN FRANCISCO EARTHQUAKE

By quantitatively measuring adjustment associations in two locations, it is possible to make predictions of future hazard response. However, the validation of such predictions requires further substantiation. Figure 9 illustrates the structure of interaction based on adjustment behavior of Nigerian farmers and urbanites of San Francisco. By comparing those to the generalized interaction structures in Figure 8, behavioral patterns can be identified, and predictions of future choice can be made.

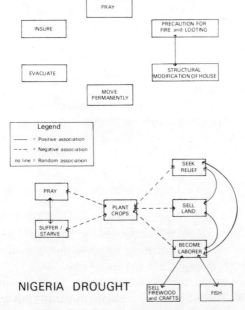

Figure 9.   Adjustment interactions: San Francisco and Nigeria.

First, consider the adjustment pattern found for residents of San Francisco faced with an earthquake hazard. Six responses are surveyed: prayer, purchasing earthquake insurance, taking precautions to reduce damages from fires and looting, structurally modifying the home to make it more earthquake-resistant, evacuating after the earthquake has occurred, and permanently moving to a lower risk location. When analyzed, the adjustment pattern for San Francisco earthquake hazard closely resembles the random interaction system in Figure 8. Current behavior lacks focus, and future choice will likely continue in a fortuitous manner. The current emphasis on loss absorption is unlikely to change.

A wider range and a different pattern of adjustment is found for Nigerian drought. Responses include prayer, bearing the loss by suffering and starving, replanting lost crops, seeking relief or aid from relatives and the government, selling land, switching occupations to become a laborer, fishing to gain added food, and selling noncrop goods such as firewood or crafts.

A more complex set of interactions is found, and elements of both extremes of negative and positive reinforcement are at work. This creates isolated subsets of adjustment behavior. One emphasizes loss bearing, a second—replanting—exemplifies preventing loss, and the third is a complex system of change, ranging from relocation to switching occupations. Negative associations between the adjustments will tend to strengthen these three behavioral configurations in future episodes of drought.

The investigation of interaction points out a need for studying human response in longitudinal frameworks which seek to explain how behavior changes and what factors account for change. As we gain greater insight into the dynamics of human response to hazard, we can gain better understanding of human cognitive processes, and at the same time formulate policy which reduces human suffering from disaster.

LINEAR TRENDS AND DISCONTINUITIES

Human response to natural hazard is difficult to predict and explain. Most change does not occur in a gradual fashion. Mixes of adjustments change in an abrupt or discontinuous manner, and do not mirror the smooth slope of a differential equation.

For example, major revisions in United States earthquake, drought, and flood policies have come on the heels of disaster. The same observation seems to apply to other countries. Efforts to redirect policy without crisis, an indicator of linear behavior, have typically met with failure. Change, when it occurs, is often large and dramatic. This is exemplified by the United States flood insurance program; or the great commitment to earthquake prediction in China.

On an individual basis, changes in response also may be abrupt. The Sahel farmer who has led a nomadic life changes his migration pattern because of environmental conditions and aid policies. The residents of Topeka, Kansas, suddenly strengthen kinship ties in the wake of a severe tornado (Drabek & Key, 1976). The migration of farmers occurs in response to short-term changes in Australian weather conditions (Heathcote, 1974).

Often rapid change and fluctuations in response to hazard are labeled unpredictable or irrational. This is both dangerous and erroneous. We must seek to identify models of human response with better predictive capability, and gain fuller understanding of the processes of decision to overcome such charges.

CULTURE AND RESPONSE

Throughout the paper, examples have been given of where differences in hazard events, resource use systems, perception or cognitions, and hazard adjustment can be observed between two or more locations with different cultural compositions. Yet, insufficient evidence exists to define the nature of the relationship between culture and behavior under conditions of risk. To illustrate this, Table 4 summarizes some relevant factors about 10 flood and drought prone study sites.

We would all agree that these locations differ with respect to culture. To some extent, we could also concur that type of development, resource use, and individual perception are, in part, a manifestation of cultural processes. Yet there is no consistent correlation between these factors and adjustment behavior. Both Shrewsbury and Malawi accept flood loss. Australia and Brazil have experienced human locational changes in response to drought. Residents of Sri Lanka and Rock River, Illinois, have a similar perception of the randomness of floods. Yucatan and Tanzania display similar resource use systems. The farmers of India and Yucatan possess nearly identical views of the consequences of hazard events, despite different natural systems.

Although we are prevented by the number of studies from drawing statistically valid conclusions, the implication is that the conceptualization of culture is inadequate. Cross-cultural differences and similarities exist. On the other hand, differences in observed behavior cannot be explained adequately on the basis of culture alone. It is to be hoped that

TABLE 4
COMPARISON OF STUDY SITES

	Type of development	Characteristics of physical event	Resource use system	Perception of physical event			Adjustment	
				Random (%)	Cyclical grouped & denial (%)	Perception of serious consequences (%)	Mode of coping	Prevent damage (%)
FLOOD								
Malawi	Folk	Intensive	Shifting farming	43	50	89	Accept	42
India	Transitional	Intensive	Intensive farming	63	33	94	Reduce	17
Sri Lanka	Transitional	Intensive	Intensive farming	78	22	89	Reduce	—
Rock River	Industrial	Intensive	Urban	76	20	24	Reduce	44
Shrewsbury	Industrial	Intensive	Urban	72	24	27	Accept	3
DROUGHT								
Nigeria	Folk	Pervasive	Shifting, mixed farming	17	83	100	Accept	0
Yucatan	Folk	Pervasive	Shifting farming	45	53	95	Accept	11
Tanzania	Transitional	Pervasive	Shifting farming	64	36	79	Reduce	47
Brazil	Transitional	Pervasive	Farming	49	46	—	Change	38
Australia	Industrial	Pervasive	Farming, ranching	81	17	—	Change	16

others can proceed from where the current research ends, to move toward a fuller understanding of this topic.

FUTURE RESEARCH DIRECTIONS

The cross-cultural efforts thus far completed have influenced public policy toward natural hazards in two ways. They have pointed out types of adjustments and social policy which merit examination with a view to possible application elsewhere. And they have led to generalizations about social process that appear to have relevance wherever policy alternatives are considered.

An elementary aspect of comparative study is that it raises the question, "Why is a practice in one place not adopted in another place?" The answer may be that there are good reasons rooted in the cultural and natural environment for not adopting a given practice. Or it may be that a transfer would not promise net benefits. In other instances, transfers have been made in a deliberate manner. Growing out of some of the studies reported above, the French government undertook a detailed appraisal of United States flood management policy, and already has adopted components of its nonstructural and floodplain information activity (Ministre de l'Equipment, 1977). Western attempts to aid sufferers from the Sahelian drought were moderated by observations of scientists who had worked in Kenya and Tanzania. The United States strategy on earthquake research has been influenced by information as to the Chinese use of folk wisdom in earthquake prediction, and social process in generating such predictions. These are relatively simple transfers, resulting from asking the same question in different settings.

It may be expected that, as public agencies appraise the suitability of adopting hazard adjustments which have proved effective elsewhere, and as they move away from single technological solutions and compare the merits of different measures, they will seek a more sophisticated understanding of how people respond. Thus, the further findings cited above on the relation of experience and hazard-mitigating behavior (Waterstone, 1978) sprang from an agency's need to know what difference, if any, the dissemination of a flood brochure and map had upon the actions of recipients. New studies on response patterns would be strengthened by more precise definition and measurement of cultural dimensions of the population affected.

Less easy to trace are the effects of broad generalizations derived in preliminary form from the comparative studies. For example, the proposition that hazard experience affects acuity of individual awareness and response to hazard information is receiving wider validation, and is suggesting strategies for programs of public information in a number of countries. The notion that a sense of efficacy and command of specific avenues of action is an important factor affecting response to hazard warnings is being translated into the design of local warning system tactics. The application of the lessons normally takes account of local culture and social organization. It is to be hoped that the expansion of local studies, and the sharpening in them of cultural and social distinctions, will permit fashioning of a more solid theoretical framework than now is available. Many of the studies to date have been limited to a single hazard at one point in time.

As new studies take account of a wider spectrum of natural and technological hazards, it should become somewhat easier to sort out the role of culture. To the extent that longitudinal investigations are mounted, the dynamics of change may be illuminated. The decisions commanding attention are those which are repeated over time, and reflect the evolving consequences of earlier decisions, as well as enduring culture traits.

For reasons stated at the outset, the cross-cultural studies have advanced further toward the suggestion of commonalities than the explanation of differences across cultural boundaries. Such explanations are still elusive, for the most part. Although the behavior patterns can be described, the response of a given pattern to a new social intervention, such as an insurance program or a relief project is difficult to predict. Where the social structure is dominant, as in the extreme of socialist states, there may be a bit more confidence; but unraveling the cultural thread in the fabric is still very complicated. The studies to date lay a partial groundwork, but are lacking much in coverage and in theoretical framework.

ACKNOWLEDGMENTS

Brian Murton and Thomas Saarinen provided useful comments on the manuscript. Graphics and cartographic work were provided by Jane Eckelman. The typing was done by Jacqueline Myers.

REFERENCES

Adams, R. L. A. Uncertainty in nature, cognitive dissonance, and the perceptual distortion of environmental information: Weather forecasts and New England beach trip decisions. *Economic Geography*, 1973, *49*, 287–297.

Baker, E. J. Public attitudes toward hazard zone controls. *Journal of American Institute of Planners*, 1977, *43*, 401–408.

Barker, M. *Specialists and air pollution occupations and preoccupations.* University of Victoria, Department of Geography, Western Geographical Series No. 14. Victoria, B. C.: University of Victoria, 1977.

Barker, M., & Burton, I. *Differential response to stress in natural and social environments: An application of a modified Rosenzweig picture-frustration test.* University of Colorado, Institute of Behavioral Science, Natural Hazards Working Paper No. 5. Boulder: University of Colorado, 1969.

Barton, A. *Communities in disaster.* New York: Doubleday, 1969.

Baumann, D., & Sims, J. Human response to the hurricane. In G. White (Ed.), *Natural hazards: Local, national, global.* New York: Oxford University Press, 1974, pp. 25–30.

Bolt, B., Horn, W., Macdonald, G., & Scott, R. *Geological hazards.* New York: Springer-Verlag, 1975.

Bowden, M. *Hurricanes in paradise.* St. Thomas, V. I.: Island Resources Foundation, 1974.

Bowden, M., & Kates, R. The coming San Francisco earthquake: After the disaster. In H. Cochrane, J. Haas, M. Bowden, & R. Kates, *Social science perspectives on the coming San Francisco earthquake.* University of Colorado, Institute of Behavioral Science, Natural Hazards Working Paper No. 25. Boulder: University of Colorado, 1974, pp. 62–81.

Burton, I. *Types of agricultural occupance of flood plains in the United States.* University of Chicago, Department of Geography, Research Paper No. 75. Chicago: University of Chicago, 1962.

Burton, I. *International Geographical Union, Working group on environmental perception, Circular no. 1.* Toronto: University of Toronto, Institute for Environmental Studies, 1977.

Burton, I., & Kates, R. The perception of natural hazards in resources management. *Natural Resources Journal*, 1964, *3*, 412–441.

Burton, I., Kates, R., & White, G. *The environment as hazard.* New York: Oxford University Press, 1978.

Cochrane, H. *Natural hazards and their distributive effects.* University of Colorado, Institute of Behavioral Science, Program on Environment, Technology and Man Monograph # NSF-RA-E-75-003. Boulder: University of Colorado, 1975.

Dacey, D., & Kunreuther, H. *The economics of natural disaster.* New York: Free Press, 1969.

Davenport, S. S. *Human response to hurricanes in Texas—two studies.* University of Colorado, Institute of Behavioral Science, Natural Hazards Working Paper No. 34. Boulder: University of Colorado, 1978.

Drabek, T., & Key, W. Impact of disaster on primary group linkages. *Mass Emergencies*, 1976, *1*, 89–105.

Dupree, H., & Roder, W. Coping with drought in a preindustrial, preliterate farming society. In G. White (Ed.), *Natural hazards: Local, national, global.* New York: Oxford University Press, 1974, pp. 115–119.

Dworkin, J. *Global trends in natural disasters 1947–1973.* University of Colorado, Institute of Behavioral Science, Natural Hazards Working Paper No. 26. Boulder: University of Colorado, 1974.

Dynes, R. *Organized behavior in disaster.* Lexington, Mass.: Heath, 1970.

Ericksen, N. *Scenario methodology in natural hazard research.* University of Colorado, Institute of Behavioral Science, Program on Technology, Environment and Man, Research Monograph No. NSF-RA-E-75-010. Boulder: University of Colorado, 1975a.

Ericksen, N. A tale of two cities: Flood history and the prophetic past of Rapid City, South Dakota. *Economic Geography*, 1975b, *51*, 305–320.

Francis, P. *Volcanoes.* Harmondsworth, England: Penguin, 1976.

Glantz, M. (Ed.). *The politics of natural disaster: The case of the Sahel drought.* New York: Praeger, 1976.

Golant, S., & Burton, I. *The meaning of hazard: Application of the semantic differential.* University of Colorado, Institute of Behavioral Science, Natural Hazards Working Paper No. 7. Boulder: University of Colorado, 1969.

Goodman, P., & Moore, B. *Critical issues of cross-cultural management research.* Graduate School of Business, University of Chicago, no date.

Gruntfest, E. *What people did during the Big Thompson flood.* University of Colorado, Institute of Behavioral Science, Natural Hazards Working Paper No. 32. Boulder: University of Colorado, 1977.

Hartman, L., Holland, D., & Giddings, M. Effects of hurricane storms on agriculture. *Water Resources Research,* 1969, *5,* 555–567.

Heathcote, R. Drought in south Australia. In G. White (Ed.), *Natural hazards: Local, national, global.* New York: Oxford University Press, 1974, pp. 128–136.

Heijnen, L., & Kates, R. Northeast Tanzania: Comparative observations along a moisture gradient. In G. White (Ed.), *Natural hazards: Local, national, global.* New York: Oxford University Press, 1974, pp. 105–114.

Hewitt, K., & Burton, I. *The hazardousness of a place.* Toronto: University of Toronto Press, 1971.

Islam, M. A. *Human adjustment to cyclone hazard: A case study of Char Jabbar.* University of Colorado, Institute of Behavioral Science, Natural Hazards Working Paper No. 18. Boulder: University of Colorado, 1971.

Kates, R. *Hazard and choice perception in flood plain management.* University of Chicago, Department of Geography, Research Paper No. 78. Chicago: University of Chicago, 1962.

Kates, R. Natural hazards in human ecological perspective: Hypotheses and models. *Economic Geography,* 1971, *47,* 438–451.

Kates, R. Experiencing the environment as hazard. In S. Wapner, S. Cohen, & B. Kaplan (Eds.), *Experiencing the environment.* New York: Plenum, 1977, 133–156.

Kates, R. *Risk assessment of environmental hazard.* New York: Wiley, 1978.

Keesing, R. M. *Cultural anthropology: A contemporary perspective.* New York: Holt, Rinehart, & Winston, 1976.

Kirkby, A. *Perception of air pollution as a hazard and individual adjustment to it in three British cities.* Paper presented at 22nd International Geographical Congress, Calgary, Alta., Canada, 1972.

Kirkby, A. Individual and community response to rainfall variability in Oaxaca, Mexico. In G. White (Ed.), *Natural hazards: Local, national, global.* New York: Oxford University Press, 1974, pp. 119–128.

Kunreuther, H. *Risk taking and farmer's crop growing decisions.* University of Chicago, Center for Mathematical Studies in Business and Economics, Report No. 7219. Chicago: University of Chicago, 1972.

Kunreuther, H. Economic analysis of natural hazards: An ordered choice approach. In G. White (Ed.), *Natural hazards: Local, national, global.* New York: Oxford University Press, 1974, 206–214.

Kunreuther, H. Limited knowledge and insurance protection. *Public Policy,* 1976, *24,* 227–261.

Kunreuther, H. *Limited knowledge and insurance protection: Implications for natural hazard policy.* New York: Wiley, 1978.

Leopold, L. *Hydrology for urban land planning: A guidebook on the hydrological effects of urban land use.* U. S. Geological Circular No. 554. Washington, D. C., 1968.

Lichtenstein, S., Slovic, P., Fischhof, B., Layman, M., & Combs, B. Judged frequency of lethal events. *Journal of Experimental Psychology Human Learning and Memory*, 1978, 4, (6) 551-578.

MacDonald, G. A. *Volcanoes.* Englewood Cliffs, N. J.: Prentice-Hall, 1972.

Man and the Biosphere. *Expert panel on project 13: Perception of environmental quality: Final report.* Paris: Programme on Man and the Biosphere, UNESCO, 1973.

Mileti, D., Drabek, T., & Haas, J. *Human systems in extreme environments: A sociological perspective.* University of Colorado, Institute of Behavioral Science, Program on Technology, Environment and Man, Monograph No. 21. Boulder: University of Colorado, 1975.

Ministre de l'Equipement et de l'Aménagement du Territoire. *Approche rationnelle des décisions concernant la lutte contre les nuisances dues aux inondations.* Paris: Direction de Ports Maritimes et des Voies Navigables, Service Central de l'Hydrologie et de l'Environnement, 1977.

Mitchell, J. K. *Community response to coastal erosion.* University of Chicago, Department of Geography, Research Paper No. 156. Chicago: University of Chicago, 1974a.

Mitchell, J. K. Natural hazard research. In I. Manners & M. Mikesell (Eds.), *Perspectives on environment.* Washington, D. C.: Association of American Geographers, 1974b, pp. 311-343.

Nichols, T. Global summary of human response to natural hazards: Earthquakes. In G. White (Ed.), *Natural hazards: Local, national, global.* New York: Oxford University Press, 1974, pp. 274-283.

Porter, P. *The ins and outs of environmental hazards.* Environmental perception research working paper number 3. Toronto: Institute for Environmental Studies, University of Toronto, 1978.

Saarinen, T. *Perception of drought hazard on the great plains.* University of Chicago, Department of Geography, Research Paper No. 106. Chicago: University of Chicago, 1966.

Saarinen, T. Problems on the use of a standardized questionnaire for cross-cultural research on perception of natural hazards. In G. White (Ed.), *Natural hazards: Local, national, global.* New York: Oxford University Press, 1974, pp. 180-184.

Schiff, M. *Some theoretical aspects of attitudes and perceptions.* University of Colorado, Institute of Behavioral Science, Natural Hazards Working Paper No. 15. Boulder: University of Colorado, 1970.

Schiff, M. Hazard adjustment, locus of control and sensation seeking: Some null findings. *Environment and Behavior,* 1977, 9, 233-254.

Simon, H. Rational choice and the structure of the environment. *Psychological Review,* 1956, 63, 129-138.

Sims, J., & Baumann, D. The tornado threat: Coping styles of the north and south. *Science,* 1972, 176, 1386-1392.

Slovic, P., Kunreuther, H., & White, G. Decision processes, rationality and adjustment to natural hazards. In G. White (Ed.), *Natural hazards: Local, national, global.* New York: Oxford University Press, 1974, pp. 187-204.

Sorensen, J. Interaction of adjustments to natural hazard (Doctoral dissertation, University of Colorado, 1977). *Dissertation Abstracts International,* 1977, 38, 3052-A. (University Microfilms No. 77-24, 295).

Tuan, Y. *Space and place.* Minneapolis: University of Minnesota Press, 1977.

Tversky, A., & Kahneman, D. Judgment under uncertainty: Heuristics and biases. *Science,* 1974, 185, 1124-1131.

Waddell, E. The hazards of scientism: A review article. *Human Ecology,* 1977, 5, 69-76. See reply in *Human Ecology,* 1978, 6, 229-231.

Warrick, R. *The volcano hazard in the United States: A research assessment.* University of Colorado, Institute of Behavioral Science, Program on Technology, Environment, and Man, Monograph No. NSF-RA-E-75-012. Boulder: University of Colorado, 1975b.

Waterstone, M. *Hazard mitigation behavior of urban flood plain residents.* University of Colorado, Institute of Behavioral Science, Natural Hazards Working Paper No. 35. Boulder: University of Colorado, 1978.

White, G. *Human adjustment to floods: A geographical approach to the flood problem in the United States.* University of Chicago, Department of Geography, Research Paper No. 29. Chicago: University of Chicago, 1945.

White, G. *Choice of adjustments to floods.* University of Chicago, Department of Geography, Research Paper No. 93. Chicago: University of Chicago, 1964.

White, G. Natural hazard research. In R. Chorley (Ed.), *Directions in geography.* London: Methuen, 1973, pp. 193–216.

White, G. (Ed.). *Natural hazards: Local, national, global.* New York: Oxford University Press, 1974.

White, G., Bradley, D., & White, A. *Drawers of water.* Chicago: University of Chicago Press, 1972.

White, G., Calef, W., Hudson, J., Mayer, H., Scheaffer, J., & Volk, D. *Changes in urban occupance of flood plains in the United States.* University of Chicago, Department of Geography, Research Paper No. 56. Chicago: University of Chicago, 1958.

White, G., & Haas, J. *Assessment of research on natural hazards.* Cambridge: M.I.T. Press, 1975.

Whyte, A. *Guidelines for field study in environmental perception.* Paris: UNESCO, 1977a.

Whyte, A. The role of information flow in controlling industrial lead emissions: The case of the Avonmouth smelter. *Proceedings of the International Conference on Heavy Metals.* Toronto: Institute for Environmental Studies, 1977b.

Windham, G., Posey, E., Ross, P., & Spencer, B. *Reactions to storm threat during hurricane Eloise.* Mississippi State University, Social Science Research Center Report 51, 1977.

9

Culture, Ecology, and Development

REDEFINING PLANNING APPROACHES

IGNACY SACHS

INTRODUCTION

Mine is a practical concern. Planning for development involves designing policies intended to shape, or, at least, influence what man does to
nature and to himself in the process of using nature. As a planner,
through my daily practice, I, therefore, relate to cultural ecology, as
defined by J. W. Bennett (1976): "This is the heart of cultural ecology: the
way man-man relations modify man-nature relations in particular representative cases, and how the results affect the future of both" (p. 310).

In this paper, I shall argue that ecodevelopment is an action-
oriented construct based on cultural ecology. Thus, I share with the
cultural ecologist the field of observation, with the notable difference that
for me it becomes a field of action. As a practitioner, I cannot choose
only representative cases with a view to arriving at a typology of situations, challenges, and responses. I must cope with situations as they
arise, atypical as they may be. In a sense, each case is unique, as it
represents a specific combination of natural and cultural factors, and as
it occurs in a particular historical and sociopolitical setting. But underlying this specificity there are general *principles*. It calls, therefore, for a

IGNACY SACHS • Le Centre International de Recherche sur l'Environnement et le Développement, Ecole Pratique des Hautes Etudes, 54 Boulevard Raspail, 75270 Paris, France.

creative response, and a design that cannot simply reproduce an historical model or apply a theoretically evolved formula. History should be
scrutinized for antimodels to be overcome, not for solutions to be replicated; theory helps the planner to ask pertinent questions, to develop
an approach by no means evident to the layman. It cannot, however,
offer ready-made solutions to cope with the complexity of real life.
These will always require an exercise in concrete social imagination in
which the population concerned has a major role to play, together with
the planner. However, the planner's and the people's social imagination
need supportive concepts in the form of comparative studies of people's
ways of dealing with similar patterns. Hence, the practical importance of
cross-cultural anthropological and historical research, and, also, the
need to expose the planner systematically to the results of such research,
to give him the sense of relativity across space and time, to broaden his
perspective both to ecological and to cultural dimensions of development. For this, ideally we would require a gigantic double entry
culture/ecosystem matrix, filled with data on selected aspects of life-
styles evolved over time in different parts of the world. Life-style, understood as a system of consistent choices based on the rules and culture
of a group faced with an environmental challenge, may be a key element
in describing how societies, both rural and urban, operate.[1] The matrix
would provide the often neglected information on vernacular solutions
to daily life problems. These must be carefully assessed without indulging in an indiscriminate and romantic praise of traditional lore. As
Rapoport (1969) has shown for housing, vernacular architecture offers
examples of extremely imaginative and successful adaptation to the
ecosystem, side by side with cases of failure. The former deserve, of
course, our attention as potential starting points for technological and
organizational innovations which better fit the ecological and cultural
environment than the across-the-board transfer of solutions evolved in
our industrial societies. From the matrix, we should be able to read how
a given culture responds to different environmental contexts, and, conversely, how resourceful different cultures have been when faced by
similar environmental challenges.

ECOLOGICAL PRUDENCE

As a planner—as distinct from an accountant, an entrepreneur or
even an academic researcher—I deal with the long-term consequences of

[1] For a discussion of life-styles in the urban context, see Rapoport (1977).

human actions. In this context, the recently acquired environmental awareness leads to an emphasis on the need to design development processes on a sustainable basis. Whenever possible, flows of renewable resources should be used, rather than depleting the stocks of nonrenewable resources. This calls for the ecologically prudent management of resources whose renewability is limited, and depends on policies: a felled forest which is not replanted becomes a mine of timber.

Restated in a more theoretical fashion, this is tantamount to respecting the steady-state-maintaining mechanisms of the ecosystem defined as the totality of life in some region, or else as a complex population of quite different organisms (Rapoport, 1974, p. 23). But, since a living system includes not only steady-state-maintaining mechanisms, but also an adaptive capacity for evolution, the postulate of the ability to sustain development processes does not lead to a rigid conservationist posture of "keep your hands off nature." It stresses, instead, the need continually to seek new forms of symbiosis between the earth and humankind. As R. Dubos (1976) rightly points out "human interventions into nature can be creative and indeed can improve on nature, provided that they are based on ecological understanding of natural systems and of their potentialities for evolution as they are transformed into harmonized landscape" (p. 480). Successes and failures in achieving this symbiosis may account for the rises and falls of civilizations throughout history, although one should refrain from hasty and unilateral explanations of complex historical processes (Pomian, 1976). In the century-old debate between geographical determinists and cultural possibilists, I am inclined to give more reason to the latter (Febvre, 1970; for a recent restatement of this controversy see Gourou, 1973). People's endurance and resourcefulness usually prove stronger than the impositions of climate and ecosystem. Moreoever, the challenge of adverse natural conditions is responsible for some of the most extraordinary achievements of mankind, both in terms of adaptation to these conditions (e.g., the Eskimos), and creation of wholly artificial environments (e.g., the spaceship).[2] But the argument should not be carried too far either, to the point of forgetting the limiting and enabling role of natural factors in the rise of civilizations.

A healthy ecology of human civilization requires, therefore, "a single system of environment combined with high human civilization in

---

[2]Quite clearly, the space program is an offspring of the armaments race, and the usefulness of travel to the moon may be severely questioned, given the large number of more urgent tasks facing humanity. Nevertheless, technically, the spaceship is a remarkable feat.

which the flexibility of the civilization should match that of the environment to create an ongoing open system; open-ended for slow change of
even basic (hard-programmed) characteristics" (Bateson, 1973, p. 470).
"High civilization" is meant here to signify that the return to the inno-
cence of primitive people is neither possible nor desirable. Bateson is
right in saying that such a return would involve the loss of wisdom that
prompted the return! We cannot do without technical gadgets and institutions to maintain the necessary wisdom and "to give physical,
aesthetic and creative satisfaction to people" (Bateson, 1973, p. 471). But
a high civilization should be able to limit itself in its transactions with the
environment, reducing to a minimum the use of stocks of depletable
resources, and turning to the flow of renewable energy and biomass.

At the normative level, this means proposing flexibility as an important societal value: uncommitted potentiality for change, diversity, preservation of options for the future, and ecological prudence in the husbandry of resources. The underlying ethical principle is that of diachronic solidarity with future generations (Sachs, 1977a). That is, it is our
responsibility to see that future life on our planet is not endangered by
irreversible decisions, by the cumulative negative effects of pollution,
heat dissipation, and resource depletion. Diachronic solidarity, however, cannot be separated from its twin principle of synchronic solidarity
with our contemporaries. Concern for ecology should not be separated
from a concern with social equity among nations and inside nations.
Particularly, since "man's use of Nature is inextricably intertwined with
man's use of Man, and . . . remedies for destructive use of environment
must be found within the social system itself" (Bennett, 1976, p. 311).
The twin principles of diachronic and synchronic solidarity have not
only an ecological, but also a cultural component. It is equally important
to preserve cultural diversity, and to help all cultures coexist in conditions of mutual respect.

The present market-dominated patterns of resource use are geared
to the maximization of short-term economic profit. Resources and
spaces are considered exclusively from the viewpoint of their availability
and prices. Ecological imbalances become a worry only to the extent to
which they create negative externalities in the production processes, and
are then dealt with on a piecemeal, remedial basis. In fact, the roots of
our ecological crisis may be attributed to our inability to get out of the
trap of *ad hoc* measures that offer short-term individual profitability, but
do not add up in a collective strategy sustainable in the long run.[3]

---

[3] Cf. Bateson (1973): "I regard the groves of destiny into which our civilization has entered
as a special case of an evolutionary cul-de-sac. Courses which offered short-term advan-

Design should stress alternative patterns of resource use, based on criteria of what may be called expanded social rationality. Sustainability of production processes implies careful husbandry and recycling of depletable resources, as well as resorting whenever possible to renewable resources.[4]

Space—the only finite resource the size of which is known once and for all[5]—should be used in such a way as to minimize irreversible decisions, harmonize multiple uses whenever possible, and keep the options open for the future: in other words, sharply departing from the present practices of transforming agricultural land into urban construction and parking lots, or locating heavy industries in coastal sites suitable for aquaculture. As one example among many of what should not be done, we may mention the continuous extension of Cairo and Alexandria on fertile agricultural lands, which are extremely scarce in Egypt. According to some estimates, the losses of agricultural land incurred in this way over the last 20 years exceeded the new additions to the arable area obtained through the construction of the Aswan dam. The Egyptian government has at last decided to build new towns in the desert, yet some planners argue on the basis of narrow economic criteria that this is not the right policy to follow.

Finally, concern for global ecological and climatic balances should permeate all development thinking. As yet, we know little about the climatic consequence of our increased intervention into nature, beyond the very fact that its cumulative effects are likely soon to become signifi-

---

tage have been adopted, have become regidly programmed, and have begun to prove disastrous over longer time. This is the paradigm for extinction by way of loss of flexibility. And this paradigm is more surely lethal when the courses of action are chosen in order to maximize single variables" (p. 477).

[4] Renewable resource is, however, a doubly relative concept: first, because a resource as such depends on the state of knowledge of a society about ways of using elements of its environment, and culturally defined ways of using it—or, indeed, whether use is appropriate; second, because renewability depends on an ecologically sound management of soils, water, and biomass; as already suggested, a felled forest where no replanting takes place is a mine of timber. On the other hand, recycling may allow for several uses of certain nonrenewable resources.

[5] In a sense, time is even more limited when looked at from the perspective of each individual. Moreover, its flow cannot be stopped or reversed. That is why, of all the forms of social wastefulness, the worst is perhaps the one of people's time, caused by the forced idleness known as unemployment or underemployment (the latter embracing the case of self-employed petty peasants with insufficient access to land to use efficiently the family's labor potential). Forced idleness should not be confounded, however, with a deliberate societal choice of limiting the working time, and using it instead for other more convivial activities, even if that entails frugality. [For a description of the mode of underproduction in primitive societies, see Sahlins, (1972)].

cant from the point of view of global balances. This lack of precise knowledge, together with the record of man-made local climatic and ecological disasters, suggests the need to behave prudently, as if outer limits (see Matthews, 1976) were known, rather than dismissing the whole issue along the lines of Berry (1974), Kahn, Brown, & Martel (1976), and other worshippers of unlimited technological fix. The dust bowl in the United States in the thirties, the negative consequences of the hasty opening of new lands to agriculture in Kazakhstan in the fifties, the recent catastrophic floods in India related to the devastation of the forests in the Himalayas, and the process of desertification in the Sahel are a few examples of local disasters striking enough to make us think seriously about global threats, such as the possible consequences of excessive dissipation in the atmosphere of heat and carbon dioxide.

SHOULD WE STOP GROWING?

The above considerations should not be equated with simplistic pleas to stop economic growth altogether. Asking for a zero rate of material growth is politically unfeasible in inegalitarian societies. Even in the most affluent nations poverty persists, and inequality breeds acquisitiveness and emulation for the so-called "positional goods"—those that improve one's relative position in the society of status seekers (Hirsch, 1976). The same goes for inequalities among nations. That is why Ehrlich and Ehrlich's (1970) call for discontinuing industrialization in third world countries met with sharp criticism, notwithstanding their verbal precautions about the simultaneous need to deindustrialize the West and to conduct a radical redistribution of wealth. It is difficult to see how this could possibly happen without growth, if even the modest target of 0.7% transfer of gross national product (GNP) in a period of unprecedented prosperity could not be achieved. Moreover, the arguments in favor of an early steady state are based on two assumptions which can be challenged.

First, one does not need to be an unqualified technological optimist in order to question the apocalyptic views expressed about the imminent depletion of energy and other resources. Such views may in fact defeat the purpose of their authors by exacerbating the struggle for the control of raw materials. The transition toward the steady state at a later stage will not be possible in any case, unless socioeconomic development of the third world is speeded up right now as a precondition for slowing down the rates of population increase in the future.

In fact, the population loop works in the opposite sense to that suggested in *Limits to Growth* (Meadows, Meadows, Randers, & Behrens, 1972). Far from being an independent variable amenable to birth control, and, in this way, conducive to higher per capita increases in income for a given rate of economic growth, it depends heavily on people's attitudes toward family size, which, in turn, reflect their social conditions and cultural beliefs, often sanctified by religion. Why should poor peasants believe that having fewer children would improve their lot, when, viewed from their perspective, evidence points to the contrary? Infant mortality being high, many, many children are needed to bring up a few sons, who will first serve as an unpaid source of labor, and then, hopefully, take care of their aging parents. Also, the tougher the competition for wage jobs, the more it pays for a family to put several persons on the labor market, in the expectation that at least one of them will get the winning ticket in the employment lottery. The conflict between family rationality and overall social rationality cannot be eliminated except by reducing infant mortality, providing jobs or opportunities for self-employment, and ensuring security for old age, that is, by means of accelerated social and economic development, geared to the satisfaction of fundamental human needs on an equitable basis. While the solutions will take different forms reflecting the diversity of cultures and religions, they must, broadly speaking, deliver the minimum package defined above in general terms.[6] Paternalistic distributional schemes that increase people's passivity and disillusionment with life, while catering to their minimum material needs, probably fail to bring the desirable changes, which require a new sense of purposiveness, and deeper understanding of the working of the society and the individual's stake, share, and roles.

Second, it is wrong to assume that the "rate of exploitation of nature" (Wilkinson, 1973) is only related to the rate of economic growth, and not to the forms, contents, and uses of growth. The parametric relation between the two rates would only be true if the societal goals, consumption and production patterns, as well as technological choices, were not amenable to purposive social control. Instead of questioning growth as such, one should rather explore alternative growth patterns based on a different goal function, organized and tooled in such a way as to minimize the negative ecological impacts and the use of depletable resources. The challenge is to redefine the forms and uses of growth,

---

[6] Although I do not share fully Marvin Harris's somewhat crude materialism, I believe that his insistence on the need to relate beliefs and practices to "ordinary, banal, one might say 'vulgar' conditions, needs and activities" (Harris, 1975, p. 5), is appropriate when discussing the population problem, which is often presented as overwhelmingly dominated by religious considerations and purely cultural problems.

rather than to give it up. In any case, the call for no growth is based on somewhat faulty logic, when it invokes the spectrum of resource depletion: even a stationary economy is resource consuming. Why, then, content oneself with a stationary state, rather than postulating negative rates of growth? Conservation for the sake of conservation, carried to its ultimate limits, amounts to the denial of the anthropocentrism which underlies all human cultures and most of our philosophies—man's primordial concern with the survival, if not progress, of mankind. Taken to these ultimate limits, total genocide would offer by far the most practical way of freeing the planet, once and for all, from its most predatory species: mankind.

At any rate, we know today that rates of economic growth are a very poor indicator of societal performance. Although development without growth is hardly imaginable, the same rates of growth may lead either to development or to maldevelopment, the difference between the two being qualitative. Development occurs when genuine use values satisfying societal needs are produced, and a situation of maldevelopment prevails when the economy turns out pseudo use values in the forms of conspicuous consumption goods and services, as well as weaponry (Sachs, 1978a).

No strictly objective criteria exist to distinguish development from maldevelopment. Value judgments are involved, which is why development planning should be participatory. Experience shows, however, that maldevelopment is often associated with imitative growth, i.e., the attempt to reproduce the historical pathway followed by currently industrialized countries. Such growth may be fairly rapid—Brazil and Iran are good instances—but, to the extent to which it is associated with social and regional inequalities, it leads to exceedingly high social costs of modernization—and, frequently, cultural breakdown. However, social inequality breeds environmental degradation, as rich people waste resources in conspicuous consumption, and the poor overuse the scarce plots of land to which they have access. Thus, maldevelopment is closely related to cultural dependence. Whether imitative growth happens by imposition (as in old colonial times), or by a more or less autonomous decision on the part of the modernization elites, it implies the acceptance of alien cultural values and life-styles as a model. In some respects, this cultural alienation is harder to overcome than economic or financial dependence. Another consequence of maldevelopment is the cultural gap between the westernized elites and the bulk of the society, as well as the emergence, in some cases, of the subculture of poverty, which cuts across regional, rural, urban, and even national boundaries (see Lewis, 1976).

Development can be normatively defined as: *Self-reliant* and *endogenous* in counterposition to the cultural dependence of the imitative model; *need-oriented* and equitable (which also implies *conviviality*); *environmentally prudent*, and, of course, open to the *institutional changes* capable of adapting to the new tasks the existing set of institutions; cultural diversity will reflect itself in the plurality of institutional designs (see *What Now?*, 1975).

Another way of looking at development is to emphasize its process character: development may be viewed as a societal learning process geared to the identification and satisfaction on a sustainable basis of *socially and culturally determined human needs, material and nonmaterial.* In its initial stages, development is also a liberation from material wants, fear, and dependence (self-reliance being an ethical concept linked to autonomy in decision making, and not to autarky). Development can also be viewed as an open-ended process of creation and preservation of cultural diversity arising from the differences in the initial natural and cultural contexts, as well as from the human potential for invention. A key word here is *resourcefulness*—the ingenuity in transforming elements of the environment (natural and cultural) into useful resources.

Far from being synonymous with affluence, development can happen at a fairly low level of material advancement. Conversely, rich countries may be maldeveloping; as a matter of fact, this is a fairly widespread phenomenon. Given a situation of maldevelopment, a high rate of growth becomes an indicator of the speed at which distortions occur, rather than a measure of societal welfare.

THE HARMONIZATION GAME

The task for the planner, then, is to harmonize cultural, socioeconomic, and ecological concerns; to define an ecodevelopment strategy by striking a balance between two complementary and closely interwoven ethical principles, the synchronic solidarity with all men and each man of our generation, and the diachronic solidarity with future generations. The former leads to emphasizing the issues of present maldistribution of wealth and income, and the consequent need for changes in the rules of access to them. The latter provides a safeguard against jeopardizing the future in the pursuit of immediate gains. As Robinson (1962) has shown, arbitrating between consumption today and consumption tomorrow is ethically a very delicate operation, as the people concerned are not the same. While the present generation may legitimately decide to give up short-term gains for the sake of a better future for their children and grandchildren (provided the decision is reached in a truly democratic way), it has no right to improve its lot at the expense of as yet unborn people by indulging in a predatory pattern of resource use.

We may review briefly the main variables of this harmonization game (Godard, 1978; Sachs, 1977b). On the demand side, the planner may manipulate the two main components of life-styles: (1) the consumption basket of goods and services, produced in the market, supplied as a welfare service by the state or self-produced by the household; (2) the uses of time by the society. In both cases, the corresponding and underlying cultural models are of great importance. Making operational the concept of life-style is a major challenge for the ecodevelopment planner. Given the complexity of the subject, I cannot develop it fully here (see Sachs, 1978b), but I would not like to leave it without two observations. The first calls for maximum intellectual honesty when dealing with consumption patterns, in order to try to avoid, insofar as is possible, mixing three quite different issues: a plea for voluntary simplicity, leading to cuts in the level of consumption; rationing, prompted by considerations of equity and/or scarcity; and the search for alternative ways of providing approximately equivalent services and goods.

The second refers to a conceptual issue. The inclusion of the uses of time in the enlarged concept of consumption can be achieved by putting a price tag on time (see Becker, 1977), and assuming that all the choices are performed on the basis of economic calculation. The construct of *Homo oeconomicus* is then supposed to reflect the true and whole nature of man. My position is diametrically opposed to the one just outlined. I believe models of societal time use to be irreducible to the economic dimension, because they reflect the pluralistic scales of values of each culture. Polanyi's (1957) question about how economy is embedded in the society offers a starting point. The higher the economic surplus and/or the surplus of time available for noneconomic activities, the broader, theoretically, are the margins of freedom for choosing a societal project (as well as individual projects) in which the role of the economy is kept within deliberate limits. In practice, both these measures of freedom—the economic surplus and the surplus of available time—are heavily mortgaged by the working of institutions, the burden of the living past, and culturally bound life-styles. How to free them is a major challenge for industrialized societies.

Let us turn now to the supply side of the harmonization game. The planner will act on four sets of variables relative to energy, space use, resources, and technology, searching for solutions that are culture-specific, and, at the same time, meet the principles of expanded social rationality already described. Thus, an ecodevelopment strategy calls for giving priority to energy conservation over additional flows of energy. The nonconsumed energy is ecologically the best, and often also the cheapest. Let it be remembered that the scope for energy conservation exists even in the most primitive economies, e.g., by redesigning the stoves, and thus cutting down the energy requirements for cooking in the Indian villages (see Makhijani, 1976). It also emphasizes the uses of renewable energy in all its forms: solar, wind, biomass, while minimizing the consumption of depletable energy resources. Ecological prudence and consideration of economic costs converge in a cautious attitude toward nuclear energy.

Spatial strategies are fundamental to an integrated view of ecodevelopment planning, for two reasons. As mentioned before, space is a unique resource: its availability is given once forever, and no human activity can take place without its permanent or temporary appropriation. On the other hand, the environmental impacts of these activities will depend to a considerable extent on their location; the carrying capacity of the ecosystems is a complex function of several variables related to climate, topography, density of human and economic occupation, patterns of land use, etc. A copper smelter built on the desert coast of Peru will require fewer antipollution devices than one located in a suburb of Lima. The planner should also keep in mind that a high degree of irreversibility is attached to many locational decisions. This is particularly true of agricultural land lost to cities and highways, as well as of coastal sites chosen for industrial plants.

In order to protect the diversity of natural ecosystems and to preserve the options for the future, the planner will be tempted to recommend the setting up of reserves and national parks. Important as this may be, the scope for such operations is limited, due to the pressure of economic interests. Excessive reliance on them may even prove self-defeating, putting the ecologists on the defensive. A far more difficult challenge consists in recommending ecologically sound positive use of land, and making compatible multiple uses of the same territory (e.g., the seacoast belt). Ecological considerations lead to an emphasis on the need for redeploying, with nations and among nations, industrial activities excessively concentrated in a few congested areas. Recent technical progress in telecommunication and data processing seems to open new opportunities for industrial decentralization, the revival of small towns, and the ruralization of a considerable range of secondary and tertiary activities. Our concepts of economies of scale and of positive externalities attached to urban concentration are becoming increasingly obsolete, although we are slow in recognizing it; more so, in that cultural preferences tend to favor urban life-styles. At the same time, the planner should realize that the opening of new economic frontiers, e.g., the Amazon region, cannot succeed unless the population is fairly concentrated in selected areas. The settlers coming from outside, culturally unprepared to cope with the fragile ecosystem of the tropical rain forest, must be provided with adequate health, educational, and social services, and therefore grouped in small urban nuclei, rather than dispersed. Practice shows that scattering small farms in an immense territory often lead to an extremely predatory pattern of resource use. Moreover, isolated settlers tend to take a hostile attitude toward the indigenous tribes, partly out of fear, partly out of greed and impunity warranted by isolation. They are, in turn, an easy prey for the middlemen who provide the only link between them and the so-called civilized world. A more concentrated pattern of human settlements would be less energy-intensive in terms of transportation needs, and would offer better chances of organizing a fair system of exchange between the pioneer settlements and the outer economy (say in form of cooperatives). The use of such nucleated settlements also allows for the provision of appropriate homogeneity, and development of appropriate social and cultural support systems. Last but not least, the creation of reserves for intensive development is perhaps the only way of minimizing the contact with the remnants of indigenous tribes, and leaving them with an extensive habitat, at least for one or two generations; buying time in this way seems a better alternative than setting reserves for the Indians.

With respect to resources other than energy and space, the eco-planner will be guided by the following considerations:

•Eliminating wastefulness in resource use, which depends to a considerable extent on changing patterns of consumption and life-styles (e.g., on a set of cultural and political variables) and on choosing appropriate technologies

•Resorting to recycling and reusing of materials and wastes

•Substituting the flow of renewable resources for the stocks of depletable resources

•Making the best possible use of the locally available resources, as far as possible on a sustainable basis

The multidimensional nature of technology explains the role played in the harmonization game by the choice of appropriate products and production processes. Hence, the importance of identifying in each case the relevant dimensions, and then making explicit the corresponding criteria of appropriateness. Such criteria make sense only in relation to a given ecological, cultural, economic, and historical context. *There are no appropriate technologies, as such, in absolute terms,* contrary to a misconception widely disseminated in the literature. The so-called green revolution is a good example. Undoubtedly, new genetically improved varieties of wheat and rice, combined with an adequate package of inputs—water, fertilizers, insecticides—produce higher yields, as compared with traditional farming methods. But the scope for the green revolution appears quite limited, and the social and ecological price paid for it quite high. First, the conditions for a successful application of the new package do not exist in most rural areas of the third world, because of the lack of irrigation facilities, shortage of capital to provide them, nonavailability of the right kinds of fertilizer in the right quantities, etc. Second, the package, when applied, often has adverse ecological impacts, such as the excessive use of fertilizers and insecticides, which is responsible for killing fish in the paddy fields, with far-reaching negative effects on the protein intake of local populations. Third, the new varieties of cereals are not always found acceptable to the concerned populations, on the grounds of taste and/or nutritional quality. Fourth, the introduction of the green revolution package by rich farmers provokes far-reaching changes on the local labor market, and further social polarization in the countryside. Thus, it would be wrong to consider the technologies of the green revolution as universally applicable. Their scope is, on the contrary, limited, and their introduction calls for very careful handling of cultural, ecological, and sociopolitical variables. Taking a different approach, the evaluation of traditional agricultural systems and nutritional patterns, both ecosystem and culture-specific, should open the way for many locally feasible improvements, as well as cross-cultural exchanges; these improvements might require a strong modern science component, which is not at all tantamount to increasing the dependence of peasant agriculture on industrial inputs. The ecodevelopment approach calls for a redirection of scientific research, not for a romantic worship of traditional techniques.

Nor is it possible to operate exclusively with intermediate, low-capital or environmentally soft technologies, as both these partially overlapping subsets are far from being able to provide all the needs of the economy. Besides, their productivity may prove too low: even a poor society must apply in its choices a minimum productivity criterion. While it is important, therefore, to update and improve traditional village technologies, to design new ecotechniques for the use of the specific resources of each ecosystem, and to broaden the range of soft technologies, the ecoplanner must be prepared to lay down and apply criteria of appropriateness all along the range of technological choices, from labor-intensive to capital-intensive. He must also learn to manage technological pluralism; a selective use at some point of a sophisticated technology often makes viable a whole chain of labor-intensive production (see Sachs & Vinaver, 1976). The advanced methods of treatment of timber with sophisticated chemicals and/or by irradiation may change its physical properties so as to make it fit for new industrial and building uses, opening in this way an outlet for a product which can generate considerable employment in forest management and timber extraction.

An important consideration for product design is its durability (for details see Ceron & Baillon, 1979). With respect to production processes, the planner will prefer low-waste technologies to the present escalation of production, pollution, and antipollution. This leads us to the place of environmental policies *stricto sensu*. The more we succeed in the harmonization game just outlined, the less scope there will be for remedial action best exemplified by antipollution measures. But this is, at best, a long-term perspective. In the short and immediate term, considerable effort is required to arrest the degradation of our physical environments on which depend our health, well-being, and quality of life. On the other hand, insisting on the potential of renewable resources makes sense only on the assumption that such resources will be ecologically managed. A major ecological, and, therefore, social disaster would follow, if we were to intensify the present pattern of predatory exploitation of renewable resources.

THREE CONDITIONS FOR ECODEVELOPMENT

Three conditions are necessary to make operational the concept of ecodevelopment. First, we need a great deal of knowledge about cultures and ecosystems, and about what different cultures have learned about their ecosystems. An extensive program of research in ethnoecology and ethnohistory, taken in their broadest meaning, is called for, in order to identify the best starting points for the processing of the specific resources of each ecosystem. Such a program might be conceived around the different societal needs. The food potential of local flora and fauna habits for indigenous people should come first. Our subsistence depends on a very small number of plants and animals. At the same time, historical and anthropological studies have shown the amazing range of foods locally consumed (Tannahill, 1975), from weeds and algae (or rather what we consider to be weeds) to insects. Some of the plants of arid zones, to mention only one example, that were important in the past (Balls, 1972) and were almost totally forgotten, seem to offer a promise for the future, and a considerable potential for improvement through genetic research (Felger & Nabhan, 1976). Intensification of game cropping and game ranching seems equally possible (De Vos, 1978), and for some regions more rewarding than cattle breeding. Domestication of certain wild species can also be advocated, since it has been shown, for example, that under conditions prevailing on foodplain savannas, capybaras are 3.5 times more efficient than cattle.

The next step consists in making systematic inventories of already available ecotechniques for food production in different ecosystems and cultures.[7]

Finally, one comes to the controversial question of orientation of agricultural and nutritional research. The green revolution cannot, as already stated, solve the problems of those peasants, a majority, in fact, who do not have access to irrigated land and the capital necessary to operate it. New production systems, ecologically and culturally adapted, are needed for the tropical areas. The pioneering efforts of the International Institute of Tropical Agriculture (IITA) in Nigeria are but a drop in the bucket (Bergeret et al., 1977; Greenland, 1975).

In this connection, it may be worthwhile to mention as particularly promising the research on tridimensional forestry (Douglas, 1973) as a source of timber, food for people, and fodder for cattle in the form of leaves and fruits,[8] as well as the patient efforts of Pirie (1971) to promote extraction of protein from leaves by means of a relatively inexpensive industrial method, which can equally be applied to weeds and aquatic plants, such as water hyacinths.

We know slightly more about vernacular architecture and house building (see in particular Fathy, 1970; Rapoport, 1969; Rudofsky, 1974), as well as about the obstacles to the application of soft technologies available for individual houses to urban settings (Baczko, Sachs, Vinaver, & Zakrzewski, 1977). Vernacular architecture, as rightly pointed out by Rapoport, offers instances of excellent adaptation to ecosystems, but this is by no means a general rule. Hence, there is a need for a patient review and analysis of all experience as an important contribution to "ecodesign."[9] The prefix "eco" here should be read in a

---

[7]For a modest start in this direction along the lines described here, see Bergeret, Godard, Morales, Passaris, and Romanini (1977), and also two monographs subsequently published by the Centro de Ecodesarrollo in Mexico: Morales (1978), and Romanini (1976).

[8]According to Pierre Gourou (1971, pp 160–161), the people from the Ukara Island on Victoria Lake were particularly skillful in using forest and aquatic resources for intensive cattle raising.

[9]The term has been coined by a Peruvian architect and urbanist, Eduardo Neira, who is at present directing a UN project on housing ecotechniques (ECLA, United Nations, Calle Masaryk, Mexico, D. F.).

double sense, as referring to ecosystems and cultures, to ecology and cultural ecology.

Space and competence prevent me from sketching what could be done, following the same approach, with respect to settlement planning, health care, education, and other systems. Let it be only said here that in the last few years the World Health Organization (WHO) has reoriented its activities, after losing some of its previous faith in the technological fix and after coming to appreciate the mass of knowledge and skills accumulated by the indigenous medicines (e.g., the value of ethnomedicine), as well as the scope of paramedical services. Once more, the issue is not to be seen in terms of either/or, but rather as an effort in integrative thinking.

Illich (1978) has brought a new dimension to the discussion with his concept of disabling professions: educators and physicians exercise in our societies a radical monopoly of decision, depriving people of their autonomy and reducing the scope for the direct production of use values in the household sector. Schooling has become a rite of passage, with little useful education in it. A thorough rethinking of the whole service sector is called for. One does not need to agree with Illich on all points to appreciate the critical power of his writings. A new look at anthropological evidence may well offer the starting point for the redefinition of educational strategies, with greater emphasis on all forms of informal education, in an effort to design the learning processes in a way which makes it possible for people to start from their own perception of the environment, and build on their daily life experience and culture; with a radical redefinition of the role of the school and also of the schoolmaster. The school could become a sort of local development agency, systematically involving the children in the management of community affairs, and conveying to them the sense of citizen responsibility as such as a quantum of scientific information and values. For this, the school should be to a large extent self-managed and economically self-sufficient, at least with respect to the food necessary to run the school canteen. The school farm could play an important role in introducing new techniques and food habits, the youngsters being encouraged and assisted to introduce the successful innovations into their household economy. The schoolmaster should accordingly act (and be trained) as a polyvalent agent of change. On the other hand, local people with professional and life experience, not necessarily with diplomas, should be invited to share in the teaching tasks.

The second condition for effective ecodevelopment planning is citizen involvement in this activity. Who, other than the people concerned, can be better placed to identify their needs, to convey the accumulated wisdom of the (micro) society and the environment, to decide about trade-offs between alternative uses of resources, and distributions of gains, and to weigh the present against the future within the local perspective? Making people participate is also a way of releasing a latent source of initiative and entrepreneurship, as Turner (1976) has shown in the specific case of self-help housing construction. The stress on self-reliance should not, however, be taken as a pretext for avoiding professional responsibility. The people involved must be granted access to critical resources that will make their creative effort possible. There can be no self-help housing construction unless land is made available, be it by peaceful means or by squatter occupation. A qualification is in order here. The insistence on local self-reliance (i.e., autonomous decision making) comes as a reaction against the blanket imposition from above of uniform blue prints, which more often than not ended up in frustration if not disaster, precisely because of lack of sensibility to the ecosystem-and-culture-specific aspects of the development process. But such self-reliance should not be understood as a negation of the potential role of the outsiders—planners, scientists, technicians; rather, it should be seen as a call for a major reassessment of their relationship to the local population. Hierarchical communication between the expert and the local population should be replaced by a mutually educating dialogue and empathy. The planner must be committed to the people's cause, and act as their advocate. Looking from outside at the microsociety, injecting into the discussion other experiences unknown to local people, pointing out opportunities not yet identified, he may play a useful role as a catalyst. The same goes, *mutatis mutandis,* for the scientist and the technician. Even so, a problem remains: how to insure that local decisions are compatible with other local decisions, and the overall long-term interest of the society? We shall return to this question at the end of this paper.

Participation is thus organically built into ecodevelopment. But its development is slow and requires patience: it cannot be learned except by experience, both positive and negative. This time dimension should not be forgotten when preparing for action.

The third requirement for ecodevelopment pertains to the institutional domain. It is pointless to attempt initiating locally a self-reliant need-oriented and environmentally sound development process, so long as the linkages between the microregion (or the township) and the rest of the economy are of such an exploitative nature, as to confiscate and syphon off all the gains accruing from development. A minimum institutional condition for ecodevelopment consists of establishing a marketing scheme that offers relatively fair terms of trade, and provides access to some critical resources that cannot be obtained locally. Even this modest requirement, far removed from a normative vision of an ideal setting, severely restricts in practice the applicability of the ecodevelopment approach, quite apart from the fact that institutional design calls for a very careful consideration of specific cultural and social contexts—something at which we are very bad indeed. The present trend is toward heavy, centralized, and self-perpetuating bureaucracies. The need is for a problem-oriented and more "horizontal" (as opposed to a "vertical") approach, for which institutions can be set up rapidly to cope with specific issues, to vanish just as rapidly once they have accomplished their task.

A PROPOSAL FOR THE PERUVIAN AMAZONIA

Ecodevelopment as a philosophy of development has been remarkably successful in the short span of years since the 1972 Stockholm Conference on Human Environment. With United Nations Environment Programme (UNEP) support it has inspired a number of research and action-oriented initiatives, both in industrialized and in developing countries, as well as a few rural and urban development projects. This is not the place to list and review them in detail. [10] I prefer, rather, to analyze briefly, as an illustration of the approach and its potentialities, one project with which I was associated: an attempt to define a new development strategy for the Peruvian part of Amazonia. The proposal was drafted in 1972 by UN and Peruvian experts (ILPES, 1972).

Although very favorably received by the Peruvian government, the project was never really implemented, to the best of my knowledge, caught as it was in the meanderings of UN bureaucracy. Nevertheless, it is still of some interest, to the extent to which the ecodevelopment approach made us ask different questions and look for unexpected resources.

The report listed that oil discoveries in the Amazon region, believed to be important at the time, made it impossible to postpone a discussion of the region's future. At the same time, it was important not to repeat the mistakes of monoproduction of oil. A substantial part of oil revenues should be devoted to building a flourishing regional economy on a lasting and sustainable basis, in this case based on the region's natural capacity for biomass production. This matter was to be studied by a

---

[10] Information on publications and organizations dealing with ecodevelopment may be obtained from the author. See also Sachs (1977c).

network of local research institutes, to be strengthened or created through UN support. We also insisted on nonorthodox approaches to food production: surveying of interesting local vegetal and animal species, domestication, game cropping and ranching, tridimensional forestry, multilevel agriculture under the cover of trees, and aquaculture, which is particularly important in the region (including feeding of fish with insects, protein extraction from aquatic weeds, etc.)

On the other hand, we thought that biomass could be used as raw material for a wide range of chemical industries, and ultimately lay the foundation of a new industrial civilization in the tropics. It should be remembered that the report was written one year before the 1973 energy crisis.

The report recommended a spatially concentrated development pattern, based on small urban centers, and asked for an international competition to produce an urban module best adapted to the Amazon ecosystem in terms of housing, urban design, use of local materials, and promotion of soft technologies for energy production, sewage treatment, etc. [11]

The futuristic aspects of the report dealt with the selection of appropriate technologies. Managing of technological pluralism (described in the report as resorting to "combined technologies") called for the introduction of a limited number of fairly advanced techniques. We thought it worthwhile to analyze whether the dirigible would offer a convenient alternative to expensive road building. The excellent river system could be used to move floating factories to the forest rather than bringing timber to mills. As workers would be spending, in this case, most of their time far from their homes, we imagined that in a not too distant future a hovercraft transportation system could enable them to join their families at weekends. This was but one among many intellectual provocations deliberately introduced in the report. The authors, as I can see now, underestimated the dynamic conservatism of the UN bureaucracy.

Our report contrasted with the pessimistic mood prevailing in the international literature on the economic potential of the Amazon region (Goodland & Irwin, 1975; Meggers, 1971; Tricart, 1978).

However, in a recent and well-documented study, Goodland, Irwin, and Tillman (1978) argue that a substantial sustained yield could be obtained for Amazonia, provided that trees were utilized as the main crop. This would mean a radical departure from the present irrational exploitation of Amazonia mainly through cattle breeding. Most of the

---

[11] United Nations Development Programme (UNDP) turned down this proposal, on the grounds that such a competition could not be financed by them.

propositions made by the authors coincide with our own intuitions, and with the conclusions of several independently conducted studies at Centre International de Recherche pour l'Environnement et le Développement (CIRED), Centro de Ecodesarrollo (CECODES), etc. This convergence is most heartening. It probably stems from similarity in methodological outlook: start by assessing the potential of a specific ecosystem, and then look for the ecologically and culturally appropriate technologies, rather than try to modify the environment in order to make it fit a transferred technology and/or crop.[12]

One gap in the report must be explained. In apparent contradiction with the approach outlined in this paper, it dealt with the potentialities of the ecosystem, and not with those of the local cultures other than the Indian tribes. As far as the latter are concerned, we recommended ethnoecological surveys. However, the remaining population, composed mainly of migrants from different parts of the highlands, is culturally uprooted,[13] ill adapted to the new environment, subject to terrible economic exploitation made possible by isolation, and undermined by illness and malnutrition to the point of sinking into total apathy, when not dreaming about ways of making money fast that would enable them to move to Lima. The contrast with many African peasant societies, where traditional culture is vigorous and well and offers many starting points to build from, is striking. It should also be said that, with the exception of one small Japanese settlement, quite successful in producing pepper, the region up to now does not have the experience of settlement by compact migrant groups sharing a common culture or living in culturally appropriate settlements and dwellings, with appropriate work, education and, other systems. Work on these aspects may well help alleviate some of the problems described above.

[12]In an important first-hand study of the Transamazonian Highway, Smith (1978) has shown that the failures of colonization there are due to the choice of wrong crop patterns: "A diversified crop base, with manioc serving as a major source of cash and subsistence during the first few years of settlement, not only reduces pest and disease damage, but provides security against oscillating prices of agricultural products. Manioc alone will not provide a panacea for all the agricultural problems of the highway, but it can help build a foundation of trust, mutual assistance and financial solvency which can foster co-operative efforts and provide a catalyst for agricultural development. Agricultural planners in Amazonia might consult the considerable cultural and ecological experience of peasants and aboriginal groups when devising colonization schemes" (pp. 415–432).

[13] For an analysis in historical perspectives referring to *caboclos* of the Amazon River Valley in Brazil, see Ross (1978).

TOWARD NEW PLANNING PARADIGMS?

The formidable challenge of ecodevelopment, then, is how to identify and satisfy on a sustainable basis genuine needs of each person and all people, respecting their diversity and creative potential for change.

For reasons already explained, it cannot be achieved by a return to the primitive simplicity and the resolution of the complex industrial societies into an archipelago of self-contained communities. Important as it may be as a symptom of malaise, and deserving a place in societies committed to pluralism as a value, the counter-culture does not provide the solution to our environmental and cultural predicament. Instead of turning our backs on the market and the state, the civil society should seek, through struggle and negotiation, a different distribution of power. It is up to civil society to exercise concrete social imagination in order to propose and experiment with innovative solutions of societal problems, based on a different mix of direct production of use-values in the domestic sector, of goods and services purchased on the market, and of those provided by the state (Sachs, 1978c; Sachs & Schiray, 1979.)

Nor should we expect development from a technological *fuite en avant*. It would bring more growth and more modernization. But, as we have seen, growth and modernization can lead either to maldevelopment or to development, the former outcome being far more probable under conditions of a market-propelled process stressing complex, technical systems. Under those conditions, vulnerability to a man-made or nature-provoked disaster is maximized. [See Vacca, 1973; also, for an open-ended view of this subject, see the contributions of McNeill (1978), and Brauscomb (1978), in a Resources for the Future symposium.]

While a zero-risk path may be impossible, the pretext of lost opportunities should not be invoked to push us into the escalation of high technology mass consumption responses, particularly since rising levels of material consumption cannot offer a compensation for alienation at work and lack of purposiveness in life: the easier it becomes to obtain a good, the lower the psychological gratification derived from it. Bettelheim (1960), among others, has pointed out this fundamental dilemma of modern civilization. Either we succeed in voluntarily imposing on ourselves a ceiling on material consumption, seeking gratification in the nonmaterial spheres of our lives and thus emphasizing the cultural dimension of human nature, or we shall be caught in the accelerating course for the acquisition of an ever greater number of goods. In that case, mankind will end up hitting against the outer ecological limits of our finite planet. True, the resource scarcity may be avoided by imaginative substitutions; but these will perforce be energy intensive, and we shall, therefore, be quickly moving into a new situation, where the amount of man-dissipated heat and released carbonic dioxide will significantly interfere with the working of great ecological cycles with climate.

Outer limits should not be considered, however, as given once and for all. They may be extended by the ways in which we husband resources and design man-made production and habitat systems, i.e., by the degree of ecological awareness of our culture. Ideally, man-made systems should take natural ecosystems as a paradigm, emphasizing complementarities between different activities, transforming waste into resource, and accommodating different ecological niches in a multilevel architecture of economy and society. This paradigmatic or methaphoric use of natural ecology is not synonymous, however, with postulating a steady climax-like state for society. Contrary to natural systems, man-made systems are open-ended through their cultural component, and their potential for change remains high, subject to the postulate of ecological prudence. The latter imposes careful articulations, case by case, of man-made systems with the life-supporting cycles of nature, i.e., the actual application of ecological knowledge in planning and managing of the economy. Both the uses of ecology—the paradigmatic and the actual—require a new awareness and sensibility, that is to say, a new education. One needs to introduce cultural ecology into primary and high schools. One needs also to revise drastically the curricula for training of planners, managers, economists, architects, engineers, and all development practitioners, so as to expose them to the theory and practice of ecodevelopment (Sachs, 1978c). On the other hand, we are confronted with the task of redefining the approaches to planning. From what was argued here, it follows that planners should identify, and strive to broaden, the *spaces for local autonomous decision making*. This task will be made possible only by a major research effort in the realm of the *anthropology of daily life*. We must know how people cope with their daily crises, mostly those which are not dealt with by the institutions supposed to take care of them; how they house themselves, rear children, commute to work, arrange jobs, grow food, play, love, chat, and pray; how they organize themselves at the household, neighborhood, and community levels, how they help each other, what mechanisms of exploitation are used within the formal and the informal sectors, and so on. This sort of information, very different from that usually at hand in planning agencies, should be gathered by advocacy planners and anthropologists with a view toward recommending action meant to support and encourage certain local initiatives, to assist them through an array of legal, administrative, fiscal, and financial methods, including a transfer of resources from rich to poor.

   While encouraging grass-root initiatives, the planner should constrain local choices, so as to make them compatible with other local choices, and with the long-term overall interest. For that, he must design and implement space use, energy, resource use, and technological policies reflecting the ecodevelopment approach. The question of how to do this, achieving a balance between local autonomy and the need for an overall harmonization, as well as for the centralized operation of certain facilities (e.g., telecommunications), is another area for action-oriented research, possibly leading to the consideration of new contractual tools for planning. A set of local projects partly supported from the center might take the form of a *contract program*, by means of which all the societal actors involved enter into a contractual arrangement. At any rate, the simultaneous broadening of the planners' outlook toward ecology is bound to produce far-reaching consequences for his praxis.

REFERENCES

Baczko, M., Sachs, I., Vinaver, K., & Zakrzewski, P. *Techniques douces, habitat et société.* Paris: Editions Entente, 1977.

Balls, E. K. *Early uses of California plants.* Berkeley: University of California Press, 1972.

Bateson, G. *Steps into the ecology of mind.* St. Albans, England: Paladin, 1973.

Becker, G. S. *Economic approach to human behavior.* Chicago: University of Chicago Press, 1977.

Bennett, J. *The ecological transition: Cultural anthropology and human adaptation.* Oxford: Pergamon, 1976.

Bergeret, A., Godard, O., Morales, H. L., Passaris, S., & Romanini, C. *Nourrir en harmonie avec l'environnement. Trois études de cas.* Paris and La Haye: Mouton, 1977.

Berry, A. *The next ten thousand years.* Bungay, England: Coronet Books, 1960.

Berry, A. *The next thousand years.* London: Cape, 1974.

Bettelheim, B. *The informed heart.* New York: Free Press, 1960.

Brauscomb, L. M. Coping with an uncertain future: Scientific perspective. In C. J. Hitch (Ed.), *Resources for an uncertain future.* Baltimore: Johns Hopkins University Press, 1978, pp. 68–77.

Ceron, J. P., & Baillon, J. (with the collaboration of Baczko, M., & Zakrzewski, P.) *La société de l'éphémère.* Grenoble: Presses Universitaires de Grenoble, 1979.

De Vos, A. Game as food. *Tigerpaper*, 1978, *5* (3), 1–7. (FAO Regional Office for Asia and the Far East, Bangkok).

Douglas, J. S. L'Agrisylviculture pour accroître la production alimentaire de la nature. *Impact, Science et Société, UNESCO*, 1973, *23* (4), 127–144.

Dubos, R. Symbiosis between the earth and humankind. *Science*, 1976, *193*, 459–462.

Ehrlich, P., & Ehrlich, A. *Population, resources, environment: Issues in human ecology.* San Francisco: Freeman, 1970.

Fathy, H. *Construire avec le peuple*. Paris: Martineau, 1970.

Febvre, L. *La terre et l'évolution à l'histoire humaine: Introduction géographique*. Paris: Albin Michel, 1970.

Felger, R. S., & Nabhan, G. P. Une aridité trompeuse. *Ceres* (FAO Review on Development), 1976, *9* (2), 34–39.

Godard, O. *L'environnement et la planification du développement: Aspects méthodologiques et institutionnels*. Unpublished manuscript, 1978.

Goodland, R. J., & Irwin, H. S. *Amazon jungle: Green to red desert?* New York: Elsevier Scientific, 1975.

Goodland, R. J., Irwin, H. S., & Tillman, G. Ecological development for Amazonia. *Ciencia e Cultura*, 1978, *30*, 275–289.

Gourou, P. *Leçons de géographie tropicale*. Paris: Mouton, 1971, pp. 160–161.

Gourou, P. *Pour une géographie humaine*. Paris: Flammarion, 1973.

Greenland, D. J. Bringing the green revolution to the shifting cultivator. *Science*, 1975, *190*, 841–844.

Harris, M. *Cows, pigs, wars and witches*. New York: Vintage, 1975.

Hirsch, F. *Social limits to growth*. Cambridge: Harvard University Press, 1976.

Illich, I. *Towards a history of needs*. New York: Pantheon, 1978.

ILPES, Instituto Latino Americano de Planificacion Economia y Social, *Informe de la mission preliminar del PNU-ILPES com respecto al programa de desarrollo del oriente del Peru*, 1972.

Kahn, H., Brown, W., & Martel, L. *The next two hundred years*. New York: Morrow, 1976.

Lewis, O. *Five families: Mexican case studies in the culture of poverty*. London: Souvenir Press, 1976.

Makhijani, A. *Energy policy for the rural Third World*. London: International Institute for Environment and Development, 1976.

Matthews, W. (Ed.). *Outer limits and human needs* (Resources and Environmental Issues of Developmental Strategies). Uppsala: The Dag Hammarksjold Foundation, 1976.

McNeill, W. H. Coping with an uncertain future: Historical perspective. In C. J. Hitch (Ed.), *Resources for an uncertain future*. Baltimore: Johns Hopkins University Press, 1978, pp. 59–67.

Meadows, D., Meadows, H. D., Randers, J., & Behrens, W. W. *Limits to growth: A report for the Club of Rome's project on the predicament of mankind*. New York: New American Library, 1972.

Meggers, B. *Amazonia: Man and culture in a counterfeit paradise*. Chicago: Aldine–Atherton, 1971.

Morales, H. L. *La Revolution azul: Acuacultura y ecodesarrollo*. Centro de ecodesarrollo. Mexico: Editorial Nueva Imagen, 1978.

Pirie, N. W. *Leaf protein: Its agronomy, preparation, quality and use*. Oxford: Blackwell Scientific Publications for the International Biological Programme, 1971.

Polanyi, K. The economy as instituted process. In K. Polanyi, C. M. Arensberg, & H. W. Pearson (Eds.), *Trade and market in the early empires*. New York: Free Press, 1957, pp. 243–269.

Pomian, K. Les limites écologiques des civilisations. *Informations sur les Sciences Sociales*, 1976, *15* (1).

Rapoport, A. *House, form and culture*. Englewood Cliffs, N. J.: Prentice-Hall, 1969.

Rapoport, A. *Conflict in a man-made environment*. Harmondsworth, England: Penguin, 1974.

Rapoport, A. *Human aspects of urban form*. Oxford: Pergamon, 1977.

Robinson, J. *Economic philosophy*. Harmondsworth, England: Penguin, 1962.

Romanini, C. *Ecotecnicas para el tropico humido.* Mexico: Centro de ecodesarrollo del Consejo Nacional de Ciencia y Tecnologia (CONACYT), 1976.

Ross, E. B. The evolution of the Amazon peasantry. *Latin American Studies,* 1978, *10,* 193–218.

Rudofsky, B. *Architecture without architects.* London: Academy Editions, 1974.

Sachs, I. Civilization project and ecological prudence. *Alternatives: A Journal of World Policy,* 1977a, *3* (1), 1–18.

Sachs, I. The harmonization game. *Mazingira,* Oxford, 1977b, *3/4,* 37–45.

Sachs, I. *Environment and development: A new rationale for domestic policy formulation and international cooperation strategies.* Ottawa: Agence Canadienne pour le Développement International (ACDI), 1977c.

Sachs, I. Développement, utopie, projet de société. *Tiers-Monde,* 1978a, *19,* 645–656.

Sachs, I. *Styles de vie et planification.* Unpublished manuscript, 1978b.

Sachs, I. Environment and development: Key concepts for a new approach to education. *Prospects,* 1978c, *8,* 439–445.

Sachs, I., & Schiray, M. *Experiences and experiments on life-style patterns in the Western world.* Unpublished manuscript, 1979.

Sachs, I., & Vinaver, K. De l'effet de domination à la self-reliance: Techniques appropriées pour le développement. *Mondes en développement,* 1976, No. 15, 481–491.

Sahlins, M. *Stone-age economics.* London: Tavistock, 1972.

Smith, N. H. Agricultural productivity along Brazil's Transamazon highway. *Agroecosystems,* 1978, *4,* 415–432.

Tannahill, R. *Food in history.* Boulder, Colo.: Paladin, 1975.

Tricart, J. L. F. Ecologie et développement: L'example amazonien. *Annales de Géographie,* 1978, *87,* 257–293.

Turner, J. *Housing by people, towards autonomy in building environments.* London: Marion Boyars, 1976.

Vacca, R. *Demain le moyen age: La dégradation des grands systèmes.* Paris: A. Michel, 1973.

What now? The 1975 Dag Hammarksjold Report prepared on the occasion of the Seventh Special Session of the United National General Assembly, Uppsala, 1975.

Wilkinson, R. G. *Poverty and progress, an ecologic model of economic development.* London: Methuen, 1973.

Index